MW00791292

THE CIA UFO PAPERS

THE CIA UFO PAPERS

50 YEARS OF GOVERNMENT SECRETS AND COVER-UPS

DAN WRIGHT

FOREWORD BY JAN HARZAN, DIRECTOR OF MUFON

MUFON
Mutual UFO Network
— est. 1969 —

This edition first published in 2019 by MUFON, an imprint of
Red Wheel/Weiser, LLC
With offices at:
65 Parker Street, Suite 7
Newburyport, MA 01950
www.redwheelweiser.com

Copyright © 2019 by Dan Wright
Foreword copyright © 2019 by Jan Harzan
All rights reserved. No part of this publication may be reproduced or
transmitted in any form or by any means, electronic or mechanical,
including photocopying, recording, or by any information storage
and retrieval system, without permission in writing from
Red Wheel/Weiser, LLC. Reviewers may quote brief passages.

ISBN: 978-1-59003-302-9
Library of Congress Cataloging-in-Publication Data
available upon request.

Cover design by Kathryn Sky-Peck
Cover image by iStock
Interior by Steve Amarillo/Urban Design LLC
Typeset in Minion Pro and Gotham

Printed in Canada
MAR
10 9 8 7 6 5 4 3 2 1

This work is dedicated to the memory of the late Walter H. Andrus Jr., cofounder and thirty-year-long International Director of the Mutual UFO Network, Inc. Walt served as my mentor and remained a true friend. If only we could interview him today to discover what else he has learned about non-human intelligences.

Contents

Foreword

Shortly after taking office as the Executive Director for MUFON, the Mutual UFO Network, I received a congratulatory email from Dan Wright, former Director of Investigations for MUFON in the 80s and 90s. It was a heartfelt moment, as I had followed Dan through his MUFON career and even heard him speak at a MUFON Symposium or two but had lost touch with him through the intervening years. He was writing to congratulate me on my new position and to offer his help with anything I might need. And there are always things that need to be done in any volunteer organization. I thanked him for his offer and told him I would keep him in mind as opportunities arose.

Then in January of 2017 I received another email from Dan inquiring what MUFON planned to do with the million or so UFO documents the CIA had just dumped onto the internet. Or at least that was the headline in an online publication announcing this momentous event. My first thought was *that's a whole lot of documents and it will take a team of MUFON volunteers years to weed through it,* but Dan insisted it needed to be done and he would be happy to lead the charge. How could I turn him down!

After a short discussion we agreed that he would make a first pass and *see* what the size and scope of the project looked like. After a few weeks I received another email from Dan stating that he had just scratched the surface but that he was finding some interesting facts about the "million" UFO documents on the CIA website. The first was that it was nowhere close to a million documents, but more like 20,000 or so documents placed in the CIA's Electronic Reading Room (ERR) on the UFO subject.

The second was that many of the documents had nothing to do with UFOs. It was as if a machine had gone through the massive CIA archives and pulled out anything with the letters U-F-O in that order in a document and placed it in the reading room under the heading UFO.

At that point Dan suggested that he dive in and take the first few years in the archive, since the documents were ordered chronologically, and give it a try to *see* what the effort would be like. And so, the journey began, Dan taking one to five years at a time, pulling the documents which might number one or two hundred and reading through them one by one to discern, first, was it UFO related, and second, what was the purpose of the document including when it was written, by whom, and for what purpose. It might be good here to remember the mission statement of the CIA, this coming from their website, ". . . to further US national security objectives by collecting intelligence that matters, producing objective all-source analysis, . . . and safeguarding the secrets that help keep our Nation safe."

The actions of the CIA with regard to UFOs was primarily gathering information on UFO events through public sources, and spending a good amount of time keeping track of individuals and organizations that were publicly following and actively pursuing the UFO subject. It's all documented here in the CIA's own documents. In the pages that follow are Dan's detailed and painstaking efforts to separate the wheat from the chaff and provide you the with the mother lode of what is in the CIA's files about the UFO subject. In doing so he has included everything that is UFO related that the CIA made public. It's all here for you in one simple body of work. He's done the hard work and provided it for you on a platter called *The CIA UFO Papers*. I hope you enjoy this fascinating look behind the veil of the CIA and what they are sharing with the public as much as I did.

Jan C. Harzan
Executive Director
MUFON, Mutual UFO Network

Preface

As an Obama farewell before his second term expired, on January 17, 2017, the Central Intelligence Agency made available on its permanent website *(www.cia.gov)* a great cache of electronic files previously released under the Freedom of Information Act (FOIA) housed at the National Archives—available for inspection onsite only. Among a variety of subject matters: unidentified flying objects. Finally, serious UFO researchers had a stockpile of reports and correspondence available to examine at home.

Wading into this volume of material, two things became immediately evident. First, the documents were in no particular order—not chronologically, not by topic, not by office or other source. More importantly, the great share of documents had no bearing whatsoever on the subject of aerial phenomena. While one might be curious about just what Bulgaria's total rail tonnage was in 1956, it would not advance the cause of UFO research. Nonetheless, sharp eyes and perseverance won the day. When the sorting was finished, 550 files were shown to be useful.

Notes

All base documents are listed in chronological order, beginning with the World War II years. Attachments are often from an earlier date.

Capitalized file identifiers, such as Office Memorandum, or Letter, indicate the document as presented was on formal Agency masthead (letterhead or memo-head)—definitely not a draft.

The Agency was amazingly inaccurate in dating its files. The Publication Date listed on the introductory web page for each document very often preceded by a few or several weeks the actual event discussed or the date typed on the correspondence. If a date is shown on the document itself, that is used here. Certain types of documents do not include such a date of origin. For those, or if the publication date was obviously incorrect, the earlier of either a Release Date or Distribution Date is substituted.

Regarding document numbering, three Agency numbering schemes were used over six decades. In those with (yes) 27 digits, variously two or three hyphens were inserted by the Agency. Two types of 10-digit numbers were also employed. This often resulted in document duplication, meaning the file was listed under one scheme, then later an identical file was included under another scheme. Care has been taken to eliminate duplicates.

Acronyms and Abbreviations

AD/SI: Assistant Director for Scientific Intelligence
ADC: USAF Air Defense Command
A/DDS&T: Assistant Deputy Director for Science and Technology
AFOSR: Air Force Office of Scientific Research
APRO: Aerial Phenomena Research Organization
ASD: Applied Sciences Division
ATIC: USAF Air (later Aerospace) Technical Intelligence Center
DCD: Defense Communications Division/Domestic Collection Division
DCI: Director of Central Intelligence (a.k.a. CIA Director)
DD/I: Deputy Director for Intelligence
DDS&T: Deputy Director for Science and Technology
DIA: Defense Intelligence Agency
Doc: Document
FBIS: Foreign Broadcast Information Service—successor to JPRS
FCDA: Federal Civil Defense Administration
FOIA: Freedom of Information Act

FTD: Foreign Technology Division (formerly ATIC)

Hq: Headquarters

IFDRB: Information from Foreign Documents or Radio Broadcasts

IAC: Intelligence Advisory Committee

JPRS: Joint Publications Research Service—later FBIS

NICAP: National Investigations Committee on Aerial Phenomena

NPIC: National Photographic Interpretation Center

NSA: National Security Agency

NSC: National Security Council

OACSI: Office of the Assistant Chief of Staff, Intelligence

OCI: Office of Counter Intelligence

OO: Office of Operations

ORD: Office of Research Development

OSI: Office of Scientific Intelligence

P&E: Physics and Electronics Division

SAFOI: Secretary of the Air Force, Office of Information

SRI: Stanford Research Institute

Acknowledgments

The editor wishes to acknowledge numerous individuals who contributed mightily to the content contained in the chapter-ending section, "While you were away from your desk . . ." While the names listed throughout the text are too numerous to repeat here, those whose contributions were especially compelling and useful include:

Jerome Clark
Timothy Good
J. Allen Hynek
Margaret Sachs
John Schuessler
Ronald D. Story
John G. Fuller
Don Berliner

This is also to acknowledge two production workhorses: copy editor Lauren Ayer and Faye Thaxton, a career typesetter and copy editor. Both made scores of technical corrections as well as numerous suggested clarifications.

Introduction

The early success of British and French spies during the Second World War impressed upon the US military and Congress the importance of gathering reliable intelligence on one's adversaries. The House, Senate, and President Roosevelt agreed in the summer of 1942 to create an Office of Strategic Services (OSS) to better understand the capabilities and intentions of the Germans and Japanese. Among OSS objectives was to skew and distort the Axis powers' understanding of our own capabilities. OSS operatives in Europe worked on effectively unmasking the Nazi machine while disguising our own.

Tangential to those black operations, as the conflict proceeded across both oceanic theaters, OSS heard stories from fighter pilots claiming that odd spheres of light or plasma escorted their planes from time to time. Moreover, German and Japanese pilots were apparently reporting the same. Discounted by some as atmospheric ball lightning, they nonetheless appeared when no thunderstorm conditions were present—which ball lightning requires—and sometimes remained in proximity to the plane over long minutes and miles, unlike ball lightning's fleeting nature.

The Allies came to call them *foo fighters*. Still, OSS and the Army Air Corps stopped short of referring to them as an adversary. Foo fighters were never aggressive per se; though an airplane's engine might run rough in its presence, no Allied aircraft plummeted to the earth as a consequence. These were simply oddities, a staple of musings at the bar between combat missions. In any event, they were decidedly not essential to intelligence-gathering efforts.

As successors to the OSS, the Central Intelligence Agency and National Security Council were born in the summer of 1947—scant weeks after Kenneth Arnold's Cascade Mountains *flying saucer* sighting and the alleged saucer crash at Roswell, New Mexico. While Agency principals would thereafter admit to a certain curiosity about such anomalies, they were not at all interested in taking responsibility for determining origins or purposes. Indeed, they were more than willing to pass that baton to the newly reconstituted US Air Force. Still, thereafter the CIA would be periodically dragged back into the UFO controversy.

Internally a decades-long sequence ensued—attraction and repulsion on this singularly peculiar subject. The Agency's Office of Scientific Intelligence (OSI) would long be at the center. But far from seeking publicity, at every turn OSI and other CIA officials insisted on anonymity, perhaps with sound reasoning. Admitting Agency involvement in UFO research would be, to some, tantamount to admitting the reality of space aliens on our planet. That could have been a can of worms the bureaucrats were loathe to open. Acknowledging that the reported saucers, spheres, wingless cylinders, boomerangs, and the rest were technologically superior machines would at once give credence to sighting reports by the public and argue against American invincibility. Either was untenable.

Some have suggested—emphatically—that *any* prominent nation openly acknowledging visits to Earth by a nonhuman intelligence could bring about the ruination of everything we cherish. Among the world's institutions, arguably one religion susceptible to such a crisis is Christianity. For every Christian cleric who accepts the presence on Earth of intelligent nonhuman beings as the greater glory of God, five or ten might proceed with a countdown to the end. Further, if aliens are an undeniable fact of life, then how could Jesus be the "only begotten Son"? It just wouldn't add up for many Christians.

Financial markets might well suffer short- or long-term setbacks in the face of an undeniable UFO reality. An old adage insists that markets hate uncertainty. In the wake of one or more nations admitting a UFO reality—without any assurance of what comes next—fewer people would be expected to invest their savings long-term or to purchase life insurance. More families would be expected to rent rather than buy a home. A greater share could be expected to collapse their time perspectives, live more day-to-day, eschew long-term financial investments of any kind. CIA officialdom long recognized that admitting a nonhuman presence on this planet would not be good for business.

Among the various industries probably affected over time, producers of canned goods and other nonperishable foodstuffs would likely flourish. Weaponry would be another winner in the post-acknowledgment era, though perhaps not so much in the United States, where the three hundred million guns already sold might prove problematic. High gun sales worldwide would probably have less to do with the prospect of human-humanoid standoffs, more to do with a general breakdown in societal law and order. When tomorrow is not assured, some people's darker motivations will surface.

Then again, such changes to popular attitudes would surely not be universal. As a friend of this editor once remarked about the prospect of an alien presence, "It's just one more thing to put up with."

The Mutual UFO Network, Inc. (MUFON) and its veteran members have of course given serious thought to the notion of an official government statement that UFOs are real—possibly even that contact has been established—and the potential negative consequences to humanity. That said, MUFON supports opening every pertinent file for inspection without redactions. All other considerations aside, the public has the fundamental right to know.

Scintillating drama is not the showcase here. No CIA file suggests information was exchanged in a dim parking garage. This is a chronicle: the sequence in ebbs and flows, from the 1940s through the 1990s, of UFO-related news that reached the Agency's attention—plus what, if anything, was done about it.

To be sure, certain threads within this tapestry were at cross-purposes. The leader of a civilian UFO investigative group, NICAP, himself a retired military officer, proved to be a persistent thorn in the Agency's backside, loudly shouting "Cover-up!" at every opportunity. Concurrently, a chemist at a New Mexico scientific research facility demonstrated stamina and single-mindedness over several years, advancing essentially baseless claims that hard evidence proving an alien presence on Earth was secreted away. As subplots in our story line, both men managed to cause great distraction and consternation within the Agency's ranks.

Long years later, in a seemingly innocuous interoffice note, came an unexpected acknowledgment that UFO-related research was still ongoing at the Agency. Scientists were collecting sighting reports, accumulating evidence, and correlating findings. Like an interminable itch, the Central Intelligence Agency necessarily kept on scratching—and may well still be doing so to this day.

These files released to the CIA website in 2017 do not constitute a tell-all file dump—though Agency officials might protest that assertion. To demonstrate, each chapter (most comprising a single year) concludes with a section titled "While you were away from your desk..." There, UFO incidents of consequence in that same year, arising in the United States or elsewhere, are summarized. These are cases that were not mentioned in the 2017 cache of documents. A majority of these involved pilots, police, and other trained observers. As officially stated concerning the US Air Force and its Project Blue Book, events potentially involving a national security threat were withheld. One could expect nothing different from the CIA. The 550 or so usable files on the Agency's website are, as a certain president under threat of impeachment once said, a "limited hangout." Still, in sum they tell quite a story.

Chapter 1

The 1940s:

War and Beyond

In July 1940, Franklin Roosevelt appointed a new Secretary of the Navy, Frank Knox. Months later, Knox introduced him to William "Wild Bill" Donovan, a much-decorated World War I commander. Two decades after that pinnacle, Donovan was a successful New York lawyer. He would ultimately be the only person in American history to receive every one of our highest service awards: Medal of Honor, Distinguished Service Medal, and National Security Medal. He also earned a Silver Star, Purple Heart, and decorations from numerous nations for his World War I service. But his efforts in the next war made an even greater difference. At CIA Headquarters, Bill Donovan was and is the Father of American Intelligence.[1]

Donovan conceived of an agency that would combine the gathering of sensitive information with propaganda and subversion. Roosevelt was impressed with his ideas on intelligence and its place in modern war. In the summer of 1941 FDR decided to force the military and civilian services to cooperate on intelligence matters. He tapped Donovan to lead the mission as the White House's Coordinator of Information.[2]

Donovan initially divided his staff into separate analysis and propaganda wings. In short order, the military branches, chafing at being assigned espionage roles during peacetime, persuaded Roosevelt to hand their respective undercover units to Donovan.[3]

Along with those staff acquisitions, Donovan was given access to *unvouchered* cash from the President's emergency fund (appropriated by

Congress to be spent under personal responsibility of the President or a designated White House official). The expenditures were not audited in detail; Donovan's signature on a note attesting to their proper use sufficed.[4]

Donovan and his staff recruited, in particular, Americans outside government circles who studied world affairs, frequently traveled abroad, or both—some of the best and the brightest at East Coast universities, businesses, and law firms. These recruits brought the practices and disciplines of their academic and professional backgrounds. Making use of their efforts, he reasoned, would forge answers to many intelligence problems. Those solutions would be found in libraries, contemporary journalism, and the filing cabinets of business and industry.[5]

Following Pearl Harbor and America's entry into the Second World War in 1942's initial months, Roosevelt endorsed the military's idea of moving Donovan and his recruits under the control of the Joint Chiefs of Staff (JCS). But FDR wanted to keep a newly formed Foreign Information Service, a radio broadcasting arm, out of military hands.

Though military pressure on the White House had resulted in Donovan reporting to the Joint Chiefs, an undercurrent of resistance within the ranks remained for a time. At issue was that the long-since civilian Donovan was on a par with the individual commanding generals and admirals. But those misgivings were eventually quelled and nothing came of the discontent.

Just as Americans were settling into the slog of what was becoming a long war, unusual sights commenced inexplicably in the months to follow. Dutch sailors on the Timor Sea near New Guinea were on the lookout for enemy aircraft on February 26, 1942, when a large luminous disc approached at great speed. For hours it flew in broad circles around the ship at moderate speed and altitude. Contrasting that peaceful event was one occurring a month later on March 25. An RAF bomber returning from a mission to Essen, Germany, was over Holland's Zeider Zee when the tail gunner noticed a luminous disc or sphere approaching. After notifying the pilot, the gunner readied his weapon and waited. When it was within 100–200 yards, he fired several rounds, apparently hitting it, but to no effect. Shortly the vehicle flew away at a speed that the crew thought to be beyond the speed of sound.[6]

Early successes of British commandos prompted Roosevelt to authorize, in June 1942, the evolution of the Coordinator of Information into a full-scale intelligence service—modeled after Britain's MI6. Renamed the Office of Strategic Services (OSS), it would likewise be under the command of General Donovan. This was to be a military/intelligence meeting of the minds. Donovan's staff now totaled 600, spending ten million dollars per year.[7]

The agency's name change may have implied a move toward a darker side of data collection. It fulfilled Donovan's wish for an office name reflecting the clandestine importance of the work. The OSS mandate was to collect and analyze strategic information—anything of potential assistance to the war effort. This was America's first organized attempt to implement a centralized system for secret military intelligence.

Nicknamed the "Glorious Amateurs," OSS even employed once and future celebrities, including Hollywood actress Marlene Dietrich and later TV chef Julia Child, as well as four future CIA directors. At its peak, the OSS was deploying over 13,000 operatives (that is, spies), a third of them women.[8] Their daring missions into Austria and Germany, especially, were essential to turning the tide for the Allies.

Contrasting those clandestine efforts was a massive, open display in the Pacific Theater on August 12, 1942. As told by an observer, a GI on combat duty on Tulagi, one of the Solomon Islands, heard an air raid siren and leaped into his foxhole, rifle at the ready, expecting an attack by Japanese warplanes. Instead he was amazed to *see* overhead a swarm of unknowns, which he estimated at about 150, in a series of straight-line formations, passing by high in the sky. He did not know their purpose or where they were headed. All he knew was that they were definitely not Japanese zeroes.[9]

When World War II reached its dramatic climax at Hiroshima and Nagasaki, resulting in Japan's quick surrender, OSS remained in service to the military but needed to be repurposed. On September 20, 1945, a Truman executive order dissolved the agency only to re-form it a few months later, out of necessity. OSS, in a reduced role, would remain part of the intelligence establishment until after the Korean Conflict.[10]

The first public mention of a "central intelligence gathering agency" appeared on a White House command-restructuring proposal to a congressional military affairs committee at the end of 1945. Despite resistance from the military, Department of State, and FBI, by executive order, Truman formed a National Intelligence Authority—the direct predecessor of the CIA—in January 1946. Its operational extension was known as the Central Intelligence Group (CIG).[11]

On July 26, 1947, Truman affixed his signature to the National Security Act of 1947, which dissolved the CIG and established both the National Security Council and the Central Intelligence Agency.[12]

A primary impetus for the CIA's creation—the desire to continue espionage efforts beyond the renewal of peace—lay in the retrospective shock of the December 1941 Pearl Harbor attack amidst diplomatic negotiations with Japanese authorities. Ears to the ground, it was reasoned, might have anticipated that attack and prepared for it.

The Agency (insiders' simplified handle) was originally housed on Navy Hill in Washington, D.C. Its stated purpose was to create a clearinghouse for foreign policy and analysis. Essentially, it would collect, evaluate, and disseminate foreign intelligence reports, while performing covert actions as necessary.[13]

Nazi UFOs?

While common knowledge has tagged the origin of saucer reports to the summer of 1947, a latent CIA internal document dialed back that date to Germany's World War II effort. In August 1953, an operative somewhere in Europe completed and distributed a by-then standard Agency reporting form, Information from Foreign Documents or Radio Broadcasts (IFDRB). The operative's source claimed personal knowledge that, as early as 1941, a large cadre of German scientists and engineers drew up preliminary plans for an unconventional flying craft.[14]

That effort was led in part by a brilliant 29-year-old aerospace engineer, Wernher von Braun. At the Breslau, Germany, complex, he was charged with creating a flying vehicle unlike any other: unconventional in appearance and propulsion. By 1944, the source continued, three if not more of the experimental vehicles had been fashioned. It is unclear from the record what became of the plans or whether the crafts were ultimately destroyed.

Nazi saucer experiments were not confined to the Breslau complex. Using tens of thousands of ethnic prisoners as slave laborers, an enormous tunnel-connected circuit of underground complexes was dug in southwest Poland. Dubbed Project Lothar—apparently for a hero in medieval German folklore—the engineering effort there intended to create a bell-shaped object, approximately three meters in diameter, either electrical or nuclear powered, with vertical takeoff ability. Later, Igor Witkowski, a Polish journalist and military historian, wrote extensively about the *bell* in his book, *Prawda O Wunderwaffe* (*Reality of the Wonder Weapon*), published in 2000.[15]

Nazi Georg Klein later publicly supported Witkowski's claim that such design efforts had been undertaken. The aeronautical engineer remarked, "I don't consider myself a crackpot or eccentric or someone given to fantasies. . . . This is what I saw with my own eyes, a Nazi UFO."[16]

Former CIA agent Virgil Armstrong stated that before World War II's conclusion, the SS possessed at least two fully formed Haunebu flying saucers (presumably named for the proving grounds where the prototypes were designed, in Hauneburg, Germany). One was capable of speeds up to 1,200 mph, plus 90-degree turns and vertical takeoffs and landings, he claimed. Armstrong said other crafts were capable of twice that speed.

On the 15th of August, 1945, President Harry Truman issued an executive order concerning what to do with a cache of German materials relating to the study of new technologies. An attendant covert operation known as *Paperclip* began in March 1946. It was, in reality, the vehicle to spirit German scientists into the United States for the purpose of developing "miracle weapons systems." The assembled group was headed by Wernher Von Braun.[17] A German-produced televised documentary in 2014, *UFOs in the Third Reich*, speculated that the Roswell, New Mexico, incident in July 1947 was linked to testing of the bell. The producers stated that the craft was the forerunner of stealth technology, crafted by Von Braun and scores of V2 rocket experts. Paperclip was fulfilling its goal of affording the United States an edge over the Soviet Union in rocket and other advanced technologies.[18]

Before and After Roswell

On August 1, 1946, an Army Air Force captain in the Tactical Air Command was piloting a C-47 cargo plane from Langley Field, Virginia, to MacDill Field, Tampa, Florida. Just northeast of Tampa, flying at 4,000 feet, the pilot, copilot, and flight engineer observed what looked like an incoming meteor. At 1,000 yards, the object turned sideways and crossed the airplane's path. They realized it was twice the size of a B-29 bomber and cylindrical with luminous portholes. A stream of fire issued from the rear. The anomaly— America's very own *ghost rocket*, so often reported in Sweden and through-out Scandinavia that year—was in view for three minutes.

Six weeks before the Roswell incident, May 19, 1947, at Manitou Springs, Colorado, seven railroad workers were eating lunch outside when they caught sight of a silvery, flat-bottom object, ovular in shape. It stopped overhead then moved "erratically in wide circles" 1,000 feet above. After 20 minutes the ship flew away in a straight line until out of sight.[19]

On June 24, 1947, the so-called *modern age* of UFOs began with a 3:00 p.m. sighting by Kenneth Arnold, a civilian pilot. As he was flying near Washington state's Cascade Mountain range, searching for a downed C-46 military transport plane, he saw nine identical, gleaming aerial objects. Thin in profile, they flew in a chain-like formation, bobbing and weaving through the mountain passes. Using two known peaks as guides, Arnold estimated their speed as over 1,200 mph. His homily to a reporter after-ward that the objects "flew like a saucer would if you skipped it across the water" gave rise to the term *flying saucer*. The Army Air Corps dismissed the sighting as a mirage.[20]

An internal FBI memorandum dated July 10, 1947, titled "Flying Discs," outlined an official request by Army Air Corps General George Schulgren. The general requested the Bureau's help with a recent spate of aerial saucer reports. When obtained later, the memo included a hand-written note at the bottom by FBI Director J. Edgar Hoover. The note read, "I would do it but before agreeing to it we must insist upon full access to discs recovered. For instance in the La. case the Army grabbed it & would not let us have it for cursory examination."[21]

For those who overlooked the August 1, 1946 anomaly observed by a military pilot in Florida (see page 6) or the broader Scandinavian ghost rocket phenomena that year, a replication in the United States took place in the predawn hours of July 25, 1948, in the skies of Alabama. The pilot and copilot of an Eastern Airlines DC-3 confronted an oncoming unknown.

"It flashed down toward us and we veered to the left," said the captain later. Streaking by some 700 feet to their right, it zoomed up into the clouds and was gone. The pilots described it as a wingless aircraft about 100 feet long without any protruding surfaces. Along its side, stretching the entire length of the fuselage, was a medium-dark blue glow. What appeared to be portals were seen along its length. Investigators from the newly minted United States Air Force determined that a C-47 transport was the only aircraft in the vicinity, and it did not report any such incident.[22]

Soon agencies similar to the young Central Intelligence Agency, patterned after Britain's successful MI6, would find their way into the governments of Australia, France, Russia, China, India, Pakistan, Egypt, and Israel. The fundamental purpose of each was to warn/inform leaders of important overseas events.

The CIA's Executive Office within the Department of Defense (DoD) provided the US military with information it gathered, received data from military intelligence agencies, and cooperated on field activities. To guard against counterespionage, CIA employees would undergo periodic polygraph exams.

At its birth—just three weeks removed from the famed incident outside Roswell, New Mexico—no one involved in organizing this new agency, international in scope, could have imagined it would eventually be dragged into the quagmire of unidentified flying objects (UFOs), known colloquially back then as flying saucers.

In the months immediately following Roswell, saucer reports rather suddenly started flooding newspaper offices nationwide, many from otherwise credible witnesses who had heard little or nothing about Roswell. These would be buttressed by periodic magazine features speculating on what the unusual machines might represent.

One such event that received little or no press attention, but may have made its way to the Agency, occurred at Muroc Army Air Field, California, which by then was on high alert, with fighter aircraft fueled and perched on a runway. A few days after Roswell, at 9:20 a.m., July 8, 1947, a lieutenant and three other servicemen at Muroc observed two spherical objects over the base, flying at an estimated 300 mph. Earlier that morning, two Army engineers at the same base reported two metallic discs "diving and oscillating" overhead. Whether discretion was the better part of valor or just out of fear, no interceptor was ordered up to investigate.[23]

The still-situating CIA leadership likely did not know how, if at all, to respond to all the UFO hullabaloo. Flying saucers were a domestic matter, after all, beyond the reach of the Agency's formal charter. Then again, the Muroc incident did originate with the military, the Agency's close ally.

On September 23, 1947, General Nathan Twining, later Chairman of the Joint Chiefs of Staff, wrote a letter to the Commanding General of the Army Air Forces, entitled "Flying Discs":

> The phenomenon reported is something real and not visionary or fictitious. . . . The reported operating characteristics such as extreme rates of climb, maneuverability (particularly in roll), and action which must be considered evasive when sighted or contacted by friendly aircraft and radar, lend belief to the possibility that some of the objects are controlled either manually, automatically, or remotely.[24]

In a heated September 27, 1947, letter to Air Force General George MacDonald, FBI Director J. Edgar Hoover terminated the Bureau's initial cooperation on UFO matters. In his letter, Hoover paraphrased a September 3, 1947, letter from Air Defense Command Headquarters that described the FBI's role. Hoover said he was not interested in "relieving the Air Force of running down incidents which in many cases turned out to be 'ash can covers, toilet seats, and whatnot.'" Four days later an FBI bulletin to its field offices formally ended the joint investigations.[25]

Mantell Incident

On the afternoon of January 7, 1948, Kentucky Air National Guard's Thomas Mantell, a 25-year-old pilot with World War II experience, was headed north past Goodman AFB in his F-51 Mustang. The State Highway Patrol had been passing along citizen reports that day of an unusual aerial object first seen over Maysville, 80 miles east of the base. Soon sightings were reported from two other towns. Three air base personnel, including the commanding officer, a colonel, spotted the oddity at high altitude. Through binoculars, the colonel later remarked, "It was very white and looked like an umbrella . . ." Its apparent size was about a quarter of a full moon. At times the top or bottom appeared to be banded in red. The three witnesses continued observing for 1½ hours; all the while the unknown was seemingly stationary.

At that point, four F-51s, including Mantell's, approached the base on their flight from north Georgia. One, low on fuel, landed. The tower directed the remaining three to pursue the unknown—per recent USAF policy. Mantell spotted it first and radioed back that it was "in sight above and ahead of me, and it appears to be moving at about half my speed or approximately 180 miles an hour. It appears to be a metallic object or possibly reflection of sun from a metallic object, and it is of tremendous size."[26]

Without first informing his companions, Mantell climbed steeply toward the object, the others in hot pursuit. At 16,000 feet one pilot donned an oxygen mask in the thinner air. Mantell's plane was not equipped with oxygen. At 22,500 feet both of the wingmen broke off the chase, while Mantell continued upward in the hope of closing further. The other pilots last saw his plane still climbing.

In minutes, two rural Kentucky witnesses separately heard a screaming sound and saw Mantell's plane headed steeply downward in a spiraling path. It exploded in midair. Upon retrieving the body, rescuers said his shattered watch had stopped at 3:18 p.m. At 3:50, the unknown was lost from view by the Goodman tower. The evening edition of the *Louisville Courier* proclaimed, "F-51 and Capt. Mantell Destroyed Chasing Flying Saucer."[27]

Note: In a separate account, MUFON's Leonard Stringfield reported he had later been told by one of the wingmen that Mantell's Mustang did indeed have oxygen onboard, the only one among the four so equipped, and that his oxygen mask allowed him to continue when the others broke off the chase. That pilot allegedly told Stringfield that he saw some type of tracers directed from the unknown toward Mantell's plane, causing it to break up.[28] Another source stated that none of the F-51s had oxygen onboard in that the flight from Georgia was to be at modest altitude.[29]

The USAF Air Technical Intelligence Center (ATIC) later stated that Mantell and the others had misidentified a high-altitude Skyhook balloon. That explanation, however, would seem problematic, given the lengthy duration of the event (1½ hours plus) asserted by the base commander, the swiftness of prevailing winds, and Mantell's airborne description of the object as reflective metallic.

Aerial peculiarities occurred elsewhere as well. On the afternoon of April 5, 1948, at Holloman Air Force Base, New Mexico, three balloon observers from the Geophysics Lab saw three round but irregularly shaped objects of either white or gold coloration. One made three loops around the area before rising rapidly out of sight. The others flew in a fast arc to the west. USAF Project Blue Book later left the case unidentified.[30]

In the wee hours of July 24, 1948, an Eastern Airlines DC-3 was en route from Houston to Atlanta. At 2:45 a.m. the captain and copilot confronted a large red light coming directly at them. They veered left as the anomaly passed to the right of the plane, turned upward, and, with a burst of flame from the rear, shot off into the clouds. The two pilots described the object as cigar-shaped without wings, approximately 100 feet long and 30 feet thick. A pointed protrusion was at the front, while two rows of rectangular windows glowed brilliantly. The underside was likewise aglow in phosphorescent blue. The red-orange flame extended some 50 feet from the rear. Another ghost rocket?[31]

On October 1, 1948, a North Dakota National Guard lieutenant was flying his F-51 Mustang over Fargo at 9:00 p.m. when a white light passed him from behind. He gave chase but could not equal its tight turns and acceleration. The sphere of light ultimately approached him on a collision course before veering straight up and out of sight overhead. The pilot noticed no sound or exhaust trail from the light. Air traffic controllers also observed it, as did a private pilot and his passenger who remarked afterward on its amazing speed and maneuvers.[32]

Following a report in autumn 1948 by USAF Project Sign declaring saucers to be potentially extraterrestrial in origin, the effort was abandoned, replaced that December by a far less accepting Project Grudge. This program continued for a year. In 1952 it would, in turn, be displaced by the more recognizable Project Blue Book.

Chapter 2

1949:

Curiouser and Curiouser

Another aerial oddity, green fireballs were seen from 1948 through 1949 in the American southwest, especially New Mexico—clustered around sensitive research installations such as the Los Alamos and Sandia National Laboratories. Meteor expert Dr. Lincoln LaPaz headed up investigations into the fireballs for the military. He concluded that the objects displayed anomalous characteristics including slow speed and horizontal paths that were unlike meteors; instead they must be artificial, perhaps Russian devices. Many individuals with solid reputations saw the fireballs, including LaPaz, other distinguished Los Alamos scientists, Kirtland AFB intelligence officers, and Air Defense Command personnel.[1]

On January 4, 1949, about 2:00 p.m. at Hickam Field, Hawaii, an Air Force captain and pilot watched an elliptical object from the ground. Flat white with a matte top, it circled the area, oscillating to the right and left, then flew rapidly away. The Air Force listed the matter as unresolved.[2]

Beginning at 10:20 p.m., January 27, 1949, an Air Force captain accompanied the acting chief of the Aircraft Branch at Eglin Air Force Base, Florida, along with his wife, who all observed a cylindrical object for 25 minutes from their location in the Cortez-Bradenton area. As long as two Pullman cars, the ship had seven lighted square windows and was throwing sparks. It descended at one point, then climbed with a bouncing motion at an estimated 400 mph. USAF files afterward listed the incident as unidentifiable.[3]

In a January 31, 1949, memo to Director J. Edgar Hoover, the FBI's San Antonio, Texas, field office stated in reference to flying saucer reports, ". . . This matter is considered top secret by Intelligence Officers of both the Army and the Air Force." The message referenced "sightings of unexplained phenomena [that] were reported in the vicinity of the A.E.C. (Atomic Energy Commission) installation at Los Alamos, New Mexico . . . No scientific experiments are known to exist in this country which could give rise to such phenomena."[4] In short, the authorities had no clue.

A February 1949 Los Alamos conference was titled encouragingly by the Air Force, Project Sign. Among those attending were H-bomb scientist Dr. Edward Teller, upper atmosphere physicist Dr. Joseph Kaplan, and other renowned scientists and military brass. On the topic of recent fireball phenomena, the conference attendees concluded, though far from unanimously, that the displays were natural phenomena.[5]

At 9:06 a.m., September 20, 1949, while flying a C-45 cargo plane northeast of Rome, New York, an Air Force lieutenant colonel observed a silvery aerial cylinder ahead. The object descended slowly until lost from view in a cloud layer at 7,000 feet. An hour later, a lieutenant piloting a C-47 in the same region spotted an object "similar in size and shape to a fighter fuselage, silver in color" diving at a 45- to 60-degree angle. The unknown seemingly vanished while in a shadow cast by clouds.[6]

In December 1949, Project Twinkle was established then quickly extinguished. It involved a network of fireball-observation installations and photographic stations. The project was never fully implemented.[7]

A spate of three similar 1949 events reported within a month argued against any easy answer to the questions surrounding aerial phenomena. Soon, ATIC was classifying commonly observed unknowns seen in daylight in binary terms: spherical or elliptical, plus those described only as shiny metallic. Some were said to be only two or three feet across; most approached 100 feet; a few were claimed to be up to 1,000 feet. Other shapes reported in daytime sightings: torpedo, pencil, triangle, even mattress-like.[8]

Nighttime sightings in the late 1940s were still of green, flaming red, or blue-white glowing/undulating fireballs. Formations varied in number. The intruders' speed ranged from virtual hovering to moderate (like a conventional propeller aircraft) to, on occasion, "stupendous" (up to an estimated 1,000+ mph in a White Sands incident). Extreme accelerations and violent maneuvering were reported in a small proportion of cases. With few exceptions, neither sound nor smell was recorded.[9]

With World War II still in the rearview mirror and a new cold war with the Soviets just underway, reasoning held that the American populace could be forgiven for a measure of mass hysteria concerning anything unfamiliar in the sky. In that context, fair or otherwise, the CIA initially chose not to respond at all to the fundamental questions posed.

Importantly, the Central Intelligence Agency Act of 1949 (Public Law 81-110) authorized use of confidential fiscal and administrative procedures. More firmly established than before, the Agency was authorized to operate in essentially unaccountable secrecy, exempted from most limitations on the use of federal funds; there would be no public accounting for what was spent and how.

As was his authority earlier as the Coordinator of Information, CIA Director William Donovan was the only official cleared for unvouchered disbursements from the president's emergency fund, spent at White House discretion.[10] The new law likewise exempted the CIA from disclosure of its "organization, functions, officials, titles, salaries, or numbers of personnel employed."[11]

In 1949, the Agency established an Office of Scientific Intelligence (much later renamed the Directorate of Science & Technology) over concerns of a possible technological surprise by way of Soviet nuclear capacity, guided missiles, or biological warfare. Its mission was to research, devise, and manage technical collection disciplines and equipment. Many of its innovations would eventually be transferred to other intelligence organizations or, as they became more overt, to the military services.[12] Credit was not OSI's frame of reference.

OSI was destined to be at the heart of the Agency's response to the UFO problem. The earliest known UFO-related document in CIA files was recorded on March 15, 1949, in an OSI memo from a Dr. Stone to a Dr. Machle (branch office name redacted). Stone responded skeptically to earlier data submitted to him by Machle, which had apparently argued for the credence of flying saucer reports.[13]

On May 5, 1949, at the Army's Fort Bliss, Texas, two majors and a captain observed two oblong white discs flying 200–250 mph overhead at 5:45 p.m. The unknowns made a shallow turn before moving out of sight. As was its habit when the witnesses were military personnel or private pilots, the USAF Project Blue Book later listed the event as unidentified.[14]

Chapter 3

1950:
Escalation

The Agency established its first staff development facility, the Office of Training and Education, in Langley, Virginia, in 1950. It is unclear whether UFOs were even a tangential subject.

At Teaticket, Massachusetts, on February 5, 1950, from the ground an Air Force lieutenant and pilot, along with a former Navy pilot and two others, observed a pair of illuminated cylinders, thin in profile, at 5:10 p.m. As they watched, a fireball dropped from one of the structures. The objects maneuvered together for five minutes then ascended swiftly out of sight. Their report to an otherwise skeptical Project Grudge was left unidentified.[1]

At 9:26 p.m., March 20, 1950, over Stuggart, Arkansas, a Chicago & Southern Airlines captain and his first officer observed a 100-foot saucer for half a minute. They noted 9–12 portholes along the lower side that emitted soft purple light. At the top a light flashed three times in a 9-second span. The pilots adjudged its velocity upon leaving as not less than 1,000 mph. Project Grudge left this case unidentifiable as well.[2]

President Harry Truman declared on April 4, 1950, "I can assure you that flying saucers, given that they exist, are not constructed by any power on Earth."[3]

On May 25, US Air Force Lieutenant Colonel Doyle Rees, the Commander of the 17th District Office of Special Investigations, wrote to his superior, General Joseph Carroll. Rees' letter concluded:

This summary of observations of aerial phenomena has been prepared for the purpose of re-emphasizing and reiterating the fact that phenomena have continuously occurred in the New Mexico skies during the past 18 months and are continuing to occur, and, secondly, that these phenomena are occurring in the vicinity of sensitive military and governmental installations.[4]

An American Airlines DC-6, soon after takeoff from Washington National Airport on May 29, 1950, confronted a brilliant object coming straight on and veered to avoid a collision. Reported the captain later: "As I looked to my left the object appeared to come to a stop. It appeared as a perfectly streamlined object without wings or tail section . . ." In seconds the intruder circled around to the right and paced the plane, then turned away abruptly. "We watched it for several more seconds until it disappeared in the east out of sight. I have never seen anything like it before or since."[5]

On July 31, 1950, an Information Report by a CIA operative in South America attached a magazine article originating in Chile. German-born physicist Eduard Ludwig of Santiago had written the piece for a German-language magazine there. He had declared that notions of saucer origins beyond Earth were absurd. Ludwig posited that nighttime observations of anomalies were actually of the exhaust from an advanced but unnamed "gas-turbine" vehicle. The remaining text was largely technical, discussing the properties of aerodynamics related to lift.[6]

Less than three weeks later, on August 18, another foreign CIA Information Report from a redacted source concerned an August 4 sighting by a ship's crew at sea, sailing from Nova Scotia to an unidentified East Coast US port. At 10:00 a.m. that day, with smooth water and a clear sky, the captain was called hastily to the deck. There he and the crew confronted a smallish "ovular cylindrical" object off the starboard bow, probably several miles away, flying low over the water. The captain viewed it through binoculars for 1½ minutes as it approached the ship then flew away with an uneven "churning" motion, its closest approach being about 1,000 feet. No sound was heard. One crewman described its shape as elliptical—like an egg cut in half lengthwise. The unknown cast a shadow on the water. He said it moved away at tremendous speed with a spinning, wobbling motion.[7]

That anecdotal report deserved the credible side of the ledger as it was reportedly seen by multiple military witnesses who, by occupation at least, were likely fairly reliable at observing things at a distance. Some of them might also well have been adept at judging the size and shape of something unusual in their seafaring environment.

Late that summer, on September 8, came an underscoring of military directives—pointedly regarding anomalous airborne objects. Air Force Major General Charles P. Cabell at Air Materiel Command wrote to Air Force commanding generals, major air commands, and US air attachés, with copies to the intelligence directors of the Army, Navy, Coast Guard, FBI, CIA, and State Department. The memo, titled "Reporting of Information on Unconventional Aircraft," defined same as "any aircraft or airborne object which by performance, aerodynamic characteristics, or unusual features, does not conform to any presently known aircraft type." Each incident was to be reported separately, with descriptive details and time of the sighting, to the Air Materiel Command, Wright-Patterson AFB, Dayton, Ohio.[8]

At the outset of the Korean War in August 1950, the CIA comprised a few thousand employees—one thousand of them engaged in various types of analysis. Raw intelligence material came largely from an obscure Office of Reports and Estimates within the Defense Department, which in turn drew the contents of its daily reports variously from State Department telegrams, military dispatches, and public documents. As yet, the CIA lacked its own intelligence-gathering function.

In its early tenure, the Agency endured disparate demands brought by the official bodies overseeing it. Truman's White House wanted a centralized group to organize the information reaching him. The DoD wanted military intelligence and spy-stuff covert action. The State Department wished it to be the agent for global political change favorable to the United States. From those inputs, the basic areas of CIA responsibility as an arm of the federal government became (a) covert actions and (b) covert intelligence gathering. The primary target was the Soviet Union, of course, which had likewise been a priority of the CIA predecessors, OCI and OSS.[9]

While you were away from your desk . . .

Though 1950 was not hectic in terms of UFO-related activity internationally, sharp Agency analysts might have bent the rules of the CIA charter a bit and thereby better served their superiors by acquiring the accounts of a few additional anomalous aerial events. However, nothing concerning those incidents was found among the files released to the CIA website in 2017.

March 8, 1950

At 7:50 a.m., four F-51 Mustangs were dispatched from Wright-Patterson AFB, Dayton, Ohio, to engage an unknown observed from the tower and tracked on radar. Two pilots came close enough to identify the object as huge, circular, and metallic. But severe weather forced them to break off the chase.[10]

March 17, 1950

At Farmington, New Mexico, on the morning of March 17, 1950, hundreds of locals over the course of an hour witnessed a great number of airborne discs—variously estimated between 500 and several thousand feet in diameter. USAF Captain Edward Ruppelt, later the first head of Project Blue Book, immediately and defensively claimed they all had seen the shattered remains of a Skyhook balloon launched that morning from Holloman AFB. University of Arizona atmospheric physicist Dr. James McDonald contended that witness descriptions of fast-moving discs did not support that. Records thereafter released by Holloman and the Office of Naval Research squelched Ruppelt's contention; no Skyhook had been released from Holloman or any other place on or near that date.[11]

April 27, 1950

At 6:20 p.m., over central Indiana, a TWA captain, his copilot, the flight attendant, and many passengers watched a dull red object overtake and pace their plane at a distance of half a mile. The pilot later reported:

> We watched it fly parallel to us for 7 or 8 minutes. I couldn't tell its shape, but I'd guess it was roughly 50 feet across. Then (the copilot) said, "Let's get a better look," and we turned to the right to fly closer. As soon as we did that, the object increased its speed and seemed to turn also, away from us. Then it descended and seemed to disappear among the lights of South Bend.[12]

May 11, 1950

About 7:30 p.m., near the town of McMinnville, Oregon, a farm couple named Trent watched as a flat-bottomed saucer, 20–30 feet across, approached. Grabbing his camera, Mr. Trent took two photos before the saucer accelerated away. In 1967, astronomer William K. Hartman, serving as an investigator for the (UFO debunking) University of Colorado UFO Project, analyzed the negatives and concluded the following:

> This is one of the few UFO reports in which all factors investigated, geometric, psychological, and physical, appear to be consistent with the assertion that an extraordinary flying object, silvery, metallic, disk-shaped, tens of meters in diameter, and evidently artificial, i.e., not man-made, flew within sight of two witnesses.[13]

June 21, 1950

At Hamilton Air Force Base, California, three air traffic controllers witnessed a flying disc make at least three passes over the base, emitting a "thunder-like roar." They followed the craft with binoculars as it buzzed the field at elevations of 2,000–5,000 feet and speeds in excess of 1,000 mph, trailing blue flame "like an acetylene torch."[14]

September 5, 1950

At 4:09 p.m., while preparing for the annual Farnborough, England, Air Display, an RAF lieutenant was among six officers in the watchtower who caught sight of something unexpected some 10–15 miles distant. (The lieutenant had witnessed the same or an identical object three days earlier.) All described it as a flat disc, light pearl gray in color, its apparent size comparable to a shirt button at arm's length. It followed a fast, rectangular flight path in addition to a "falling leaf" motion—upward as well as downward. Finally, it left for the horizon at great speed.[15]

October 15, 1950

Three security staff at the Atomic Energy Commission facility witnessed the approach of two shiny silver objects at 3:20 p.m. in Oak Ridge, Tennessee. Roughly bullet shaped, they dove toward the witnesses, trailing smoke. One simply vanished; the other stopped 5–6 feet above the ground and hovered some 50 feet from the observers. In the ensuing minutes it left and returned several times to spots somewhat farther distant. Eventually it left the area. Project Grudge ruled the intruders unidentified.[16]

November 21, 1950

Wilbert Smith, Director of Project Magnet, the first Canadian government UFO study, wrote a secret memo on "Geo-Magnetics" following a meeting in Washington, D.C. On the subject of UFOs he related:

> The matter is the most highly classified subject in the United States Government, rating higher even than the H-bomb. Flying saucers exist. Their modus operandi is unknown but a concentrated effort is being made . . . The entire matter is considered by the United States authorities to be of tremendous significance.[17]

Chapter 4

1951:

Calm Before . . .

For all of calendar year 1951, since-released CIA files were bereft of any documented Agency memo, interagency correspondence, or incoming foreign report concerning unidentified flying objects. Supporting the notion of a drop-off in public interest, the Air Force was reporting ever-reduced numbers of sighting reports.

Within the USAF and CIA staffs alike, gratitude was no doubt quietly expressed for not having been caught up further in that no-win situation: trying to prove a negative—that every letter to a local newspaper editor, every phone call to the police, airport tower, or radio station was mistaken. There were more than enough credible issues occurring in the world; unusual things seen in the sky were not a necessary concern.

That attitude would change—shortly and abruptly.

While you were away from your desk . . .

February 10, 1951

At 12:55 a.m., a Douglas RSD four-engine Navy transport, with a second crew plus 31 passengers aboard, was at 10,000 feet on a return flight from Kevlavik, Iceland, to Naval Air Station Argentia, Newfoundland, when a brightly glowing unknown appeared in the distance, 1,000 or 1,500 feet above the water. Suddenly it rose at great speed toward the plane, clarifying its appearance as a disc with reddish orange at the perimeter. Upon its close approach, the plane's hydraulic and magnetic directional gyros began oscillating, along with a magnetic compass and two auto direction finders. The intruder reversed course, zooming into the night as the instruments returned to normal functioning. The crew was extensively debriefed afterward and the pilot was visited months later by an officer from Naval Intelligence who showed him multiple UFO photos, seeking a match.[1]

February 26, 1951

At Ladd Air Force Base, Alaska, a sergeant observed a gray metallic object at 7:10 a.m. He estimated the unknown to be about 120 feet long and 10–12 feet thick. After hovering above the base grounds for over a minute with puffs of smoke escaping, it suddenly sped away. USAF Project Blue Book listed the case as unidentified.[2]

August 25, 1951

About 9:00 p.m., a Sandia Corporation staffer and his wife saw a huge, silent vehicle pass low over them in Albuquerque, New Mexico. They described it as a V-shaped wing with dark stripes and glowing bluish lights along the after edge.

Twenty minutes later in Lubbock, four Texas Tech professors walking on campus observed a similar shape with 20–30 lights visible. Just over an hour later a second such anomaly passed overhead, followed by a third before midnight. All the groups of lights appeared suddenly, high above the horizon, and disappeared just as abruptly. The next morning a nearby Air Defense Command radar station reported that two sets of equipment had reported an unknown target moving 900 mph at 13,000 feet. An F-86 Sabrejet was scrambled, but too late. On the 31st a college freshman and amateur photographer took five photos to the newspaper office—what became famously known as the Lubbock Lights.[3]

Undetermined Date, 1951

Future astronaut L. Gordon Cooper scrambled his F-84 Thunderjet into the sky from Neubiberg AFB, Germany. He and his fellow pilots expected to confront MiG-15s, which frequently crossed over the border. Instead, as they reached their maximum altitude of 45,000 feet, well ahead of and above them, and traveling far faster were multiple unknowns.

> I could *see* that they weren't balloons or MiGs or like any aircraft I had seen before. They were metallic silver and saucer-shaped. We couldn't get close enough to form any idea of their size; they were just too high.[4]

Chapter 5

1952:

A Genuine Wave

As the calendar flipped to 1952, the United States found itself knee-deep in yet another war—this time in Korea, undeclared by Congress. Manufacturers were back to building Jeeps and artillery even as new models of Fords, Chevys, and Packards rolled off assembly lines. Harry Truman entered the final year of his presidency hugely unpopular, his candid and unrefined personal style not nearly the winner it would become in retrospect. Jim Crow would remain, in practice, the law of the land across the South for another decade and more. Plus, the potential for a nuclear-tipped Russian ICBM pervaded the American public's consciousness.

While decisive victories over the Nazis and Japanese were a source of great American pride, the world was now a more complicated place geopolitically; the period of binary wartime political philosophies was over now. Analyzing a hodgepodge of critical intelligence data from multivarious sources dominated the Agency's attention.

In the midst of that hubbub of activity arrived an official yet enigmatic Information Report originating in the Uzbek Republic of the Soviet Union—later Uzbekistan. The report was dated February 11, 1952, but it concerned events dating from May into September 1947.

From a work camp 50 km southwest of the capital, Tashkent, a worker claimed that three (in modern UFO parlance) nocturnal lights moved across the sky about 15 minutes apart, between 9:00 and 10:00 p.m., nearly every night from May into September 1947. He implied it was common knowledge among the rest of the workers.[1] Recall, the Kenneth Arnold sighting of flying saucers in the Cascade Mountains took place in the final week of June 1947; the Roswell, New Mexico crash—a cornerstone of any UFO discussion—was traced to the first week of July.

The early-May peak of the Eta Aquarids and mid-August's Perseids peak, both major meteor showers, might be suspects for the Uzbek activity. But it was improbable at best that the early- and late-date meteors associated with those showers, visible for a second or less as streaks of light, were responsible. The notion of a comet also had to be dispelled; to the ground observer's eye, over a given hour a comet always appears stationary.

The Agency's source detailed the informant's nightly observations, in the company of others, in far different terms: A dark-red ball of fire was seen first; after about six seconds it reached the apex of a long, drawn-out trajectory. During this time the ball developed a trail of fire. Its color, which was bright red at the apex, changed from pale green to white. No smoke trails, noises, or detonations were noticed. In apparent size to the eye, each unexplained light was reportedly about one-fifth the diameter of a full moon. The lights' trajectory was generally from southwest to northeast.

If taken at face value, the work crew witnessed something unexplained in either astronomical or meteorological circles. Operating in anti-communist mode, CIA analysts no doubt entertained notions of long-range Soviet artillery or rocketry as strong possibilities. No published Agency records support that contention, but alas, for want of a follow-up record the world will never know.

After what had been an absolutely *quiet* 1951—at least in terms of the CIA's recorded interest in UFOs—official files on the subject rose inexplicably across 1952 to include thirty formal communications to, from, or within the Agency on the flying saucer subject.

With one of its wordy, catchall form titles, the CIA had developed an open-ended retrieval document for such communication purposes: Information from Foreign Documents or Radio Broadcasts—the IFDRB. The foreign documents in question were usually newspaper articles.

On March 29, 1952, a Vienna, Austria, daily paper published what became an IFDRB file titled "Flying Saucers over Belgian Congo Uranium

Mines." It was distributed more widely across the Defense Department in August. Allegedly, two fiery discs glided through many turns over the mines in Elisabethville District (date uncertain) for 10–12 minutes, then suddenly left in a zigzag fashion, emitting a hissing-buzzing sound. A nearby pilot and military commander jumped into his jet and chased the unknowns, reportedly coming within 120 meters of one. He described it as 12–15 meters in diameter, the color of aluminum. The undercarriage rotated at great speed and emitted a fiery effect, he said. The intruding vehicles left in unison at greater than Mach 1.

Following a two-month calm on such matters, warm-weather reports would cause the hair on the collective necks of Agency analysts to stand on end.

June 1, 2:40 a.m., at Port Gentil on the coast of the west African nation of Gabon, the master and first mate of a cargo ship at anchor saw an orange luminous object rise up behind the port, do two right-angle turns, pass overhead, and continue out of sight.[2]

On July 9, 1952, a newspaper in Athens, Greece, published an article titled "Flying Saucers in East Germany." A former village mayor who had escaped East Germany with his family related an incident that occurred at some unspecified time while they were on the Soviet side. At dusk, he and his 11-year-old daughter were returning home on his motorcycle when it blew a tire. As he was tending to the flat, the daughter called his attention to something odd some 140 meters away in a wooded area. They were curious enough to investigate. When within about 40 meters, the father realized what they'd seen initially was actually two "men" dressed in "shiny metallic clothing." One of them had a "lamp on the front of his body, which lit up at regular intervals."

Apparently unnoticed, father and daughter continued through the trees toward the men. Just ten meters short of them, he discovered a round metallic object on the ground beyond in a clearing. It had the over-all shape of a handle-less frying pan. He estimated it to be 13–15 meters in diameter. Two rows of holes, just under a foot in diameter each, were spaced around its periphery. Atop the saucer body was a black conical tower three meters high. As he continued to examine it, his daughter spoke to him. This drew the attention of the intruders, who immediately scampered into the tower and disappeared.

The object rose slowly from the ground at first, the father continued in his later testimony. It was surrounded by a ring of flames. Intermittently they heard a slight hum plus a whistling sound similar to that of World War II bombs dropping. Seconds later the object accelerated rapidly into the sky and was gone. The witnesses found a fresh depression in the ground matching the vehicle's diameter. For good measure, the father swore to all of his observations under oath in court.[3]

If UFO reports were only grudgingly and barely considered by American officialdom, they were both commonplace and openly speculated on elsewhere. Algeria was host to numerous events during July.

On July 11 at Lamoriciere, a man noticed an apparent meteor followed by two other bodies, all trailing yellowish smoke. These vanished and a longish fiery oval appeared from nowhere then moved out of sight.

Four nights later, at approximately 11:00 p.m. at Boukanefis, two bakers saw a plate-shaped object move across the sky with unusual agility, emitting greenish smoke that lit the air.

On or around July 25 at 2:35 p.m., several workers at an Algiers factory and elsewhere saw a luminous white mass glide across the sky. Two minutes later a newsman and two others saw a brilliant disc flying at great speed over the coastal city of Oran.

That late evening at Lodi, southwest of Algiers, at 11:30 p.m., a yellowish object crossed the sky at great speed. Twenty minutes later a larger inverted cone was observed.

The next morning, July 26, at 10:45 a.m. in Tiaret, five persons saw a shining cigar-shaped mass with a darkened center silently traverse the sky.

That same night at 11:30, three women at Eckmühl spotted a red-orange "patch" of sky in a flattened-egg shape that left momentarily after the sighting.

On the morning of July 30, an Algiers resident observed a shining black disc on the horizon; it ascended vertically then suddenly moved horizontally out of sight. That night at Sainte Barbe du Tlelat, two policemen, a judge, and a lawyer saw a luminous unknown in the sky.

The same night, at 3:30 a.m., July 31, an object was observed at Oued Taria, making right-angle turns. At 4:00 a.m., an object trailing whitish smoke was seen at Tlemcen, likewise executing impossible turns. Several hours later at 11:30 a.m. back in Oran, a couple driving outside the city watched a tapered spindle shape cross the sky at great speed.[4]

In the midst of Algeria's sightings, in the Netherlands, during late July, a woman and her four children, ages 10–16, reportedly witnessed a formation of discs in view for long minutes as the objects passed slowly overhead:

> On July 24 at about 6:30 p.m., presumably a big formation
> of "Flying Saucers" was seen above Arnhem. Together
> they saw the unknowns coming in "V" formation from
> the North. They could *see* them for several minutes before
> the anomalies suddenly disappeared to the South.[5]

UFOs were seemingly ubiquitous, including multiple ventures over metropolitan Washington, D.C., in the latter half of July 1952, when separate radars detected unknowns also observed by pilots and from the ground. Curiously, no report of those events was included in the Agency's official record.

Unfamiliar objects were said to have appeared over Barcelona, Spain, and Sousse, Tunisia, that summer. Many Moroccan citizens claimed sightings at Meknes, Taourirt, Marrakesh, and Casablanca.[6]

In Roseville, Michigan (a Detroit suburb), on April 27, 1952, a minister and three other adults witnessed three aerial events in 45 minutes. At 4:45 p.m., a silver oval tumbled, descended, hovered, then flew away. Soon two silver cylinders, followed by one more, meandered about the area and departed at high speed. The same day at Yuma, Arizona, an off-duty control tower operator and his wife had eight sightings of bright red or flame-colored discs in a two-hour period. Seven were of a single object, one of two that were identical in appearance. All occurred below an 11,000-foot overcast. USAF Project Blue Book left both cases unidentified.[7]

At 9:10 a.m., May 1, 1952, over Davis-Monthan Air Force Base, Arizona, two shiny round objects overtook a B-36 Peacemaker bomber in flight. The intruders paced the bomber for some 20 seconds, turned an impossible 70–80 degrees and accelerated away. Before reaching the horizon, one stopped suddenly without decelerating. No contrail was seen and no sound heard from the unknowns. The incident was observed in flight by the bomber crew, from the ground by an airman, and also by the Air Intelligence major in charge of analyzing local UFO sightings by the public. Somehow their written reports became lost. USAF Project Blue Book listed the case as a misidentified aircraft.[8]

On the same morning, at 10:50 a.m. on the George Air Force Base, California, three men on the firing range, plus an officer four miles away, observed five matte-white discs, all about 100 feet in diameter. The unknowns flew rapidly overhead in a formation of three followed by two. The saucers executed a 90-degree turn then darted about for perhaps half a minute before departing. USAF Project Blue Book listed the incident as unidentifiable.[9]

Within a week at Keesler Air Force Base, Mississippi, about 12:15 p.m. on May 7, 1952, a captain, two sergeants, and an airman on the ground watched a silvery cylinder dart in and out of clouds for 5–10 minutes. USAF Project Blue Book left the event unidentified.[10]

At San Antonio, Texas, around 7:00 p.m., May 29, 1952, an Air Force pilot on the ground watched a bright tubular object in the sky. It tilted from horizontal attitude to vertical for eight minutes before slowly returning to horizontal. It then accelerated, turned red, and appeared to stretch out as it went. The entire sighting lasted 14 minutes. USAF Project Blue Book left the event unidentifiable.[11]

From 11:40 p.m., July 19, until 5:00 a.m. the next morning, seven objects were detected near Andrews AFB, Maryland, and by separate radarscopes at Washington National Airport. Reports by commercial pilots in the vicinity verified their paths up, down, and sideways at 100+ mph, routinely violating restricted airspace. One air traffic controller referred to the maneuvers as "completely radical compared to those of ordinary aircraft."

Nearby Bolling AFB, D.C., had no interceptors to send out due to runway repairs underway. The interceptor unit was instead called in from its temporary home in Wilmington, Delaware. After an unexplained delay, two fighter jets entered D.C.'s radar range at 3:30 a.m. But as soon as they arrived, the intruders left. Over the next 90 minutes, alternating pairs of interceptors played a cat-and-mouse game with the interlopers. On a final pass, they did not disappear; instead the approaching pilots witnessed an enormous fiery-orange sphere pace them from above.[12]

Following a brief visit on the 23rd of July, the intruders were back in numbers on the 26th. Beginning at approximately 9:00 p.m., between six and twelve unknowns were tracked by radar over the District and surrounding areas. At 2:00 a.m. two interceptors were scrambled from Wilmington. Having been present and mockingly apparent for several hours, the unknowns once again retreated when the jets reached D.C. radar range. Following a pass and return covering ten minutes, the pilots were directed back to Wilmington. Reportedly at the moment they left D.C.'s radar range, the unknowns reappeared on the screens. Finally, on retreat, one of the pilots gained visual recognition of multiple objects, which he described as blue-white lights tremendous in size.[13]

On the heels of all this activity, on July 29, Ralph Clark, Acting Assistant Director of the CIA's Office of Scientific Intelligence (OSI), advised the Agency's deputy director (DDI) that verified UFO reports were ongoing. "In the past several weeks a number of radar and visual sightings of unidentified aerial objects" were received. Clark added that OSI had stayed on top of such matters around the world in the three years since its inception, but a study group had now been formed to review all that had been experienced. OSI would be participating in that study.[14]

Three days later, on August 1, the acting chief of the CIA Weapons and Equipment (W&E) Division wrote to the DDI informally. Of the roughly 1,000–2,000 reports of anomalies recorded by the US Air Force's Air Technical Intelligence Center (ATIC), mostly from inside the country, the majority were "phoney" [sic]; fewer than 100 remained unexplained. Among those, there was "no pattern of specific sizes, configurations, characteristics, performance, or location." Better information, the chief added, might have explained most or all of those recent unresolved incidents as well. That information shortfall included misidentified conventional equipment, basics of the night sky, and things that were airborne but not yet identified.[15]

Because an alien origin could not be thoroughly discounted, caution required continued monitoring of the subject, he determined. The chief stressed that CIA interest or concern should not reach the press or public due to their alarmist tendencies. A thorough briefing by ATIC would follow.

In a later untitled note regarding a phone call from the FBI, on August 8, 1952, the W&E chief declared: "So long as a range of reports remains 'unexplainable' (interplanetary aspects and alien origin not being thoroughly excluded from consideration), caution requires that intelligence continue coverage of the subject."[16]

Muddying the waters was an attached untitled radio teletype (translated from French) summarizing an article written for the German magazine *Der Flieger* (The Aviator). The text outlined an alleged UFO crash at Spitsbergen, an island off Norway. The saucer had allegedly been studied by Norwegian and German rocket experts. Described as 47 meters in diameter and pilotless, it was outfitted with a radio piloting transmitter containing a plutonium nucleus. On its periphery were "46 automatic jets." An inscription in Russian was discovered inside. There was no firm evidence either to confirm or cast doubt on the credence of the teletyped report.[17]

An OSI branch, in an August 8 meeting, discussed an upcoming project that would originate in the Agency's Physics and Electronics (P&E) Division to evaluate unidentified aerial objects reported to date. P&E's Dr. Todos M. Odarenko took charge of the gathering. He was a Czech-trained electrical engineer and recipient of a civilian award from the US Navy for his electronics work at Bell Laboratories during World War II. He would later consult for the Joint Chiefs.

Dr. Odarenko suggested maintaining a file to permit the division and branch to take a stand and form an opinion as appropriate. Already underway, the Air Force's ATIC was examining the subject, keeping records, and informing the CIA. All P&E members were to review the materials and determine how to contribute. Outside inquiries would be handled by ATIC via its standard form. A P&E project officer was appointed and directed to learn who handled such cases, get a past history, and find out what had been learned in meteorology, radar, and other technologies relative to the aerial events.[18]

On August 20, after an OSI briefing, Director of Central Intelligence (DCI) Walter Smith ordered the preparation of a formal document for consideration by the National Security Council, advising on the great numbers of UFO reports and "stating the need for investigation and directing agencies concerned to cooperate in such investigations."[19]

Attached to CIA Director Smith's directive was a July 29, 1952, draft memo to unknown parties, enclosing a memo from the Acting Assistant Director of OSI to inform them that UFO visual and radar reports were ongoing. Also attached was an undated NSC directive for Smith to establish procedures for identifying unknown aerial objects.[20]

Tasked with drafting that set of Smith procedures based on supportive staff studies, the deputy CIA director and his OSI staff determined that the broader problem was essentially one of research and development. Though OSI had continually reviewed anecdotal reports from Agency sources and others over its first three years, that material was all unevaluated. A special task force of experts was needed, one devoted to reviewing the entire UFO subject to date. If such a group were formed, OSI would participate.[21]

The DDI decided to contact an Air Force R&D resource, no doubt in hopes of sharing the burden of this sticky wicket. An interagency conference soon followed. The Air Force, specifically ATIC, had been analyzing incoming written reports from the public since 1948, most from within US borders. By the second half of 1952, those reports numbered around 1,500. Hoaxes were few, but at least 80 percent were resolved to the military command's satisfaction as ordinary objects (aircraft, weather balloons, meteors, Venus, and the like). Common sense suggested that many of the misidentifications stemmed from hopeful delusions.

Within that 80 percent rejection pile was every single-witness account anywhere at any time—disqualified out of hand for lack of corroboration. Given sufficient resources, most of the remaining 20 percent would likewise be explained, the argument went. Still, a small percentage of reports continued to involve multiple, credible observers describing seemingly incredible things. To some within the Agency, at least, that was puzzling. Still, it was legitimate to pose a fundamental question: For what, if any, reason was the Central Intelligence Agency involved in this odd business?

The Agency's assistant director for operations wrote to the DDI on August 22. The FBI had latently intercepted the transcript of a June 10, 1951, Moscow radio program on the UFO subject—the first-ever mention by the Kremlin-controlled state service. Responding to a question in the "Listener's Mailbag," the Soviet broadcast proclaimed, in reference to purported misidentification of weather balloons:

> The Chief of Nuclear Physics in the US Naval Research Bureau explained them recently as being used for stratospheric studies. US Government circles knew all along that these objects were of a harmless nature, but if they refrained from denying "false reports," the purpose behind such tactics was to fan war hysteria in the country.[22]

The DDI in response requested the FBI director to alert field stations to convey any mention of flying saucers in Iron Curtain countries.

Coincidentally, that summer there arose a revealing, if non-sourced, 29-page statement, "The Air Force Stand on Flying Saucers—As Stated by CIA, in a Briefing on 22 August 1952." The statement's cover sheet revealed that ATIC was responsible for handling UFO reports to the Air Force, backed by the USAF Office of Special Investigations for authenticity and witness reliability. The USAF officially denied that flying saucers were US or Soviet secret weapons, nor were they evidence of extraterrestrial visitors. All sightings, it said, were (a) well-known things (for example, balloons, aircraft, meteors, clouds) or (b) atmospheric phenomena (refractions, reflections, temperature inversions, ball lightning, and so forth). "Not a shred of evidence exists" that any report lay outside those categories. Sightings were frequent near atomic energy plants due to the numbers of security staff observing the sky and grounds there. Other less well-advanced ideas were also offered. The notion that byproducts of atomic fission might produce flying saucers was likewise advanced. Cumulative data showed 78 percent of cases to be explainable as (a) or (b); 2 percent were hoaxes; and 20 percent were left unexplained due to the ambiguity of the accounts.[23]

The Air Force was mainly interested in the psychological warfare factor. Key members of *saucer societies* who kept the subject alive were of dubious loyalty and open suspicion. Some had suspect financial sources. A public "made jumpy by the 'flying saucer' scare would be a serious liability in the event of air attacks by an enemy."[24]

Attached to the August 22, 1952, "Air Force Stand" document was one from three days before, "Flying Saucers." A semi-formal Air Force-OSI Study Group had pondered "the implications of the 'Flying Saucer' problem." They had reviewed available intelligence, official reports, press and magazine articles, and popular books leading up to their findings:

Following the June 1947 Mount Rainier, Washington/Kenneth Arnold incident plus great numbers of claimed sightings in the months to follow, the Air Force had begun a study, initially titled Project Saucer. In December 1947, its task force released sections of a secret report that concluded the sightings resulted from mass hysteria, hoaxes, hallucinations, and misinterpretation of known objects. The public, the report went on, was initially satisfied, but in the years to follow read popular but "highly speculative books and magazine articles" by "sensational writers."[25]

Those, plus increasing sighting numbers overall, prompted the Air Force in early 1951 to institute worldwide reporting and alert USAF bases to "intercept the unidentified objects."[26]

USAF General John A. Samford had offered to the press that study's interim conclusions: Analysis showed: (a) no threat was posed to the United States; (b) recent Washington, D.C., reports were likely caused by temperature inversions; and (c) no American experiment or test was responsible.

Despite those findings, the authors concluded, "There are many who believe in them (UFOs) and will continue to do so in spite of any official pronouncement . . ."[27]

In light of all the aerial phenomena reported in Europe, America, and worldwide, ongoing Agency monitoring of the Soviet press curiously revealed no mention of the subject whatsoever. CIA staff concluded such an utter silence had to be official Soviet government policy in order to somehow use the data in psychological warfare.

As alluded to in the paper, civilian saucer groups had formed in the United States. The unnamed leader of one was perhaps of questionable character and could set off mass hysteria. USAF was already monitoring that group.

The report had concluded that, for a given month, perhaps a dozen sightings by the general public remained unidentified.

Also attached to the "Air Force Stand" document was a non-sourced, untitled, 14-page draft paper dated August 15, 1952 (page 12 was missing). The author or authors asserted that four issues bore on the subject of aerial anomalies: (a) earnestness of the witness; (b) absence of a reference point for objects seen against the sky; (c) difficulty of estimating size, distance, and speed without a reference point; and (d) absence of material evidence.

Psychological factors impacting an individual's veracity included mental conditioning from earlier stories in print, emotional response to the unknown, and a potential desire for publicity.

Physiological factors—the person's general physical condition—included possible fatigue or anemia, eye strain, and adaptation to night viewing.

ATIC attested that the most commonly misinterpreted sources were balloons, aircraft, astronomical bodies, atmospheric phenomena, instrument errors, and windblown objects. Examples:

- The Mantell Incident (see pages 9–11) and a later observation at Wright-Patterson AFB were misperceived Skyhook balloons.

- Conventional aircraft were misidentified during the day (reflections) and at night (running lights).

- Astronomical sources of routine visual mistakes included planets (especially Venus) and meteors.

- Atmospheric sources distorting optics or even radar returns included ball lightning, temperature inversions, turbulent air masses, the Aurora Borealis, and jet streams.

- Also mistaken were birds in flight as well as clouds masking the moon or illuminated by searchlights.

These sources explained 80 percent of all sightings. Another 10 percent would be explained with more accurate details and investigative follow-up. "This still leaves ATIC with a possible 10 percent of sightings for which there is no available explanation." Little-understood natural phenomena could have caused optical or electronic aberrations, while some of the unknowns could have been electromagnetic or electrostatic in nature. However, "we still are left with numbers of *incredible reports from credible observers*" (emphasis added).[28]

A fourth attachment to the "Air Force Stand" file was a nine-page, non-sourced August 14, 1952, document titled "Flying Saucers"— seemingly a prepared speech. A "phenomenal increase" in reported sightings in recent weeks had been accompanied by great numbers of requests to the Air Force for information, the paper exclaimed. NSA Director and Air Force General John Samford had already spoken out that there was "no pattern of anything remotely consistent with any menace to the United States."[29]

That paper outlined various types of misidentifications and denied the US government was responsible for any sightings, adding that the Air Force would emphasize instrumentation in its continuing efforts. The report recalled two military interceptions previously ordered. The first and more prominent occurred on January 7, 1948, resulting in the pilot's death—the much-publicized case of Captain Thomas Mantell of the Kentucky Air National Guard. (See "Mantell Incident," pages 9–11)

Despite explanations from American officials to the contrary, reports of inexplicable airborne objects continued to stream in from across the Atlantic. An IFDRB distributed August 27, 1952, referenced anomalies in southern Europe and North Africa in the spring. A newsman's personal account published in the Tangiers, Algeria, newspaper described a rocket-shaped object that passed over Barcelona, Spain, on May 21, 1952, at an estimated 2,000 meters altitude. The object traveled on a straight line, he said, trailing smoke.[30]

From the same document, on June 3 an unknown trailing pale-green light and travelling at a high rate of speed over Sousse, Tunisia, was seen by many. Four days later, an incident in Meknes, Morocco, involved a flying saucer trailing white smoke and moving at great speed. Also, a June 15 incident at Taourirt, Morocco, as viewed by multiple dock workers, was described as a "disc of white flames surrounded by two circular strands" that flew past the witnesses. Saucer sightings were also reported on June 15 over Marrakesh and Casablanca.[31]

The July 16 Casablanca news carried reports from various locations:

1. On July 12 at night, two policemen saw an elongated object at high speed with a white trail.

2. Also July 12 at 9:30 p.m., a diminutive yellow object (under one meter) passed overhead at high speed.

3. On July 13, a blue-green sphere with a short tail was observed at great speed; in seconds it was gone.

4. Also July 13, three "white fires" were observed in the sky at 9:30 p.m. Additional 9:00–10:00 p.m. reports described a "luminous flying object" near Casablanca.

The July 18 Casablanca daily reported that a "phosphorescent, ovoid object" 20 meters long allegedly rose rapidly from the ground with a bluish trail—date uncertain.[32]

An undated, heavily redacted Information Report was distributed September 2, 1952. The lone untouched section outlined an Arnhem, Netherlands, incident occurring on July 24 (see page 29).[33]

Also distributed was an IFDRB relating UFOs reportedly seen in North and West Africa, originating in the Dakar, Senegal, and Casablanca, Morocco, newspapers. In Dakar, at 6:08 a.m., July 3, a flat yet tapered object was observed, estimated to be 1,500 meters high and traveling at great speed, issuing red and blue flames.[34]

Another UFO-related IFDRB was distributed on September 27, 1952, from a source who covered Spain, Algeria, and French Equatorial Africa. At 8:00 a.m., April 21 over Almansa, Spain, "many people saw a series of four glowing spheres crossing the sky" in succession, at great height and speed. On the night of July 30 in Andujar, Spain, many residents saw a round red object at great speed and silent, trailing greenish light.[35]

The same report conveyed other aerial oddities from various sources. On June 1, at 2:40 a.m. at Port Gentil, Gabon, the master and first mate of a cargo ship at anchor saw an orange luminous object rise up behind the port, execute two right-angle turns, pass overhead and continue out of sight.

On October 13, 1952, mid-level manager James Reber typed a lengthy draft memo to the Agency's deputy director of intelligence. It was titled "Flying Saucers."

With the Eisenhower-Stevenson election less than a month away, surely neither wanted such a distraction. America was now in a full-blown cold war with the Soviets, who were quickly marching from atomic to hydrogen bombs. Of necessity, the Air Force had been analyzing UFO reports out of concern for a possible Soviet attack on the United States. Further, the USSR could use any social confusion to launch an air attack.

Thus far, the memo strove to convince, the Defense Department had relied on ATIC research and that 80 percent of reported sightings had, to OSI satisfaction, been resolved. Further, "(OSI) review of existing information does not lead to the conclusion that the saucers are USSR created or controlled."[36]

Lacking, Reber said, was some fundamental scientific research "to clarify the nature and causes of Flying Saucers and to devise means whereby they might be instantly identified." The paper, though, projected scientific intelligence problems: What was the Soviets' knowledge of these phenomena? Could the Soviets use them against the United States? How did flying saucers affect our threat warning system? Among its basic conclusions:

1. The Defense Department had primary responsibility for scientific research on these matters.

2. The CIA Director should communicate with the IAC or NSC.

3. It was premature to do US psychological warfare planning.

4. A National Estimate on Flying Saucers should be the "basis for a public policy to reduce or restrain mass hysteria."[37]

As autumn 1952 proceeded, voices across the Agency's Office of Scientific Intelligence came to a singular conviction: The saucer problem would never be resolved to the public's satisfaction unless recognized experts brought hard science to bear.

In the aftermath of Eisenhower's victory, the first week of December served to focus Agency attention on "the problem" and a potential resolution. On December 2nd, OSI's Director, H. Marshall Chadwell, sent a memo titled "Unidentified Flying Objects" to Walter B. Smith, Director of Central Intelligence. Chadwell expressed an urgency over the matter: "At this time, the reports of incidents convince us that there is something going on that must have immediate attention." Sightings of unknowns at great altitudes and speeds near defense installations were neither natural phenomena nor known aerial vehicles. He further informed the DCI that OSI was establishing a group of consultants to review the matter and convince authorities that research and development must be undertaken.[38]

The next day Philip G. Strong, OSI's Acting Deputy Assistant Director, wrote a memorandum for the record (a common Agency practice) to summarize a meeting on the 2nd with MIT executives Julius Stratton and Max Millikan. Strong outlined recent valid UFO cases. Stratton reiterated his call for an academic study, but because of delicate relations with the Air Force, any such study would need its concurrence soon thereafter. He added that Cal Tech would be one preferred site and asked to be kept informed of new developments. Over lunch a CIA colleague suggested enlisting the help of a Columbia University professor, an expert on "magic and general chicanery." That aside, Strong concluded that no new study would be viable without the expressed approval of the CIA director.[39]

Then on the 4th, the Agency's Intelligence Advisory Committee held a meeting in the director's conference room, the Acting DDI Robert M. Amory Jr. presiding. On UFOs, according to the minutes transcribed, "It was recognized that the problem is best approached if directly related to specific problems of intelligence and defense." Selected scientists should appraise the evidence "in light of pertinent scientific theories."[40]

Still that week, one staff member informed another via informal memo of the "Proposed Study on the Flying Saucers Phenomena; Intelligence Advisory Committee," December 5, 1952. "[T]he military members suggested a logical approach which would call for a group of scientists to make a study of the new 'saucers' data." But a recent African encounter had argued against all such phenomena being explainable.[41]

The following week, on December 9, OSI staffer H.U. Graham wrote to his superior, Philip Strong, via formal Office Memorandum entitled "FCC Monitoring and Flying Saucers." Graham referred to certain unexplained radio signals intercepted by the Federal Communications Commission. He proposed that any panel of scientists formed to consider reports of unidentified aerial objects ought to review said signals for possible connection to the phenomena.[42]

A week after his earlier memo to the CIA director, on the 10th, OSI Director Chadwell wrote to Walter Smith again. In this memo, "Unidentified Flying Objects," Chadwell cited recent incidents:

1. Movie footage of ten unknowns at Tremonton, Utah, unexplained as either natural phenomena or known aircraft

2. A brilliant light over the coast of Maine, at least twice the altitude of any known device, which remained aloft for four hours

3. A claimed saucer in Florida that left effects as yet unexplained

4. At various locations, lights or objects not resembling known aircraft, not of a celestial origin, not weather based

Chadwell suggested a panel of experts to examine the evidence, headed by Howard P. Robertson, a distinguished physicist at the California Institute of Technology.[43]

Chadwell's typewriter was busy once more on the 13th. Again titled "Unidentified Flying Objects," his memorandum (signed by subordinate H. L. Clark) to the CIA director was to amplify the earlier conveyance and to present current thinking on the subject.

Clark determined a preliminary review by the Air Force's young Project Blue Book was complete. A day before, Cal Tech's H. P. Robertson, CIA agent and missile expert Fred C. Durant, and others visited ATIC at Wright-Patterson AFB. There they acquired selected case materials. Review of those concluded there was "no reasonable evidence that the objects sighted are of foreign origin." Though not a direct threat to national defense, certain dangers remained.[44]

The memo went on. OSI was considering whether to round up a small group of respected scientists to continue extensive examination of the evidence. OSI would also decide on investigative methodologies, select instruments to obtain data, and decide methods of rapid identification. It would recommend whether to enlist a larger panel—which would not be soon convened; so far, that was not justified.

An enclosure to the memo described in some detail the July 2, 1952, Tremonton, Utah, film; the October 10–11, 1952, "orange object" seen at the Presque Isle and Limestone (later Loring) AFB weather stations in Maine (both episodes subsequently assessed by Ohio State University astronomer Dr. J. Allen Hynek as Jupiter); and an August 19, 1952, report of an alleged close encounter by a Florida scoutmaster and four of his scouts.[45]

In West Germany on November 20, 1952, an inventor applied for a patent for his "elliptical flying object," which he claimed was 40 meters in diameter and capable of hovering, with a top speed of 4,000 km/hour.[46]

Taking Stock

Since the summer of 1947, it was generally agreed that the Air Force's Air Technical Intelligence Center (ATIC) had received around 1,500 official reports of sightings from the public—250 in July 1952 alone. ATIC listed 205 cases as unexplained from 1947 through 1951, plus 285 in 1952. Four hypotheses from the military contemplated possible explanations for the unknowns: (a) US secret weapon development, (b) Russian development, (c) "men from Mars"—spaceships—interplanetary travelers, or (d) given adequate resources, an explanation for all as either known objects misidentified or little-understood natural phenomena.

OSI would evaluate the multifaceted Air Force study to determine intelligence implications, if any. But public awareness of CIA involvement risked hardening perceptions of the subject's seriousness. The Agency review would include its own intelligence, many official reports, press coverage, and popular books. In preparation, OSI spent a day at Wright-Patterson AFB speaking with Blue Book principals, then conferred with its own consultants.

A meeting of scientific minds was in order.

While you were away from your desk . . .

No doubt scurrying about for explanations of the mysterious airborne vehicles that had frequented our nation's very capital, CIA analysts might have missed some of the other 1952 incidents involving aerial phenomena. For the events below were not included in the major release of UFO-related materials to the Agency's website in 2017.

March 29, 1952

Near Glen Burnie, Maryland, a car's engine died as the driver neared a 50-foot silver disc with a lighted rim and off-centered dome. The ship moved overhead and hovered with a vacuum cleaner sound. The motorist retrieved a submachine gun and stepped outside. A second driver stopped in the near distance but quickly retreated at the sight of the craft, the weapon, or both. After three minutes, the disc turned on edge and shot away, tumbling as it went. The auto's wiring had been magnetized and the paint was damaged. USAF Project Blue Book ruled the incident unidentified.[47] Note: The driver's occupation, other pursuits, or purpose that night in carrying an automatic weapon were not specified.

May 1, 1952

"May Day!" was never more apropos. A major was leaving George AFB in Victorville, California when he spotted a formation of five enormous discs over the base. Momentarily they moved into a V formation and left the area. The major returned to the base to meet with the security officer only to find that he was interviewing a group of airmen who had also witnessed the anomalies. This would turn out to be the first of nine sightings at the base over a three-week period.[48]

On the same day, at the Davis-Monthan AFB outside Tucson, Arizona, a B-36 Peacemaker bomber was closely approached by two discs. Apart from the crew, witnesses on the ground included the Air Intelligence officer charged with investigating UFO sightings. The observation lasted approximately three minutes.[49]

At 9:27 p.m. still that day, 12 unknowns appeared over Randolph AFB, Texas. Flying in three tight formations, they crossed the expanse at a velocity estimated between 1,500 and 2,000 mph—roughly 2–3 times that of any experimental aircraft's top speed to that point.[50]

June 5, 1952

At Offutt Air Force Base, Nebraska, about 11:00 p.m., three personnel watched a red airborne object, stationary for 4–5 minutes, speed away emitting a short tail. One of the witnesses was a top-secret control officer for the Strategic Air Command and formerly in the Air Force Office of Special Investigations (AFOSI). USAF Project Blue files listed the incident as unknown.[51]

July 14, 1952

At 8:10 p.m., a Pan American Airways DC-4 was approaching Norfolk, Virginia, on its way to Miami. The captain and third officer noticed a red brilliance in the sky, headed generally their way but at a much lower altitude. As the brightness grew nearer, it resolved into six separate bright objects at perhaps 2,000 feet. The captain later described their shape as clearly outlined and circular with well-defined edges, i.e., not phosphorescent or fuzzy. The upper surfaces glowed red-orange. They could now tell that the six unknowns were in narrow echelon formation, each vehicle successively higher. The men estimated the diameter of each as 100 feet.[52]

Suddenly the lead object decelerated; the second and third wavered and seemed to almost pass the first as all six slowed down. When almost directly below the plane, they all flipped on edge simultaneously. The pilots could now *see* that the saucers were coin-shaped, their edges unlit, and about 15 feet thick. The top surfaces appeared to be flat, not domed. While still tilted, the formation reversed its echelon order then tilted back to horizontal. The group made a sharp turn and moved a distance away. Now the pilots caught sight of two more identical but still brighter UFOs as they darted into view from below the plane. These two proceeded to join the original six anomalies. All eight extinguished their lighting momentarily. Then they arched up over the airliner and sped west, blinking out non-sequentially.

Upon landing, the crew was questioned at length by representatives of AFOSI who told them of several other groups of observers, including one USAF officer. AFOSI's classified cable outlining the event was sent to Army and Navy intelligence, the Armed Forces Security Agency (forerunner of the NSA), the Joint Chiefs of Staff, and (son of a gun) the CIA.[53]

September 1952: Mainbrace

Operation Mainbrace comprised twelve days of NATO maneuvers in September 1952, held primarily in northern Europe and the North Atlantic. In the early hours of September 13, a participating Danish destroyer was north of Bornholm Island (off the southeast coast of Denmark) when the lieutenant commander and several crew members watched a triangular object, emitting a bluish glow, travel southeast at an estimated 900 mph. Over the next week four more incidents were witnessed by well-qualified observers.

On September 19, 1952, just before 11:00 a.m. at RAF Topcliffe, Yorkshire, two RAF officers and three crewmen witnessed a silver disc following a Meteor jet fighter as it banked in preparation for landing. "But after a few seconds it stopped its descent and hung in the air, rotating as if on its own axis. Then it accelerated at an incredible speed to the west . . ."[54]

About September 20, personnel of the aircraft carrier USS Franklin D. Roosevelt, participating in the Mainbrace activities, observed and photographed a silvery sphere. (The photos were never made public.) The object moved across the sky behind the fleet. A reporter aboard the Roosevelt took several color photos, subsequently examined by Naval Intelligence officers and by Captain Edward Ruppelt of the USAF Project Blue Book. Ruppelt remarked, "[The pictures] turned out to be excellent. Judging by the size of the object in each successive photo, one could *see* that it was moving rapidly." The possibility of a balloon being responsible was checked out, but none of the ships had launched any. A poor print of one of the photos later appeared in the Blue Book files released.[55]

At 7:30 p.m., September 20, at Denmark's Karup Field, three Danish Air Force officers sighted a shiny metallic disc as it passed overhead from the direction of the Mainbrace fleet. It moved through clouds and out of view.[56]

On September 21, six British RAF pilots in formation over the North Sea observed a shiny sphere's approach from the direction of the Mainbrace fleet. It eluded their pursuit and left the area. Later returning to base, one of the pilots noticed it following him, but when he turned to give chase it sped away.[57]

October 17, 1952

At Oloron, France, in the early afternoon, the family of the local high school superintendent were among the witnesses to a narrowly formed, whitish cigar-shaped object in the sky, inclined 45 degrees and accompanied by about thirty small spheres with a yellowish ring. These moved in pairs, zigzagging as they went. When two pulled apart, something like an electric arc was produced between them. All the objects were expelling an abundant trail of an unusual substance likened to strands of fiberglass— what would become known colloquially as *angel hair*—which drifted down and clung to trees, power lines, and house roofs. When held, the material gelatinized and disappeared.

October 27, 1952

Ten days later, at 4:00 p.m., an eerily similar incident occurred. A hundred Gaillac, France, residents observed a formation of 16–20 discs, arranged in pairs, traversing the sky. The revolving objects were said to emit bluish light. Many among the witnesses also noticed an elongated cylinder within the formation, which marched directly over the town for ten minutes. All the objects discharged shining white material akin to fiberglass. Much of this angel hair was caught by trees and powerlines. But gathered samples quickly disintegrated. After ten minutes in sight, the formation reportedly continued along a straight path. Minutes after the Gaillac event, a single disc plus a cylindrical anomaly were sighted over 125 miles northeast at a meteorological station.[58]

October 21, 1952

An RAF lieutenant and his student pilot took off from RAF Little Rissington, Gloucestershire, that afternoon, in a Meteor twin-jet trainer for a planned exercise at 35,000 feet. As they broke through cloud cover at about 14,000, three luminous white discs came into view. The jet drew closer and they determined that the objects had a flat plate shape. When the bogeys moved across the jet's path, the student suggested they pursue them. Recalling rumors of planes disappearing in such a circumstance, the pilot replied that that was a terrible idea.[59]

Chapter 6

1953:

Cold Water from Robertson and Others

On January 9, 1953, OSI Director H. Marshall Chadwell communicated with the Agency Director, Walter Bedell Smith. The subject of the Memorandum was "Consultants for Advisory Panel on Unidentified Flying Objects."

Prior to the selected panel members convening, this memo proposed adding, in advisory capacities, radar expert Luis Alvarez and Thornton Page, astronomer and astrophysicist. Chadwell emphasized, "Every effort has been made to consider the most competent scientists whose dispositions are suitable to this complex study."[1] Attached were two single-page documents that were completely illegible.

Organized by OSI and coming together quickly, the core group of five scientists formed the Scientific Advisory Panel, headed by Cal Tech's physicist Dr. Howard P. Robertson. The group met at OSI's offices for several hours over four days, January 14–17, 1953.[2]

Soon to be known broadly, if informally, as the Robertson Panel, the academics each argued for and against the claimed evidence. Informal commentaries regarding the integrity of film and photographic cases included Tremonton, Utah; Great Falls, Montana; and Yaak, Montana. Considerable discussion was also devoted to incidents at Port Huron, Michigan; Bellefontaine, Ohio; Presque Isle Air Force Base, Maine;

Limestone (later Loring) AFB, Maine; and Haneda AFB, Japan. Among fifteen additional cases the panel paid significant attention to was an alleged close encounter involving a Florida scoutmaster and four boy scouts. In total, 75 case files from 1951–52 were addressed. The remaining fourteen cases reviewed stemmed from 1950 or before.[3]

Fred C. Durant of OSI, who served as the panel's recording secretary, began preparing a report of its findings while the sessions were still ongoing, finalizing it a day after the meetings ended, on January 18. The Durant Report contained the official Robertson Panel Report materials plus minutes of the group's discussions, lists of all staff and participants, and related details and would prove superior to the more basic Robertson Report.

Perhaps the most contentious case evaluation of a supposed aerial anomaly concerned motion pictures at Tremonton, Utah, as taken by a military photographer using a state-of-the-art movie camera and film. The panel determined the photographer had captured either polyethylene balloons or a flock of seagulls in flight. The panel was seemingly unimpressed overall by the meager amount of quality data to bolster the countless anecdotal accounts nationwide.

Rather than recommend steps to improve fact gathering, the members' findings were predictable, setting a tone for the scientific community's attitude toward the subject thereafter. Foremost was their conclusion that UFOs offered no direct threat to national security.

The panel had found no evidence to suggest basic principles of science beyond what was already known. They recommended abandoning any effort to improve the quality of data received since it would only serve to show that UFOs do not exist.

In the panel's opinion, most cases had a reasonable explanation, while better data, deductive reasoning, and the scientific method would likely have explained the rest. Sighting brevity and unclear witness statements left some cases unexplained. Solving most or all incoming sighting reports "would be a great waste of effort," the group concluded.[4]

As an aggressive and controversial assertion, the Robertson Panel concluded that national security agencies should "take immediate steps to strip the Unidentified Flying Objects of the special status they have been given and the aura of mystery they have unfortunately acquired." Such debunking efforts, the panel recommended, would preferably include media airtime, military training, and monitoring of civilian ufology groups.[5]

The next week, the group issued its formal report, "Scientific Advisory Panel on Unidentified Flying Objects, 14–17 January 1953." The group followed up with a detailed 21-page document expressing a variety of thoughts generated during the four days of panel sessions.[6]

The majority of sightings could in all likelihood be measured in seconds, not minutes, the panel asserted. Further, in many cases the witness statements were either convoluted or otherwise unclear, leaving them unexplained for the wrong reasons. The Air Force or other government agency attempting to solve most or all sighting accounts would be a wasted effort unless it aided training or education of the public. Charles Fort had written on "strange things in the sky," and how over the centuries no single explanation accounted for "things seen."[7]

The Formalized Report

The Robertson (Durant) Report, assessing numerous factors arising from the group's discussions, emphatically proposed an ongoing program of incident debunking and public education in order to rid the nation of supposed UFO mischief once and for all.

Evidence Presented

Twenty-two forms of evidence were included within its (arguably) broad inquiry:

1. ATIC's 75 best-documented cases, 1951-52, plus 14 earlier cases

2. ATIC status and progress reports on Projects Grudge and Blue Book

3. Progress reports on Project Stork

Note: This interagency group was quoted in the minutes of the panel's first meeting: "It is very reasonable to believe that some type of unusual object or phenomena is being observed as many of the sightings have been made by highly qualified sources."[8]

4. Summary report of sightings at Holloman AFB, NM

5. USAF report on Project Twinkle (green fireballs)

6. Outline of Project Pounce (Kirtland AFB proposed UFO investigations)

7. Films of sightings at Tremonton, Utah, July 2, 1952, and Great Falls, Montana, August 8, 1950

8. Summary report of 89 selected cases

9. Draft of ATIC manual

10. Unexplained sightings, by US location

11. US balloon-launching sites

12. Selected balloon flight paths in respect to sightings

13. Sightings frequency, 1948-52

14. Categories of sighting explanations

15. Film transparencies of balloons in bright sunlight

16. Film of seagulls in sunlight

17. Intelligence reports of USSR interest in US sightings

18. USAF reporting forms and Air Force, Army, Navy orders on the subject

19. Sample polyethylene *pillow* balloon

20. JANP (Joint Army-Navy Publication) manual on radar characteristics

21. Official letters, foreign intelligence reports

22. Magazine, newspaper articles

On Lack of Danger

"[T]here was no evidence of a direct threat to national security." During World War II, foo fighters, a.k.a. balls of light, may have been electrostatic (akin to St. Elmo's Fire), electromagnetic, or reflections from airborne ice crystals—the question was never resolved. They were the flying saucers of the 1943–45 period.[9]

Air Force Reporting System

Public pressure probably caused some of the Air Force's concern. In a true crisis, mass low-grade reports of nocturnal meandering lights could over-load communications, mislead the public, and hide genuinely hostile acts. A concerted program to de-emphasize the subject needed to be carried out.[10]

Artifacts of Extraterrestrial Origins

The panel agreed that Earth may one day be visited by ETs, but it rejected the material at hand as evidence thereof. All the cases reviewed were raw and unevaluated. "[P]resent astronomical knowledge of the solar system makes the existence of intelligent beings (as we know the term) elsewhere than on the earth extremely unlikely . . ."[11]

Concerning the July 1952 Tremonton, Utah, incident, US Navy photographer and officer Delbert Newhouse, who had taken the footage, used Kodachrome film (1600 frames/minute), which strengthened the case. He testified afterward that there were twelve metallic saucer-shaped discs in his viewfinder. The team of USN and ATIC personnel who initially investigated the case argued that it eliminated birds, balloons, aircraft, and reflections; thus by deduction it must be a genuine unknown. The panel rejected that conclusion. Polyethylene pillow weather balloons, released in that area routinely, offered one alternative. Note: This expla-nation, of course, begged the question of why so many weather balloons would be sent aloft simultaneously.[12]

The August 1950 film from Great Falls, Montana, purportedly captured two rotating discs. The panel pondered, "in bright sunlight, the apparent motions, sizes, and brightnesses [*sic*] of the objects were considered strongly to suggest birds . . ." Alternately, they were reflections from an aircraft known to be in the area.

Note: The Great Falls film seen by the Robertson Panel—taken in bright daylight by a minor league baseball manager tending his ballpark—was particularly problematic, for they may not have viewed the best of it. The film taker had voluntarily loaned the film to the Air Force, likely Project Grudge or someone on its behalf, in October 1950. When the man later received it back, he realized about thirty-five frames were missing. These had shown the discs at their clearest and obviously rotating, he claimed. So, did the panel *see* the full-length Great Falls film or the shortened version?[13]

The panel asserted parenthetically that the Tremonton and Great Falls cases should not have been linked by the USN/ATIC team.

Follow-up on all 1,000+ sightings per year (1,900 in 1952) would waste limited resources. Further, long delays in reaching conclusions diminished their intelligence value. Scientists, the panelists stipulated, should accept that a phenomenon, to be accepted, had to be completely and convincingly documented. The burden of proof was on the witness.

Potential Related Dangers

While a direct threat to national security from these events was wholly lacking, the public's fascination with them posed other threats. Those included the misidentification of an actual enemy attack, an overload of emergency channels with false UFO claims, and efforts by a foreign nation to engage in psychological warfare, subjecting the United States to mass hysteria. An educational program could help filter out invalid sighting reports and keep the subject in proper perspective.

Geographic Locations of Unexplained Sightings

The ATIC map showed clusters of sightings near sensitive areas such as Los Alamos, New Mexico. This may have been an expected result, given the numbers of security staff stationed outdoors at such sites.

Instrumentation to Obtain Data

Placement of cameras at airports would not likely produce valuable data but might allay public concerns. No striking unidentified object had been recorded by astronomers watching the sky.

Radar Problem of Mutual Interference

Given the fact that radar as a technical field was still very young, occasional overlaps of radar signals could cause false UFO reports.

Unexplained Cosmic Ray Phenomena

Two recorded cases of radioactivity were not strong; that factor in UFO reports was rejected.

Educational Program

Such an effort should have two aims: training and debunking. Educating the public would improve witness recognition of conventional objects and natural phenomena and thereby reduce false sightings. That would involve enlisted, command, and research personnel.

Debunking sighting reports would be expected to reduce public interest. Television, movies, and magazine articles would be involved, focusing on cases originally puzzling but later explained. This would "reduce the current gullibility of the public and consequently their susceptibility to clever hostile propaganda." Using true cases would be a forceful argument.

A training/debunking program would take up to two years. By then, the "dangers related to 'flying saucers' should have been greatly reduced if not eliminated." Psychologists, writers, and a film producer would be necessary. The remnants of ATIC could focus on cases of scientific value.[14]

Unofficial Investigating Groups

"[S]uch organizations should be watched because of their potentially great influence on mass thinking if widespread sightings should occur.

The apparent irresponsibility and the possible use of such groups for subversive purposes should be kept in mind."[15]

Increase in Number of Sightings

All factors considered, overall reported sightings could be expected to increase.

On January 28, 1953, OSI Director Chadwell wrote to Robertson to indicate the report was "on its way up the ladder with our concurrence..." The full report plus lists of evidence received and personnel involved would be sent separately. These would collectively become known as the Durant Report.[16]

This file contained a January 20 letter from Robertson to "Chad" in which the scientist exulted, "Perhaps that'll take care of the Forteans for a while."[17]

Note: The Fortean Society, founded in 1931 and continuing in some form to the present, celebrated the works of Charles Fort, best known for his collection of accounts of anomalous phenomena entitled *The Book of the Damned* (1919).

Reflecting the hectic 1952 pace of citizen reports was a provocative IFDRB prepared on February 9, 1953, by (redacted), an Algerian intelligence source. The three-page submittal contained material spanning July 3 to November 20, 1952. It was titled "Reports of Unconventional Aircraft in French Africa, Corsica, and Western Europe." The document drew from multiple newspaper accounts.[18]

According to one press account, on July 3, 1952, 7:00 p.m., at Oran Department, Algeria, a man driving home had noticed a small silvery disc in the distance, rotating rapidly and maneuvering slowly. After three minutes, the unknown raced toward the sea. The Algerian weather bureau proclaimed a weather balloon as the source.[19]

On October 2, 1952, several Corsicans had observed a luminous spindle-shaped object at altitude. Four days later, at 6:30 p.m. on the Algerian coastline, numerous persons had watched a flaming cigar-shaped object cross the sky.[20]

Immediate Aftermath

Having finalized the CIA-commissioned Robertson Panel Report days earlier, in the last week of January 1953, OSI Director Chadwell wrote to Dr. Julius Stratton, Provost at MIT.[21] As earlier promised, this six-page letter was to update Stratton on the "problem of 'unidentified flying objects.'" At a December meeting the Intelligence Advisory Committee (comprising representatives of the Army, Navy, Air Force, Joint Chiefs of Staff, State Department, Atomic Energy Commission, and FBI) had recommended that the CIA assemble a panel to examine the problem. Experts in physics, radar, and astronomy were desired. Thus had Robertson's group come together.[22]

The panel recommended improved training of relevant personnel and a debunking effort to reduce public interest. Also, civilian investigative groups should be watched because of their potential influence on mass thinking and the possibility of subversive behavior. National security agencies should take "immediate steps to strip the Unidentified Flying Objects of the special status they have been given and the aura of mystery they have unfortunately acquired."[23]

The CIA concurred in the conclusions and recommendations of the Robertson Panel. Since the problems identified were operational, not intelligence related, the Agency would be only indirectly involved in the future. Knowledge of the CIA's interest would be restricted in view of probable misunderstanding by the public.

And Then Durant

The lengthier Durant Report was prepared by Fred C. Durant, CIA special agent and missile expert, who served as the Robertson Panel's recording secretary.[24] Two Durant Report attachments, both plain non-sourced sheets, explored "possible explanations" for UFO sightings: (a) psychological—hysteria, hallucinations, hoaxes; (b) misidentification of conventional aircraft, other known objects, or nature, including reflections, missiles, searchlights, balloons, kites, birds, bugs, airborne dust, or seeds; (c) natural phenomena—light aberrations, reflections, refractions, anomalous radar propagation, ionization, static electricity, ball lightning, planets, meteors, other astronomical bodies; (d) unconventional man-made devices in the United States, USSR, other foreign nations; (e) extraterrestrial origin— living creatures or machines.

Among the notable suggestions made by panel members was to expand the size of ATIC and insist that sighting reports be declassified ASAP.[25]

USAF Stands Down

In the wake of the Robertson Panel Report and the follow-up Durant Report, the Air Force continued to maintain a UFO interest but with reduced emphasis. At least that was their intention. ATIC transferred Project Blue Book to the Air Defense Command (later NORAD) headquarters in Colorado, from which it would perform any necessary investigations. ATIC continued to check sighting reports against meteorological, astronomical, aircraft, and balloon data. Findings were cross-referenced by date, location, source, type of observation, and conclusion drawn. About 10 percent of sightings remained unsolved.

Following the Robertson Report's release, the CIA decided not to prepare a National Security Council Intelligence Directive on the matter. UFOs were of only minimal intelligence interest, one of the universe's unsolved mysteries, as it were.

Operationally, though, the subject would remain on a front burner. Another wave of reports such as in 1952 could potentially interfere with air defenses, overload lines of communication, or serve as an enemy's psychological offensive timed to an actual attack.

The Agency embarked on the recommended two-pronged effort. A program to educate the public to recognize conventional aircrafts and natural phenomena would reduce the volume of sighting reports, while debunking new cases would serve to retard public interest in the subject.

Concurrently, it was agreed internally that civilian groups, such as the Aerial Phenomena Research Organization (APRO), should be surveilled because of their influence on public opinion and potential for subversive behavior. The Tucson, Arizona-based civilian investigative group, headed up by Coral and Jim Lorenzen, had garnered some interest nationwide and was in a position to feed a potential public frenzy.

A January 30 openly private Memorandum for Record by OSI's Philip Strong was mysteriously titled "Briefing of ONE Board on Unidentified Flying Objects, January 30, 1953." While the composition of the "ONE Board" came to be partially identified, precisely what its purpose was could not be defined outside government circles. Assisted by agent Fred Durant, Strong advised eleven high-ranking officials, including a general, an admiral, an ambassador, a future CIA director (William Bundy), and "Dr. Edgar Hoover."[26]

Among other materials in the same file were summary statements regarding the Tremonton, Utah, and Great Falls, Montana, films.

A West Coast civilian UFO investigations group likely became an early target of the aforementioned initiative to monitor such organizations. In a February 9, 1953, Office Memorandum to the Contact Division's assistant for operations, the (redacted) staffer was emphatic in citing the California Committee for Saucer Investigation (CCSI) for potential scrutiny. As evidence, he pointed to a German rocket scientist then working in the United States, Dr. Walter Riedel, who had spoken to someone about that civilian group; apparently, he was a member. Riedel mentioned that CCSI was planning a deliberate hoax in the Los Angeles area in order to track the volume of reporting witnesses and test variations in their accounts. The Air Force, he added, was already well aware of the group and its applied scientific methods; a copy of the UFO case reports Aerial Phenomena Research Organization (APRO) considered credible was always sent as a courtesy to Wright-Patterson AFB. Note: Was that subversive or patriotic?

The writer went on to say that Riedel showed interest in how the population of the USSR was reacting to UFO-sighting accounts—now publicized by *Pravda* after years of presumed official silence. The National Aeronautical Association had apparently advised Riedel not to maintain his CCSI membership.[27]

Apart from the Robertson connection early in the year, ufologically speaking 1953 was a fairly quiet year for the Central Intelligence Agency, evermore convincing officials there that its program of public education and debunking was working.

Still, enterprising analysts here and there engaged in chatter.

NICAP, Et Cetera

A January 4, 1953, internal document (not sourced) was titled "National Investigations Committee on Aerial Phenomena." The anonymous report writer assessed NICAP as loosely structured but efficient, with a newsletter, media relations, special reports, programs, and a localized investigative network. At the top, the organization consisted of an executive director and staff, an advisory board with ties to the scientific community, and an editorial review board with press connections. Regional staff maintained contact with local investigators.

The NICAP advisory board included recognized experts in physics, astronomy, anthropology, medicine, and psychology. A computer project to develop pattern analyses of the 15,000 raw reports on hand was underway.

The writer praised NICAP's policy for investigator acceptance and assignment as "a good one." Individuals selected had to be at least 25 years old, with "formal training or experience in some form of science, or other specialized background applicable to systematic collection of information." The United States was now divided into regions, with investigators in each.[28]

As of 1951, NICAP had 35 investigators nationally, a growing number, and an overall dues-paying membership of 3,500, which was expected to rise due to the spate of reported sightings in the news in 1952. As an organization, NICAP had an annual operating budget of $40,000.[29]

Without saying as much, the writer broadly implied that this group was worthy of careful watch, one that, at a time of cold-war strife, might stir up trouble.

Meanwhile, the Robertson-Durant reports continued to filter their way down the Agency ranks. On February 6, as an example, a bureau chief, Alan Warfield, mentioned them in a memo to fellow bureau heads titled "Unidentified Flying Objects." He broadly outlined the Robertson Panel's findings and recommendations.[30]

A long skirmish for America's hearts and minds on the possibility of life elsewhere was only beginning. Backing the CIA's Office of Scientific Intelligence (OSI) was a plainly nationalistic administration in regard to both current and previous enemies. Hence, no "woo woo" speculation was permitted.

Tidying Up

On March 12, 1953, the CIA Intelligence Advisory Committee (IAC) sent a copy of the Robertson Panel Report's two-page summary, plus an accompanying two-page document, "Evidence Presented," to a redacted source. The roster of panel members, associate members and interviewees was also included. The same materials were forwarded to the Secretary of Defense, the Federal Civil Defense Administration, and the National Security Resources Board. A handwritten note (sender and receiver redacted) related a phone call from a redacted source: "He said Mr. (redacted) would like to have you get someone to look over the material on the Scientific Panel on Unidentified Flying Objects. There may be something of interest there which should be reported to the (redacted) deputies."[31]

The following day, IAC Secretary Richard Drain enclosed the same materials with a letter to the Defense Secretary. Drain outlined the Robertson panel's conclusions, identified dangers to national security, and suggested ways to eliminate them. The CIA, he added, did not consider this subject primarily its concern but would assist in any action deemed advisable.[32]

On March 31, OSI's Fred Durant, the Robertson Panel recording secretary, sent a formal Office Memorandum to Philip Strong, OSI's Acting Deputy Assistant Director. Durant explained that the Agency's Office of Counter Intelligence (OCI) was no longer studying UFO reports and sought a place to send its files. OSI interest lay in the Air Branch of the Applied Science Division (ASD) and should continue to follow anomalous aerial developments through the summer months. He recommended that OCI, meanwhile, send its files to the ASD. Except for unusual events, ASD would destroy those files. All future OCI communications on UFOs would be sent to the ASD. In the event of a "future flap," the ASD would be valuable for critical analysis by Durant or Strong.[33]

OSI Director Chadwell sent a letter to Dr. Samuel A. Goudsmit of the Brookhaven National Laboratory on April 7, 1953. He was responding to a March 26 "Dear Chad" from "Sam" letter in which Goudsmit remarked tartly:

> When I spent those few days in your section last January, the
> file we studied contained one, or perhaps two, pamphlets
> from a crack-pot organization somewhere in the west. I
> am interested in following up this angle and, would like to
> get the name of that pamphlet and the address . . .

In reply, Chadwell identified the "crack-pot organization" as the Aerial Phenomena Research Organization, which published the *APRO Bulletin*, outlining civilian sighting investigations. On behalf of OSI, Chadwell expressed his appreciation for Goudsmit's previous help in that area and that he might call on him again.[34]

Having received a copy of the Robertson Report, on April 18 the head of the Federal Civil Defense Administration wrote to the secretary of the CIA Intelligence Advisory Committee to express FCDA's contin-ued interest in the UFO subject. As an item for follow-up, on the 21st, IAC Secretary Drain indicated that FCDA Administrator Val Peterson suggested a formal conference for a thorough discussion. Drain referred the correspondence to OSI.[35]

In a memo for the record on the 23rd, OSI's Strong wrote that a meet-ing to include the FCDA and CIA to review the Robertson Panel findings would be held in the Virginia governor's office if he planned to attend, otherwise at OSI. Strong said H.P. Robertson would be there.[36] In another memo for the record the following day, Strong indicated the meeting was set for the 30th. The governor would not be in attendance but three or four of his staff would be there.[37]

Perhaps as a consequence of that meeting with the FCDA and governor's staff, the accumulated data on UFOs would soon be transferred to new management within OSI. On May 27, 1953, OSI Director Chadwell wrote an Office Memorandum to Todos M. Odarenko, Chief of the Physics and Electronics (P&E) Division, the subject being "Unidentified Flying Objects." Chadwell began without fanfare: "Responsibility for maintaining current knowledge of reports of sightings of unidentified flying objects is hereby assigned to your division." Chadwell relatedly requested that the Applied Science Division (ASD) provide assistance "from a weapons and hardware standpoint." He directed the P&E staff to interact with the Air Branch of ASD, where the "major files" were kept, and with the Operations Staff office, which held key documents and administrative papers.[38] UFOs were now appropriately assigned, at least; staff attitudes notwithstanding, physics and electronics were central to the puzzle.

A month and change later, Odarenko responded to Chadwell. The assignment to take custody of such materials did not specify its priority, he mentioned prominently. Without asking per se, he was inquiring what that priority might be. Separately, the communication said, P&E staff, Air Force personnel, and the Scientific Review Board (called on by the CIA in 1952) had been contacted. Such a review would entail the need for two analysts plus clerical staff. Given the Board's findings of no direct threat to national security, the P&E division presumed "the project will be considered inactive." Incoming material would be reviewed periodically to leave only compelling cases meeting the "unidentified" definition. Unless involving immediate national security, all material would be filed for future reference. This level of effort required two staff part-time plus a filing cabinet.[39]

Voices from Elsewhere

On the 13th of July, 1953, an IFDRB copied from the Stockholm daily included the proclamation, "Danish Defense Leaders Take Serious View of Flying Saucers." Reports from trained observers and Danish Air Force radar of unknowns over Denmark and adjacent waters had led the military to suspect they originated from Soviet bases in the Arctic Ocean. The same week, an officer and seven others at Karup Air Field observed an aerial object basically resembling an aircraft but moving faster than anything known.[40] The airfield had served as a refugee camp after World War II. With the creation of the Royal Danish Air Force in 1950, it was renamed Air Base Karup.[41]

More recently, the crew of a Norwegian anti-aircraft battery had observed an unknown at great height. A jet aircraft sent to investigate could not reach the unknown before it "disappeared at a terrific speed." The Danish Defense Command remarked that the "flying saucer traffic" over Scandinavia was of immense aero-technical interest.[42]

Another IFDRB, distributed August 18, conveyed accounts of anomalies from newspapers in Athens, Greece; Brazzaville, Congo; and Tehran, Iran. The events outlined covered the previous months of March, April, and May.[43]

In one headline-grabbing story, a German engineer claimed that flying saucer plans, drawn up by Nazi engineers before World War II's end, had come to be in Soviet hands. The source claimed German saucer blueprints were already underway in 1941. By 1944, three experimental models were ready, one in disc shape. All could take off vertically and land in a confined space. After a three-month siege of the Germans' Breslau (now Wroclaw, Poland) facility at the war's conclusion, Soviets stole the plans on saucer construction.[44]

The same IFDRB related a November 22, 1952, account. A missionary and five companions in French Equatorial Africa had had a close encounter. Driving at night, they had witnessed four motionless discs overhead that lit up like suns when in motion but were silvery when stationary. Over 20 minutes the four moved about the area, seemingly performing tricks, then hovered momentarily before leaving non-uniformly. Later the six witnesses saw four objects forming a square at cloud level. One lit up vivid red and rose vertically; the other three joined it to form a square again. Luminous aerial objects were seen in the same time period above Homs, Syria, and the oil fields at Abadan in west-central Iran.[45]

In an undated (post-August 24, 1953) letter from the CIA's Legislative Counsel, John S. Warner, to Congressman Gordon H. Scherer, Warner responded to the concern of a constituent who had seen photos from Brazil of an alleged UFO, which had appeared on the morning *Today Show* with Dave Garroway. Warner stated that the photographer's processing of the film could not be independently verified and thus might have been faked. The inquirer to Scherer's office had a history of contacting officials on this subject. The Agency had nothing to add.[46]

Back to Robertson

Philip Strong, Deputy Assistant Director of OSI, wrote to Dr. Thornton Page of Johns Hopkins University, probably sometime in late August 1953. Dr. Page had been a member of the Robertson Panel. Strong advised him that recently the Air Force had requested declassification of the panel's two-page summary of conclusions so it could be shared with the press. In response, Dr. Robertson and the CIA had agreed to *partially* declassify the material—leaving out verbiage on debunking new sightings and monitoring civilian investigative groups, plus any mention of CIA involvement. Further, Strong went on, names of the Panel members could be withheld, but leaks might still occur. He asked Page to indicate approval or disapproval of such a partial release and whether his name could be used in it.[47]

In the weeks following, Strong repeated this letter-writing exercise, communicating with the remaining panel members. Ultimately, they all agreed to the proposed restricted release and to the publication of their names.

Donald Keyhoe versus the Company

In December 1953, Philip Strong and Todos Odarenko made more waves. First, in a strongly worded Office Memorandum to the OSI Assistant Director, Ralph Clark, Strong critiqued a popular book by Donald Keyhoe, a retired major in the US Marine Corps. The purpose of the book review was to ascertain any CIA security violations.

Keyhoe had been a USMC naval aviator. He wrote numerous aviation articles and fictional short stories for leading publications in the 1920s and 1930s. He also managed promotional tours for some aviation pioneers, in particular Charles Lindbergh. He returned to active duty in World War II, joining a naval aviation training division.[48]

Following the June 1947 Kenneth Arnold sighting, Keyhoe began to study the flying-saucer subject. Initially skeptical, he eventually became convinced that aerial phenomena were real. As their shapes, maneuvers, and speeds were apparently beyond the capacities of any nation, he determined that they had to be the products of alien technology. Approached by the editor of *True*, a popular men's magazine, Keyhoe wrote an article entitled "Flying Saucers Are Real," which appeared in the January 1950 issue and caused a sensation. Captain Edward Ruppelt, the first head of the USAF Project Blue Book, subsequently carried forward a rumor floating across publishing houses that the *True* article was among the most widely read magazine articles in history.[49]

Keyhoe then expanded his article into a book, *The Flying Saucers Are Real* (1950), which sold over a half-million copies. He argued that the Air Force knew the UFOs were extraterrestrial but downplayed sighting reports to avoid public panic. Keyhoe proceeded to write several more books on the subject, most prominently *Flying Saucers from Outer Space* (1953).[50]

In 1956 Keyhoe would cofound the National Investigations Committee on Aerial Phenomena (NICAP), whose reputation was burnished by a board of directors that included several prominent figures in the sciences and technology. A year later he assumed the directorship. NICAP would be his platform from which to challenge officialdom.[51]

In his "Report on Book Entitled 'Flying Saucers from Outer Space,'" Philip Strong decided the content was highly distorted, including many half-truths and inferences drawn by author Donald Keyhoe. Further, Albert Chop, a public information officer in the Air Force Reserve, was quoted extensively, claiming the Air Force deliberately concealed UFO-confirming positive conclusions. Claimed but unnamed sources had said the CIA instructed the Air Force to debunk the subject, state that it had ended all UFO investigations, then carry them on in secret.[52]

Further tightening the air seals against leaks, on December 16, Philip Strong issued a terse clarification to Operations staff on the subject of "Flying Saucers." In a memo to the chief of the Operations staff, he declared:

> In view of the fact that over-all substantive responsibility on the above subject has been assigned to the Physics and Electronics Division and action responsibility within that division assigned to Lt. Colonel Oder, Operations staff must coordinate any matter concerning FLYING SAUCERS with Colonel Oder or in his absence, with Dr. Odarenko.

Since the Agency's overall responsibility regarding this subject rested with the Physics and Electronics (P&E) Division, any matter concerning the subject was to be forwarded there.[53]

The next day, responding to a verbal request from OSI executives and likely also bearing on their reaction to the Keyhoe book, came a Memorandum from Dr. Todos Odarenko, Chief of the P&E Division, to Ralph Clark, OSI Assistant Director. This memo thoroughly explained the Division's UFO-related duties since May 27, when P&E assumed those tasks, as well as those of other principals in this matter. The P&E efforts heretofore had been confined to remaining aware of UFO activities by other agencies (notably USAF) and maintaining files.

Dr. Odarenko explained that Defense Department activities, such as they were, centered on OSI's Air Force counterpart. "The Air Force continues to maintain, but with apparently decreasing emphasis, its interest in UFOB's." The USAF Directorate of Intelligence, he underlined, offered only cursory cognizance of the project in Air Technical Intelligence Center (ATIC), code named "Bluebook No. 10073."[54]

Odarenko continued: "At ATIC the project is carried by one officer (Capt. Charles A. Hardin), one airman (A-10 Max O. Futch), and a secretary, operating as the Aerial Phenomena Section of the Electronics Branch, Technical Analysis Division. In spite of this limited staff, as well as several changes of project officer, the project records appear to be up to date. ATIC personnel no longer conduct field investigations of UFOB sightings." Those, he clarified, would have to be by request of an Air Force intelligence officer—prominently from Air Defense Command (ADC) or Airways and Air Communications Service (AACS), whoever was nearer to the sighting.[55]

Bluebook staff performed a series of minor tasks relative to new reports:

- Receiving and checking the incoming reports
- Requesting additional field investigation, where necessary
- Performing necessary checks against meteorological, astronomical, aircraft, and balloon data
- Recording their findings and conclusions in a cross-referenced system by date, location, source, type of observation
- Conclusion drawn[56]

The Aerial Phenomena Section also deals directly with the Public Information Office at USAF headquarters, regarding information for public release. For about the past year, approximately ten percent of the reported sightings have been tagged as unsolved.[57]

Odarenko explained why Bluebook was transferred to the Air Defense Command. ADC had been the go-to military entity for the project's hands-on investigative work. Per Lieutenant Colonel Harry Johnston, Chief of the Electronics Branch of P&E, ". . . if it turns out that these things (UFOB's) are spaceships or long range aircraft from another country, ADC is the (Air Force) Command that would have to take action." He then injected his own thinking into the transfer.

> It is undoubtedly true that ADC is the Air Force Command primarily concerned with UFOB's at the present time in that their interceptors are occasionally dispatched "against" UFOB's and that their reporting stations and communications systems are involved in a considerable portion of the UFOB activity. ATIC will maintain liaison with the project.[58]

As related by Odarenko, sometime in the spring or summer of 1952, ATIC initiated a program to situate cameras at "selected ADC radar sites and AACS control towers in locations where consistent UFOB reports were received in the hopes of photographing UFOB's." In all, 74 cameras were distributed and installed. But a failure in attendant equipment negated the possibility of spectrographic analysis by most of the cameras. A recall and retrofit was expected.[59]

Other nuggets dropped by Odarenko in his insightful December 17, 1953, memo:

- ATIC had planned to concentrate instrumentation in the Albuquerque area; that effort was abandoned.

- Project STORK, with a Secret designation, was a comprehensive statistical UFOB report, prepared at ATIC's request, covering the years 1947 through 1952. It was expected to be completed that December.

- ATIC continued to issue quarterly Blue Book statistical reports—twelve in all since its inception. The Navy's effort regarding aerial anomalies consisted of one intelligence analyst part time.

- The Army, meanwhile, "evidenced little or no interest in UFOB's except to cooperate with the Air Force in reporting sightings and pertinent data . . ."

- Under the header "Investigations or Interests of Foreign Governments," three topics were entirely redacted.

- An IFDRB was distributed several months after an event at 10:25 p.m., August 11, 1953, originating in the town of Drama, Greece. The anomaly was described by villagers as luminous and rocket-shaped. It hovered low in the sky for 3-4 minutes before leaving.[60]

Another latent IFDRB covered sightings over several previous months. On May 26, 1953, a doctor driving from Capetown to Uppington, South Africa, at 5:10 a.m. noticed yellowish-green light penetrating the cloud cover. It then emerged as a light 10 times brighter than any star and emitted three streaks of light. It paced the driver until 6:00, often moving up and down. Whenever he stopped the car it ascended. In Djougou, Benin, on October 11, 1953, at 11:30 p.m., many residents observed an oblong luminous object at high speed. On the night of December 21, 1953, two brilliant objects emitting red and green flames were seen over Peshawar, Pakistan.[61]

Kinross Intercept

Readers may find it puzzling that no CIA evaluation and no recorded correspondence to, from, or within the Agency resulted from a reprise of the 1948 Mantell incident, this one taking place on the evening of November 23, 1953, over Lake Superior. Air Defense Command radar tracked an unknown traveling at 500 mph over this the northernmost Great Lake. In minutes an F-89C Scorpion jet interceptor was dispatched from Kinross AFB in Michigan's Upper Peninsula. Lieutenant Felix Moncla Jr. was at the controls along with radar observer Lieutenant Robert Wilson. As ADC radar tracked the jet closing on the unknown, the two blips on the radar screen appeared to merge into one, which then faded from view completely. Communication with the interceptor ceased. An extensive search of the lake and surrounding land masses afterward found no trace of the aircraft or its two crewmen.

The next day, Wisconsin's Truax AFB (which handled public information matters for bases in the Upper Midwest) released a statement claiming the jet was still miles from the unknown when it disappeared from radar. That release did not account for the absence of communication from the F-89 that the plane or crew was in trouble. A day later, a USAF spokesman at the Pentagon issued a brief statement: The F-89 assigned to the task had indeed located the unknown—a Royal Canadian Air Force twin-engine cargo plane, a Douglas C-47. The jet did not actually collide with that prop aircraft, the spokesman said, but something unspecified happened, resulting in the interceptor's crash. This explanation, of course, implied gross incompetence by the F-89's pilot or radar man. The RCAF, in turn, vehemently and repeatedly denied that any such incident involving one of its aircraft took place.[62]

Beyond those Canadian denials, the US Air Force's resolution of the matter suffered from a fatal flaw. As originally determined by the ADC, the unknown on its radar screen was moving at 500 mph. By comparison, the C-47, a venerable aircraft in use from World War II through Vietnam, was more than substantially slower. Even a souped-up model introduced in the late forties, the Super C-47, had a top speed of 250 mph, not the 500 mph recorded at the ADC.[63] Surely, the radar jockey there would have recognized such a stark difference as he plotted the unknown's velocity.

Unlike the 1948 Mantell incident, which received nationwide media coverage, the failed intercept from Kinross AFB garnered minimal newspaper attention. As importantly, while the event was never explained satisfactorily, it did result in an unnecessary dustup with the Royal Canadian Air Force.

From a CIA perspective, one might well conclude that, five years after Mantell, "the fix was in." The Agency had made an effort to abandon the UFO subject after the writing of the Robertson Panel Report, and no peculiar circumstance—even one costing two servicemen their lives—could drag it back into that muck and mire. The Central Intelligence Agency had washed its hands of unidentified flying objects, period . . . sort of.

At 4:20 a.m., December 7, 1953, a pilot for Sabena Airlines, preparing to land at Melsbroek, Belgium, spotted a fireball on the horizon—white edged in green with a long trail and illuminating the whole sky. It was assumed he saw the same type of anomaly identified a few weeks later at Dieppe, France (see page 75), which French astronomers concluded was a very large meteor. Seven minutes later, at 4:27, a fiery object with a long trail was seen at Arras, France. A witness said it was motionless for an instant then flew over the horizon. In that general time period, residents of Gemeaux, Nouvelles-les-Champlitte, and Langras, France, reported an airborne red ball surmounted by a triangle, which flew past without leaving a trail.[64]

In France, on December 9, 1953, at 3:45 p.m., an Emilion man observed a round, luminous golden object motionless in the sky. After some 10 minutes it changed position and assumed the form of several horseshoes,

100 meters in diameter, enveloped in smoke trails. The display then disappeared. Near the same time a couple in Surgeres observed a round object glowing in all colors and flying at great speed.[65]

On December 12 at 9:00 p.m, a man in Montluçon, France, saw a luminous white disc. After two minutes it moved off at great speed. Shortly, the man observed a red crescent shape, which likewise flew away at high speed. Five days later on December 17, a commercial airline pilot flying over Hassleholm, Sweden, spotted what he discerned was a saucer. Then, back in France, on January 4, 1954, just after 9:00 p.m., a man saw a luminous object land at the Marignane airfield. It left while he was phoning the control tower. At 10:45 p.m. a man driving to Marseilles saw a large, round, reddish fiery ball in the sky.[66]

From a December 10, 1953, news report (no sighting date or time shown), thousands over several parts of Algeria witnessed a cigar-shaped object with a smoke trail, high overhead and moving northeast. Near Constantine, Algeria, on December 12, 1953, 10:30 a.m., a school's director, staff, and students saw a luminous disc move overhead, leaving ribbon-like trails. Not especially swift, it continued beyond the horizon. In the same general time frame, Algiers residents witnessed a yellow-orange object in the sky. Its apparent size grew to 2–3 times that of the sun, then it diminished and soon passed seemingly into the sea.[67]

On the afternoon of December 17, 1953, a Swedish pilot and his flight mechanic, in a Transair commercial aircraft, were flying over the town of Skaane when they noticed a round metallic object, about 10 meters in diameter, suddenly approaching. It flew past them at what they considered roughly the speed of sound.[68]

Afterward, the pilot detailed their experience: "What I saw was a completely unorthodox, metallic, symmetric, round object . . . a 'flying lozenge.'" Its surface, the pilot continued, had a metallic luster. It left no exhaust or condensation trail. The sighting lasted about 10 seconds. The next day, Sweden's Defense Staff postulated a Geminids meteor, though a balloon or unknown foreign aircraft was not ruled out. On the 19th a Swedish perfume manufacturer announced that it had released more than 300 small (15–30 cm) promotional balloons of various colors and that some had reached the Skanne area.[69]

While you were away from your desk . . .

The Robertson Report and its aftermath may perhaps have dominated the Agency's attention, time, and efforts, but a few other matters would perhaps have been expected to capture some interest. The incidents to follow were not found in 2017's major release of files to the CIA website.

January 8, 1953

From the ground at Larson Air Force Base, Washington, a round, glowing green object was observed from 7:15 to 7:30 a.m. by the commander and men of the 82nd Fighter-Interceptor Squadron. The vehicle exhibited a bobbing motion and sideways movements below the cloud cover. It could not be explained by USAF Project Blue Book.[70]

January 10, 1953

Around 4:00 p.m. in Sonoma, California, retired Colonel Robert McNab along with a Federal Security Agency employee observed a flat object high in the sky. It performed three 360-degree loops and abrupt 90-degree turns to the left and right. After pausing to hover, the vehicle ascended out of sight in a vertical climb at great speed. USAF Project Blue Book files left this anomaly unidentified as well.[71]

February 11, 1953

A month later, about 10:00 p.m., a Marine Corps lieutenant on intercept-ready status was scrambled aloft in his F9F Panther to check out an unknown blip on Norfolk Naval Station radar. He was ordered to "run black" (without running lights). Finding nothing, he was returning to base at 20,000 feet when he noticed a blob of light at or near the water. Momentarily, it rose in an instant to his altitude. As the pilot approached, he discerned a disc shape with red blinking lights on the hull. Suddenly, blue-white light bathed his cockpit. Glancing down, he saw through his gloves and flesh to the bones of his hands. "It was like an X-ray." For several seconds he seemed motionless in his surroundings; all sound had ceased, even the roar of the engine. Then, with a flash of light, the intruder moved away at great speed as sounds and motion returned to normal. A second pilot sent to investigate spotted the unknown in the distance, receding along the North Carolina coast. On his return, the lieutenant with the close encounter was extensively debriefed. When finally released, he was warned sternly to "say absolutely nothing" about the matter.[72]

March 27, 1953

Near Mount Taylor, New Mexico, an Air Force F-86 fighter chased a bright orange circle for 4 minutes. The jet's 700 mph speed was not enough to catch the intruder traveling at an estimated 900 mph. The case was left unidentified in the USAF Project Blue Book files.[73]

June 7, 1953

A sworn statement (non-sourced, with redactions) by Arthur Stansel, a former member of the US Air Force, concerned his involvement in a May 21, 1953, recovery effort following a flying saucer crash:

> . . . I assisted in the investigation of a crashed unknown object in the vicinity of Kingman, Arizona. . . . The object was constructed of an unfamiliar metal which resembled brushed aluminum. It had impacted 20 inches into the sand without any sign of structural damage. It was oval and about 30 feet in diameter. . . . [Inside were] 2 swivel seats, an oval cabin, and a lot of instruments and displays. . . . A tent pitched near the object sheltered the dead remains of the only occupant of the craft. It was about 4 feet tall, dark brown complexion, and had 2 eyes, 2 nostrils, 2 ears, and a small round mouth. It was clothed in a silvery metallic suit

and wore a skull cap of the same type of material. It wore no face covering or helmet.[74]

October 19, 1953

At midnight, an American Airlines DC-6 was passing over Conowingo Dam, north of Baltimore, on its way to Washington, D.C. Without warning it confronted an unknown on a collision course. The pilot executed a dive, which threw passengers into the aisle, injuring some. The object streaked overhead and into the night. The captain described it as having a size similar to the length and breadth of his own plane's fuselage. Ground control insisted that no other known aircraft was within a 100-mile area.[75]

November 3, 1953

Two weeks hence, an RAF lieutenant and his navigator, piloting a de Havilland Vampire fighter jet at 30,000 feet from their base at West Malling, England, confronted a bright circular object straight ahead. The glow was more intense around its periphery. In about ten seconds, it flew away and out of sight. The object did not appear on their onboard radar.[76]

December 16, 1953

Lockheed aircraft engineer Clarence "Kelly" Johnson (designer of the F-104, U-2, and SR-71), along with his wife, observed an enormous flying wing over the Santa Barbara Channel from their home in Los Angeles County. One of Johnson's test crews, coincidentally in flight aboard a Lockheed EC-121 surveillance aircraft, spotted the intruder from Long Beach.

In due course, the Air Force—presumably Blue Book—concluded these trained observers had misidentified a lenticular cloud. During the observation Johnson considered and ruled out that explanation.[77]

Chapter 7

1954:

Through a Long Winter's Night

Following a brief holiday break, the strangeness returned in Europe. On France's northern coast at Dieppe on January 7, 1954, residents were awakened by a loud crash and saw a dazzling airborne light in the night sky. The powerful sound shattered windows and set doors ajar. A railwayman near the Belgian border claimed to *see* a luminous saucer cross the sky at great speed.[1]

Two days later at 4:16 p.m., a fireball crossed the west coast of Sweden, emitting a long trail of sparks. Observers speculated it exploded over Copenhagen. The Swedish Air Force received many calls.

On March 1, numerous beachgoers near Montevideo, Uruguay, saw a metallic disc reflecting the sunlight. The anomaly reportedly remained stationary for two minutes at high altitude before leaving the area.[2]

In an untitled communication from OSI Director Chadwell to his general counsel, Walter Pforzheimer, May 4, 1954, Chadwell returned to the Agency's unwritten but firm policy of anonymity in all matters related to aerial phenomena. He attached a draft letter for the OSI attorney to review. It was in reply to a letter from Senator Edwin Johnson who had forwarded a constituent concern. The reply asked the senator not to mention the CIA in his response to the citizen. Within the text was sample wording to state that most sighting reports had been resolved and with better information the rest would be.[3]

A monthly French periodical by the Study Committee on Military Aeronautics—headed by the Air Force chief of staff—included an article postulating supersonic interstellar ships powered by cosmic energy. A Paris newspaper speculated that the mere appearance of the article indicated the French Air Force was admitting the existence of flying saucers.[4]

Renowned German aircraft engineer Georg Klein, in a German newspaper interview, described his work on experimental flying saucers from 1941 to 1945. He claimed the first piloted craft reached 1,300 mph in 3 minutes. Three large designs evolved, two of which he described: a non-rotating disc, 135 feet in diameter; and a rotating ring surrounding a stationary circular crew cabin. He named other designers (only surnames given) Miethe, Habermohl, and Schreiver. Before the Soviets occupied Prague, Germans destroyed everything saucer-related at a research facility there. However, in Breslau, Poland, Klein claimed, Soviets captured a saucer of Miethe's design.[5]

A Genoa, Italy, inventor was given a patent for a flying disc, which he claimed could reach 3,000 km/hr. The vehicle would weigh 5 tons and take off from an 18-meter tower. In construction, it would consist of a plastic disk-shaped wing, an aluminum central sphere, and a cockpit containing two jet engines. The gentleman offered his plans to the Italian government but he was turned down. As a result he intended to emigrate and offer them elsewhere.[6]

Given design-construction efforts underway in Canada and England and by the US Air Force, OSI assumed responsibility to initiate and exploit "all intelligence measures required to identify, to assess, and to report the use by any foreign power or nation of non-conventional types of air vehicles, such as or similar to the 'saucer-like' planes presently under development . . ." The OSI project on UFOs would retain and keep up its central file and make material available to assess non-conventional vehicles developed by other countries relative to certain potential weapons systems.[7]

In another Memorandum for the Record penned June 14, 1954, OSI's Assistant Director Herbert Scoville Jr. shifted internal arrangements. The text of the document, "Office Responsibilities for Non-Conventional Types of Air Vehicles," called for a transfer to the Applied Science Division.

"Henceforth, the ASD will conduct all surveillance of available information on this subject." OSI branches would be instructed to forward all such files to the ASD, terminate their own filing, and offer consultation if and when necessary.[8]

On July 30, an Agency source distributed an extensive IFDRB covering reported sightings over a four-month period in western and northern Europe as well as Africa and the Far East. The header of the dispatch read "Sightings of Unidentified Flying Objects." The report chronicled a January 18, 1954, incident in Setif, Algeria, where at 2:30 p.m. inhabitants saw a cigar-shaped vehicle arrive at modest speed from the east. It was emitting a bluish trail. After circling the town for several seconds at high altitude, "it suddenly headed back in the direction of Saint Arnaud at great speed."[9]

British Malaya had hosted a double header in March. On the 12th, harbor workers at Swettenham, Kuala Lumpur, sighted a cigar-shaped object at altitude leaving a trail. It moved into the clouds and out of sight. Five days later, residents of three towns in Kuala Lumpur likewise witnessed an airborne cylindrical vehicle without wings.[10]

In France, on April 15 two residents of Saint Mexant saw an elongated cone shape at high altitude, with red and green lights at the base. A week and a half later on the 26th, a group on a walk near the town of Sare, near the Pyrenees Mountains, saw a wingless cigar shape flying rapidly at about 2,000 meters, headed toward Spain.[11]

On the 16th of April at 8:00 p.m. in the town of Worcester, South Africa, a man saw what appeared to be a blood-red star in motion. Through a telescope, he detected moving objects around it. "The 'star' climbed obliquely at a very fast rate and moved upward with a jerky motion, alternately starting and stopping. It seemed to sway like a balloon and became brighter as it rose. Finally, the object headed north."[12]

On May 13 in the Hammerfest Province of northern Norway, a V formation of unknowns was spotted at great height, passing over the town of Kautokeino at very high speed. A deputy constable with binoculars claimed that they were not ordinary airplanes. "He added that they seemed to be red on one side and white on the other and appeared to be rotating.[13]

Also on the 13th of May, in the morning three persons at different locations in the Norrbotten Province of Sweden observed a "brilliant silver-colored sphere with a tail." Then, at 12:10 p.m., a sheriff, three deputies, and two clerks at Kautokeino, Norway, observed three objects in a V formation at a low altitude estimated to be 2,000 meters. Binoculars were employed during the 4–5 minutes they were in view. Each unknown was described as "reddish brown on the underside and shiny on the upper, and moving with a rotary motion." The objects left no trail. The weather at that hour was clear and visibility was unlimited.[14]

The next day, Norway's Air Command North received numerous calls concerning unknowns over its Finnmark Province. The callers dismissed conventional aircraft or meteorological balloons as identifiers.[15]

Their accounts were enhanced a few days later by other provincial residents. On or about the 17th of May, back in Norrbotten Province, Sweden, a sphere with an attached meter-long rod and a fiery tail 70–80 meters long was observed low in the sky. It appeared to descend into a forest half a kilometer away, but no trace was found afterward.[16] Note: The Eta Aquirids meteor shower peaks on May 5; meteoric fireballs may occur anytime.

On June 18, 1954, a Roman Catholic missionary in the Middle Congo confided he and others sighted an unknown at 7:35 p.m. "A luminous globe, it came from the North toward the Laketi Mission. It suddenly stopped, rose, and dropped, stopped again, gyrated, and seemed to shake. A noise like that of an airplane engine, heard until that moment, also stopped." Binoculars revealed the object as having a dark mass and light rays of unequal length. After 15 minutes of the seemingly nonsensical lights and movements, the vehicle shot back over the horizon at great speed.[17]

Near Spjellerup, Sweden, a military-assisted excavation was planned to unearth an object that landed in a field in late 1953, digging a hole 3.5 meters deep but only 25 cm wide. The landowner had pushed a long rod into the hole and located something he determined was metallic.[18]

Another IFDRB, distributed August 25, 1954, related news accounts from early May to mid-June in Europe and beyond. On May 6 at 11:30 a.m., people in Mersin, Turkey, spotted an unknown over the nearby Taurus

Mountains. It appeared to be about 10 meters in length and travelled slowly in a straight line. After a few minutes it was lost from view.[19]

Between Frankfurt and Darmstadt, Germany, near the Rhein-Main AFB in early June, two people saw a pair of glowing discs descend almost vertically, then rise rapidly. They were in view for about 10 seconds. The base's radar did not detect the intruders. At the Duesseldorf airport, in early or mid-June employees of various airlines watched a shiny UFO—described by one as a saucer—approach from the south at high speed, turn west, then ascend through the 6,000-meter overcast.[20]

Police in Norrbotten Province, Sweden, announced that two additional persons had come forward to relate their recollections of the May 13 incident there. One eyewitness declared that he had seen a "silvery football-shaped object" (a soccer ball to Americans) coming from the nearby border with Finland. With a fiery tail 70–80 meters long, it appeared to descend to earth about half a kilometer from where he stood. Separately, a second witness also described the object as spherical; she said it passed by her and descended into a wooded area a short distance away.[21]

During a June 30 total eclipse whose path crossed Scandinavia,[22] in Helsinki, Finland, several photos were taken of an aerial unknown. The round object was said not to be the moon or a cloud. Informed sources further clarified: "One photograph differs from the others in that the upper edge of the object is illuminated as if the sun were shining on a hard surface. The center of the object appears as a dark blotch."[23]

Likewise during the eclipse, in Norway a pilot at 4,500 meters took color motion pictures of two shining aerial discs with vapor trails, moving at great speed. Within 30 minutes after the eclipse, a "strange object was photographed in the sky in Maarianhamina, Finland. The cigar shape appeared on several pictures taken as a result."[24]

On July 7, 1954, at Hallein, Austria, three men reportedly observed an unknown, stationary above the Tennen Mountains. It was described as a shapeless bright red mass with a diagonal streak; its size was about three times the size of Venus. The men added that it moved "spasmodically," both vertically and horizontally.[25]

On an evening prior to July 25 south of Salisbury, Rhodesia, a policeman and friends observed six unidentified objects in the sky. Almost immobile, they were visible for about 20 minutes before leaving as night fell.[26]

About 10:00 p.m. August 6 at Darmstadt, West Germany, several residents, the local weather station crew, and a night-duty officer at police headquarters separately observed three flying saucers. Fiery red-yellow in coloration, the anomalies alternately hovered and darted to and fro. They remained in the area for 1½ hours. The same night between 10:00 and 11:15 p.m., at Schleawig, West Germany, two anomalies were observed. "They were described as faint, fiery red points of light, which finally approached close enough to be made out as disks. Greenish-white rays are reported to have been emanated from the center of the disks."[27]

On the afternoon of August 17, in central France an industrial engineer claimed to have seen an unknown over the town of Montluçon. He described it as a "luminous, brilliant white, disk-like object." After several seconds, it proceeded behind a cloud and out of sight.[28]

Several days before another incident was published on August 25, at least two-dozen persons at Rastatt in southern West Germany witnessed a pair of unknowns pass over the city in seconds. "The two disk-like objects were lighted like white neon lamps and made no noise. The radar sets at the nearby airfield of Soellingen, where Royal Canadian Air Force jet fighters are based, failed to pick them up, because of their high altitude." Several similar sightings had been reported in the region.[29]

On August 19, 1954, at 8:45 p.m. in Bregenz, Austria, three men reportedly observed a disc that abruptly reversed direction and displayed phenomenal movements. Viewed from their homes on Lake Constance, residents described a small gleaming disc-shaped object, about twice as large as Venus, that came from the southwest. One of the witnesses said, ". . . [I]t turned and went in the opposite direction, making some abrupt zigzags over Bregenz. After about two minutes it disappeared into a bank of clouds."[30]

In northern France on the night of August 22, a man in the town of Vernon spotted a "large, luminous, cigar-shaped object" motionless in the sky. Momentarily, "a flying saucer detached itself, assumed a vertical position, descended a short distance, leveled off, and silently disappeared at great speed." Over the next 45 minutes, four more saucers emerged and did the same. The final one to exit went to a lower level before flying away, revealing itself as red in the center and edged in black. Two Vernon constables also reported sighting an elongated, luminous airborne object that night. None of the witnesses mentioned the manner of its departure.[31]

On unspecified days prior to August 29, members of the Swiss Air Force and others reported flying saucers to authorities. Five objects in formation were reportedly seen in the mountainous terrain around Lake Constance. A newspaper had earlier carried a sighting report from August 19, it too involving five unknowns around Lake Constance.[32]

A man in Lyon, France, reported sighting an aerial oddity at 10:15 p.m., August 31, 1954. The "short, fat cigar" was moving east to west over the city. "The object was bluish-green in color and emitted sparks from its tail." It headed toward a radio beacon mounted outside the city.[33]

About 8:20 p.m. (date uncertain, but prior to September 4), various people in Angers, France, watched as a disc passed over the city. "The object was generally described as being brown and emitting a smoke trail of an odd hue of green." A local nurse said it "gave off a soft drone, and its glow was reminiscent of the light in neon tubes. The phenomenon was visible for several minutes."[34]

In the first week of September 1954, outside Dakar, Senegal, on Africa's west coast, a mason and his assistant saw a "gray object resembling a truncated millstone with a large inverted plate lying on it in a field about 200 meters from the road where they were bicycling . . . The object oscillated slowly and seemed to have a closed door on its side. . . ." The men left their bikes and ran toward the object. When they had covered roughly 50 meters:

> [T]he object began to fly away. Smoke was then visible from
> a sort of exhaust pipe on the underside. After an oblique
> flight of about 15 meters, the object rose vertically and

disappeared. Police later found no traces of the object . . .
They stated that the object never touched ground, but
hovered above the ground like a helicopter. It was about 10
meters in diameter and 3 meters in height, did not glow,
and departed noiselessly, trailing smoke as it took off.[35]

On the 7th of September at 12:30 a.m., a couple plus an in-law were
driving in France's Aisne Department when they spotted a red-orange
disc following a railroad track; it stopped suddenly across the road, some
300–400 meters off the ground. "It seemed to have on its upper side a
small luminous tail forming an integral part of the object." When they
reached a particular bridge, they saw the flying saucer increasing in altitude. Their headlights beamed on it, and the object flew at great speed
toward a nearby town, soon lost from view.[36]

On the night of September 14 over Helsinki, Finland, several individuals watched a circular object 800 meters in the sky that issued intense light
and left broad reddish smoke three times as broad as the vehicle.[37]

At 8:00 a.m., September 15, a man in Calvados Department, France,
witnessed the appearance of a white point of light in the sky, which grew
in size, resolving into an oval of unusual brilliance. The sighting lasted two
minutes. "The witness stated that he was not subject to hallucinations." A similar phenomenon was reported by a farmer—also in Calvados Department.[38]

In Tuscany, Italy, two residents of Pitigliano reported sighting a round
white object on September 14 that made a "strange, loud noise." The object
stopped "then disappeared at high speed."[39]

On September 17 in the afternoon, tower controllers at Rome's
Ciampino air base "observed a mysterious object shaped like half a
cigar flying slowly at an altitude of about 1,200 meters. Leaving a trail of
luminous smoke, the anomaly was visible for about 40 minutes. Those
manning the tower watched the object make a 400-meter dive then rise
again, moving from a horizontal to a vertical attitude. As the object took
off toward the sea, the Ciampino tower notified the Practica di Mare
(military air base) control tower, 30 kilometers from Rome, which picked
up the object and followed it on its radar screen for about 20 minutes.

"The radar showed the presence of an antenna located at the center of the widest part of the object."[40]

All other factors aside concerning the validity of published saucer reports of the time, a conditioning of sorts was underway. Eerie accounts of things in the sky that ought not to have been there were becoming commonplace in local newspapers. Whether true, exaggerated or hoaxed, the stories were often thought provoking. The general public across many lands— even in the Soviet Union—were now somewhat accustomed to reading or hearing of them in the news periodically. UFO headlines and their implications, sparked by a free press or otherwise, remained in one's subconscious. The accounts were not quite as astonishing as they had been only a scant few years before.

While you were away from your desk . . .

Some publicized events involving anomalous aerial phenomena occurred around the world in 1954 without the CIA's notice—at least as recorded on its website in 2017.

March 1954

The Defense Department issued an ominous warning to both military and commercial airline pilots in the form of a new regulation. Joint Army/Navy/Air Force Publication (JANAP) 146(C) was titled "Communication Instructions for Reporting Vital Intelligence Sightings from Airborne and Waterborne Sources." Listed with suspicious aircraft and missiles were unidentified flying objects. Those sightings were now an intelligence matter.[41] The Air Force followed up with its own regulation, AFR 55-88, Communications Instructions Reporting Vital Intelligence Sightings (CIRVIS). To ensure pilots would no longer talk to the media, a heavy fine or imprisonment was threatened.[42]

May 14, 1954

Just after 12:00 a.m., at Maxton, North Carolina, a patrolman and passenger encountered a bus-sized triangle hovering above the trees of a mobile home park. As related afterward by the officer: "The craft gave off a real bright light, yet the ground wasn't lit up at all. There were about 30 lights, each about one foot in diameter, and they were so bright and intense that they blinded us from a block away." The men gave chase for 20 minutes. Outside the town near the passenger's home, the intruder landed, then "just vanished."[43]

July 1, 1954

Tragedy struck the town of Walesville, New York: before noon that day, air traffic controllers at Griffiss AFB tracked an unknown moving across the state. An F-94 Starfire with a two-man crew was scrambled. Onboard radar vectored the plane to the targeted area. Breaking through cloud cover, the men spotted a gleaming disc. As they closed in, a suffocating heat suddenly filled the cockpit. They were unable to continue and bailed out. The jet careened downward, striking a building in the town then a passing auto. Its occupants—a couple and their two children—were killed. Five others nearby were injured. The pilot and radar operator parachuted to safety outside the town. They were still dazed from the experience when a news reporter came upon them. The pilot was conveying to him the circumstances in the air and the onset of extreme heat when a sedan with an Air Force logo arrived. The men were whisked into the car, which immediately left.[44]

August 16, 1954

At Tananarive, Madagascar, at 5:00 p.m.:

> [A] green ball was seen in the sky and disappeared behind a hill. It reappeared a minute later and flew over the higher part of Tananarive. When the object flew in front of them, some witnesses could *see* a lentil-shaped

device with silvery metallic aspect enveloped in electric luminous gas.[45]

August 29, 1954

At Prince Christian Sound, Greenland, at 11:05 p.m., the crew of a Royal Dutch Airlines DC-4 saw 3–4 dark, lens-shaped objects veer north and change position in formation.[46]

September 15, 1954

At Manbhum, in the Bihar district of India, a UFO was seen in the afternoon by about 800 people living in three proximate villages. Some witnesses described the object as shaped like a saucer, about 12 feet in diameter with a gray exterior.[47]

From September 12 to November 30, a great influx of UFO sightings occurred in western and southern Europe. The greatest number occurred in France, followed by Italy. This was the first large-scale European UFO wave.[48]

October 14, 1954

In the afternoon, a Meteor jet aircraft, part of the Middlesex Squadron of the Royal Auxiliary Air Force, was flying from RAF North Weald, Essex, England, at 16,000 feet when three discs suddenly approached; the Meteor and the intruders were on a collision course. Two broke off and away while the third continued on a direct line. When within a few hundred yards, it finally veered away. The pilot banked to give chase but the discs were nowhere in sight. Each vehicle "was saucer-shaped with a bun on top and a bun underneath, and was silvery and metallic. There were no portholes, flames, or anything."[49]

October 30, 1954

Two weeks later, an R7V-1 Super Constellation, a four-engine military transport with 42 passengers aboard, left Patuxent River Naval Air Station, Maryland, headed for the Azores Islands. After passing over Bermuda, the plane was not heard from again. An intensive search failed to find any trace of wreckage. The Naval Board of Inquiry later concluded:

> It is the opinion of the Board that R7V-1 BuNo 128441 did meet with a sudden and violent force, that rendered the aircraft no longer airworthy, and was thereby beyond the scope of human endeavor to control. The force that rendered the aircraft uncontrollable is unknown . . .[50]

Yes, *that* Bermuda Triangle.

Chapter 8

1955:

The Ham Radio Flap

The previous year had been as busy in western and northern Europe, plus parts of Africa, as it was quiet in the United States. CIA analysts were left to wonder whether the so-called delusions and hallucinations afflicting the American populace in 1952 and beyond had somehow moved into the collective subconscious across the Atlantic.

In a brief February 25, 1955, memorandum the deputy chief of OSI's support staff notified the contact division chief in the Office of Operations (OO). Someone (redacted) had acquired a wire recording of an electrical transmission of unknown origin. An attachment (not shown) explained details of the acquisition. It was requested that OO obtain the recording for investigation by the OSI Physics and Electronics (P&E) Division.[1]

In the first week of March, OSI's contact division chief followed up on the support staff's appeal for further information on the suspicious recording. The chief wrote to the Agency's Chicago office, asking to take possession of, or at least borrow, the program recording, which contained an unidentified code.[2]

Two weeks later, the contact division chief in OSI responded to someone in OSI—the Support Staff Office or other (addressee illegible). Apparently, the undefined message had been heard and recorded by a ham radio operator in metropolitan Chicago who alleged it was a "message from outer space." The recording was now received. The chief added that other Chicago-area ham radio operators claimed similar communications; those could be tracked down.[3]

On April 6, the chief of the P&E Division threw a bucket of cold water on the mystery of the ham radio recording. In his memo to the Office of Operations, the P&E manager related that the tape recording forwarded earlier was familiar. It "has been analyzed and positively identified as a known signal of US origin."[4] But that resolution would not be the end of the matter—not by a long shot. A tempest was brewing in this teapot.

Battelle's Input

On May 5, 1955, the Air Force released Special Report No. 14, "Analysis of Reports of Unidentified Aerial Objects" (Project No. 10073; Study No. 102-EL-55/2-79).[5] Readers might wonder, whatever happened to the special reports numbered 1–13. Those remained classified.

Special Report No. 14 was prepared for the Air Force by the Battelle Memorial Institute, which in the 21st century bills itself as a "global research and development organization committed to science and technology for the greater good."[6] It was and is located in Columbus, Ohio.

Battelle researchers gave attention—from, no doubt, dismissive glances to serious appraisal—to "a number of reports considered large enough for a preliminary statistical analysis, approximately 4,000 reports."[7] Those emanated largely from the general public but also trained observers such as police and airport personnel. However keen the individual's awareness, though, from Battelle's perspective the mere observation of a UFO without something physical as evidence merited nothing.

As part of its summary, Battelle stated: "In general, the original data upon which this study was based consisted of impressions and interpretations of apparently unexplained events, and seldom contained reliable measurements of physical attributes."[8] Shades of the January 1953 Robertson Panel Report.

The special report's authors claimed to have made "(1) a systematic attempt to ferret out any distinguishing characteristics inherent in the data or any of their segments, (2) a concentrated study of any trends or patterns found, and (3) an attempt to determine the probability that any of the UNKNOWNS represent observations of a class, or classes, of 'flying saucers.'"[9]

The report went on about its thoroughness and fairness before wrapping it up:

> An attempt to determine the probability that any of the UNKNOWNS represent observations of a class, or classes, of "flying saucers" necessitated a thorough re-examination and re-evaluation of cases of objects not originally identified; this led to the conclusion that the probability was very small.
>
> Therefore, on the basis of this evaluation of the information, it is considered to be highly improbable that reports of unidentified aerial objects examined in this study represent observations of technological developments outside of the range of present-day scientific knowledge ... [T]here was a complete lack of any valid evidence consisting of physical matter in any case of a reported unidentified aerial object.[10]

All rhetoric aside, the report went on to reveal in all its marvelous detail that, statistically, those hard-to-dismiss cases still listed as "unknowns" (multiple credible witnesses, some in close proximity to the source) constituted three percent of the cases: around 120 incidents from 1947 through 1954. When all the cases Battelle reasoned had "insufficient evidence" were included, the total unidentified rose to 21 percent.[11]

Note: Later that year, former Project Blue Book director Captain Edward Ruppelt commented: "This is not a good study . . . I saw the unpublished draft and had written it off as worthless."[12]

On July 12, 1955, the P&E chief notified the acting assistant director of OSI of a preliminary report from Pepperrell AFB, Newfoundland (not shown). The pilot of a tanker aircraft in flight (exact date not stated) observed an unknown that was simultaneously tracked by the base's radar.

The pilot radioed the intruder's repeated changes of direction, which corresponded with what the radar screen in the tower was showing. The anomaly remained on radar for 49 minutes.[13]

OSI's assistant director two years before, on May 27, 1953, had designated the P&E Division as the keeper of the UFO flame, as it were. A July 3 reply by its chief, Todos Odarenko, outlined those responsibilities as he foresaw them:

- In that the project had been deactivated, further incoming reports would be reviewed only periodically.

- Material not identified as a known source was to be filed— unless of immediate national security interest.

The three OSI division chiefs further clarified those duties on June 14, 1954. Case review and filing activities used between 10 and 25 analyst hours per month, plus half of that in clerical time.

Odarenko now requested that P&E be relieved of the tasks since no information of intelligence value had been derived. The project did not fall under the Critical National Intelligence Objectives, while meeting fiscal year 1956 data production quotas in other pursuits necessitated ending nonessential activities. Consequently, this project would be terminated and the files placed in dead storage.[14]

While awaiting the okay from above to abandon the UFO files, the next day, August 9, 1955, an Information Report was received at P&E. It carried forward an account from 1953 that originated in the Soviet city of Shakhty, a coal-mining town at a spur of the Donetsk Mountains in southwestern Russia. On a warm night in August (the 12th or 13th) at a work camp near Rostov, three objects were seen at a distance—all moving southeast to northwest. The first was spotted at 9:45 p.m., the second an hour later, and the third after another hour. No sound was heard from the unknowns. Each was described as exhibiting "a fiery gleam in a reddish color which was similar to that of planet Mars. It looked like a comet or shooting star." Afterward, the camp workers disagreed as to the true nature of the three; some believed they were rockets, though no detonation was heard.[15]

OSI's Assistant Director, Herbert Scoville Jr., sent a Memorandum to the Director of Central Intelligence on September 4 (typeface deteriorated and mostly illegible). Scoville mentioned Project "Y," an effort underway by Avro Aircraft Ltd. to build a replica saucer. The Air Force supported the project.[16]

On the same day, AD/SI Scoville wrote for the record a narrative of an interview with one of four travel companions aboard a moving train outside Baku, Azerbaijan, on September 4, 1955. Whereas three mates believed they had witnessed a "flying saucer" take off two miles or so in the distance, describing its glow as it rose, the fourth had a different take on the incident:

> The size of the object was comparable to that of a jet fighter, with a squat shape and in the form of an equilateral triangle. There were three lights on the object, one on each point of the triangle, presumably two wing lights and a taillight. As we watched, it was ejected from its launching site, making not less than three and not more than seven fast spirals, after which it climbed extremely fast at about a 45 degree angle.

He concluded that he had seen the launch of a triangular-shaped rocket.[17]

A month later, on October 4, CIA Director Allen Dulles responded to Congressman Gordon Scherer, who had written to the Agency on behalf of a constituent. The latter wished to pursue mail fraud charges in connection with George Adamski's book, *Inside the Space Ships*. Dulles explained that the Agency had no jurisdiction in the matter. He suggested that the complainant contact the Department of Defense or the National Science Foundation, either of which would presumably be better suited to the matter.[18]

Wilton E. Lexow, Chief of the OSI Applied Science Division—the latest archive for UFO-related documents—penned a Memorandum for Information on the subject on October 19. The chief concluded that recent sighting reports related to an old Nazi-founded saucer-building program that had since been adopted by the Soviets. Lexow's thoughts crossed seven topics:

1. The objects reportedly sighted were similar in description to the (disc-shaped) vehicle, still in design stage, conceived by Avro Aircraft Ltd., a British-Canadian firm under contract with the US Air Force to build a flying saucer. That effort was codenamed Project "Y."

2. The most recent of several Avro design studies called for specific targets:

   a. Circular wing 30 feet in diameter and 1.1 foot thick

   b. Top speed of Mach 3

   c. Rate of climb of 120,000 feet per minute

   d. Ceiling of 102,000 feet

   e. Range of 700 nautical miles

3. The Air Force had committed $800,000 to wind-tunnel testing of the Avro vehicle.

4. Project "Y" was directed by John Frost. John Carver Meadows "Jack" Frost was a pioneering British aircraft designer whose seminal work included British and Canadian jet fighters capable of supersonic speeds.[19]

5. "Since two objects were reportedly seen in operation at one time in an area where it is most unlikely that experimental flying would be conducted, it is likely that these objects were in service. This would indicate very rapid progress in this development for the Soviets. It does, however seem inconsistent that the Soviets, if they have such an object in service, would continue their large development and production programs on conventional type aircraft."

6. ASD had been on the alert for information that the Soviets were working on such a project. Prior to the recent (redacted) observation, no such information had been forthcoming.

7. More information was needed to evaluate the sighting report. The Air Force would have technically competent people question the reporting party.[20]

The next day, OSI Assistant Director Herbert Scoville sent a memorandum to CIA Director Allen Dulles. Having interviewed three of the four observers in an alleged "flying saucer" event, "there still remains nothing to confirm the existence of these or other particularly unconventional type aircraft." The objects observed were very likely normal jet aircraft. At best, Scoville noted, whatever was observed had a "high rate of climb." He was clearly suspicious of the motives of one individual. "Since (redacted) seems to have been the prime mover in sending the original dispatch and ascribing so much confidence to the observation of these saucers, it is imperative that he be interviewed alone."[21]

On October 31, 1955, Scoville communicated via memo with OSI Director Chadwell. After the debriefing was finished, Scoville recounted the stories by four travel companions aboard a train in Soviet-controlled Azerbaijan on the 4th of September. A particular paragraph in the communiqué by one of the train passengers appeared to be the key to resolving the matter: "I wish to emphasize that this was no ordinary take-off but a launching procedure more like a missile ejection.

"Our companion from next door reported that this was the second launching in rapid succession." That statement clearly indicated that a conventional vehicle was observed.[22]

The final UFO-related dispatch of 1955 was again by Herbert Scoville. On November 10 the assistant director wrote to a redacted party about guided missiles observed in Afghanistan. OSI was unable to compare those unknowns with other flying saucer reports, but the staff would have a great interest in any debris found after a landing. An attached Kabul news article stated the Soviets were testing a revolutionary bottle-shaped craft that issued flames and traveled through a corridor of Afghan land.[23]

While you were away from your desk . . .

January 1, 1955

On New Year's Day over Cochise, New Mexico, at 6:44 a.m. a US Air Force instructor and student pilot in a TB-25 bomber-trainer were paced for 5–7 minutes by a metallic disc-shaped object, 120–130 feet in diameter. The intruder at one point flipped on edge without changing its path. Eventually it flew away into the pre-dawn darkness. The incident was left unidentified in the case files of the Air Force's Project Blue Book.[24]

February 2, 1955

At the Miramar Naval Air Station, California, a Navy commander noticed a highly polished, reddish-brown sphere in the sky at 11:50 a.m. The orb began a descent, then instantly accelerated to a velocity estimated by the commander as 1,000–1,500 mph. His report on the incident was left unidentified by USAF Project Blue Book.[25]

April 8, 1955

At 9:30 a.m. four adults in a neighborhood of Rockford, Illinois, observed a UFO and phoned authorities. Soon three jet fighters arrived. At this point the witnesses saw a small disc emerge from the "parent" vehicle and ascend out of sight. The jets then fired on the larger unknown, which exploded. Afterward, the witnesses reported that Air Force personnel had contacted them, warning them to say nothing about what they had observed. The editor of the *Rockford Register* contacted O'Hare Field (outside Chicago) on their behalf and was told that the jets had fired on a weather balloon. On July 28, Air Force Captain Robert White contradicted that assertion by declaring, "Our aircraft do not fire on balloons, nor would they fire on any target in a residential area unless we were invaded by an enemy force."[26]

June 16, 1955

At 11:00 p.m., a Flying Tiger Airlines crew, 40 miles northeast of Springfield, Missouri, spotted a blue-white disc flying at tremendous speed toward the plane. After executing a tight circle around the aircraft, the saucer tilted up steeply and streaked out of sight.[27]

June 23, 1955

A week later, a Mohawk Airlines captain and crew on a routine flight over upstate New York discovered an elliptical object, estimated at 150 feet long with lighted openings, 500 feet above them. Moments later it was spotted by Colonial Airline pilots, another airliner, and control tower operators at Albany. It was also picked up by radar in Boston. From the recorded times after the Mohawk sighting, its speed was computed as between 4,000 and 4,800 mph.[28]

August 21–22, 1955

Although the CIA's charter did not include domestic issues, the thoroughly bizarre incident at Hopkinsville, Kentucky, given its eventual widespread tabloid fame, must have come to Agency staff's attention at some point. Two families in the same house allegedly sighted a disc-shaped object in the night sky. Soon, "a group of strange, goblin-like creatures are reported to have repeatedly approached [their] farm house and looked inside through the windows. Family members present shot at them several times with little or no effect. The encounter lasted from evening until dawn."[29]

CIA-released files for 1955 do not include such mention. Posts from any source that mentioned phenomena surely would receive a degree of attention before being dutifully filed. That was standard operating procedure. But again, domestic affairs were stated to be outside CIA purview; they said they looked away.

Chapter 9

1956:

Transitive

Sometime in calendar year 1956, someone in the Agency compiled and internally distributed 109 pages of non-sourced photographic prints of aerial vehicles claimed to be unconventional. As released, nearly all were very grainy and of generally poor quality. Few were accompanied by any explanation.[1]

Likewise undated was a handwritten note, its author anonymous—presumably a person of some stature within the Office of Scientific Intelligence. He stated that, while the subject was not a specific OSI responsibility, it was of Agency interest. (By this time, the term "flying saucer" had lost favor in light of the particular shape implied; the more generic "unidentified flying object" had caught on both within and outside government circles.) By whatever handle the phenomena were described, this note warned of the implications: "Mass UFO reports could: (a) produce mass hysteria, (b) overload our radar (illegible) system, (c) overload communication facilities."[2]

On the 6th of January, an unnamed party in the Belgian Congo sent along a CIA Information Report. The document was in actuality a request for a "fine telescope" to be shared with the author's sky-watching group in order to spot the aerial anomalies that frequented that country.[3]

On January 9, OSI Assistant Director Herbert Scoville Jr. wrote a Memorandum for the Record, updating responsibilities related to anomalous aerial phenomena.

Henceforth, ASD (Applied Science Division) will conduct all surveillance of available information on this subject. All other OSI Divisions will provide such technical consultative assistance to ASD as it requires to discharge its assigned responsibility in this field. ASD will request a project of the requisite scope when appropriate for inclusion in the OSI Production Program.

Relatedly, the ASD was charged with maintaining all files on the subject. Other divisions were instructed to forward their relevant files to ASD and terminate their filing activities. This document superseded a similar June 14, 1954, Memorandum for the Record (see pages 76–77).[4]

In a February 9, 1956, Memorandum for the Record, Wilton Lexow, ASD Chief, referenced a statement for the record a month earlier by AD/SI Scoville titled "Responsibility for 'Unidentified Flying Objects.'"[5]

Scoville's memo had asserted three basic points:

1. The June 1954 memorandum assigning responsibility for tracking aerial anomalies to OSI's Physics and Electronics (P&E) Division was rescinded.

2. ASD was tasked with conducting "all surveillance of available information on this subject," with consultative assistance by other divisions as necessary.

3. Every file on the subject, old or new, was to be kept at ASD.

   To those ends, Lexow established several procedures:

   • ASD would maintain incoming raw reports potentially bearing on foreign weaponry research or development.

   • Where such reports might involve advancements in basic science, ASD would share the information with the Fundamental Sciences Area for review, requesting its return for filing.

- Reports not bearing on foreign weaponry but which might involve science advances would be forwarded to the Fundamental Sciences Area for retention or destruction.

- Reports which fit none of the above would be destroyed.

- ASD would maintain a chronological file of "all OSI correspondence and action taken in connection with the United States U.F.O. program . . ."

- ASD would maintain completed UFO-related intelligence reports published by the intelligence community.[6]

These procedures would prevent the accumulation of reports that could not be analyzed in ways useful to OSI. Raw UFO intelligence and obsolete finished reports would be destroyed. The long and short of it: The Applied Science Division was assuming full responsibility for UFOs within OSI; that authority had been afforded earlier but apparently had not been truly executed. Procedures were now outlined for retention or destruction of report submittals. Everyone was again pencil ready.[7]

Attending a conference at the palatial Arden House outside New York City, CIA Deputy Director Robert Amory Jr. had his attention directed to the March 17, 1956, issue of a popular French magazine, *Match*. It contained an especially challenging radar-visual *mysterious object celestial* (MOC) case. A control tower's radar photo of an unknown was verified by the direct observation of a commercial pilot.

Upon his return to Washington, Amory wrote an informal memo to OSI Assistant Director Herbert Scoville Jr. Amory asked, "Are we keeping in touch with the Air Force center on these things? Does it concern itself with foreign 'sightings' such as [this]?" Amory went on to say the planet Mars would be making an especially close pass by Earth soon, implying this would engender many false UFO reports. He concluded with a directive of sorts: "Outlandish as it may seem, I do feel that OSI has the responsibility to keep its finger on this general subject if for no other purpose than to arm the front office with the refutation of the more spectacular published reports".[8]

Scoville replied to Amory on April 13. He argued that the incident reported in the French magazine *Match*, noted above, was explainable—though he offered no specifics. With proper investigation, he insisted, that case would have been resolved as identifiable. The USAF Project Blue Book staff had reduced unexplained cases from 25 percent to 10 percent by interrogating all witnesses (a dubious claim, given the absence of staff to do so). In other countries, by comparison, he said, that standard was haphazardly applied. Scoville added that a liaison had been maintained with the Air Force's ATIC on domestic cases. The impending approach of Mars to Earth, he agreed, would no doubt result in false UFO reports. Though asked by Amory, Scoville did not reply as to whether the Air Force tracked foreign cases—which it did not.[9]

A redacted source sent in an Information Report on behalf of a relative on April 17, 1956. His niece, then living in Budapest, Hungary, had penned a letter to him the previous November in which she referred to a formation of unknowns that had flown over the city. She stated, "The so-called flying saucers (rockets) for several weeks kept the people in a nervous state. These very fast speeding flyers kept scientific groups very busy."[10]

An Information Report from a redacted source was forwarded on August 2, 1956, pertaining to events in spring 1954 over Stalingrad, Russia. The writer and other Stalingrad hospital patients twice witnessed an unknown fly from horizon to horizon in one minute. "I could not *see* the object itself, but I did *see* disturbance in the air which seemed to envelop it." The object, the person added, issued a "screeching, whistling noise."[11]

The final episode in a generally slow year domestically occurred on the east coast of Florida. On December 10, 1956, CIA communications officer J. P. Anderson wrote to OSI to explain an incident occurring two days before at Patrick AFB, Cape Canaveral. Multiple witnesses described a red glowing anomalous light high in the sky and moving rapidly. Patrick explained that it was in reality a flare ejected from a missile one minute after a test launch. He estimated its altitude as 15,000–20,000 feet, with a velocity immediately after ejection of 750–1,000 mph. Those factors matched witness descriptions.[12]

While you were away from your desk . . .

CIA analysts, perhaps distracted by President Eisenhower's reelection campaign, seem to have overlooked certain incidents reported by police as well as the military—one from an American ship, another from neighboring British and American air bases.

January 18, 1956

On the evening of the 18th, at Redondo Beach, California, a glowing saucer came to rest on the ocean surface, 75 yards from shore. Local and Hermosa Beach police officers came to the scene. Finally, the craft sank in 25 feet of frothing water, its surface continuing to glow. A lifeguard rowed to the site, spotted the object on the bottom, and left to organize a diving team. An officer also rowed out with a Geiger counter, which gave a normal reading. By the time the divers arrived, nothing could be seen on the seafloor.[13]

July 26, 1956

From the aircraft carrier USS Franklin D. Roosevelt, at anchor in the port of Rio de Janeiro, crewmen were startled to *see* two disc-shaped vehicles, one directly over the other, hovering above the flattop. Momentarily the upper disc ejected a fireball, which entered the top of the other. Both then left at great speed.[14]

August 13, 1956

At 9:30 p.m. a radar station at RAF Bentwaters, Suffolk, England, detected a target 25–30 miles east-southeast of the base, moving several thousand miles per hour. Within 30 seconds it was 15–20 miles northwest. A few minutes later a group of perhaps a dozen targets appeared eight miles southwest of Bentwaters, all separated and covering an expanse of 6–7 miles, moving northeast at about 100 mph. In front of them were three more in V-formation. At that point, checks for radar malfunctions proved negative. Suddenly all the targets on the screen merged into one very large blip, which remained stationary for 10–15 minutes. This oversized target moved a bit, only to halt again for a few minutes. Then it was lost to the radar as it headed north. Perhaps five minutes later another strong blip appeared on the screen, moving several thousand mph. Traveling west, it was within 25 miles of the base when it vanished from radar. At 10:55 p.m. still another target appeared 30 miles east and moving west at 2,000–4,000 mph. It passed nearly overhead, seen by both a C-47 pilot in the air and personnel on the ground. It was lost beyond the radar's reach 30 miles west of the base.[15]

The action then shifted to Lakenheath AFB, located northwest of Bentwaters. Having been alerted during the earlier activity, both radar and visual observations were made of a luminous unknown that abruptly stopped then shot off in another direction. Soon two white lights arrived from the distance and seemingly merged. It moved away in fits and starts, accelerating rapidly before suddenly halting. At midnight, Lakenheath phoned the RAF station at Natishead, Suffolk, which dispatched a Venom jet fighter. The pilot reported seeing a target well ahead that soon moved out of sight. The two-man crew was directed to another target, locating it ahead both visually and with onboard radar. They were amazed momentarily when they recognized it was suddenly *behind* their plane. Low on fuel they returned to base. Intermittently until 3:30 a.m. Lakenheath recorded anomalous radar returns.[16]

Chapter 10

1957:

Ham Sandwich

At the turn of the calendar to 1957, the US Air Force was under pressure from NICAP, news organizations, and many interested individuals to release the 1953 Robertson Report and requested CIA permission to do so. But complying wasn't quite so easy. OSI prepared a two-page summary of the findings for declassification and contacted all of the scientists from the panel individually, seeking approvals to use their names in connection with a limited distribution.

Throughout those efforts, CIA correspondence to the Air Force and others emphasized that no mention of Agency involvement would be permitted. Its stated reason was that public knowledge of those ties would give credence to the UFO subject.

The letter dated January 1, 1957, to Dr. Thornton Page of Johns Hopkins was identical to those sent to the remaining panel members. The Robertson Panel Report was referenced and a copy of the two-page summary enclosed. Drs. Howard P. Robertson, chairman of the Cal Tech physics department, and Samuel Goudsmit, physics department chairman at the Brookhaven National Laboratory, agreed the report could be partially but not entirely declassified. Air Force brass, meanwhile, insisted that names of panel members be used for official communications only, not given to the press. Still, OSI asserted, those names might become common knowledge.[1]

Recording Redux

As conveyed in a telegram from the Agency's Chicago office on March 4, 1957, Leon Davidson, a chemist at the Los Alamos National Laboratory, had recently written to CIA Director Allen Dulles, requesting all Agency information regarding a certain tape recording OSI acquired in February 1955 (see pages 87–88). The recording was of an electrical transmission of unknown origin. Apparently, the undefined recorded message had been heard and recorded by a ham radio operator in metropolitan Chicago who alleged it was a "message from outer space."

The (redacted) recipient of the Chicago telegram was requested to indicate any correspondence with Davidson plus how he justified writing to the Agency director.[2] Davidson told Chicago CIA staff that he had recently testified before a House subcommittee on the UFO subject.

Among the correspondences with Davidson was an informal note (to/from redacted) mentioning that Leon Davidson had inquired whether the tape had been evaluated by ATIC at Wright-Patterson AFB. The note writer informed Davidson that the tape was sent to "proper authorities" and that no further information was available. In a second letter, Davidson asked where to inquire about flying saucers. The writer replied, as Davidson knew, the place was the Air Technical Intelligence Center (ATIC) at Wright-Patterson.[3]

In an Information Report sent April 1, 1957, the (redacted) writer remarked that, in early May 1956, unknowns passed over Budapest at great height. "Nothing was done to disturb this flight, the probable reason being that the (illegible) Air Defense Command had no weapons at its disposal to research these intruders." Throughout May and June, objects in formation were reported on radar at over 75,000 feet on a near-daily basis. Reports came from all sections of Hungary.[4]

Soon enough, Leon Davidson was back on the Agency's radar. On May 8 the deputy assistant director for operations wrote to J. Arnold Shaw, Assistant to the Director, Allen Dulles. The deputy's memo attached a suggested reply to Davidson. It read, "[T]he recording in question was forwarded to OSI and found to be Morse code of US origin." The Air Force's ATIC would contact Davidson to inform him of that finding.[5]

So, just what were the motivations of this Davidson fellow? Was he, an otherwise accomplished chemist at a prestigious laboratory, merely a UFO nut who accepted at face value the notion of an alien origin for an innocuous ham radio transmission? Perhaps he had an entirely different take on UFO matters.

According to one source, by 1957 Davidson had "concluded that every aspect of the mystery led back to the CIA. He argued that they had deliberately concocted the major UFO reports and fed them into the public arena as a cover for experimental aircraft and rocket tests at best and psychological warfare experiments practiced on its own citizens at worst."[6]

CIA officials had insisted that Agency involvement in sponsoring the 1953 Robertson Panel, and in various situations thereafter, be kept from the public because attaching its name to analysis of the phenomena would lend credence to claims of a UFO reality. Davidson intended to upend that apple cart. To him, the CIA was continuing to perpetuate a flying saucer myth in order to conceal the true identities of planes and rockets of experimental design. By that reasoning, the tape-recorded code in question was not some extraterrestrial communication but rather CIA obfuscation, part of its nefarious program to confuse the public and keep the UFO rumors alive. That as a be-all-end-all explanation, of course, was likewise out there.

Whatever the truth of Davidson's motives, he would remain a front-burner personality and irritant in Agency affairs.

On May 10, 1957, J. Arnold Shaw, AD/CI, wrote to Davidson in reply to his April 21 letter. The tape in question, he stated, was being assessed by a separate government agency, which would reply to him directly.[7] That separate arm of the government was the US Air Force, specifically the Air Technical Intelligence Center at Wright-Patterson AFB, echoing the assertions of the previously received (sender redacted) note.

Also on May 10, 1957, the chief of the contact division sent a memo to the chief of the Chicago CIA office. An attached memo from OSI sought "analysis of the tape." Also attached was a suggested letter to Davidson from USAF. The Chicago staff was directed to ask the Air Force to follow through and obtain a copy of said letter for OSI.[8]

Following a hiatus of several weeks, like a bad penny, the matter of Leon Davidson renewed. In a July 2 note between redacted parties, Davidson came up. "Based on your conversation with ATIC, we told the CIA Director that Leon Davidson would receive a reply. Were you copied on the response? If not, was it in fact written?"[9]

A few weeks earlier, on June 11, the director of the Agency's planning and coordination unit wrote a formal Memorandum for one or more parties (redacted) as a primer of sorts on CIA involvement in the UFO subject over the previous several years. Though the Air Force and CIA continued to follow reported UFO events, responsibility had not shifted to the Agency. OSI's Philip Strong headed the CIA effort.[10]

As background, by January 1953 OSI had formed a panel of seemingly informed outside experts in the sciences to study the situation. Panel members included:

- Lloyd Berkner, President, Association of Universities; also President of the International Council of Scientific Boards; also a member of the President's Scientific Advisory Committee

- H.P. Robertson, Chairman, California Technical University Physics Department; also an OSI consultant

- Samuel Goudsmit, Physics Department Chairman, Brookhaven National Laboratory; formerly a member of the Combined Scientific and Military Team (which examined German nuclear capabilities during World War II)

- Luis Alvarez, University of California at Berkeley physicist (later Nobel Prize winner)

Astronomer Thornton Page of Johns Hopkins University and J. Allen Hynek, observatory director at The Ohio State University, were also substantially involved.

The Air Force and Navy supported the outcome and aftermath. The June 11 Memorandum added, "Since the study was made (January 17,

1953), OSI has maintained a watching process on UFO. The relatively few reports received by OSI are examined by the appropriate division."

Those involving natural phenomena were examined by the Geo-Physics Unit of the Fundamental Sciences Division.

Those concerning hardware aspects of flying craft were turned over to the former Weapons Unit in the Applied Science Division.[11]

"Gen. Watson, ATIC, (Phil Strong believes) maintains one or two officers following the UFO question. This ATIC effort is all that is left of an earlier larger Air Force Project called 'Blue Book.'"[12]

As previously noted, Project Blue Book never consisted of more than two low-ranking officers among four staff, including clerical assistance.

"I asked Phil point-blank if the unexplained category could include actual secret Soviet advanced aeronautical equipment. He replied, 'Conceivably, yes.'" But, more likely, with better data all the reports of unknowns would be explained as mundane. He emphasized that:

> OSI has no information concerning new Soviet design which would indicate possible construction of flying saucer type aircraft. The Applied Science Division of OSI and ATIC work closely together in following radical new designs and advances by the Soviets.

A joint British-Canadian project was underway to design a jet-powered flying saucer intended to reach 80,000 feet altitude. "[T]he Air Force has 'some projects' along this line."[13]

A mix and match of incoming foreign reports and in-house chatter followed:

An Information Report emanated from Azerbaijan on July 2, 1957, describing an event along the border separating Iran and Azerbaijan—then a USSR republic. At 11:00 a.m. on June 12, someone spotted a sphere one-half meter in diameter at an estimated 2,000 feet overhead. It sped laterally on a course from Iran into Azerbaijan. The object had a half-meter "tail" and left a brief smoke trail. Another party in the area witnessed a similar object at the same time and altitude.[14] Note: A bolide meteor is a strong possibility.

Sometime after July 8 (date illegible), Philip Strong, OSI's deputy assistant director, wrote to the deputy director for coordination. The subject was "Flying Saucers," in particular a meeting with a controversial figure. On the DD's behest, the chief of the fundamental sciences division had contacted Morris K. Jessup at the physical sciences integration committee. Jessup referred to Wayne Aho and a meeting resulted. A report of that conversation (not shown) was attached.[15]

Note: Wayne Sulo Aho was an American *contactee*, claiming repeated contact with extraterrestrial beings. He was one of the more obscure members of the 1950s wave of self-described contactees who followed George Adamski.[16] Morris K. Jessup was the author of *The Case for the UFO*, 1955.

The Charleston, West Virginia, daily (via INS) carried a news article on July 12 that voiced NICAP's claim of multiple supersonic airborne objects. The article quoted a NICAP spokesman as stating, "Civil Aeronautics Administration control-tower operatives have tracked four 'flying saucers' over California, operating at speeds up to 3,600 miles an hour."[17]

Retired US Navy Rear Admiral Herbert B. Knowles, a NICAP member, criticized what he called the veil of secrecy surrounding the UFO subject. Presaging a fellow Navy admiral (see below), he declared: "There is a real need to break through the official Washington brush-off and get the truth to the people."[18]

An NEA staff correspondent wrote in the Harlan, Kentucky, newspaper on July 20 a story headlined, "Spot a Flying Saucer and Afraid the Neighbors Will Laugh? Then Tell It to New Confidential NICAP." The article featured Donald Keyhoe, NICAP director, a retired Marine major who said NICAP offered confidentiality to witnesses reporting UFOs, while secrecy would likewise be extended to those choosing to join the civilian organization.[19]

The article continued by remarking that the first issue of NICAP's periodical announced the appointment of its newest board member, Admiral Roscoe H. Hillenkoetter, career Navy officer and—importantly—former CIA director. Keyhoe continued his scolding of Washington: "It has been Keyhoe's contention all along that the Air Force has a big plot cooking to keep the real facts on saucers from the public."[20]

Wayne Aho, the contactee who met with Agency staff, apparently failed to impress. In a July 26 memo from (redacted) to the OSI deputy assistant director for collection, the Agency staff person said up front that Aho claimed to possess the powers of extrasensory perception (ESP). The information conveyed went predictably weird from there. "He explained that spaceships are all about travel in a fourth dimension . . ." The visitors, Aho said, are here only for good. He was able to travel in the fourth dimension while asleep, in his "twin body."[21]

Two years before, Aho said, he had first encountered a saucer; he claimed six friendly beings appeared on a screen before him. Ten weeks before, on the night of May 11–12 in the desert he allegedly saw a white light resolve into a red orb, diameter 20–30 feet, hovering nearby for five minutes. He spent the night walking about 20 miles in the desert, as directed by a magnetic force. He encountered an invisible ship and felt the presence of visitors. No classified information was offered during the interview.[22]

An August 20, 1957, note from Support (to/from redacted) indicated that, based on communication with the Air Force's ATIC, the CIA Director was told that Leon Davidson would receive a reply to his inquiry regarding a coded ham radio transmission. Was this note's recipient aware that such a letter had been sent or drafted?[23]

A month later on September 20, Air Defense Command tracked an unknown at 50,000 feet, its speed a consistent 2,000 knots (2,300 mph) from Long Island to Buffalo, New York. (The air speed record in 1957 was 1,207 mph by a McDonnell 101A Voodoo.[24]) Radar *jamming* was reported at several locations along the way. It was unlikely to be a Soviet advanced aircraft or missile launch in a military taunt—though no specific intelligence on any Soviet activities was available. Weather phenomena might well have explained the early radar returns, but none were forthcoming. Consequently, no Intelligence Advisory Committee meeting needed to be called regarding this event.[25]

In an October 1 exchange between anonymous parties in the Agency, one shared with the other: ". . . I accept the fact that people *see* things in the sky and cannot identify them." Ninety percent or more, he went on, were known objects—planets, balloons, birds, high-flying aircraft. Having spent time studying the subject:

> I saw no evidence of "intelligently controlled" objects. . . . [T]he likelihood of truly inexplicable phenomena is vanishingly small. . . . [T]hey are not a uniform class but a hodge-podge of widely disparate, partly described phenomena. . . . [T]he subject, by its nature, precludes any rigorous proof or dis-proof.[26]

Philip Strong, OSI's Deputy Assistant Director, continued to contact former members of the 1953 Robertson Panel, this time Lloyd V. Berkner on October 2. As Strong had explained to the others, the Air Force requested that the Robertson Panel's conclusions be declassified for press purposes. The CIA agreed with partial declassification, deleting any mention of Agency involvement. As a panel member, did Berkner agree with the partial declassification proposal? Would he allow mention of his name?[27]

An anonymous Agency staffer, who had written a UFO-related book intended for publication, replied to someone critical of his argument for a UFO reality. In his October 5 return letter, the author remarked:

> It was refreshing to receive a negative letter that evidenced clear and sound thinking. Unfortunately, I cannot say the same for some seven or eight-odd letters from scientists who, although thinking much the same as you, have shown sarcasm and ridicule in expressing themselves . . . Whether or not I can use your opinions in the book remains for the publisher to decide . . . It would interest me to know with what USAF project you were associated.[28]

Philip Strong notified his superior, the OSI assistant director, via Office Memorandum of a UFO-related development. His October 26 dispatch conveyed that, per a phone call from Howard Robertson, Air Force Major James F. Byrne had contacted Robertson for permission to release the Robertson Panel conclusions. Strong added that he would follow up with Major Byrne.[29]

"Dr. Leon Davidson is on our backs again. He wants a verbatim translation of the 'space' message and the identification of the transmitter from which it came." The sender of this November 3, 1957, telegram (to/from redacted) was evidently irritated by Davidson's persistence in the matter. The message went on to say that ATIC's Captain Wallace Ellwood had written to Davidson, explaining that the recording in question "was in identifiable Morse code from a known US licensed radio station." Would the assistant director be willing to obtain the translation and transmitter ID from the Air Force? "We'd like to dismiss this man once and for all."[30]

In a follow-up the next day, someone in authority (redacted) sent a note indicating no translation of the code was available. ATIC had twice attempted to contact Leon Davidson. This case was closed. The person suggested his letter be ignored.[31]

Another telegram from the Chicago office, this one on November 5, clarified that its contact with Leon Davidson was in person when he was in Chicago for a meeting. Davidson was preparing an article for a "space magazine" and demanded either (1) the translation of the message and emitting station to prove the message was a hoax, or (2) permission to display CIA and ATIC letterheads in the article to show the government was avoiding his inquiries. "He explained that he had received no satisfactory answer to his request of us and ATIC in nearly a year." The Chicago staff was seeking an escape route.

> Davidson was calm and pleasant but very determined . . .
> We wish to bow out of this thing, but urge that headquarters, (redacted), and ATIC concern themselves with this man and try to satisfy him. Please do not let us down on our agreement to communicate with him. We are committed.[32]

Philip Strong contacted Cal Berkeley's Dr. Luis Alvarez for the purpose of enclosing a citizen letter to the Air Force on the UFO subject, plus the declassified Robertson Panel Report.[33] Strong wrote identical letters to Dr. Lloyd Berkner, President, Associated Universities, Inc.,[34] and to Dr. Thornton Page, Operations Research Office, Johns Hopkins University.[35]

A November 7 interoffice memo from a redacted party to the chief of another (illegible) office included photographs printed from a strip of 16 mm movie film taken in 1952. The photos were on loan to the Agency for 30 days. The movie camera used had a focal length of 63 mm and took 24 frames per second. The cameraman and other observers present estimated the unknown to be 2,000 feet high, at a camera angle of 45 degrees. The lens aperture was f:2.7, while film emulsion was fast panchromatic. The original negatives were in Air Force hands. The witness stated his willingness to make more negatives from the prints if they would be useful.

"The object appeared to have the shape of a saucer, i.e., a rotating oblate spheroid which seemed to flatten out as speed increased. The UFO was in view for about three minutes and was of a bright orange color."[36]

In the wake of the Soviet Union's first two Sputniks, a former CIA Director, Admiral Roscoe H. Hillenkoetter had a different take on that story line. In a November 18 news article (publisher not shown), he made a prediction:

> Satellite and space exploration programs should give us new, valuable information on UFOs, affording definite evidence as to their reality, and this will result because of a tremendous increase in observation of the sky, by radar and telescope tracking systems and by naked-eye observations.

Such an increase in sightings volume was underway, this member of NICAP's board of governors added. "There are already increases in authentic UFO reports since the Russian satellite drew public attention to the skies. Also, spotters of Operation Moonwatch, the US satellite tracking network, have sighted a number of UFOs."[37]

On December 4, 1957, Dr. Thornton Page of Johns Hopkins University wrote back to OSI Deputy Assistant Director Philip Strong to express his opinion that after nearly five years since it was written, the Robertson Panel Report should be declassified. Page added that he did not object to the release of his name in connection with the report. Further, he had no strong opinion on withholding some of the information. A separate exchange of their letters was enclosed (not shown).[38]

On the 12th of December, a (redacted) staff person sent a memo to the chief of an OSI (illegible) division regarding five photographs of an unknown he had returned to a private party on the 10th. In the conversation that ensued, the staffer clarified the Agency's position on such matters and the individual's rights and obligations.

The staff person asked whether an evaluation of the photos might be done by OSI. The staffer said they would not be but that his desire would be sent on within the Agency.

He explained that a television show was planned in order to inform the public and encourage UFO witnesses to take photos whenever possible. To that end he asked if it would be permissible to state on air that an intelligence agency had viewed the photos and found them of interest. The answer was negative.

Finally, he asked about writing to the director of central intelligence to seek an evaluation and the Agency's permission to show the photos on the program. The staffer told him he had that right.[39]

By mid-December Leon Davidson and his cover-up allegation concerning some Morse code, recorded from ham radio, was consuming Agency time again. A telegram from the Chicago office to a redacted source (probably in ATIC) on the 19th expressed a growing consternation: "As we informed your office there is no translation available nor is there any record available except for what you know." Davidson had been approached recently by ATIC staff:

> [T]he same message was given him again. He asked for it in writing which (redacted) refused to do. Davidson then said he would write to ATIC. We are all resigned to more letters . . . He has already received a couple of letters from ATIC, two from the DCI's office, and two visits from (redacted).

The sender suggested ignoring the latest Davidson letter.[40]

On the 20th, OSI's Deputy AD Philip Strong communicated to Howard P. Robertson, now chairman of DoD's Defense Science Advisory Board. Five years before he had agreed to chair a small group of physicists to examine the best evidence gathered in support of an ET hypothesis of UFO reports. On this occasion Strong was sharing a citizen's letter to the Air Force, plus the two-page declassified statement of the Robertson Panel's conclusions (neither shown).[41]

Strong wrote similar letters that day, enclosing the sanitized Robertson Panel Report, to the other panel members: Samual Goudsmit of the Brookhaven National Lab, Thornton Page of Johns Hopkins, Luis Alverez of Cal Berkeley, and Lloyd Berkner of Associated Universities.[42]

As if to wrap up all the presents and tie them with bows during Christmas week, Strong completed his December 20 correspondence with a letter to the Air Force assistant chief of staff for intelligence. Respecting the stated wishes of USAF brass to declassify the "Report of the Scientific Panel on Unidentified Flying Objects" (a.k.a. Robertson Report), Agency staff and the panel members came to agreement that the report could be released to the press and public but only in a brief, sanitized form, as stipulated. Moreover, any mention of Agency involvement was strictly *verboten*—"no connection with the CIA may be disclosed." Strong added that no panel member objected to use of his name. The report as revised was enclosed.[43]

Calendar 1957 and its repeated call to anomalies ended in a to/from telegram exchange between redacted parties. The Chicago CIA office expressed that, in all respects concerning the Leon Davidson matter, "we wish to bow out of this thing."[44]

1954-57 from Blue Book's Perspective

The USAF Project Blue Book's accumulated data on UFO reports in America from 1954 through 1957 reveals some consistencies as well as certain trend lines—as dutifully collected and assessed at their desks by a low-ranking officer and one noncom, whose job was to collate data collected from numerous sources.[45]

- Total cases received and evaluated rose year over year.

  1954—487

  1955—543

  1956—669

  1957—1,005

- Astronomical sources—planets, especially Venus and Mars; the four or five brightest stars; meteors and the occasional comet—were the most repeated misidentifications in each of the four years.

  1954—28%

  1955—25%

  1956—33%

  1957—34%

- Conventional aircraft ranged from 16–22% of the total cases each year.

- Balloons accounted for 11–19% of the cases.

- "Insufficient data," including momentary events and ambiguously described sightings, accounted for 17–21% of the total.

- Confirming the wisdom of a long-term education and debunking program, officially unidentified cases as a portion of the total descended from 9% in 1954 to less than 2% in 1957. For 1956 and 1957 combined, only 31 incidents were left unexplained.[46]

While you were away from your desk . . .

Other significant cases in 1957, in America and overseas, might have captured CIA interest—had it been paying attention. The volume of records placed on its website in January 2017 included none of those described below.

March 9, 1957

At Wilcox Field (later Miami International Airport) air traffic controllers sent a flash message to the Civil Aeronautics Board concerning an incident at 3:30 a.m. To avoid an oncoming unknown, the pilot of a Douglas DC-6A four-engine prop aircraft took violent evasive action. The intruder was described as having a brilliant greenish-white center with an outer ring reflecting the glow from the center. Seven other pilots in the air offered similar descriptions. No missile flight or jet aircraft activity accounted for the incident.[47]

May 3, 1957

Two men, on behalf of test pilot and later astronaut Gordon Cooper, were filming installations at Edwards AFB, California, when they observed the landing and departure of a silent flying disc. Their film evidence was sent to the Pentagon (a.k.a. the black hole). No evidence suggests they heard back.[48]

May 20, 1957

During the Cold War era of the 1950s, the US Air Force used RAF Manston, located at Kent in England's East Anglia area, as a Strategic Air Command base. That night, two F-86D Sabre jet interceptors, already on routine scramble alert, were ordered into the air and east out over the North Sea. The lead pilot, Lieutenant Milton Torres, later recalled conversing with the Ground Controlled Intercept (GCI).[49]

> The initial briefing indicated that the ground was observing for a considerable time, a blip that was orbiting the East Anglia area. There was very little movement . . . [I]t was suggested to us that the "bogey" actually was motionless for long intervals.[50]

After a final turn he was told to look 30 degrees left, and there it was, 15 miles distant. Though still in heavy clouds, the blip on his radar was now intense—equivalent to a "flying aircraft carrier." His radar locked onto the target and he was preparing to fire the salvo when the bogey proceeded to bounce all over the screen, breaking the radar lock. A moment later it moved beyond the 30-mile maximum distance for radar tracking. The attempted interception was over, and the pilots returned to their base.[51]

July 17, 1957

Two months later in the predawn hours, a US Air Force RB-47 Stratojet reconnaissance bomber, equipped with the most advanced electronics of the time, returned across the Gulf of Mexico at 34,500 feet altitude and 500 mph on the final stage of a training mission. As it moved over Gulfport, Mississippi, onboard equipment picked up something that appeared to be pacing the plane. A bit later, after the bomber turned west, multiple sets onboard, plus ground radar, kept track of the unknown. At one point the crew spotted a huge white light in the distance, which in the darkness vaguely appeared to be attached to something airborne that was still larger. At another juncture, the bogey was in front of the plane, seemingly on a collision course, and the pilot veered to avoid it. By the time the Stratojet turned north toward its home at Forbes AFB in Topeka, Kansas, the UFO had been in its company for 700-800 miles. Blue Book and the Air Defense Command both investigated the case, though no account appeared in print until 1969 as part of the *Scientific Investigation of Unidentified Flying Objects*, a.k.a. the Condon Report. In the interim, shortly after this incident, Blue Book officially declared the intruder to be a commercial airliner while offering no data.[52]

August 14, 1957

At 10:55 p.m., a Varig Airlines C-47 cargo transport was passing over Brazil's state of Santa Catarina at 6,300 feet on its way to Rio de Janeiro. Suddenly it confronted a luminous object ahead that crossed its path laterally. Without warning the plane's engines began coughing and the cabin lights dimmed severely. At that point the unknown dove downward into a cloud and was gone. The C-47 immediately returned to normal operation.[53]

August 20, 1957

At approximately 11:30 a.m., near Enoshima Miani Beach, Japan, a gentleman's sister called his attention to an approaching airborne oddity about 3,000–4,000 feet up. He snapped one photo of the object, which they reported as silvery and glowing brilliantly. When directly overhead, the object made a 90-degree turn and sped up from an estimated 250 to 500 kph. It was quickly lost in the clouds. A few minutes later about 15 bathers at the beach spotted the same or a similar vehicle racing silently overhead.[54]

September 4, 1957

While flying on a path over Portalegre, Portugal, under the command of Captain José Lemos Ferreira that night, the crews of four Portugal Air Force fighter-bombers at 25,000 feet spotted a large luminescent object above the horizon. As they looked on, the anomalous light appeared to grow in size then diminish. After several minutes the pilots noticed a small yellow circle emerging from the larger unknown. Later three more circles appeared. Near the town of Coruche, the bigger object (*mother ship*?) rose up and away while the smaller ones left the area. The bombers landed without any problems, following which Captain Ferreira declared: "After this, do not come to us with that Venus, weather balloons, aircraft, and similar stuff which have been being used as general explanations for almost every case of UFOs."[55]

November 2–3, 1957

During the night, from disparate locations surrounding the town of Levelland, Texas, frightened callers told the sheriff's office that an oval/egg-shaped object, perhaps 200 feet in length, rose from fields and charged their vehicles, passing low overhead with a thunderous sound. As it went past, each motorist claimed, the engine and headlights of the car/truck died—only to return to normal operation once the anomaly was gone.

The first call came from a pair of Latino farmhands at 10:50 p.m. After a flash in an adjacent field, a yellow-white light lifted off the ground, accelerated, and "passed directly over the truck with a great sound and rush of wind." As it approached, the truck's headlights went dark and the engine died. When the light had passed out of sight, the engine was restarted without a problem. Another call to the sheriff at 12:05 a.m. from a college student told much the same story. He estimated the vehicle when stationary was about 125 feet across—most callers that night estimated around 200 feet—and glowing blue-green. After a few minutes it rose straight up and out of sight. The witness had no trouble restarting his car. Among the reporting witnesses across several hours were the sheriff, a deputy, and the local fire marshal.[56]

November 3, 1957

Just hours after the spectacular series of sightings around Levelland, Texas, at the White Sands Proving Grounds, New Mexico, a tantalizing if brief series of encounters ensued. Two military policemen were patrolling about 3:00 a.m. when they spotted a brilliant red-orange, egg-shaped object descending to about 50 yards above a bunker; it suddenly vanished before their eyes. The men estimated its expanse as 75–100 yards. A few minutes later it blinked on again and descended, this time at an angle, toward the same bunker, only to disappear once more. It did not reappear and a later search party found nothing.

Seven hours later at 10:20 a.m., two military policemen patrolling White Sands observed a brilliant red-orange, egg-shaped object descend to within 50 yards of a bunker, then vanish. Minutes later it blinked on again, descended on a slant, and disappeared in broad daylight once more. A search party found no trace of the intruder. About 8:00 p.m. that evening, a separate patrol spotted a brilliant light, 200–300 feet long, over the same bunker. The light pulsated as it ascended slowly at an angle, then imploded to a point of light and disappeared.[57]

November 4, 1957

At Fort Itaipu, Brazil, about 2:00 a.m., two sentries noticed what they at first thought was a star. It rapidly descended and slowed, at which point they realized it was a disc about 100 feet in diameter and surrounded by an orange glow. It stopped 150 feet above the grounds, issuing a humming sound. The sentries, standing within the light being cast, were too frightened to move. Suddenly a blast of severe heat engulfed them; one fell to the ground, the other raced away screaming in pain and terror. The sleeping men of the garrison leaped from bed only to have their interior lights go out. Then the surroundings became strangely hot. A minute later, the heat lifted and the lights came back on. Some of the soldiers running to their battle stations saw the glowing UFO as it sped away. The burned sentries were treated medically and survived. US Army and Air Force advisors were at a loss to explain the intrusion.[58]

Chapter 11

1958:

Insurgencies Peak

Samuel Goudsmit of the Brookhaven National Laboratory, and a member of the 1953 Robertson Panel, had written to the OSI Deputy Assistant Director Philip Strong on December 26, 1957, concerning the inclusion on the retrospective panel of astronomer J. Allen Hynek and physicist Lloyd Berkner. In his reply on January 3, Strong explained that Hynek, though attending some of the panel meetings, was not a full member and did not sign the report. Berkner was a member and did sign the report.[1]

Leon Davidson refused to give up. On January 9, a redacted Agency person sent a memo to the chief of the support branch in the Chicago office. Davidson had been told firmly that the CIA "cannot resolve his problem concerning the space message and its transmitter because records on the matter have been destroyed by the evaluating agency." Davidson informed the writer that he had written a second article about sightings of unknowns. (A presumably important paragraph was deleted.) The writer ended with, "We are sure more will be heard from Davidson."[2]

A January 31 telegram to the Agency's support staff in Chicago from (redacted) once again addressed the CIA irritant, Leon Davidson. The writer said that Davidson was demanding an interpretation of the tape recording in question—a translation of the Morse code, as well as answers to irregularities he perceived in the CIA investigation thereof. Additionally, contrary to a statement the chemist had made, "(Redacted) did not ask Davidson to keep secret the location of the Agency's Chicago office, but advised him not to use CIA letterhead in his forthcoming article . . . without first clearing with CIA authorities in Washington."[3]

Air Force Regulation 200-2, titled "Unidentified Flying Objects (UFO)," was released February 5, 1958. It displaced identically numbered regulations from August 26, 1953; November 2, 1953; and August 12, 1954. This iteration reestablished emphasis on procedures for information and evidence material pertaining to UFOs. Its further purpose was to set forth "the responsibility of Air Force activities in this regard. It applies to all Air Force Activities."[4]

In its introduction, the Department of the Air Force made clear that the USAF role with respect to the reported aerial anomalies was fourfold: detection, identification, interception, and, ominously, destruction. The Headquarters more broadly outlined the Air Force's responsibilities in addressing this subject:

- Determine any security threat to the United States posed by unknowns.

- Ascertain technical or scientific characteristics, within or beyond present-day knowledge.

- Explain or identify *all* sightings.

These tasks would be handled by one low-ranking officer, a noncommissioned officer, a part-time secretarial assistant, and a filing cabinet: Project Blue Book.

Since UFOs could be hostile or foreign unconventional aircrafts, it was imperative to ensure rapid, factual, and complete reports of sightings by the public. The Air Force needed up-to-date information on new or unique designs, propulsion systems, and weapons. The academic fields of geophysics, atmospherics, and astronomy could benefit from the study of UFOs and other aerial phenomena, was one current of CIA thinking.

In the quest to minimize the number of reported unknowns remaining unexplained, in all but a comparatively few sighting events, subsequent analysis had identified them as prosaic: conventional aircraft, planets and stars, atmospheric phenomena, balloons, and so forth. With better data from the reporting witnesses and others, the remainder could probably have been explained, the Agency insisted.

US Air Force interest in the UFO subject and objectives were declared to be twofold: (1) to thwart possible threats to the security of the United States and its forces, and (2) to determine the technical aspects of the so-called phenomena involved.

Until then, the flying objects reported had posed no threat to US security or that of its possessions. However, the possibility that new air vehicles, hostile aircraft, or missiles might first be regarded as unknown flying objects was real. Therefore, sightings needed to be reported as rapidly and as completely as information permitted.

These efforts had thus far failed to provide a satisfactory explanation for a number of sightings reported.

> The Air Force continues to collect and analyze reports until all sightings can be satisfactorily explained, bearing in mind that:
>
> - to measure scientific advances, the Air Force must be informed on experimentation and development of new air vehicles;
>
> - the possibility exists that an air vehicle of revolutionary configuration may be developed; and
>
> - the reporting of all pertinent factors will have a direct bearing on the success of the technical analysis.

UFOs were, once again, serious business to the Air Force.[5]

Readers might question the timing of this regulatory release. America was in the midst of a cold war with the Soviet Union, certainly, and "duck and cover" was the naïve response in public service announcements to the threat of Russian bombs or missiles. Now they had launched a pair of Sputnik satellites. In such an atmosphere of potential hysteria, using military resources to nip the buds of reported anomalous lights in the sky could certainly be justified.

Or might there possibly have been a watershed moment—per chance a change in perspective on what UFOs might mean, by the Air Force Chief of Staff, the Defense Secretary, a White House adviser—at some point over the 30 months since the Air Force's most recent regulations on the same subject?

To be clear, this directive stipulated that all base commanders were responsible to report information on UFO sightings, regardless of source. The Air Force base nearest to the sighting location was responsible for the initial investigation and efforts to resolve it. The Air Technical Intelligence Center (ATIC) at Wright-Patterson AFB, Ohio, would analyze the findings and investigate further if necessary. The CIA Office of Information Services (OIS) would release sighting statistics and respond to inquiries from the public. The USAF Office of Legislative Liaison would respond to congressional inquiries and utilize ATIC as necessary. All bases and offices were to assist USAF investigators.[6]

Screening and evaluating sighting accounts meant assessing the logic, consistency, and coherence of the witness account. That had to be painted against the person's age, education, and occupation. A theodolite (a surveying instrument used for measuring angles) would assist in some aerial measurements. Airborne interception and ID or air search might be necessary. Contact with local air traffic controllers, ground crews, private pilots, airlines, astronomers, weather forecasters, and other sources of factual data was thereby encouraged. Photography was invaluable, and to be used whenever possible. ATIC sometimes needed additional materials (for example, maps, drawings) and was authorized to request them.[7]

OIS, meanwhile, was responsible for coordinating with ATIC on technical matters as well as sighting and investigative information and to process correspondence from the public.

A base commander could release information regarding sightings in the base's vicinity: "If the sighting is unexplainable or difficult to identify, . . . the only statement to be released is the fact that the sighting is being investigated and information regarding it will be released at a later date." If newsmen or individuals intended to release unofficial information, efforts would be necessary to disassociate the Air Force. OIS staff were not to contact or share information with unauthorized persons unless so directed. USAF reports transmitted within three days of the sighting were to be tabbed "Priority." Older reports would be "Routine."[8]

A detailed Air Force reporting format included the object's description, aerial course, manner of observation, sighting time and date, observer's location and identifying information, weather conditions, any unusual activity or condition, aerial interception or ID, action taken, air traffic in the area, and existence of physical evidence. Instructions were offered for handling still photos, motion pictures, negatives and supplemental prints, camera specifics, and radar tracking.[9]

As he had promised, Leon Davidson sent a copy of his magazine article to the Pentagon, which forwarded it to OSI without comment. OSI handed it to Colonel Stanley Grogan, Special Assistant to the CIA Director for public relations, stating nothing could be done about it; Grogan agreed. The sender declared, "We do not want any business with Davidson. If he wishes to contact the Agency he already knows enough names. . . . So, unless there are overriding reasons in the future we do not want (redacted) involved in this mess."[10]

Herbert Scoville, OSI Assistant Director, sent a memo titled "Unidentified Flying Objects" to his counterpart in the Office of Operations on March 21. He attached two letters (not shown) recently sent to the Director of Intelligence (presumably from Donald Keyhoe and Leon Davidson, respectively) and forwarded to OSI for reply. Scoville asked for OO comment as soon as possible—especially regarding the final two paragraphs of the letter from Keyhoe, the retired Marine Corps major who headed NICAP. Scoville commented warily, "The statements and inquiries made in these letters involve a number of rather critical matters." Three days later the AD at Operations assigned a staff person to prepare a memo for Scoville's signature. On the assignment buck slip the AD remarked, "I hope Major Keyhoe is not referring to any of our field personnel."[11]

Also on March 21, retired Air Force General Charles P. Cabell, CIA Deputy Director, responded to a Donald Keyhoe letter of March 13. Having reviewed various UFO reports cited by Keyhoe, Agency staff determined that further inquiries and coordination with other organizations were needed. Cabell conditionally promised, "dependent upon the findings of my staff," to advise Keyhoe on these incidents.[12]

The CIA was dealing with a salvo of criticism, courtesy of Keyhoe, NICAP's chairman, who charged that the Agency was silencing UFO eyewitnesses. (Think *Men in Black*.) If true and if made public, the CIA would suffer a serious embarrassment and deservedly so. It was not authorized to contact US citizens, let alone attempt to intimidate them.

An internal memo attempted to clarify the matter: Witnesses were to be told that their relationship with the Agency must remain confidential in order to minimize disclosure of CIA involvement. But there was no intent—at least not by the people in Langley, Virginia, who set policy— to impose any security restrictions on the content of their accounts. Conceivably some witnesses, or agents, were confused.

Shortly thereafter, the Operations acting AD responded to Herbert Scoville at OSI. Regarding Major Keyhoe's allegation, agents may have misinterpreted policy on communicating with UFO witnesses.

> [T]he relationship between the source and the Agency
> is confidential in nature. This caveat is not intended to
> impose a security restriction on the information imparted
> by the source but to minimize the disclosure of the
> Agency's relationship with the source.[13]

In other words, it was all right to tell a UFO witness that "this conversation never happened," since the agent was not permitted to contact the witness in the first place. But insisting that the person remain silent about the circumstances of an incident was over the line.

Scoville wrote to the Operations AD again on the 23rd. He attached copies of letters to the CIA Director. To prepare replies, he requested the AD's comments on part of Donald Keyhoe's letter (not shown).[14]

On April 1, the Operations AD wrote to OSI's Scoville again. Major Keyhoe's question concerning CIA silencing of UFO witnesses suggested a possible misinterpretation by Contact Division staff. There was no intent to impose a security restriction on the content of eyewitness accounts.

Conceivably some sources were confused. Separately, the Contact Division had accumulated a detailed history of Dr. Leon Davidson's activities in the UFO field and alleged outer space communications.[15]

On the 4th of April, an executive officer in the CIA Director's office, J. S. Earman, wrote to Keyhoe. Earman explained that, since the subject of Keyhoe's March 13, 1958, letter was of primary concern to the Air Force, it had been forwarded there for reply to him.[16]

The chief of the OSI Applied Science Division (ASD) prepared an Office Memorandum for AD/SI Herbert Scoville on April 4. Back in 1953, the Robertson Panel had assessed potential threats to national security posed by UFOs and found nothing of significance. Edward Ruppelt, an Air Force captain, had attended panel meetings because he was the first head of Project Blue Book. But his 1956 book on his investigative experience (*The Report on Unidentified Flying Objects*) implied that the panel's mission had been to identify UFOs. The chief asserted, "Ruppelt's statements regarding the mission of the panel are in error. He has led the reader to believe the panel's mission was to identify the flying objects and to make recommendations on methods to further identify such objects."[17]

An interview with Captain Ruppelt by pugilistic television journalist Mike Wallace revealed the CIA/USAF connection in selecting Robertson Panel members. Concurrently, the misinformation in Ruppelt's book, the division chief continued, "is the basis for the apparent contradictions" which arose during that interview. Further, recent letters from both Donald Keyhoe and Leon Davidson had not jibed with the major focus of Ruppelt's book.[18]

In October 1957 Air Force Major James F. Byrne had formally requested that the full Robertson Panel Report be declassified. Now Davidson and Keyhoe desired copies of it. Since panel members were already disclosed, it would be expedient to send them the full version. "[E]ither the Air Force should answer the letters (to Davidson and Keyhoe) or we should make it plain to the recipients that we obtained the panel report from the Air Force," the ASD chief concluded.[19]

Oh, really? The CIA's handpicked panel wrote its report for the Air Force?

Wilton Lexow, the ASD Chief, had asked the Secretary of the Air Force about releasing the declassified portion of the Robertson Panel Report to Donald Keyhoe and Leon Davidson. The Air Force Secretary's Office of Information (SAFOI) responded. Major Lawrence J. Tacker wanted OSI to instead send the letters and report drafts to him for follow-up; he implied that his office was the nexus for UFO inquiries. Lexow now wrote of his relief at this sudden turn of events. "I think we can use this procedure as a precedent henceforth in all inquiries regarding UFO's."[20]

It did not take the Agency long to react to this welcome news. That same day, on behalf of Wilton Lexow, CIA Executive Officer J. S. Earman wrote back to Major Tacker, enclosing copies of the latest letters received from Leon Davidson and Donald Keyhoe concerning UFOs, along with the Agency's replies. Also enclosed were three copies of the declassified portion of the Robertson Panel Report.[21]

Two weeks later, on April 17, Earman attempted to put out a fire of the Agency's making. In a terse letter to Donald Keyhoe, Earman denied emphatically a potentially explosive charge:

> I have had the records of this Agency checked and find nothing therein reflecting that any CIA employee, at any time, caused any witness to an unidentified flying object to remain silent concerning said witness' observations of said UFO.[22]

OSI's Wilton Lexow wrote himself a memorandum for the record on May 16 after meeting with Air Force personnel. The purpose had been to outline actions to deal with persons such as Leon Davidson. The chemist, whose superiors may have excused his words or not, had been "most insistent" upon getting the entire Robertson Panel Report released. The report had not been declassified entirely because it cited potential enemy actions harmful to US national security. Panel members later agreed that, "while they had no objection to their names being used in connection with the report, they did not want their names connected to the Central Intelligence Agency. So far it is believed that all connections between the panel members and the CIA have been made by unofficial personnel."[23]

In dealing specifically with Dr. Davidson, Major Lawrence Tacker of the Air Force Office of Information (SAFOI) would henceforth speak for both the Air Force and the Director of Central Intelligence. Davidson had sent his most recent letter to both USAF Major Tacker and the CIA director. To forestall future such inquiries, SAFOI would draft a press release using the Robertson Panel's conclusions. Major Boland, USAF Legislative Liaison, agreed that this would best serve congressional requirements.[24]

NICAP head Donald Keyhoe drew credibility from the presence on the NICAP board of governors of Vice Admiral R.H. Hillenkoetter, the late-1940s CIA Director. Air Force representatives "suggested that perhaps if the Admiral were shown the Secret panel report he would understand and take appropriate actions."[25]

A second Agency staffer in attendance at the May 16 CIA/USAF meeting, (redacted), an assistant to the legislative counsel, likewise registered in the assembled memorandum for the record that day. He noted that the Permanent Investigating Subcommittee (chaired by Senator John McClellan) of the Senate Committee on Government Operations wanted the Air Force to "dispel the air of mystery surrounding the flying saucer report of 1953." To that end, the Air Force proposed a press release. Major Tacher [sic] of the Air Force Information Service [sic] "indicated that he is being badgered constantly by UFO groups and various individuals concerning the subject of UFOs generally and the 1953 report specifically."[26]

In a draft USAF reply to Davidson, no mention was made of the OSI or that the CIA convened the 1953 panel. Tacher [sic] would also draft a press release using "the strongest possible language." The draft release would be reviewed by CIA offices: OSI, General Counsel, and Office of Security.[27]

Admiral Hillenkoetter's association with Major Kehoe [sic] and his group was discussed. The Air Force felt that the group was keeping the UFO subject in the public's eye and that "the position which it has taken is not entirely sound." Further, the admiral's presence gave the group "considerable prestige." The legislative counsel's assistant doubted Hillenkoetter was aware of the position taken by the group on the Robertson Report. The CIA attendees agreed to look into the matter and to consider approaching Hillenkoetter.[28]

A related Memorandum for Record sprang up on May 22, penned by LaRae L. Teel, the deputy division chief in OSI's Applied Science Division. Teel had met with Frank Chapin, assistant to the CIA director, on replying to Leon Davidson's latest letters. That was followed by a phone call with Major Lawrence Tacker of the Air Force. Chapin agreed to merely acknowledge receipt of the letters and inform Davidson again that this was a USAF matter. The next day, Tacker stated that he had already replied. He inquired in turn whether the Agency had contacted Admiral Hillenkoetter. Teel would find out.[29]

On the 26th, J. S. Earman, Executive Officer for the DCI, sent a brief letter to Leon Davidson. Recalling the chemist's earlier letters, Earman declared once more that those were forwarded to the Air Force for appropriate reply.[30]

Philip Strong, Deputy Assistant Director at OSI, wrote to Dr. Samuel Goudsmit at the Brookhaven laboratory on May 29. The purpose of his letter was to offer a heads-up. Strong said Howard P. Robertson, chair of the UFO study panel on which Goudsmit served over five years before, as well as panel member Lloyd Berkner had been "besieged" by Leon Davidson letters regarding their participation on the panel. To prepare Goudsmit for potentially similar treatment, Strong enclosed copies of pro forma correspondence to Davidson, including one that Robertson had put together. Strong suggested Goudsmit adopt the same tenor. Should the occasion arise, Strong added, Goudsmit should tell Davidson that the Air Force handled all such matters.[31] (Similar letters were sent to panel members Thornton Page and Luis Alvarez.)

That same day, Strong wrote to Lloyd Berkner, one of the aggrieved parties. This was to extend Strong's remarks on Leon Davidson[32]—"Mr. Davidson has kept the pot boiling hard . . ."—and to enclose a copied letter from Dr. "Bob" Robertson to Davidson and suggested Berkner employ the same tone. Strong also enclosed copies of a Robertson-Davidson exchange (also sent to Alvarez, Goudsmit, and Page) in a call for a united front. "He is taking far too much of all our time and effort."[33]

The next week, on June 4, Strong sent a letter to USAF Major Lawrence Tacker at SAFOI. Strong enclosed correspondence from Leon Davidson, who "continues to inquire about UFO's." Strong also enclosed a copy of an OSI reply to Davidson informing him that his letter was forwarded to the Air Force for reply.[34]

Strong might as well have added the phrasing, this isn't funny anymore. The human cost in terms of expenditures of time devoted to this man's fanaticism were by now intolerable. Hours continued to be taken from other pressing demands, real problems arising around the world. This distraction was beyond annoying.

In yet another OSI meeting to discuss Leon Davidson, this one held July 25, it was agreed not to reply to his July 3 letter, wrote Wilton Lexow of ASD in a memo for the record afterward. Consensus was also reached for OSI to inform the FBI of a potential charge of subversive activity.[35]

In a July 30 letter, Philip Strong thanked Thornton Page for sending a copy of his letter to Leon Davidson. "This letter should do much to quiet down the large furor which Mr. Davidson has raised around the community." Strong asked for a copy of Davidson's letter to Page that expressed Davidson's concern over UFOs. If one were to consider the term "building a case," this circumstance fit the phrase.[36]

Tag Team

An August 2, 1958, news article in the *Pittsburgh* (PA) *Press*, "Saucer Data Suppressed, Admiral Says," must have raised hackles across OSI. It could only be that nemesis behind Door No. 2, retired USMC Major Donald Keyhoe—still the signature figure at NICAP—encouraging Hillenkoetter.

Keyhoe claimed that secret congressional hearings on UFOs had been held, which the Air Force denied. Meanwhile, the admiral and other NICAP board members issued a statement: "[T]he Air Force is still withholding information on unidentified flying objects—including sighting reports. We believe this policy to be dangerous."[37]

The Air Force, and by extension the Central Intelligence Agency, had no capacity to prove a negative, that secret congressional hearings on UFOs had *not* been held. The Air Force denied the charge, of course. But Admiral Hillenkoetter and the NICAP board were adept at inserting themselves into the public's awareness whenever they chose to do so.

To many who paid attention, the Defense Department's response to the UFO subject—which once again was capturing public attention after a bit of a hiatus—was awkward and not entirely convincing. The man in the street may well have begun to question just what Washington knew about UFOs. But the culmination thereof was still years away.

Picked up in the daily sweep of news foreign and domestic was a letter to the editor of the *Akron Beacon Journal*. Its writer responded to a letter writer who had criticized Swiss psychiatrist Carl Jung for his belief that the US Air Force was hiding what it knew about UFOs. Other prominent persons held the same view, he noted, adding that the House Armed Services Committee was looking into the matter.[38]

OSI's deputy assistant director wrote to Dr. Samuel Goudsmit again on August 19. With "Dear Sam" informality, Philip Strong thanked the Brookhaven physicist for his letter (not shown) criticizing newspaper editor Fred Kirsch on the UFO subject. Goudsmit's words were "exactly what is needed in present context."[39] On a separate matter, Strong told Goudsmit that all materials at hand on Robert Jungk had now been sent to him. "I am sorry it took so long but my people apparently had difficulty prying the information loose." A 1956 book *Brighter than a Thousand Suns: A Personal History of the Atomic Scientists*, by the Austrian visionary writer and journalist Robert Jungk, was translated into English in 1958. Jungk claimed a group of German atomic scientists, the "pacifists," balked at building atomic bombs.

Wilton Lexow, OSI Applied Science Division Chief, sent off a spate of memos on August 22. In a formal Office Memorandum, he thanked Air Force Major Lawrence Tacker for volunteering to be "the official authority in these (UFO) matters." He enclosed a letter from the newspaper editor Fred Kirsch.[40]

In another Office Memorandum the same day, Lexow informed Frank Chapin, assistant to the CIA Director, that the Air Force's Major Tacker would reply to the letter writer (see note 38 above) that the Air Force was the sole UFO authority. Said person (Kirsch) had written some twenty letters to the Air Force.

Then, in a Memorandum for Record at day's end, Lexow noted that his recommendation not to answer Leon Davidson's July 3 letter had been followed.[41]

An unnamed (illegible) party sent a buck slip to the DCI assistant Frank Chapin. In a prior phone call to USAF Major Tacker, Chapin had agreed to respond to Donald Keyhoe as before, to explain that the Air Force was the only government entity qualified to address the UFO subject. Tacker said he had told Keyhoe that the undisclosed portions of the Robertson Panel Report did not pertain to UFOs. The sender suggested the Agency write to Keyhoe to clarify that his letter had been forwarded to Tacker.[42]

The August 22 letter from Keyhoe to J. S. Earman, Executive Officer, was attached to the buck slip. Keyhoe had inquired, ". . . I am writing again to ask what part the Central Intelligence Agency plays in the official investigation of the unidentified flying objects." After citing Air Force denials regarding the Robertson Panel Report, Keyhoe declared:

> Despite the published conclusions of the 1953 scientists group, we have found that there is an increasing public belief that the UFOs may possibly be unfriendly. We have absolutely no evidence to prove that they are hostile and I cite this only to prove the danger of the present secrecy policy. Secrecy breeds ignorance of the subject and it could lead to hysteria or even panic under certain conditions. I believe that an open discussion of the problem would serve the best interests of the country.

Keyhoe also requested an interview with a CIA staffer qualified to speak on the subject.[43]

Earman responded to Keyhoe in an October 10 letter, clarifying that his August 22 correspondence had been forwarded to Major Tacker at the

USAF information office. Earman further commented, "I believe the Air Force is the executive agency and perhaps the only government agency qualified to speak on the subject of unidentified flying objects."[44]

A District of Columbia resident, using new types of film and emulsion, claimed to have photographed groups of unknown objects crossing between Earth and the moon on several occasions over the previous few months. The photo processing allegedly delivered very high resolution images. The unidentified memo writer, who had been investigating the photographic process independently, sent a representative to interview the photographer. At the person's home, ". . . one of my men did notice the objects reported . . ." The writer "would not like to overlook some evidence of an often-reported phenomenon" that might interest the intelligence community. "[T]hese objects were remarkably clear and certainly indicated a phenomenon . . ."[45]

The memo writer sought counsel on how to obtain the materials to examine firsthand. The photographer had said he was out of work at present but had previous contracts with the Air Technical Intelligence Center. ATIC verified that the man had no current contract. Without question, he would deliver the materials for examination—only at a price.

The writer also mentioned that a House committee had addressed the problem of UFOs and sought to review all such evidence. It had suspended its hearings but intended to reopen them later.[46]

An overseas Information Report issued October 10 recalled an incident from July 1958 while aboard a train, an hour outside Leningrad, Russia. The writer and others saw two bright lights ascending in the far distance that trailed gray smoke. The lights remained in view for 10 minutes, still ascending. They seemed to move too slowly to be rockets.[47]

Probably concerning the same incident, another Information Report arrived in late October. As stated by the report preparer, about 10:00 p.m., July 10, 1958, he and others aboard a train one hour outside Leningrad observed a bright light trailing black smoke. The object was estimated to be under 2,000 feet above the ground and 5-15 miles distant. A tour guide joked that it was probably a flying saucer.[48]

Philip Strong of OSI wrote to Director Gilmore of the National Photographic Interpretation Center on October 29 concerning alleged UFO photos taken by a Mr. Fine. Strong explained that OSI had a certain level of interest in the subject, but overall responsibility rested with the Air Force. The CIA had been "flooded by queries concerning UFO's" since part of the Robertson Panel Report was declassified and released. Those were all forwarded to the USAF's Major Lawrence J. Tacker, who handled public relations at the Pentagon. Investigative problems were likewise directed to the Pentagon. With his permission, Strong would send the memo describing the photos of unknowns to Gilmore for investigation as appropriate.[49]

On the 2nd of December, an assistant to the CIA director, F.M. Chapin, wrote to George Popowitch, leader of a civilian group, The Unidentified Flying Objects Research Committee. Popowitch had made an inquiry (not shown) on November 19. Chapin carried forward "Company" policy with his brief remarks in return. "We have forwarded your letter of inquiry concerning Unidentified Flying Objects to the Department of the Air Force for action. Contrary to your statement, we do not take an active interest in the unidentified flying objects picture."[50]

A December 11 Teletyped Information Report (to/from redacted) was titled "Unidentified Flying Object Observed in the Sky." It referred to an event on the 6th, originating from "USSR/India." A person observing Mars via telescope watched a light move across his lens. Unlike a meteor, it did not disintegrate, smoke, or issue flames; no sound was heard. The witness assumed he had just seen a Sputnik or its rocket carrier. But a check of records ruled that out. Besides, he added, the north-to-south path of the unknown was not used for satellites.[51]

The final UFO-related file for calendar year 1958 was a December 17 letter from OSI's Deputy Assistant Director Philip Strong to Larry W. Bryant, who represented a group self-titled the Citizens Against UFO Secrecy (CAUS). Concerning Bryant's November 30 letter, Strong replied that it had been referred to the USAF Office of Information Services. "This Agency has no responsibility in the matter of unidentified flying objects." The Air Force "is the only agency of government qualified to speak on UFO's." The company line.[52]

While you were away from your desk . . .

A smattering of additional incidents and announcements, some involving US military personnel, apparently escaped the CIA's attention in 1958. None, at least, were mentioned in the Agency's release of declassified UFO files to its website.

February 5, 1958

On this day came the release of a revised Air Force Regulation 200-2. It ordered individual air base commanders to conduct initial investigations of all reported UFO sightings in their areas, adding the stipulation, "Air Force activities must reduce the percentage of unidentifieds [*sic*] to the minimum."[53]

April 14, 1958

Air Force pilot D.G. Tilley was flying a C-47 transport near Lynchburg, Virginia, at about 1:00 p.m. when he spotted what he described as a gray-black rectangular object which rotated very slowly on its horizontal axis for four seconds before leaving the area.[54]

May 5, 1958

Three weeks later, a pilot well known in the local area was flying his Piper Cub near Pan De Azucar, Uruguay, when he had a brief encounter with a brilliant object he described as "top-shaped" (that is, shaped like a child's toy top). When the intruder drew near, the pilot felt intense heat within the cabin.[55]

May 9, 1958

A Philippine Airlines pilot was crossing Bohol Island (part of the Philippines chain) at 11:05 a.m. when he noticed an airborne object with a shiny metallic surface. It was continuously falling and spinning for a minute and a half before he lost sight of it below.[56]

May 15, 1958

A Venezuelan Air Force pilot observed a formation of circular discs as they moved rapidly to the northwest until lost from view.[57]

Mid-May 1958

At Malmstrom AFB, Montana, one night, an unknown approached from the north and hovered about 1,000 feet over the alert hanger. It appeared to be a round metallic object of indeterminate size—termed a flying saucer by guard personnel there. The base radar picked up the object as did FAA radar about five miles away at Great Falls. The object also hovered over the atomic missile and bomb storage building nearby. It then glided slowly down the length of the runway before heading away toward the municipal airport at Great Falls. There it hovered over the National Guard (F-89) parking ramp. Finally, it flew off into the darkness.[58]

June 20, 1958

At Fort Bragg, North Carolina, at 11:05 p.m., a battalion communication chief noticed a silver circular object above. Its lower portion was shrouded in a green haze. He watched for ten minutes as it hovered and oscillated before moving away at great speed.[59]

September 1, 1958

At 12:15 a.m., at Wheelus Air Force Base, Libya, a Philco technical representative employed at the USAF base observed a round, blue-white luminous object. As he watched, it flew at varying speeds in the distance. The object was twice in view, the first time for two minutes, then for 1.5 minutes.[60]

October 3, 1958

Beginning at 3:20 a.m., between Wasco and Kirklin, Indiana, five crew members on a moving Monon Railroad freight train had a close encounter with four disc-shaped objects over a period of 70 minutes. Periodically the crew aimed their flashlights at the objects, which maneuvered in response to them. The witnesses included the engineer, fireman, and head brakeman in the locomotive plus, in the caboose, the conductor and flagman. Due to the train's half-mile length one or the other group had a better sight line at a given moment. They all watched four "big, white, soft lights" in the distance. The trained nighttime observers knew these were peculiar by nature and were obviously moving across the sky. Abruptly the lights cruised down low over the track half a mile ahead of them momentarily. "They were moving pretty slowly, too, at no more than about 50 miles an hour . . ."[61]

The fireman continued relating the crew's account:

> After the lights crossed the tracks in front of us, they stopped and came back. This time they were headed east. They shot off toward the east and were gone a few minutes—out of sight—but when they came back and we all saw them again, I turned on the microphone. We have radio between the engine and caboose. I told the boys in the caboose what we were watching. . . . [They] got the best look at the things. Especially when they came right down over the whole train.[62]

The conductor, who was in the caboose's cupola looking forward over the train, took up the account:

> This time they came down over the train, a little way in back of the engine. They were coming toward the caboose. . . . I'd say they were only a couple of hundred feet above the train as they came toward the caboose. And they weren't moving very fast—maybe 30 or 40 miles an hour. . . . I think they were silent, or nearly silent, at least.

Remaining just above the treetops, the vehicles tilted on edge, revealing shapes roughly 40 feet in diameter and 10 feet thick. The conductor also noticed the objects' coloration: bright white when moving fast, softening to yellowish at slower speeds, and rusty orange when very slow.

Over an hour after they had first been spotted, the four vehicles swept over the length of the train in the opposite direction and continued to follow the railroad track until lost from view.[63]

Had the Agency made a concerted and continuous effort, using various among the government's best resources to determine the true nature of these pesky intruders, it might very well have concluded instead that the unknowns defied definition by the terms of our fundamental sciences. Overcoming gravity and, especially, inertia appeared to be nothing short of magic. Moreover, they left virtually no hard evidence behind. Whatever "factory" constructed them, they never dropped a muffler, as it were.

This (*essentially* foreign) intelligence service, having at times been caught up in these baffling episodes years before, certainly did not wish to repeat the experience. Tasked with investigating *identifiable* security threats from *outside* the nation's boundaries, the attitude remained: no security threat, therefore no interest. UFOs would remain one of the universe's great mysteries; there was no benefit to be gained from studying them. To borrow the essential line from *Waiting for Godot*, "Nothing to be done."

Chapter 12

1959:

Same Cast of Characters

The year began with a familiar figure rapping on the front door. On January 22 came a Memorandum from (redacted) to the Assistant to the Director, J. Arnold Shaw. NICAP's Major Keyhoe was "persisting" in his query concerning CIA agents allegedly silencing UFO witnesses, a charge from his original March 13, 1958, letter. Quoting Keyhoe in that letter, ". . . I am seriously concerned—as is our Board—with this apparent censorship . . ."[1]

Five days later, the Agency underscored its position in communicating with Keyhoe. Executive Officer J. S. Earman was quite blunt, perhaps demeaning, in his response: The CIA did not normally release positive or negative information on an "inquiry such as yours." Earman asked Keyhoe why he required such information.[2]

That attitude carried over to February in a letter on the 6th from Earman to George Popowitch, head of the citizens' group, The Unidentified Flying Objects Research Committee.[3] Earman was replying to a January 21 letter from Popowitch asking how UFOs affect national security and whether information was withheld from the public. Earman made two points:

- In 1953 a panel of experts concluded there was no threat; that assessment was made public in 1958.

- Responsibility for answering such questions rested with the United States Air Force.

A February 6 buckslip from (redacted) to Frank Chapin, assistant to the D/CI, brought up an old concern. Donald Keyhoe had written to J. S. Earman requesting the full Robertson Panel Report. The Agency had long since deferred to the Air Force and its spokesman, Major Tacker, on all such matters and should again inform Keyhoe that the Air Force was the only qualified authority on UFO concerns. Attached was a letter from Keyhoe to Earman dated sometime in August 1958 (illegible date).[4]

A February 18 letter from Chapin to UFO enthusiast Fred Kirsch answered Kirsch's question whether the CIA objected to his group investigating UFOs and publicizing the results. "Since CIA has no jurisdiction over unidentified flying objects, we are not in a position to answer the questions you posed." Kirsch had asked the same questions of the Air Force, and Chapin was confident the USAF response would be prompt and appropriate.[5]

In a February 22 four-page letter to CIA Director Allen Dulles, attorney Richard Ogden, on behalf of contactee George Adamski, claimed that an FBI agent threatened him with arrest. Ogden had a December 7, 1953, radio interview with Adamski to support the allegation. A key question by the interviewer: "Was the real purpose of this visit a conspiracy to intimidate you into silence so as to discourage you from telling the American people the truth about flying saucers and the people who ride in them?" Adamski's reply: "Yes." Ogden accused the CIA of attempting to discredit and silence authors and witnesses, of sending "men in black suits" to confront them, and of using the FBI to those ends.[6] Note: If readers wondered about the origin of Men in Black, this mention may have been it.

The Agency's Executive Officer J. S. Earman wrote to Donald Keyhoe on March 5. Acknowledging Keyhoe's letter of February 12, Earman said he still had insufficient information to answer questions about alleged silencing of UFO witnesses by CIA operatives. Earman's earlier reply to Keyhoe's March 13, 1958, letter, he remarked, included all the information available to the Agency.[7]

While all this intrigue was playing out, a report of actual aerial activity arrived sometime in March, referencing a January 20 news article in a Stockholm daily. Sometime "recently," eight reliable individuals had observed an unknown over Stigsjoe in the Vaesternorrland Province of northern Sweden. The object approached slowly to within 300 meters of the witnesses. It was disc-shaped, 6–8 meters in diameter, "surrounded by a luminous ring about 2 meters wide. The underside emitted reddish-yellow light. It was visible for three minutes before departing and was reported afterward to military authorities.[8]

Beginning about 8:10 p.m. on an unstated evening in March 1959, several individuals near the town of Bergen, Norway, observed a series of five bright lights cross the sky north to south, minutes apart. As reported by the Oslo daily *Cibservation Aftenposten*, each anomaly crossed the sky in about two minutes. In size and appearance, they were remindful of Sputniks. No sound was heard, and employing binoculars added no insights.[9]

In 2004 the Agency released a May 28, 1959, Journal entry by the Office of Legislative Counsel (OLC). Of the four topics contained therein, three were redacted. The fourth had information on retired Vice Admiral Roscoe Hillenkoetter. It was learned that the admiral and retired USMC Major Donald Keyhoe had been classmates at the United States Naval Academy, both graduating in 1919. That partly explained their connection on the UFO subject and why Hillenkoetter was on the NICAP board of governors. Of late, he had needled USAF General Thomas White, saying the Air Force was withholding UFO information that the public had a right to know. The writer in the OLC said, "This information should be handled very carefully in discussing the matter with the Air Force."[10]

On the 2nd of July, 1959, OSI Assistant Director Herbert Scoville wrote a one-paragraph letter to a George Wyllie, a Tennessee resident. Wyllie had sent a book to Director of Central Intelligence Allen Dulles titled *They Knew Too Much about Flying Saucers*. Dulles had forwarded it to Scoville with a note to return it to Wyllie when he was finished with it. Presumably without turning a page, the AD/SI was enclosing the book and thanked Wyllie for the loan.[11]

On July 21, 1959, a James Maney, describing himself as deputy director of the civilian Interplanetary Intelligence of Unidentified Flying Objects, wrote to CIA Director Allen Dulles. Maney posed four questions:

1. "Is the CIA responsible for the official secrecy on UFOs?"

2. Did the Agency cancel a planned showing of motion pictures of UFOs taken by US Navy Warrant Officer D.C. Newhouse on July 2, 1952?

3. Did CIA files disclose that CIA personnel communicated with (redacted)?

4. George Adamski was allegedly visited by a CIA agent on December 17, 1953, warning him not to mention the government again. Was this true?

On behalf of Mr. Dulles, assistant Frank Chapin enclosed the letter with a buckslip to (redacted) which read, "Before I refer this on to the Air Force which is our normal procedure, will you please check and *see* if any of your people have ever had contact with any of the individuals named in the last few paragraphs of this letter?" The handwritten reply on the returned buckslip was, "Frank, no record of contact here."[12]

The chief of the Contact Division sent a buckslip to Frank Chapin, Assistant to the Director, on October 2: "Keyhoe's insistence in pursuing this matter re-enforces my conviction that it would be (illegible) . . . Ultimately we may have to give in (illegible)."[13]

An Information Report distributed October 22, 1959, redacted 12 of 13 subjects. Number 11 stated that in late August or early September in Ukraine a luminous orange ball seen in flight seemingly vanished. No other details were given.[14]

On November 3, a C.H. Marek Jr. wrote to the Agency on the subject of airplane accidents. He raised "a possibility that the unidentified flying objects is the cause of many of these accidents." He referenced two commercial airline crashes; in the first, in 1955, the pilot allegedly reported a fireball in the sky just before the plane went down. The writer also mentioned two recent accidents, one involving a USAF jet fighter. In replying, (redacted—Frank Chapin, Assistant to the Director) remarked, "This is a subject which is not within the purview of the Central Intelligence Agency . . ." He suggested Mr. Marek contact the Department of the Air Force.[15]

In a November 25 letter to Dr. Thornton Page, Wesleyan University, OSI Deputy Assistant Director Philip Strong referred to Page's November 19 letter regarding "freshman papers" on the subject of UFOs.

> I have checked with my people here who have followed this subject and they would be very much interested in having a chance to look these papers over. . . . I would suggest that, if you mention the papers being sent to Washington, you not identify the agency, but simply indicate that they are being reviewed by a part of the national defense establishment.[16]

Two weeks later, Philip Strong's secretary, Alnora Belt, wrote back to Dr. Page, acknowledging receipt of fourteen UFO-related freshman papers. "[W]e will return the essays and our comments as soon as possible."[17]

While you were away from your desk . . .

While no one at the Central Intelligence Agency seems to have paid attention, a number of intriguing and important UFO cases and circumstances arose in the United States and abroad over the course of 1959.

The foremost pioneer in rocketry, Dr. Wernher von Braun, commented (date unclear) on the deflection from orbit of an American Juno 2 rocket:

> We find ourselves faced by powers which are far stronger than we had hitherto assumed, and whose base is at present unknown to us. More I cannot say at present. We are now engaged in entering into closer contact with those powers, and in six or nine months' time it may be possible to speak with some precision on the matter.[18]

February 24, 1959

Near Williamsport, Pennsylvania, American Flight 139, piloted by Captain Peter Killian and First Officer James Dee, was on its way from Newark to Detroit in a DC-6B. They were 13 miles southwest of Williamsport when they noticed three lights in the south-southwest direction at 30-degree elevation. The lights changed their relative position, separation, and color (yellow-orange to brilliant blue-white), drawing the pilots' further attention.[19]

Project Blue Book's J. Allen Hynek assessed the Williamsport case as radar-visual (RV). Thus, a radar installation somewhere had captured the unknowns on screen. Jacques Vallee classified the case as MA2, defined as a UFO observed traveling in a discontinuous trajectory—vertical drops, maneuvers, or loops. Also, a physical effect was caused by the UFO.[20]

June 26 and 27, 1959

In Bosinai, Papua New Guinea, on the evening of the 26th and again on the 27th, an Anglican priest, Father William B. Gill, saw an anomalous airborne disc with "humanoids" at the top, one of whom communicated via gestures in response to signals by the locals. Joining Rev. Gill were some 25 New Guinea residents as witnesses, including teachers and medical technicians. Their encounters involved one large vehicle and two or three others that hovered beneath overcast skies. Their reports were among some sixty UFO sightings around the island over a few weeks. The case was investigated by Dr. Hynek, USAF Project Blue Book consultant.[21]

June 30, 1959

Along Maryland's Patuxent River, at 8:23 p.m., US Navy Commander D. Connolly observed a gold oblate-shaped object, nine times as wide as it was thick. The metallic intruder had a sharp round edge. It was in sight for 20–30 seconds, flying straight and level.[22]

August 10, 1959

From Goose AFB, Labrador, a USAF Strategic Air Command base, at 1:28 a.m., a Royal Canadian Air Force pilot on the ground observed a large star-like light move across more than 50 degrees of the sky in 25 minutes.[23] About 3:00 a.m. a resident of Newfoundland employed at the

Goose motor pool was driving two USAF pilots to a nearby lake for fishing when a "BIG" UFO of indeterminate shape emerged from treetops and moved extremely slowly 100–200 feet overhead, blocking the sky and taking most of a minute to cross the road with a light humming sound. The men turned around and headed back to the base as the driver alerted the control tower. After several minutes the huge intruder finally passed from view low over the forest. The Newfoundlander reported his experience to MUFON many years later.[24]

September 13, 1959

At 4:00 p.m., at Bunker Hill AFB, Indiana, at least two tower control operators and the pilot of a private airplane witnessed a pear-shaped object, white, cream, and metallic in coloration. A trail was seen underneath. The unknown showed little movement over three hours. An attempted intercept by a T-33 trainer failed.[25] Note: No celestial comet appeared in the sky in 1959.[26]

October 4, 1959

At Quezon, Philippine Islands, for 15 minutes beginning at 9:25 p.m., a USN lieutenant and a chief petty officer watched a round or oval object fly straight and level as its appearance changed from red to red-orange.[27]

October 6, 1959

At 8:15 p.m., in Lincoln, Nebraska, a lieutenant colonel (in Selective Service) and his wife observed a round, yellow-white light execute several abrupt turns before it sped away. Their sighting lasted two minutes. Project Blue Book declared the object unknown.28

October 19, 1959

At Plainville, Kansas, 9:25 p.m., a USAF captain and engineering instructor at the US Air Force Academy was flying a T-33 jet trainer when a bright yellowish light approached head-on. The pilot used an evasive maneuver to avoid a collision and the light dimmed.[29] No other conventional aircraft was reported in the vicinity.

November 16, 1959

Commencing about 8:00 p.m., at a Czechoslovakian Air Force base, two officers were driving when their engine suddenly died. They then saw an odd ring of light crossing the night sky. Concurrently, pilots and ground personnel watched a "flaming ball" fly silently at great speed across the terrain, execute a 90-degree turn, then leave the area. Tower radar tracked its movements. Moments later it returned and stopped 100 meters over a runway. Personnel described it as a disc, at least 150 meters in diameter, with a ring of light around the perimeter. For reasons left unexplained, none of the jet aircraft present were able to take off. After hovering for two minutes, the machine shot into the night.[30]

Chapter 13

1960:

What's This All About?

As what would be a tumultuous decade societally got underway, genuinely unidentified flying objects would not stay away.

The 1960s awoke with an unusual turn. One or more anonymous CIA staffers, on plain sheets of paper, drafted ten instructions, "Guidance to UFO Photographers," then eight more titled "UFO Photographic Information Sheet." These were practical tips, from setting the camera's shutter speed and focal length to physically changing one's shooting angle and including terrain in the viewing frame. Most of these instructions remain relevant today. Both documents were prepared in the first week of January 1960 and seemed to appear in CIA files out of nowhere— and out of context. The first sheet especially provided tips to maximize one's chance of capturing imagery of an unknown object that would pass muster with skeptics:[1]

1. Set the focus scale of the lens to infinity.

2. Use fast film. (400 ASA/ISO or higher is more sensitive, permits photography in low light, allows the freezing of motion, minimizes the effect of camera shake, and allows a large depth of field. In all, fast film can result in sharper pictures.)[2]

3. For moving objects, set the shutter speed no slower than 1/100 second.

4. Keep the camera still during exposure.

5. Take several shots; include the terrain if possible. Note: A film processing technique called "edge enhancement" compares the relative focus of the unknown's outline with other known objects in the frame, for example, a tree limb or telephone pole, to aid in determining the unknown's distance from the camera.

6. If the object is a few hundred feet away or closer, photograph it from different angles, moving 40–60 feet between shots. If a mile or more away, drive toward it between shots. "This establishes what is known as a base line and is helpful in technical analysis of your photography."

7. After taking the UFO shots, take overlapping pictures of the surroundings while swiveling 360 degrees.

8. Process the original negative or negatives with care.

9. Make a second negative from the original.

10. Any reproduction for analysis should be from the entire original frame including borders and sprocket holes.

Accompanying the "Guidance to UFO Photographers" draft and likewise issued in the first week of January 1960 was another single-sheet draft document (likely by the same author or authors), a form for completion by the photographer titled "UFO Photographic Information Sheet."[3] This form was composed of eight areas of questioning—strikingly similar to the elements covered in the original MUFON Photographic Cases form of a decade later:

- Camera model and manufacturer, lens number, and other data printed around the lens. Also, if known, the focal length of the camera lens and any external lens used.

- Date the pictures were taken.

- Time of day the pictures were taken "(to the nearest minute if you can)."

- Direction in which the pictures were taken.

- Using a roadmap or the like to illustrate, the photographer's location and direction faced when taking the pictures.

- Using a map or sketch, the direction faced for each of the 360-degree ground-orientation pictures.

- Sketch of details of area where standing when photography was taken; include such things as telephone poles, fence posts, buildings, and the like.

- Place where each original negative was processed and when.

To borrow a mid-century phrase uttered by plain folks in America, it's *mighty curious* that, at a time when CIA officials were trying to swear off UFOs, congratulating themselves on their dual impulses (to educate the public about observational errors and debunk the strongest cases by whatever means), amid that supposedly unified front lurked an outlier. Someone was seeking documented proof of a UFO. But what name or office might we ascribe? Someone from the Physics and Electronics (P&E) Division? Maybe he toiled in the Applied Science Division, the most recent unit in the Agency assigned UFO-related responsibilities. Or perhaps the person was not in the CIA at all but rather connected to the Air Force, the instructions emanating from Wright-Patterson or thereabouts. Project Blue Book was limping along as a USAF entity, as it were, so its lone officer may have doodled these drafts out of boredom. The record does not inform us who within the Defense Department was paying enough attention to UFOs to desire better photographs.

The research papers written by Dr. Thornton Page's freshman students (see page 143) had now been reviewed at OSI's Applied Science Division. Its chief, Wilton Lexow, penned a memo to the deputy assistant director at the OSI Collection Division on January 26. Lexow noted that most of the papers "reflect a solid intellectual attempt to evaluate the evidence." He added, "It seems significant that no essentially new substantiating evidence emerged from this exercise."[4] Readers might be amused by

Lexow's assertion that nothing groundbreaking was unearthed by a dozen or so 18-year-olds asked for the first time in their young lives to consider the UFO subject.

On February 28, 1960, United Press International reported on a new set of Air Force regulations released on Christmas Eve 1959. These were directed to air bases in particular and USAF personnel generally. In sending out the seven-page directive as an Operations and Training pamphlet, the Air Force's inspector general was forceful and clear: "Unidentified flying objects—sometimes treated lightly by the press and referred to as 'flying saucers'—must be rapidly and accurately identified as serious USAF business . . ."[5]

The UPI article quoted Air Force statistics: Since 1947 it had investigated 6,312 reported sightings, including 183 in the latter six months of 1959. In citing those numbers, the Air Force inspector general implied that USAF's concern lay with the danger of foreign attack veiled as an extraterrestrial presence, not with ETs per se: ". . . [N]o physical or material evidence, not even a minute fragment of a so-called flying saucer has ever been found."[6]

After learning of this new emphasis on an old policy, NICAP's retired Admiral Roscoe Hillenkoetter responded, "It is time for the truth to be brought out in open congressional hearings." He insisted that, "behind the scenes, high-ranking Air Force officers are soberly concerned about the UFO's."[7]

A separate take on the same topic was in print the next day, February 29, in the form of an editorial in the *Telegram* (city not shown).

> The Air Force, it appears is in trouble again. . . . This time the complaintants [*sic*] are the flying saucer people. (NICAP) has charged that the Air Force really believes in the existence of unidentified flying objects while, at the same time, it tries to kid the public into thinking that they are nonsense.

NICAP and similar groups had never made clear "why they believe that officialdom would sit on such information if they actually have it, or how, in the nature of things, they would be able to do so even if they wished."[8]

Still another printed reaction to the Air Force's Operations and Training pamphlet appeared as an editorial on March 4 in the *Journal* (city not shown), "Flying Saucer Alert." This item outlined the USAF's directive to commanders that UFOs were "serious business," before expressing an opinion: It conveyed that a retired Navy admiral, Roscoe H. Hillenkoetter:

> . . . charges that through official secrecy and ridicule many citizens are led to believe flying objects are nonsense. He says the Air Force has operated to hide the facts. . . . He had added, "We suspect the Air Force simply doesn't know the answer and hesitates unduly to alarm the public."[9]

According to an Information Report from within the Soviet Union, sometime in 1959 in a desert region of Kazakhstan, "glittering" objects were frequently seen in the sky moving at high speed, accompanied by explosive sounds. Local Kazakhs and other tribesman abandoned the area out of superstition.[10] Note: an aircraft reflecting sunlight and exceeding Mach 1 would be a potential explanation.

An FDD Note on the 17th of March concerned aerial objects seen and photographed in Sweden. This was an English translation of a March 8, 1960, article appearing in the Stockholm daily *Dagens Nyheter*, "Light in Sky New Satellite, Experts Believe." On the morning of March 6, shortly after 5:15 a.m., a photographer in Norrtaelje, near Stockholm, captured on film two luminous objects, each remindful of a satellite, moving southeast. Suddenly both reversed direction. Minutes later a Bromma resident saw a light moving laterally that abruptly dropped straight down out of sight. That evening, shortly after 10:00 p.m., a light believed to be a satellite was spotted by an airliner and at an observatory.[11] Note: Because satellites neither travel in pairs nor reverse direction, the initial sighting would necessitate a different headline. Either the witness misspoke or the event was truly anomalous.

On behalf of NICAP, Richard Hall offered commentary to *The Hartford Times* on June 9, 1960. He referred to having "documentary proof" of a "cover-up" by the Air Force in UFO reporting. A NICAP colleague, Dewey Fournet, claimed a 1948 USAF top secret intelligence estimate referred to the unknowns as "interplanetary spaceships." Reluctance by Air Force brass to discuss the matter in detail made a meeting of minds difficult. Events involving US Navy personnel were also cited in the interview.[12]

In response to the suggestion of secret weaponry as the source of UFO reports, NICAP board member Roscoe Hillenkoetter, a retired Navy vice admiral and the CIA Director after World War II, addressed the question in a special NICAP bulletin. "I know that neither Russia nor this country had anything even approaching such high speeds and maneuvers."[13]

A few days later on June 12, the *Worcester Evening Gazette* carried further, related remarks by Hillenkoetter: "The unknown objects are operating under intelligent control. It is imperative that we learn where the UFO's come from and what their purpose is." He thereafter called for prompt and thorough congressional hearings on the matter.[14]

The writer of the article issued a broadside then posed accusatory questions.

> In the light of the Air Force handling of the UFO matter, insisting against plain evidence to the contrary in certain cases that the UFOs can all be explained as familiar objects mistakenly identified, the question inevitably arises: Is the Air Force following a prearranged plan of public statements on the strange objects? Is the Air Force deliberately misleading the public?[15]

Perhaps in part from the heat brought by a growing list of clamoring news sources, on July 21, 1960, the Office of Public Affairs at the Department of Defense brought a boatload of statistics on the Air Force experience relative to aerial anomalies, titling the work "Fact Sheet Air Force UFO Report."

For the six months encompassing January through June 1960, 173 sighting reports reached the Air Force. Of those, 139 were analyzed, with 34 pending. Foreign countries—mostly in the Pacific and Far East— accounted for an additional 41 cases in that six-month period.

Of the 139 addressed, over a third (51) had insufficient evidence to render a conclusion. Among these discarded were 37 simply because they were single-witness sightings—comparable, in the Air Force's judgment, to a science experiment conducted only once.

The first half of 1959 tallied 175 reports. In the latter six months there were 189. Only one for the entire year was declared a hoax.[16]

Astronomical sightings were prominent in the spring of 1960 due to April's meteor shower and Jupiter's proximity in June. Refraction, diffraction, reflections, and illusions accounted for many mistaken reports. Other misidentifications resulted from a startling natural object, for example a meteoric fireball. A single report was of a satellite.

Objects reported as anomalous from 1947 through June 1960 totaled 6,523, highlighted by 1,501 in 1952, and 1,178 in 1957.

Analysis of the sighting reports was done by a group of open-minded scientists, engineers, and other professionals under USAF supervision. Astronomer J. Allen Hynek was the chief scientific consultant.

Identification categories were: balloons, aircraft, astronomical, other, insufficient data, satellites, and unidentified.

Reason suggested that some of the 4,000 balloons released daily across the country accounted for substantial numbers of misidentifications, alongside conventional aircraft—sun reflections, jet pods, vapor trails.

Under the "other" category: generalized reflections, searchlights, clouds, birds, kites, blimps, sun dogs, spurious radar returns, fireworks, flares, meteoric fireballs and bolides, ice crystals, and hoaxes.

A report would be listed as unidentified "when the description of the object and its maneuvers cannot be correlated with any known object or phenomenon." Air Force Project Blue Book's Special Report #14, October 1955, determined that 3 percent of all reports remained unidentified.[17]

From 13 years in this peculiar pursuit (6,500 reports), the Department of Defense had reached five basic conclusions. No evidence suggested the reported objects: (a) were inimical or hostile, (b) were interplanetary spaceships, (c) represented technology or principles beyond present-day scientific knowledge, (d) threatened national security, or (e) left any fragment.

"[I]f more immediate detailed objective observational data could have been obtained on the unidentified or unexplained sightings, these, too, would have been explained satisfactorily."[18]

The December 24, 1959, USAF Inspector General's Brief to all unit commanders stressed that "UFO reports are serious business since they are vitally involved in the Air Force's air defense mission." They were to be evaluated quickly, the public was to be kept informed, and the reports were not to be classified. The Air Force was charged by UFO groups with possessing information proving the existence of interplanetary space-ships. That was untrue, DoD responded. Meanwhile, the costs associated with UFO investigations were difficult to tally.[19]

An August 5, 1960, news article in the *Chicago Daily News* reported that, according to a certain UFO enthusiast, the Senate majority leader and vice-presidential candidate Lyndon B. Johnson had issued a standing directive to the Senate Preparedness subcommittee to keep a "close watch" on UFO matters. The claim came from retired Marine Corps Major Donald Keyhoe, the NICAP director. He added that Johnson ordered "subcommittee staff to report to him any 'significant' sightings of saucers along with an analysis of the Air Force investigation of them . . ." Keyhoe also said NATO's General L.M. Chassin had warned that "unrecognized UFO's could accidentally set off a war with Russia."[20]

OSI's deputy assistant director, Philip Strong, replied to Deputy Assistant Director Cary for collection on August 31 regarding an inquiry by Congressman Gordon Scherer about certain photos supposedly taken on January 16, 1958, aboard a Brazilian Navy ship off the coast of Trindade. They were soon shown on the popular morning *Today Show* with Dave Garroway. A viewer, Catherine Carter Golden, had sent the attached August 15, 1960, letter asking Representative Sherer about the validity of the photos. Strong wrote that photographic evaluation by the Naval Attaché confirmed the pictures were fakes. The person who snapped them was a known trick photographer, and no one else was present when he processed the film. Mrs. Golden had frequently written to the Air Force and others about UFOs.[21]

In a partially duplicative file from the same day, in addition to the Strong-Cary exchange, the reply to an internal note was included. In a letter of August 29 from USAF Major Lawrence J. Tacker, Air Force Office of Information Services, to Mrs. Golden, Tacker underscored the government's contention that the UFO photos purportedly taken from a Brazilian Navy ship in 1958 were the products of trick photography, a hoax.[22]

An Information Report had been prepared on March 11, 1958, by USN Captain M. Sunderland, Office of Naval Intelligence, titled "Brazil Navy— Flying Saucer Photographed from Almirante Saldanha." The photos had created something of a sensation in the Brazilian press. On February 21, 1958, Rio de Janeiro dailies carried the images, allegedly taken a month earlier on January 16 from the deck of a Brazilian Navy ship anchored off the Trindade coast. The report stated that the photographer, Almiro Barauna, "has a long history of photographic trick shots and is well known for such items as false pictures of treasure on the ocean floor." [23]

Due to the alleged presence of many crewman on the ship's deck when the photos were taken, on February 24, 1958, the Brazilian Navy stated: "Clearly, this Ministry will not be able to make any pronouncement concerning the object seen because the photographs do not constitute sufficient proof for such purpose." No sworn statements were obtained from crewmen to authenticate the incident and photos. Captain Sunderland was inclined to accept that they were hoaxed.

> Details of the land are extremely sharp but the disc is hazy and has little contrast and shows no shadow effect. It also appears that the object was inverted in photograph 2 compared to 1 and 3. . . . [T]here appears to be no lateral blurring as would occur with any reasonable shutter speed.[24]

In December 1960 John Warner, CIA Legislative Counsel, responded to a letter (not shown) from Coral Lorenzen, cofounder and head of the civilian Aerial Phenomena Research Organization (APRO). As the Agency had replied to many other cases seeking UFO-related information or statements, Warner said her letter would be forwarded to Lawrence Tacker of the Air Force (now upgraded from major to lieutenant colonel). Lorenzen had expressed concern that in an earlier letter from the Agency to Congressman Scherer, a typing error (dropping the word "by") potentially changed a meaning; ". . . provided by the Air Force" became "provided the Air Force." A misimpression—of just what, is not clear—could have been drawn over the absence of a preposition. Like diplomacy per se, intelligence work was an exacting profession.[25]

A month before the Kennedy administration took office, Washington correspondent Bulkley Griffin for the *Worcester Evening Gazette* made an appeal on behalf of those everywhere who were intrigued, confused, or both by claims of anomalies in the sky. Simultaneously, the piece served as a biting indictment of the CIA. His December 15 *Gazette* article stated in pertinent part:

> Maybe the new administration next year will quietly give the green light to some Congressional committee to investigate the unidentified flying objects (UFOs). Put this down as a long-shot possibility. It is not a probability. The Central Intelligence Agency is still in on the matter, as it always has been. The CIA, by the nature of its duties, does not squander facts among the public.
>
> Yet, the UFOs demand attention. They continue to be seen in the sky by pilots, sundry officials, and others (say, who had some special cognizance of the atmosphere above us and by others with some reputation for reliability—especially at night). The Air Force disclaimers that these strange objects relate to anything but familiar objects mistakenly identified, often damage the patent truth, and sometimes approach the ridiculous. A Royal Canadian Air Force CF-100 Canuck interceptor was on a routine mission over Lake Ontario on September 27, 1960, with a second CF-100 trailing by a few miles. Visibility was excellent

under light cirrus clouds. When the first jet entered the cirrus, it simply vanished. The other pilot reported that its contrail did not disperse to indicate an explosion. "It simply ended as though both engines had simultaneously flamed out." The pilot did not radio that he was experiencing any problem and did not bail out. Neither the interceptor nor its two-man crew was ever found. The US Air Force left the case unexplained.

Increasingly, security officials were determined to shield the public from their plainly indicated truth, which is that a clear minority of the mysterious objects represent something real which the Air Force has been unable to identify.[26]

The writer went on to explain that, initially, the Air Force didn't know the origin of some objects but feared public panic and so claimed they were all misidentified familiar things. "[N]ow the Air Force keeps repeating this because it is stuck with that story." Referencing the Air Force's scientific consultant J. Allen Hynek: "Some of his explanations . . . strain credulity beyond the limit of common sense."[27]

The Agency's chief of the Detroit office sent a memo to (illegible) on December 16, titled "Sighting of Unusual Object." The chief himself had seen a luminous greenish-white light descend across the sky at 6:54 p.m., December 14. Note: the Geminids meteor shower peaked about 7:00 p.m. one night before on December 13.[28]

While you were away from your desk . . .

A pair of California highway patrolmen witnessed an enormous vehicle descend from the sky at 11:50 p.m., August 13, 1960, two miles from the town of Corning. They presumed at first it was an impending plane crash. The object pulled up short, rose back up to 500 feet and performed aerial acrobatics over a lengthy period. Shaped like an elongated football at 150 feet long and 40 feet in breadth, it was covered in white luminescence, with red lights at either end, and, intermittently, five white lights along the side. Its movements combined incredible speeds, inertia-defying changes of direction, and frequently a sweeping red beam. The patrolmen radioed the local sheriff's office to request a radar assist, which soon confirmed the target. Whenever the object approached the cruiser, radio interference resulted. In a later letter, one of the officers remarked, "[W]e made several attempts to follow it . . . But the object seemed aware of us and we were more successful remaining motionless and allow it to approach us, which it did on several occasions." The only sound they heard was the static on their radio whenever the object approached. Eventually it moved away and the patrolmen followed. Then an identical craft joined the first. Eventually both flew over the horizon.[29]

Chapter 14

1961:

Old News

OSI Deputy Assistant Director Philip G. Strong, a retired brigadier general, penned a brief letter to (now Lieutenant Colonel) Lawrence J. Tacker at the Air Force Office of Information on January 10, 1961. Strong thanked Tacker for sending along a copy of Tacker's new book about UFOs. "Unfortunately, there seems to be a fair sized 'lunatic fringe' that will never be really convinced of Air Force objectiveness [*sic*] and forth-rightness on this subject."[1]

With the new Kennedy administration in place, whatever constraints Congress might have experienced under Dwight Eisenhower—a career military officer—on the UFO subject were apparently dissolved. Calls for congressional hearings on the UFO subject were no longer confined to voices in the wilderness such as Donald Keyhoe. Indeed, no less a figure than John McCormack, Speaker of the House of Representatives and a towering Washington figure, added his weight to the matter. McCormack declared to the press, "I feel that the Air Force has not been giving out all the information it has on Unidentified Flying Objects." He did not claim that UFOs were of extraterrestrial origin. Instead he referenced the ever-growing contingent of witnesses with observational expertise—pilots and others—who had made their accounts public. "What these reliable witnesses have seen can't be disregarded." McCormack mentioned further that some incidents were simultaneously observed firsthand and caught on radar, calling that compelling.

"You can't put it down to atmospheric phenomena." In speaking out, he joined former CIA Director Admiral Roscoe Hillenkoetter, who had long since called for hearings.[2]

Perhaps McCormack had yet to read Tacker's book. Nonetheless, whether the speaker was sincere or simply blowing smoke, no such congressional hearing was convened until four years later, a one-day affair held by the House Armed Services Committee; two years after that the House Science and Astronautics Committee would hold another single-day hearing.[3]

On behalf of The Americana Institute, a think tank devoted to the study of American history and culture, Robert J. Palmer had inquired about the Agency's position on the UFO subject. On April 5, 1961, OSI's Philip Strong again sang the Company's theme song: All governmental responsibility regarding unidentified flying objects was charged to the Air Force.[4]

Gone but Not Forgotten

Lawrence Houston, an Agency attorney, geared up for another round of biting correspondence by and about the single-minded chemist, Dr. Leon Davidson. Forwarding a letter from a member of Congress to an unnamed "Exec" (presumably the Executive Registry) on the 4th of June, Houston groused about the amount of mail that Davidson had generated.[5]

On an indeterminate date sometime after June 30, attorney Houston replied to Congressman Joseph Karth's inquiry. Dispensing with notions of discretion, Houston said Dr. Davidson's belief that the Agency withheld any knowledge of UFOs, that it engaged in psychological warfare on this subject, was "entirely uninformed."[6]

An attachment to Houston's letter listed a variety of correspondence from or regarding Davidson dating back to March 1958. Following that list, he added a cryptic note:

> In addition we have on file letters from Mr. Davidson to
> Members of the 1953 Panel requesting in essence their
> supporting him in obtaining information which would

implicate CIA or the OCB in a "*1984* type of thought control developing in America."[7]

A return buckslip from Executive Registry staff to Houston stated there was no previous record of Leon Davidson.[8]

Herbert Scoville, OSI's assistant director, wrote to Houston on July 12, attaching a draft letter (not shown) to Congressman Karth concerning Leon Davidson. Scoville pointed out that Davidson had been writing to the Agency since 1958. More recently, his correspondence had been forwarded to the Air Force, the "Executive Agent in such matters."[9]

On an indeterminate date thereafter, Houston sent the OSI-prepared letter to Congressman Karth, pointing out that Leon Davidson had had "extensive correspondence with this Agency since early 1958 on the matter of UFO's." Davidson believed the Robertson Panel and the CIA withheld vital information, he continued. In an attempt to allay Davidson's concerns, a copy of the declassified Robertson Panel Report was sent to him. The portion remaining classified pertained to unrelated intelligence matters.[10]

USAF's public information officer Lawrence Tacker also wrote a lengthy letter to Davidson to refute his belief that the CIA used the UFO topic in psychological warfare, which he said was entirely unfounded. At Lieutenant Colonel Tacker's request, the Agency had since been forwarding all such correspondence to the Air Force information office. Perhaps by this time the Agency considered Davidson's terrier-like persistence an annoyance it could have done without.

Non-Davidson Business

On September 11, 1961, the White House released a statement that was UFO-related in the sense that misidentifications might result:

> Soviet Missile Tests. The four range instrumentation ships are now taking up positions in the "closed" area announced yesterday by the USSR, about 6500 nautical miles from Tyura Tam, while the Soviets have made their usual claim that they are testing boosters for space vehicles. We believe

these tests, like those in January and July of last year, are part of the ICBM development program, probably extended range testing of the second generation missile.[11]

The pot was at a vigorous boil. On October 23, 1961, the *Roanoke* (VA) *World-News* carried a story originating from the North American Newspaper Alliance, "Congress Is Being Pressed for Flying Saucer Probe."[12] It revealed that, earlier in the year, Congressman Joseph Karth had been named to head a subcommittee of the Science and Astronautics Committee for the purpose of sorting through the important UFO-related issues. But when Congressman Karth called for a public hearing, the committee chairman, Overton Brooks, denied his request.

Could the UFOs sighted actually be some Air Force secret weapon? Or Soviet? Serious questions were going unanswered. Prominent persons who had spoken out included a former CIA Director (Vice-Admiral R.H. Hillenkoetter) as well as Rear Admiral D.S. Fahrney, former Air Force UFO spokesman Albert Chop, and astronomer Dr. Clyde Tombaugh, discoverer of Pluto.

Senator Barry Goldwater was the newest political voice calling for opening the UFO question. A *Bangor* (ME) *Daily News* editorial of November 17 endorsed that position. The Air Force insisted for years that all UFO reports were normal things misidentified. Now, Senator Goldwater, House Speaker McCormack, and retired Admiral Hillenkoetter had called for renewed hearings. "So, we say get on with the inquiry. We'll be listening."[13] One is left to ponder, all other political issues aside, whether the UFO subject would have been treated differently had Goldwater been elected president three years hence.

While you were away from your desk . . .

March 16, 1961

A Brazilian meteorologist, aboard the USS Glacier, was taking part in a US Navy exercise, Operation Deep Freeze, at Admiralty, Antarctica. He and five others witnessed the flyover of a sharply defined, egg-shaped object, estimated as about the length of a small aircraft. It soared slowly across the sky, 50 degrees above the horizon. Multicolored rays extended back in a V formation—primarily red, blue, and green and changing continually. The vehicle left a narrow orange trail. Suddenly the front and rear split apart, each forming a complete egg shape. Then both vanished.[14]

September 1961

All abuzz over a Kennedy presidency well underway, executives at the Company could not have foreseen that the signature case in American UFO annals would occur in central New Hampshire. As details of that and similar encounters to come played out across America, CIA analysts were forced to become familiar with a new term in the UFO investigative lexicon: *abduction*.

On the evening of September 19, 1961, Barney and Betty Hill were returning home from a trip to Quebec. With the Labor Day weekend well past, the tourist season was essentially over. They drove through the White Mountains alone in the darkness, following Highway 3 toward their home in Portsmouth. As they passed the Indian Head rock formation at the town of Lincoln, they heard beeping sounds—as if inside their car at the rear. Hours later they neared Ashland, some 35 miles farther south and heard the beeps again as they both came out of a stupor. What happened in between has for half a century and more been the subject of amazement, late-night speculation, endorsement, skepticism, and even ridicule. For the Agency, it was one more challenge posed by a subject it wanted nothing to do with.[15]

Chapter 15

1962:

Blinders

On April 23, 1962, OSI Deputy Assistant Director Philip Strong sent a Memorandum to US Air Force Headquarters at the Pentagon. Its purpose was to transmit a letter from Thomas B. Scott, a young South Carolina resident, plus Strong's reply. The lad had contacted the CIA regarding his April 2 UFO sighting. Strong's stock reply informed Thomas that the Air Force handled all such matters.[1]

A non-sourced, multiple-topic report was received from Argentina on May 25. Under the subject headed "Unidentified Flying Objects":

- At Bahia Blanco, south of Buenos Aires, Argentina, on May 21 many people observed a "strange luminous body suspended for several minutes over the city." One local resident took two photographs, the prints of which revealed an oval shape.

- A luminous anomaly crossing the sky was photographed several times by a reporter for the *Nueva Principia* (Argentine) newspaper. He stated that the object stopped and changed course.[2]

- A Venezuelan observatory investigated multiple reports around the country and asked the public to submit observations in order to determine whether the phenomenon was "a cluster of meteorites, part of an artificial satellite, or due to other causes."[3]

While you were away from your desk . . .

April 19, 1962

A "huge object" was tracked by radars at Colorado's Air Defense Command and at Nellis AFB, Nevada, following an original alert in upstate New York. Along the way the unknown was chased by armed interceptor jets. It landed near a power station at Eureka, Nevada. Immediately, electricity to the community was cut and remained off for over an hour until the vehicle left. As it rose into the sky, a brilliant flash was seen in Reno and parts of California.[4]

April 30 and July 17, 1962

Surely the CIA gained the particulars of two incidents involving the X-15 rocket plane. But for some reason no internal communications resulted— at least none prompting documents contained in the 2017 file dump.

NASA pilot Joseph A. Walker was aboard the X-15 on April 30, when two disc-shaped objects overtook him as he sped along at 3,400 mph, well over Mach 4. "Two UFOs just passed overhead," Walker radioed as they came within 200 feet and were captured on film by the plane's aft fuselage cameras. The discs climbed past 200,000 feet and were finally lost from view. Walker later remarked that this had been the second time he observed UFOs while flying the experimental aircraft.[5]

Then on July 17, Major Robert White was piloting the X-15 at its maximum altitude of 314,000 feet when he reported to the NASA flight control center that "several" anomalous objects were flying in formation with him. "There *are* things out there. There absolutely is!" *Time* magazine quoted his radioed exclamation.[6]

August 7, 1962

Just after midnight at a Titan missile site near Oracle, Arizona, a crewman spotted a brilliant object descending from overhead and called to a second man. As the intruder drew closer, now likened to a full moon in apparent size, they ran inside and telephoned the Davis-Monthan AFB. The unknown was hovering directly over a missile silo. In minutes two jet interceptors approached, and the intruder streaked northward out of sight. The jets circled the site boundary then left. A few minutes later the object returned and hovered momentarily over the missile silo again before ascending swiftly and vertically into the night.[7]

Chapter 16

1963:

Cooper Spills the Beans

A May 2, 1963, letter to the editor of the *Hartford Courant* was titled "Aerial Phenomena." The writer pointed to Air Force Regulation 200-2, issued July 20, 1962, which called UFOs "serious business." Per the new regulation's strictures, base commanders were now allowed to release information to the press and public only if the incident involved an identifiable source. USAF personnel were permitted to discuss the subject only with prior approval and only on a need-to-know basis. Further, the letter writer quoted Vice Admiral Roscoe Hillenkoetter, a former CIA director: "Behind the scenes, high-ranking Air Force officers are soberly concerned about the UFOs. . . . The A.F. has assumed the right to decide what the American people should or should not know," the admiral had added. The letter writer plugged NICAP as the source of truth on the subject.[1]

One letter of criticism as the entire year's correspondence on UFOs? Surely self-congratulating by now, the CIA had backed away from the subject with no consequences.

While you were away from your desk . . .

No accounts of aerial intrusions gained the Agency's official attention that year, but reports of autos besieged by airborne oddities, and others of crowds witnessing aerial acrobatics continued to reach first responders.

These were not broadly publicized. However, one very notable incident, in space, made the press big time:

Orbiting Earth in the Mercury 9 spacecraft on May 16, 1963, astronaut Gordon L. Cooper spotted an object nearby that he determined to be nothing recognizable. It was definitely flying and it was substantial, a genuine object of some sort. It was by definition a UFO. He, of course, gained some celebrity from the experience and was thereafter asked about the subject incessantly.

Later Cooper related a two-day spate of high-altitude encounters in the early 1950s in West Germany where he was stationed as a USAF test pilot. Cooper ultimately expressed his personal conclusions, straightforward and unequivocally:

> Intelligent beings from other planets regularly visit our world in an effort to enter into contact with us. . . . NASA and the American government know this and possess a great deal of evidence. Nevertheless, they remain silent in order not to alarm people. . . . I am dedicated to forcing the authorities to end their silence.[2]

1964:

From a Lull to a Quickening

Officially dated January 1, 1964, the National Investigations Committee on Aerial Phenomena (NICAP) published *The UFO Evidence*, 195 pages of sharp sticks in the Agency's eye. The document was prepared by NICAP's de facto director, Richard Hall: "Evidence is presented in support of the hypothesis that UFOs are under intelligent control, making plausible the notion that some of them might be of extraterrestrial origin."[1]

Its contents were divided by section.

A. Sample cases showing general features of UFO reports

B. Cases indicating intelligence: pacing of vehicles, reaction to stimuli, formation flights

C. Sightings by Air Force pilots, navigators, other officers, and men

D. Reports from other military personnel

E. Observations by airline, military, and private pilots

F. Observations by professional scientists and engineers, including astronomers, and aeronautical engineers

G. Sightings by police officers, civil defense, and ground observer corps; cross-section of citizens' reports

H. Electromagnetic effects; radar cases; photographic evidence; physical and physiological effects; sound; angel's hair

I. Background of USAF secrecy; official regulations; history and analysis of the official UFO investigation

J. Survey of reports from other countries, attitudes of foreign governments, and worldwide interest in UFOs

K. Chronological listing of sightings, statements, and events

L. Statistics and analyses of consistent physical appearance, maneuvers, flight characteristics, recurrent concentrations

M. Survey of Congressional interest in UFOs

N. Discussion of the implications of UFOs, and what is needed as a scientific investigation

A January 22, 1964, newspaper article written by a NICAP member outlined the UFO problem, chastised the Air Force and CIA for brainwashing the public, and warned of changes in human thinking when the truth is revealed.[2]

On the 3rd of March, a letter to the editor of the *Atlanta Constitution* was very provocatively titled "An Earthly Explanation? CIA Must Have Brainwashed You." The writer sought to say that the Agency and the Air Force had joined forces and "brainwashed everybody" to believe that UFOs were simply misidentified natural phenomena and prosaic machines—aircraft, satellites, and such. The reader predicted changes to come in religions, science, governments, and militaries when the truth of ET visits finally came out.[3]

A NICAP letter-writing campaign continued with a March 16 missive to the *Cleveland Plain Dealer*. The writer called attention to the "very dangerous problem" of UFOs. He claimed the Air Force, CIA, and National Security Council had conspired to convince the public that all such reports were normal things mistaken. He praised Donald Keyhoe and said the use of rockets for space exploration was obsolete and primitive. Presumably the USA and USSR were attempting to duplicate saucer technology.[4]

The *Amarillo Globe-Times*, in its April 27 issue, printed the same letter by the same writer. The news staff titled it, "People Are Talking about . . . Little Green Men."[5]

The same letter and letter writer as to the *Cleveland Plain Dealer* and *Amarillo Globe-Times* struck again on April 30, this one to the *Dayton (OH) News.*[6]

Once more for good measure, on May 13, 1964, the Binghamton (NY) *Sun-Bulletin* posted the same letter by the same, dedicated writer. This time the entreaty was titled "Space tests branded as propaganda."[7]

Anonymous handwritten notes outlined an incident at Naval Air Station Patuxent River, Maryland, on December 19, 1964. From 3:15 to 3:30 p.m., a chief petty officer detected unknowns on three radar sets: First, two objects were located 10 miles apart. Next, something 39 miles from the station approached at an estimated 6,000 mph. Then from 8 miles away something suddenly turned 160 degrees and swiftly left the screen. Altitudes of the unknowns varied from 3,000 to 25,000 feet. The FAA station at Salisbury, Maryland, "picked up messages from US Coast Guard reporting UFOs." (Redacted) asked the OSI to evaluate any sightings over the previous 10 weeks. Reference was made to USMC retired Major Donald Keyhoe (NICAP).[8]

Keyhoe, NICAP cofounder, continued to charge that the Air Force just didn't want the public to know the truth. Nationally, newspapers were running articles on the UFO subject with regularity.

While you were away from your desk . . .

Diplomatic barriers perhaps prevented the Agency from recognizing the importance of an event that transpired in Shanghai, China.

Sometime in January 1964

Many Shanghai citizens watched a huge, cigar-shaped aerial object fly overhead, moving southwest. Multiple MiG jet fighters from the People's

Liberation Army Air Force gave chase but failed to force the UFO down. The intruder was later officially labeled an American missile.[9]

April 24, 1964

At Socorro, New Mexico, Deputy Sheriff Lonnie Zamora was chasing a speeder when he heard a roar and saw blue and orange flames in the sky less than a mile off the highway. He broke a path across the rolling desert floor until coming upon the scene still 800 feet away, below a steep incline. A shiny egg-shaped object sat in a shallow gully. Outside it were two individuals in white coveralls, both the height of a very short adult or tall child. One of the figures apparently noticed his presence and acted startled. Zamora drove closer for a better look, his view blocked temporarily by the ridge. He stopped the car 100 feet from the craft. Now he noticed it was resting on landing gear and had a strange insignia on its side. The two figures were no longer in view. Hearing another roar, Zamora took cover. The object slowly rose, issuing blue and orange flames and moved out of sight. Soon he was joined by his police sergeant. The two examined the site where the craft had been, finding burned brush and four depressions in the ground. Note: This case has been featured in numerous televised documentaries over the years.[10]

June 2, 1964

About 4:00 p.m. at Hobbs, New Mexico, a woman stepped outside when her grandson screamed and saw a smallish tan object, shaped like a toy top. Hovering over him, it discharged a black exhaust before rising swiftly out of sight. The boy's hair was singed, while sooty deposits were imbedded in his face, ears, neck, and shirt. Although he experienced no pain, one ear was badly burned and facial swelling soon obscured his nose. He was hospitalized for five days. Local authorities took skin and clothing samples, reportedly giving them to the FBI.[11]

Chapter 18

1965:

A Gathering Storm

Memorandum for the Record by (redacted), "Morning Meeting of 18 January 1965." Among multiple subjects in a meeting with the Agency's deputy director for intelligence, one pertinent statement came forth: "ExDir" (executive director, presumably the CIA director) asked whether the DDS&T (deputy director for science and technology) and the OSI director were kept abreast of the UFO reports in the area.[1]

In a January 19, 1965, private meeting with acting NICAP director Richard Hall, OSI borrowed NICAP case narratives for an upcoming report to (redacted). Note: As longstanding NICAP practice, a complimentary copy of investigative reports, including eyewitness accounts, had been sent to Air Force bases near the events.

In turn, Hall was very interested in the December 19, 1964, Patuxent Naval Air Station radar tracks—which the Air Force had claimed were from faulty equipment. Bolstering the accuracy of those radars was visual confirmation of the intruder by a Coast Guard vessel at sea (see page 171). Hall added that a week or ten days earlier, several Washington, D.C., government employees had reported a sighting from a window in a munitions building.[2] So, was a deal struck perchance, giving NICAP those Patuxent radar tracks in return for continued eyes and ears on the ground?

The next day, as per the Agency director's earlier request, the Office of Scientific Intelligence provided a statistical summary of 1964 UFO reports evaluated by the Air Force. Of 532 sightings reported:

- Astronomical (118)

- Aircraft (65)

- Balloon (18)

- Satellite (142)

- Other (77)

- Insufficient data (85)

- Unidentified (16)

- Pending (11)

As expected, a disproportionate share of reports occurred from May through August, when more people would likely be out-of-doors.

Among several cases with wide media coverage, one was resolved as an aircraft, another as radar reflection, but the rest were potentially left valid. The Patuxent Naval Air Station radar tracks, despite dual sources, had been officially determined as "malfunctioning radar circuitry" (see also page 144). Overall, no object was considered of foreign origin or a threat to national security.[3]

In early February OSI Deputy Director Donald Chamberlain sent a UFO statistical report to the Agency's assistant director for special activities. Detailed analysis of five reports from (redacted) during the period November 16–24, 1964, concluded that the object "was no high-altitude, ultra-high-speed UFO." As observed by a Navy pilot on the 19th, it was a delta-wing object the size of a jet fighter, flying at 50,000 feet in excess of Mach 3, hence, it was logical that the remaining sightings were also unknown aircraft of Soviet or Western origin.[4]

On February 26, a NICAP representative (Donald Keyhoe, Richard Hall, or other) wrote to CIA Director John McCone. The writer referenced NICAP's publication, *The UFO Evidence,* and asked whether McCone believed a formal congressional investigation or inquiry could be justified.[5]

That summer, a CIA source in Argentina submitted an informal multi-topic report. Under "Antarctic Flying Saucers," the writer related a July 6, 1965, Buenos Aires news article declaring that flying saucers displaying red, green, and yellow were observed over Deception Island, detected from Chilean and British Antarctic bases. "The flying saucers were also seen flying in formation over the South Orkney Islands in quick circles."[6]

A July 26, 1965, letter to the editor of the *Hartford Courant* was titled "Let's Get the Facts about the UFOs." Retired Vice Admiral Roscoe Hillenkoetter, the CIA's director after World War II, openly reiterated:

> Behind the scenes, high-ranking Air Force officers are soberly concerned about UFOs. But through official secrecy and ridicule, many citizens are led to believe the unknown flying objects are nonsense. . . . The Air Force has assumed the right to decide what the American people should or should not know.

The letter writer urged congressional hearings.[7]

While you were away from your desk . . .

January 11, 1965

From their Munitions Building office windows in Washington, D.C., Army Signal Corps engineers observed anomalous objects in the distance. As the unknowns zigzagged toward the Capitol, two delta wing jets approached. With great acceleration, the UFOs quickly outpaced the planes. News reporters pursuing the story were told by military and Defense Department officials that the incident simply never occurred.[8]

A UFO encounter with a planeload of US military officers would seem very likely to reach the Company's attention. Still, the incident described below and others were not included in the 2017 files release.

January 15, 1965

On that night, a Flying Tiger Line aircraft chartered by the US Defense Department was transporting a group of Army and Air Force officers to

Japan. An hour away from landing at Tokyo, the plane's onboard radar detected three huge fast-approaching objects. Surrounded by a reddish glow, the enormous ovular anomalies descended toward the plane. The captain was preparing to turn the aircraft away when the objects, in close formation, veered to one side, decelerated, and leveled out to pace the plane at a distance of five miles. Even that far away they appeared gigantic—roughly 2,000 feet in length, maybe more. A crewman beckoned an Air Force officer to the flight deck where the pilot asked whether he should call for jet interceptors from Okinawa. The officer replied that the fighter jets would likely be helpless in the face of such crafts and might instigate a confrontation. After several more nervous minutes, the unknowns angled away, accelerated to 1,200 knots, and were swiftly gone.[9]

March 15, 1965

At approximately 1:00 a.m., from a swamp buggy in the Everglades, Florida, a hunter noticed a bright light sweeping back and forth. Curious, he motored toward it and came upon a hovering, whining object in the shape of a flat cone, 70 feet at its base, with four rows of windows, hovering close to the ground. When he walked underneath it, a beam of light struck him. He awoke over 24 hours later, nearly blind. His doctor recorded serious hemorrhaging of one eye and deep tendon numbness in his arms and legs. He and the doctor returned to the spot and photographed scorched treetops, depressed vegetation forming a circle, and scuff marks on bordering trees.[10]

March 18, 1965

Around 7:00 p.m., near Hiroshima, Japan, three workers sighted a triangular airborne object whose top radiated brilliant light. At 7:06, the captain of a TOA Airlines Convair 240 headed to Hiroshima at 2,000 meters altitude noticed a "mysterious, elliptical, luminous object." Initially fearing a collision, he lurched the plane 60 degrees to little avail. The intruder now positioned itself along his port wing, emitting a greenish light, affecting his automatic direction finder—his radar and radio. The anomalous vehicle followed him for a while, discontinued for three minutes, then "followed along my left wing across the Inland Sea for a distance of about 90 kilometers . . . then disappeared." Along the way, the copilot heard frantic calls from a Tokyo Airlines Piper Apache; the pilot said he was being paced by an unknown luminous object.[11]

August 2, 1965

Six Oklahoma Highway Patrol officers plus a seventh man from the OHP communications tower in Edmond observed a multicolored unknown. A photograph of the object was later analyzed by Air Force and civilian investigators. While, of course, the USAF results were not forthcoming, earlier private analysis indicated the object in the frame was about a mile away and perhaps 50 feet in diameter.[12]

That night and the next day, August 3, from South Dakota on into Mexico, many thousands of people were witness to waves of anomalies overhead, hundreds of unconventional lights/objects in all. It was the most massive exhibition of sightings ever recorded in the United States. By and large they were authenticated by radar at several Air Force bases and by photos taken by civilians.[13]

September 3, 1965

At 12:30 a.m., an Exeter, New Hampshire, policeman found a hysterical woman parked along Route 101. She claimed to have been paced for 12 miles by an anomalous object that displayed a halo of bright red light.

At 1:00 a.m., an 18-year-old hitchhiker confronted an aerial object similar in shape to a rugby football, 80–90 feet long and silent, with five bright pulsating red lights on its near side. It had risen from a wooded area nearby and proceeded to hover over a house, bathing it in red light. The youth caught a ride into Exeter and went to the police at 1:45 a.m. The officer on duty reported that the young man was visibly pale and agitated. Another officer returned with him to the place of his encounter. In short order the anomalous object rose from the woods again. The officer radioed an alert and soon a second cruiser arrived. The young man and the two officers watched it dart to and from locations in the fields faster than they could track visually. It was so brilliant that it was painful to look upon. At one point it moved within 100 feet of the witnesses then floated over an adjacent field. Finally, it flew out of sight, rocking as it went.

Exeter police later contacted nearby Pease AFB, which sent two officers to investigate. Apart from interviews, they checked the area for radiation but found none. Soon the case attracted newspaper and then magazine attention. In UFO investigative circles it became a staple as recounted by John G. Fuller, the "*Incident at Exeter.*"[14]

October 21, 1965

A Minnesota deputy sheriff, his wife, teen son, and another couple were returning from a hunting trip. A scant few miles from the town of Saint George at 6:10 p.m., they noticed an odd light in the sky, perhaps 2,000 feet up and a quarter-mile distant. They stopped the car for a better look, remaining there for 10 minutes as the deputy viewed it through 7x power binoculars. They drove another half-mile and stopped again. The deputy got out and snapped a photo with his Kodak Instamatic, using Ektachrome color-slide film, just as the unknown started in motion against the wind. It continued for several seconds then halted, at which point its lighting changed from bright white to dull orange and back again multiple times. It then sped away out of sight. As it moved overhead, all the witnesses heard a high-pitched whine. The deputy, who alone had viewed the anomaly through field glasses, described it thus:

> The outline was unmistakable through my binoculars as that of a flying saucer. . . . The rounded top of the dome was a metallic-silver gray that reflected the rays of the setting sun, turning the object into a large orange ball. Surrounding the dome were four small portholes that emitted a bright yellow light. Just below the windows or ports was an area that glowed a light blue. This light seemed to be a reflection of some inner light or perhaps exhaust. From the edge of the blue light's reflection to the edge of the flat saucer-like surface (outer edge), the ring

was rotating counterclockwise, causing it to throw off an aurora or halo of light that changed from orange to white with an overall tinge of blue and green. The extreme outer edge of the saucer glowed a bright orange, and this part did not move or rotate.[15]

November 9, 1965

A major electrical blackout occurred along much of the eastern seaboard of North America, from South Carolina through the eastern provinces of Canada, affecting tens of millions of customers. The outage coincided with scores of reports from the public of anomalous lights moving around electrical substations and at key points along the power grid.[16]

December 9, 1965

What has been widely known ever since within UFO investigative circles as the "Kecksberg incident" took place in the rural western Pennsylvania locale 40 miles from Pittsburgh. On that day, plenty of locals saw *something* fall from the sky, seemingly into an identifiable part of the surrounding woods. Army and Air Force personnel were on the scene within a few hours, according to some locals. Numerous media staffers made the trek as well. Considerable acreage around the alleged crash site was cordoned off; no reporter or other civilian was allowed near. From among hundreds of residents gathered along a nearby county road, a few dared to sneak into the woods but were said to be turned back by the military. Late that night, witnesses claimed they saw a flatbed tractor-trailer rig leave the area. On the bed was something large and tarpaulined. Though speculation continued for years leading to decades, no other unimpeachable facts came forth.[17]

Note: An alternate potential explanation for such military attention would be an artificial satellite. The United States had been launching satellites for just under eight years, beginning with Explorer 1. A fall from orbit would necessitate just such a response, lest someone capture it on behalf of the Soviets.

Chapter 19

1966:

All Hell Breaks Loose

At 5:45 a.m., February 6, 1966, in Nederland, Texas, the lights in a home as well as the nearby streetlights went out. The owner arose and looked outside. He confronted a tadpole-shaped object about 500 feet above, casting red and yellow pulsating light onto his property. He described the structure as consisting of a main body eight feet in diameter, with a six-foot tail section. He watched as the object proceeded slowly toward the local airport. A moment later, when an airplane began its takeoff, the intruder's lights were extinguished—only to come back on after the plane passed by. Gradually the UFO rose up until lost from view in an overcast sky. The utility company later confirmed that a transformer had failed. Project Blue Book listed the sighting as unidentified.[1]

Following the Michigan UFO incidents in March 1966 (see "While you were away . . ." later in this chapter), Grand Rapids-based Congressman Gerald Ford called on the House of Representatives to investigate. That prompted APRO's Coral Lorenzen to remark that it could make the United States "look like damn fools in the eyes of the world if the government admits UFOs exist." She favored a more scientific study. NICAP's Donald Keyhoe, in contrast, endorsed a thorough congressional inquiry.[2]

The Agency received a copy of a letter prepared by the Office of the Assistant Secretary of Defense and sent to a Hollywood production studio on April 12. The letter expressed strong disagreement with multiple factors expressed in a potential film, "Project Saucer." The DoD strongly suggested several changes:

1. Delete a reference to the CIA. "It would not be appropriate to place one of their men in the position fictionalized."

2. "The UFO investigation is not set-up [sic] factually." Enclosed was a February 1, 1966, resource from Project Blue Book.

3. The character of the Air Force general at a testing site was uncomplimentary—unnecessarily so.

4. The Air Force's role in the testing was unclear.

5. Regarding an airdrop in China, the Air Force should not be included.[3]

A heavily redacted Agency report, prepared in May 1966, referenced fragmentary evidence discovered in Congo. The remaining text, verbatim:

> On file in CIA Library is an exploitation report on a metallic fragment approximately 2" x 2" x 1" that was recovered near Kerekere, Republic of the Congo. The fragment was recovered by ground search after a UFO fell to earth in the area. The report concluded that the fragment was originally part of an electrical component, constructed of 0.010-inch thick silicon-steel laminate.[4]

On June 17, 1966, a commercial pilot, 25 miles from the Teheran airport under a clear sky, saw a "brilliant white sphere" with an apparent size of three moons. The light was in view for 4–5 minutes on the Soviet side of the border. Another pilot observed the phenomenon and exchanged radioed remarks. The unknown grew in size as its brilliance diminished. "Toward the end of this period it became very faint and its enormous size seemed to fill the sky." Persons on the ground saw nothing unusual. The report writer mentioned as hypotheses a reflected *false* moon or a sphere of gasses from an explosion.[5]

A teletyped message transmitted June 26, 1966, contained a news article from Moscow's ITAR-TASS World Service. At 12:30 a.m., June 25,

10 kilometers outside the Lithuanian capital, Vilnius, two patrol officers came upon an anomalous glowing globe hanging motionless 20–30 meters above the ground. The oddity issued a "crackling" sound and alternately expanded and contracted. The officers alerted the Vilnius police headquarters. In minutes, vehicle loads of soldiers and special forces from the ARAS Rapid Reaction Force arrived, along with civil defense staff, sniffer dogs, and police reinforcements. After half an hour, the officers approached to within 50 meters, whereupon the sphere departed. Below where it had hovered, tall grass was flattened in a 20-meter circle. The crackling sound continued for several more minutes.[6]

The Air Force Grows Impatient

Sara Hunt, Secretary of the Air Force, Office of Information (SAFOI) had visited OSI on July 19, 1966, to request a copy of the 1953 "Report of the Scientific Panel on Unidentified Flying Objects," a.k.a. the Robertson Report. Hunt referenced a recent episode of the television program *CBS Reports* that aired May 12, on which Howard P. Robertson mentioned CIA involvement in the study. This triggered a press reaction. Hunt verified that Philip Strong, OSI's deputy assistant director, approved a 1957 release to the Air Force of the sanitized report (meeting minutes, case histories, and CIA mentions deleted). Hunt now sought the unabridged report; the Air Force wished to declassify all government UFO materials. Further declassification would require significant revisions, so the chief asked Hunt to submit a second, more specific request.[7]

A buckslip (date illegible) from (redacted), OSI, to (redacted) attached a five-page newspaper article published on August 7, 1966, by the *Sunday Star* of Hammond, Louisiana. The writer reviewed the June 24, 1947, Kenneth Arnold sighting at Mount Rainier, Washington, and the 1965 event at Exeter, New Hampshire, addressed in detail by John G. Fuller in *Incident at Exeter*. (See pages 6 and 177–178 respectively.) Fuller's basic charge: The Air Force had been secretive and told untruths about the reality of UFOs. He contended that UFO history went back over a century, even to biblical times. He outlined a January 12, 1838, event in

Cherbourg, France involving a luminous, rotating unknown with a dark cavity. Also covered were an 1880 event near Trakehnen, Germany, as well as one in 1893 in Japan, both reported by the British science journal *Nature*. The writer added, "There was no Project Blue Book in those days to patiently explain to them that (1) they probably saw nothing and should stop being hysterical, or (2) it was a weather balloon, a mirage, or marsh gas." Also mentioned were the 1896-97 airship incidents over Oakland, California, Omaha, Chicago, and Iowa farmland.[8]

Also attached was a four-page news article in the *London Observer*, reprinted by *The Washington Post*, "Is There Possibly Anybody Out There?" on August 7, 1966. Astronomers Carl Sagan and Russian Joseph Shklovskii concluded that at least a billion habitable planets could exist in the Milky Way alone. "Our own technical civilization has existed for a very short time on the cosmic time scale. Thus, if we are not unique, there should be many technical civilizations which are much older." But all speculation was drawn from inferences, for humans had never truly seen the universe, the writer added.

OSI Deputy Director Karl Weber wrote to Colonel Gerald Jorgensen at SAFOI on August 16, 1966, regarding Jorgensen's July 27 request for declassification of the unabridged Robertson Panel Report. After further review, OSI determined that no additional material could be released. Permission had not been obtained from the personnel and organizations involved. The panel members themselves agreed only to a limited release. Moreover, as indicated by Philip Strong in his December 20, 1957, memorandum to Air Force principals: "We are most anxious that further publicity not be given to the information that the panel was sponsored by the Central Intelligence Agency."[9]

On July 12 and again on the 27th, the Air Force had requested the report be fully declassified, citing prior publicity of CIA involvement. Then on August 10, the same USAF representative had indicated Air Force intent to make the report public. On August 15 the complete report as sanitized was forwarded. Before its receipt, phone calls from SAFOI inquired about the extent of the sanitizing. On the 18th, SAFOI requested the return of its copy that had earlier been sent for sanitizing.[10]

SAFOI's Sara Hunt phoned three times from August 16–18, 1966, on the matter of obtaining a declassified version of the full 1953 Robertson Panel Report. She asked about the extent of necessary sanitizing. OSI's David Stevenson responded that all mentions of the CIA and its staff, plus other material, had been withheld. Hunt said John Lear, a newsman, had written an article appearing in the previous week's *Saturday Review*; SAFOI sought to offer him the best information.[11]

On September 1, 1966, Walter Mackey prepared a lengthy draft document for the CIA director's perusal—the chain of events concerning declassification of the complete 1953 Robertson Panel Report. Following a two-page cover letter were several attachments—53 pages worth.[12]

Mackey's attachments included the following:

Memorandum from USAF Colonel Eric T. de Jonckheere, Deputy for Technology and Subsystems within the Foreign Technology Division Headquarters, Wright-Patterson AFB, to CIA Deputy Director for Scientific Intelligence, "Declassification of the 'Report of the Scientific Panel on Unidentified Flying Objects,'" July 12, 1966. "This particular (January 17, 1953) report has been referred to in a number of articles by the news media and by some of the more vocal UFO hobby clubs." The colonel requested the report be downgraded to "Unclassified" or "For Official Use Only."

Memorandum from USAF Colonel Gerald R. Jorgensen, Chief, Community Relations Division, Office of Information, to CIA Deputy Director for Scientific Intelligence, Attn: (redacted), "Declassification of 'Report of Meetings of Scientific Advisory Panel on Unidentified Flying Objects' (Robertson Panel) Convened by Office of Scientific Intelligence, CIA, January 14-18, 1953." Jorgensen requested declassification of the panel's report, a copy of which was attached.

Memorandum for Record, by David B. Stevenson, "Air Force Request to Declassify CIA UFO Report," July 20, 1966.[13]

Letter from Karl H. Weber, OSI Deputy Director, to USAF Colonel Gerald R. Jorgensen, Chief, SAFOI Community Relations Division, August 15, 1966.

> The Office of Scientific Intelligence feels that the report, as originally drafted, cannot be downgraded. As an alternative, an unclassified version has been prepared which edits names of personnel and participating organizations, and we are agreeable to the release of this version.

Authorized panel members and organizations would receive only the edited summary and conclusions in P. G. Strong's December 20, 1957, memo. "We are most anxious that further publicity not be given to the information that the panel was sponsored by the Central Intelligence Agency." (See page 183.)

The October 4, 1966, issue of *Look* magazine carried a lengthy article written by John G. Fuller, "Aboard a Flying Saucer." His detailed account of Betty and Barney Hill's close encounter on September 19-20, 1961, rendered them synonymous with the word "abduction."[14]

An undated October 1966 document by the CIA Office of Legislative Counsel, titled "Journal," was prepared over four days, October 4-7. Of ten OLC topics addressed, three were entirely redacted. One entry pertained to a request by NICAP's Richard Hall for a copy of the unsanitized Robertson Panel Report. Hall had made the request to Congressman Jack Matteson, a member of the House Foreign Operations and Government Information Subcommittee. Matteson indicated he would offer Hall the name and title of the Air Force office handling such matters. No further Agency action was necessary.[15]

An October 7 article titled "National U.F.O. Probe Slated" (publisher not shown) quoted the *Denver Post*, which conveyed that the University of Colorado would oversee a new scientific study of UFO reports. The announcement followed longstanding criticism by Congress and the public of the government's handling of sighting reports. Theoretical physicist Edward U. Condon would head the effort.[16]

As a coconspirator, not surprisingly the CIA came to be criticized for generally lacking candor on the UFO subject. Condon and his esteemed group, it was envisioned, would "analyze all the phenomena associated with UFO sightings and will review the Air Force's methods of receiving, investigating, and evaluating the reports." It would not, however, have the power of subpoena or to take sworn testimony. The 15-month, $330,000 contract could be extended. Its report was to be sent to the USAF Office of Scientific Research. The National Academy of Sciences offered to review Condon's report when finished. Of 11,000 sighting reports since 1948, the Air Force said it had left only 655 unexplained. Its firm conclusion: no UFO had posed a threat to national security or appeared to be from outer space. Note: The UC contract was elsewhere declared to be for 18 months and $325,000.

McDonald on the Attack

Also on October 7, the *Arizona Republic* ran an article titled "UFO Hush Blamed on CIA Men." Atmospheric physicist James McDonald had told an audience of University of Arizona students and faculty that he reluctantly accepted the ET theory of UFOs as the "least unacceptable explanation." He added that the sighting patterns suggested peaceful reconnaissance, while rejecting time travel, ESP, hoaxes, hallucinations, secret aircraft, and natural phenomena as overall explanations. He called the Air Force claim of explaining 95 percent of reports grossly exaggerated, that it was closer to 50 percent.

McDonald declared that the CIA orchestrated an Air Force debunking effort, its written order attached to the 1953 Robertson Panel Report he had reviewed at Wright-Patterson AFB, where UFO reports were stored. When he later requested an unsanitized copy of the panel report, the CIA reclassified it off limits. He said the CIA believed less official recognition would diminish public interest and reduce sighting reports. The Agency, he added, favored surveilling civilian groups (for example APRO) for possible subversion. He blamed the Air Force for a regulation criminalizing contact by airmen with civilian research groups, which resulted in official silence regarding pilot sightings, radar returns, and detection from space.[17]

The New York Times had an entirely different take on the commotion, concentrating on the local scene. The University of Colorado Project would be conducted on the Boulder campus, but USAF investigative teams would visit communities where prominent sightings were reported. Earlier, the Air Force had addressed the problem with one officer, one sergeant, and a secretary. Project Blue Book was now to notify the Condon group of any new cases that would "merit special investigation." UC would provide specialists in the physical sciences and psychology who would be "solely responsible for the conclusions drawn." Classified military and space surveillance data and certain psychiatric evaluations of UFO witnesses would not be made public. To counter potential public ridicule, witness anonymity would be offered. In contrast to this weighty assignment, in the early 1950s Condon himself had twice been denied a secrecy clearance.[18]

The next day the *Baltimore Sun* added its two cents: University of Arizona physicist James McDonald claimed the CIA ordered the Air Force to debunk UFO accounts, a policy he said throttled any scientific investigation. Now the Air Force announced a research grant to the University of Colorado to evaluate UFO reports. McDonald said he discovered the CIA debunking instruction—and directive not to disclose the Agency's role—while researching the Robertson Panel Report at Wright-Patterson AFB. Major Hector Quintanilla, successor as Project Blue Book chief, said the Report's aim was only to "remove the aura of danger from UFO sightings."[19]

So, under the tutelage of Major Quintanilla, the Robertson Report's snarky critique of the "aura of mystery" surrounding UFO reports was itself sanitized, evolving into an "aura of danger" in need of elimination.

The Chicago *Daily News* concentrated on the fallacies of Blue Book's so-called investigations: James McDonald, the U of Arizona atmospheric physicist, said he believed some UFOs have to come from beyond Earth, "operated or controlled in some way by thinking beings." He criticized swamp gas and ball lightning as explanations. He dismissed Air Force investigative methods as "a scientific scandal," stating the professed investigators were untrained in the sciences. He declined to speculate on UFO origins. The writer said a University of Colorado in-depth study would continue 15 months.[20]

The *Washington Evening Star* took its turn announcing the Colorado study, saying the physicist Edward Condon would be given a "free hand." In response, NICAP said the scientific inquiry was "superficial."

In 1948, as director of the National Bureau of Standards (NBS), with ties to the American-Soviet Science Society and a wife from Czechoslovakia, Condon was considered a possible security risk by the House Committee on Un-American Activities. By 1951 he was being pressured to leave the NBS. In 1954 he lost his Navy security clearance—blaming Vice President Richard Nixon. By 1966 he was editing a science journal and was on an advisory board for another. Asked why he would tackle the UFO question, he said, "It's an intriguing mystery that hasn't really been looked into thoroughly."[21]

The *Los Angeles Times* weighed in on October 9, featuring Blue Book skeptic Dr. James McDonald, who claimed that the CIA's Philip Strong "signed the order to debunk UFO sightings." Rather than a cover-up, he regarded the Air Force efforts as a massive foul-up.[22]

McDonald referenced the April 17, 1966, Ravenna, Ohio, hour-long UFO chase by police. Afterward, McDonald said, the Air Force interviewer had begun the debriefing with, "Now, what about that mirage you saw?"[23] McDonald claimed hundreds of reports never reached the public because of this debunking policy. The silence, he insisted, dated back to a rash of sightings in 1952. As to the reality of these events, McDonald offered, "[S]ome of the objects may carry persons from outer space on reconnaissance missions over the earth." He came to an extraterrestrial conclusion reluctantly, he added, as the only hypothesis that made enough sense.[24]

On October 12, 1966, Agency staffer L. K. White (title redacted) penned himself a memo on a meeting held that day in which briefs on potential Vietnam battlefield scenarios were discussed for the CIA Deputy Director's attention. Someone noted tangentially that a UFO series in the *Washington Evening Star* would begin in a matter of days.[25]

On October 28, the Agency's deputy director of research and development met with representatives of the Air Force scientific research office, at the request of the latter. That office was a channel for Agency grants and contracts. The deputy wrote to himself the next day, "Apparently AFOSR is somewhat nervous about the university problem." One of the AFOSR attendees had asked whether the Robinson [sic] report from 1963 [sic] could be formally declassified and then released, that it "would appreciably assist them in their current difficulties over UFO's."[26]

The Air Force and its miniscule and underutilized Project Blue Book staff indeed found themselves in a bind. They could not satisfactorily *explain* the phenomena, nor could their best debunking outreach put an end to the periodic flaps of sightings. After nearly two decades of halting, half-hearted efforts, they had finally punted. The Colorado study would utilize four physicists and three psychologists. They would ostensibly analyze all the phenomena associated with UFO sightings as well as review Air Force methods of receiving, investigating, and evaluating sighting reports.

Yet, this development might not have been entirely a matter of good riddance from the USAF perspective. By the phrase "university problem" in the deputy director's memo for the record, he might well have been signaling friction, either within the Condon Committee itself or between elements of the Air Force and the committee.

At 7:30 p.m., November 4, 1966, a man driving on I-77 between Marietta, Ohio, and Parkersburg, West Virginia, encountered a "dark long object" that stopped on the road before him. A "man" stepped out, approached his vehicle and communicated via "thought waves or mental telepathy." The being began, "Have no fear. We come from a country that is not nearly as powerful as yours. We mean no harm." He claimed the conversation had proceeded for perhaps 5 or 10 minutes.[27] Note: Readers might question the likelihood that a "dark long object" could rest on an interstate highway for several minutes without attracting attention from passersby.

A December 7 letter from (redacted) to an Auburn, Washington, resident acknowledged receipt of his letter and suggested that he contact the Air Force. No specifics were given.[28]

On the morning of December 23, 1966, on his popular radio program, interviewer Joe Pyne had as his guest Frank Stranges, author of *Stranger at the Pentagon.* Stranges claimed he had met a Venusian. Pyne in turn challenged him to take a polygraph test. Stranges instead related a letter he had sent to the CIA, thereafter forwarded to the Air Force. In reply, Stranges said the USAF "wrote me a letter saying by faith, f-a-i-t-h, flying saucers are real."[29]

Much was written and spoken in the fifties, and into the sixties, about the contactees—a handful of individuals who claimed not just rudimentary contact but intelligent conversations with nonhuman beings. Most claimed either repeated encounters or to be of alien origin themselves.

While you were away from your desk . . .

The ever-expanding US military involvement in Vietnam warranted, and received, the government's primary attention. War dominated the print and televised media as well. This left Michigan's Congressman Gerald Ford as something of a lone voice on the House floor, calling for a hearing to make sense of whatever it was over those Michigan towns of Hillsdale and Dexter that March.

March 20 and 21, 1966

About 8:30 p.m., outside the village of Dexter in southeast Michigan (not far from Ann Arbor), an object dropped meteor-like out of the sky and landed in a wetland half a mile past a farm. The farmer and his adult son walked to within 500 yards of what they described as a dark, cone-shaped object with a "quilted" surface, hovering just over the swampy terrain. Momentarily the anomaly flew past them and was gone. They immediately reported what they had observed. Soon a crowd of fifty townspeople, including the local police, gathered and watched similar objects perform aerial maneuvers. Six separate patrol cars chased the elusive crafts that night—to no avail.[30]

The next night, an hour away at Hillsdale College, a small liberal-arts college in south-central Michigan, the county's civil defense director, a college staffer, and 87 coeds at a dormitory watched for four hours as a glowing football-shaped object meandered erratically over a swamp a few hundred yards away. When law enforcement arrived, the object's exterior dimmed, only to brighten again when the police left. At a later point the oddity approached the dorm, stopped, then retreated to the marsh. Using binoculars, the civil defense director concluded it was some kind of unknown craft.[31]

Major newspapers and televised news picked up on the back-to-back, multiple-witness accounts, assailing the Air Force in particular for remaining on the sideline. Project Blue Book's Major Hector Quintanilla sent the project's scientific consultant, Northwestern University astronomer J. Allen Hynek, to the dual scenes. After two days of interviewing witnesses, which he later termed "chaotic," with the press biting at his backside for a statement, Hynek issued his dreadful determination that "swamp gas" was probably responsible. He and the Air Force immediately assumed the role of laughingstocks.

Note: The colloquially termed "swamp gas" is the product of an actual chemical reaction under the right conditions. Buildup of methane amid wet rotting vegetation may indeed ignite into candle-like flames. But two provisos: First, such conditions are *far* more likely to occur in the heat of summer, not late winter in Michigan. Second, the effect is indeed *candle*-like flames, not the formidable displays related by observers in both communities.

March 28, 1966

The following week, NICAP held a press conference at the National Press Club, Washington, D.C., to support Congressman Gerald Ford's call that day for UFO-related hearings. Relatedly, it also called for the establishment of a government tracking network.[32]

Humiliated by the press and public over his patently absurd resolution, Hynek would ultimately undergo a metamorphosis in his thinking. Having begun his association with the Air Force most of two decades before as a hardcore debunker of all things UFO related, ultimately his cynicism faded. As he would one day tell this editor privately, he reached a point of critical mass in his thinking. "How long could I go on believing *all* these people were lying or gullible?" In 1973 Hynek would found the Center for UFO Studies, which now bears his name.

At the urging of Congressman Ford, the House Minority Leader, the Armed Services Committee held the first open Congressional hearing on the matter of UFOs on April 5, 1966. Air Force Secretary Harold Brown, Project Blue Book head Major Hector Quintanilla, and Blue Book's consultant Hynek testified. Mr. Brown asserted that UFOs posed no threat to national security and were not from outer space. Dr. Hynek bristled at being called a "puppet of the Air Force" in the press. He stated his opinion that "the body of data accumulated since 1948 . . . deserves close scrutiny by a civilian panel of physical and social scientists . . ." Afterward, the committee announced that a new outside scientific study would be undertaken. Formally titled the University of Colorado UFO Project, that group came to be known as the Condon Committee.[33]

April 17, 1966

In Portage County, Ohio, about 5:00 a.m., two sheriff deputies on patrol near Ravenna were outside their cruiser checking on an apparently abandoned vehicle when an unconventional object rose up behind trees nearby and hovered directly above, bathing them in light, before moving into the predawn darkness. Racing back to their car, the men spoke by radio with their sergeant, who ordered them to give chase and keep it in sight while he assembled a photographic team. The aerial object, ovular with a flattened bottom and a vertical projection (fin) at the rear, meandered about while remaining 300–500 feet above the ground. The officers used various roads in pursuit, speeding to over 100 mph at times to keep up.[34]

An officer in East Palestine, Ohio, (near the Pennsylvania state line) was monitoring radio traffic, spotted the object and joined the chase. Making their way across the border, at the town of Conway, Pennsylvania, they saw a parked cruiser. The aerial object had halted and was hovering in place nearby. The four officers stood by their cruisers and watched the sight. Someone on the radio remarked that Air Force jets had been scrambled to intercept the intruder. Moments later they saw the planes arriving in the distance. "When they started talking about fighter planes, it was just as if that thing heard every word that was said; it went PSSSSHHEW, *straight* up; and I mean when it went up, friend, it didn't play no games; it went *straight* up."[35]

In time, Blue Book's Major Quintanilla declared that the police officers had misidentified variously a satellite and Venus. In a personal meeting with the men, said to be acrimonious, Quintanilla refused to reconsider his conclusion.[36]

Note: At 5:00 a.m. EDT for Portage County, Ohio, the moon and Venus were both below the horizon. By 6:00 a.m., a sliver of the waning moon was visible on the east-southeast horizon; Venus was at 11 degrees altitude, also in the east-southeast. The sun rose at 6:43 directly east. By 7:00, the moon was at 13 degrees altitude and Venus higher at 21 degrees but fading in the morning light.[37]

April 22, 1966

Shortly after 9:00 p.m., numerous Beverly, Massachusetts, residents saw three gray-white saucers circling low over the high school and other buildings. Each displayed red, green, and blue flashing, rotating lights. Three women were among those on the campus grounds observing. When one of them waved her arms, one of the ships glided silently over and halted directly above them. Two Beverly PD officers arrived, then retreated when a disc descended over the school gym. The objects finally moved away, only to be seen minutes later by many people over Gordon College in nearby Wenham.[38]

August 24 and 25, 1966

The ICBMs at Minot AFB, North Dakota, drew oversight from the 91st Strategic Missile Wing, the 862nd Combat Support Group, and the 786th Radar Squadron. On August 24, and again on the 25th, multiple personnel stationed at three far-flung missile sites were witness to aerial intruders, confirmed by radar, for a total period of 3½ hours. As reported officially by the base director of operations, radio communication with a missile combat crew 60 feet underground was interrupted by static when the UFO hovered low overhead. From there the intruder rose to 100,000 feet whereupon the radio returned to normal. At another point an object descended and began to "swoop and dive," then it appeared to land some 10–15 miles away. A strike team headed toward the landing area but was still a number of miles short when heavy static disrupted its communications.[39]

Chapter 20

1967:

The Tempest Rages

A letter to the editor of the *Syracuse Post-Standard* on January 7, 1967, claimed that UFOs were being observed in ever-increasing numbers, for longer periods of time. Since the March 1966 sightings in southeast Michigan, "virtually every national magazine has printed something on UFO's." Meanwhile, physicist James McDonald cited a 1953 CIA report persuading the Air Force to debunk UFO reports on national security grounds. Now the Air Force had teamed with the University of Colorado to engage in a lengthy and, purportedly, scientific study.[1]

In February 1967 came a translated article from the popular Russian magazine *Cmena* (Change). For centuries major science discoveries had been met by popular resistance initially. Dr. Felix Ziegel of the Moscow Aviation Institute argued such was the situation with UFOs. Did the problem actually exist? Were there really indisputable facts pointing to the existence and reality of UFOs? It was easier to just say no.[2]

Dr. Ziegel outlined some recent history: In August 1947 and July 1948, US airline pilots veered to avoid collision with a cigar-shaped object; in the latter, the object's exhaust violently shook the plane. Various attempts in the same time period to pursue UFOs were met by great accelerations and sharp maneuvers. In January 1948, a Kentucky ANG pilot crashed pursuing an unknown. In August of 1949, astronomer Clyde Tombaugh and family observed anomalous rectangles cross the sky.

More recently, in the summer of 1965, air traffic controllers at Canberra, Australia, witnessed an unknown that hung overhead for 40 minutes. At a space tracking station nearby, an unknown seemingly interfered with Mariner 4 (satellite) signals. On August 1, 1965, four unknowns at great height were tracked on radar over Kansas and Colorado. UFOs were caught on radar in the US, USSR, Australia, India, and Japan. Ziegel summarized, "[T]he riddle of UFOs has become a scientific problem and highly-qualified specialists . . . have been called upon to solve it."[3]

Possible explanations according to Ziegel's thinking:

1. All UFO reports were nonsense, either fabricated or from care-less observations.

2. UFOs existed but were not what they seemed to be, for example, atmospheric optics at work. Too simplistic, he concluded.

3. UFOs were secret aircrafts of a world power. Initially the US military spread rumors they were Soviet. This notion lost sway over the years.

4. They were little-understood natural phenomena, such as plas-mas. This argument was worthy of attention but hardly a full explanation.

5. They were from other planets, surveying Earth. "[This] is an extreme point of view and at first glance completely improbable," Ziegel noted. But terrestrial organisms would not endure the enormous accelerations.

Separately, he concluded, none of the existing hypotheses could be the final answer. "[T]he only correct course is clear—to subject the mysterious UFO phenomenon to thorough and careful scientific study."[4]

NPIC Enters the Fray

The US Air Force contracted with the University of Colorado for a study to be completed in early 1968 but with the potential for an extension if warranted. USAF Brigadier General Edward Giller and physicist J. Thomas Ratchford monitored the project from Washington, D.C. General Giller established an informal liaison with the National Photographic Interpretation Center (NPIC) and its Director, Arthur C. Lundahl, for technical services including measurements and enlargements. Early on, Dr. Lundahl stipulated the limited degree of the center's involvement: "These photos are rare so very little work and no commitment of NPIC are involved."[5]

Dr. Ratchford requested five scientists, including Condon, to attend a meeting at NPIC to inspect its special photographic gear. Lundahl then sought approval from the Agency's deputy director for the visit.

> I have told USAF representatives that I can have no part in writing whatever they might conclude on this UFO phenomena but that I might be able to help them technically. . . . At the same time I might be able to preserve a CIA window on this program . . .[6]

The deputy director called the director's attention to an Air Force contract with the University of Colorado concerning UFOs. Dr. Condon had called NPIC's Lundahl for technical support. "The amount of work would be minimal," he promised. The DD/I and DCI agreed to offer the services of NPIC.[7]

A memo from NPIC responded to a request from (redacted) for analysis of four photographs—three of an alleged UFO and one of a helicopter claimed to be in the area—supplied by the Foreign Technology Division (FTD, formerly the Air Technical Intelligence Center). The four photos were reproduced from second-generation negatives of poor quality. The originals were from a Polaroid camera and not available for analysis. A USAF major used an identical camera for five photos of the Lake St. Clair, Michigan, surroundings.[8]

NPIC's assumptions and conclusion:

- The UFO was a quarter-mile away.

- Measurements supplied by the officer were accurate.

- The photos were full-format.

- The object shot was circular with a plane of tail section perpendicular to the camera.

- Adjustments to the camera focal length were not necessary.

An artist's conception offered approximate dimensions based on certain assumptions. "The quality of the photography, the crude estimation of the distance from the camera station to the object, the lack of original prints and precise camera data all tend to invalidate the answers." No definite evidence of a hoax was present. "On the other hand, for one to assume that this object is a UFO is equally as dangerous. . . . [T]he photo analysis of this UFO photograph has resulted in inconclusive answers."[9]

A nearly illegible memo concerned the photographic analysis of five non-original prints. The NPIC conclusion: "None definite. To decide the authenticity of the image as being a UFO is not possible from the furnished prints. It is possible that an analysis of the original photograph would provide added information which would enable a definite conclusion."[10]

The Air Force's contract with the University of Colorado named General Edward Gillers [sic] as senior contact, Dr. Thomas Rachford [sic] as senior Air Force scientist, and Dr. Edward Condon as senior UC scientist. On February 20, 1967, Condon and four team members visited NPIC to familiarize the team with photogrammetric and photographic analysis capabilities. A clearance level of Secret was declared for the meeting. The center redoubled its sideline capacity: "Any work performed by NPIC to assist Dr. Condon in his investigation will not be identified as work accomplished by CIA." NPIC would not prepare written comments, draw any conclusion, or prepare written reports. Its assistance would be strictly technical.[11]

NPIC briefings at the February 20 session included: (a) what photogrammetry is and what it can do; (b) problems encountered when basic information was not known, for example, camera focal length, camera make, unspecified enlargements; (c) microdensitometer and image analysis; (d) isodensitometer experiments; and (e) measuring instruments.

The fourth edition of the Agency's [massive] topical index, called the Intelligence Subject Code, listed "UFO" and "Unidentified Flying

Objects" in alphabetical order, both with the numerical code 657.260—seemingly added in March 1965. In the listing of "Subject Modifiers in Numerical Order," 079 was shown as "Possible, Suspicious, Unusual Sites or Sightings, Activities or Events," apparently added in February 1961.[12]

As the third item of a non-sourced anonymous report, the writer stated that, on February 20, 1967, Dr. Edward Condon and his group toured the National Photographic Interpretation Center (NPIC) and received a demonstration of photo analysis techniques. The sixth item, mensuration (geometric measurement) of unnamed photographic prints was closed with no conclusion reached regarding authenticity of the image. Note: All remaining items in the report were redacted.[13]

In a March 1967 piece, *Look* magazine printed a stern assessment by Warren Rogers regarding the Air Force's handling of UFO cases. Air Force Intelligence and the CIA had jointly addressed UFOs beginning December 30, 1947. Months later code name *Sign* was changed to *Grudge*, then, on August 1, 1952, to *Project Blue Book*. Its two officers (later reduced to one) and one sergeant took reports from 100+ military bases plus the Pentagon. Very few cases were directly investigated. Largely the unit compiled data for annual reports to the USAF chief of information. "Every now and then . . . the Pentagon was hit by a wave of flying-saucer stories, and mostly it was failing to cope." By 1966 the Air Force was mocked by the press and the public and was ready to pass the baton.[14]

The University of Colorado UFO study group employed five physicists and three psychologists. Over a hundred UC scientists were available for ad hoc assignments. Dr. Robert Low was effectively chief of staff. Condon claimed no preconceptions but declared, "I won't believe in outer-space saucers until I *see* one, touch one, get inside one, haul it into a laboratory, and get some competent people to go over it with me." If unable to do that, Condon would inherit the Air Force problem, Rogers said, criticized by "the fanatics who have made them a religion, the hallucinated—the whole gamut of oddballs and hustlers."[15]

Dr. Carl Sagan, a Harvard astronomer, brought in a religious angle: "The saucer myths represent a neat compromise between the need to believe in a traditional paternal God and the contemporary pressures to accept the pronouncements of science."[16]

Condon realized the UFO problem meant trying to prove a negative. He believed 90 percent of reports were misidentified everyday objects but also that 10–20 times as many sightings were never reported. Blue Book bungled cases, spoke up only after major press coverage, or never spoke at all. Of 10,147 official reports between 1947 and 1965, Blue Book left 646 unidentified—303 in 1952 alone. The contract with the University of Colorado would expire in early 1968 with a formal report from Condon's group, which the National Academy of Sciences would review.

Skeptic Philip Klass, *Aviation Week & Space Technology* editor, who initially dismissed all UFO reports as ball lightning, had by now expanded that into an identified flying objects (IFO) list including clouds of charged dust or ice particles, dust devils, or light shining on any of those. Astronomer J. Allen Hynek and physicist James E. McDonald both applauded the appointment of Condon to sort it all out.

McDonald—de facto inheritor of Donald Keyhoe's mantle of chief critic—was back on the stump. In late April the University of Arizona atmospheric physicist told an assembly of newspaper editors that in 1953 the CIA had proposed a systematic "debunking of flying saucers" in order to reduce public interest. He said he stumbled upon and examined the classified report instructing the Air Force to challenge and disallow sightings by the public; the Agency later refused his request to declassify the sensitive declaration. That was "entirely understandable when seen from a solely national security viewpoint," McDonald interjected.[17]

In a speech to the American Meteorological Society, McDonald called the extraterrestrial hypothesis "the least unsatisfactory." He said a flood of UFO reports to air bases in 1952 elevated UFOs to a security risk with the potential to clog channels of communication and strain investigative staff. Consequently, Air Force Regulation 200-2 forbade air bases from giving out information; sighting reports were to go through Blue Book; that would reduce public input. Of those reaching the Air Force, McDonald said most were "categorized as conventional objects with little attention to scientific principles." Another regulation criminalized the release of UFO information by military personnel and even airline pilots. McDonald said these regulations "have not only cut off almost all useful reports from military pilots, tower operators, and ground crews, but even more serious from a scientific viewpoint, has been the drastic effect on the availability of military radar data on UFO's."[18]

McDonald said CIA officials initially suspected UFOs were from a hostile foreign power—a notion since discounted. He claimed the country was misled, while the problem was mishandled and Project Blue Book then downgraded to low priority. But he believed "scientific and official concern is beginning to change." The University of Colorado/Condon study was a good start, he added, "but they have not taken the problem seriously enough to muster the scientific strength to do justice to the problem." Air Force Major Hector Quintanilla, Blue Book chief, disputed McDonald's assertions. He said UFOs did not threaten national security, represent futuristic technology, or come from beyond Earth.[19]

The *Boston Herald* expanded on Dr. McDonald's assertions in an April 24 editorial titled "UFO's and the CIA." The charge by a science professor that the CIA ordered the Air Force to debunk UFO reports "raises again the question of the role of the CIA in domestic policy-making." In summary, the editorial board observed, "The CIA is by law an intelligence-gathering agency restricted from interfering with the internal affairs of the country. In its activities with student organizations and labor unions, however, and with its attempt to censor UFO reports, it has disregarded these restrictions." Congress had to take actions to control it.[20]

A particular division chief, (redacted), at NPIC summarized the testing of photographs taken at Zanesville, Ohio. [Note: A Zanesville barber and amateur astronomer concocted two fake daytime photos of a saucer-like object, which he initially claimed hovered over the town on November 13, 1966. He later confessed to the hoax.] Also present were Drs. Robert Lowe, University of Colorado (UC); William Hartman, University of Arizona; Charles Reed, National Research Council; J. Thomas Ratchford, USAF; and (redacted). All attendees were said to be enthusiastic. The examination included ground survey techniques, a new mathematical analysis, photogrammetry, and densitometric traces. "Dr. Condon stated he had for the first time a scientific analysis of a UFO that would stand up to investigation." The group questioned (redacted) and were said to be very impressed. Dr. Low at UC would contractually arrange his continued work for both UC and the Air Force. Dr. Condon wished to "keep a channel open into [NPIC]."[21]

They all agreed the photogrammetric method needed more publicity. Analyzing all the strong NICAP photos was suggested. "This would put Dr. Condon in a position to say that he had reviewed and analyzed all the photography in NICAP files, and was now depending on the American public to furnish him new photography." Also discussed was the prospect of making Polaroid cameras available to police, military posts, airline pilots, and others. The report on the Zanesville photos would be sent to Drs. Condon and Ratchford soon.[22]

Two months later the *Philadelphia* (PA) *Inquirer* captured McDonald's remarks to Australian reporters. He was down under primarily to interview UFO eyewitnesses—among some 500 persons who related their accounts to him over time. The physicist told newsmen that scientific proof of flying saucers and the acceptance of their existence had been delayed by a deliberate debunking program arranged by many governments and CIA-backed. He said the Agency was "trying to sweep the problem under the carpet."[23]

Attached to a non-sourced note from (redacted) to "Walt" in the OSI (presumably Walter Pforzheimer, general counsel) was a letter (not shown) from "the Englishman" who had written to the Vice President. OSI's comments were sought. The letter had been shared with security staff. Dr. James McDonald in a lecture in Australia had issued the same charge—that the CIA was continuing to debunk UFO reports from the public.[24]

A July 18 memo was sent to "Mr. Duckett" (presumably Carl E. Duckett, head of the CIA's Foreign Missile and Space Analysis Center) from an anonymous party. The communication concerned an upcoming meeting of a group calling itself "1,000" and confirmed those to be in attendance (all redacted). The writer had asked OSI for, and was assured a copy of, the 1953 Robertson Panel Report, which would be shared at the meeting.[25]

The same day, John A. Larson of the Brookings Institution wrote to Vice Admiral Rufus L. Taylor, CIA Deputy Director. Larson thanked

Taylor for hosting a lecture. He noted a question posed at the session regarding Russian belief in UFOs.[26]

In a "Reply to Vice President's Letter from (redacted)," prepared July 19, 1967, for Mr. Duckett (presumably Carl E. Duckett), the writer recommended that the vice president be implored to ignore (redacted's) letter. If the VP did reply, it should be noncommittal, remarking that the person's letter was forwarded to the Air Force. Five earlier responses to the same letter writer had indicated the CIA was no longer involved with the UFO problem.

The writer also mentioned that Dr. James McDonald was gaining press attention for lectures that accused the CIA of concealing the complete Robertson Panel Report. Did the Agency "wish to release the report and put out any further fires . . .?"[27]

An Information Report from inside the Soviet Union spoke of interactions with scientists there on the UFO subject. A radio astronomer knew of no anomalies, while an astronomer had heard of an incident in the Caucasus. "The general feeling one gets is that no official treatment of the UFO problem has been given in the USSR. . . . At the same time, there is almost a universal awareness of the history and characteristics of the phenomenon often associated with considerable interest." The writer then offered a treatise on Soviet theories.[28]

The *Arizona Daily Star* was the source of selected quotes from Dr. James McDonald's speech to the American Society of Newspaper Editors:

"This is not a nonsense problem, as it has been made out. A lot of you have had fun, I suppose, writing feature stories about little green men and hoaxers and so on. Believe me, that is the wrong part of this problem to look at."

"The problem has been misrepresented by many interacting factors including yourselves and scientists such as myself."

"My examination of the problem strongly indicates that the Air Force expertise has had very little to do with Project Blue Book, and that this is the heart of the trouble."

"Project Blue Book . . . tells you that there is nothing in the unidentified flying objects that defies present-day explanation in terms of science and technology, that's balderdash; it is utter rot, I assure you."

"People have suggested that maybe Blue Book is only a front organization and doesn't know that it's only a front organization. . . . I do not think it is a grand coverup. It is a grand foul-up . . ."

"The swamp gas theory is nonsense."

"There are many radar sightings. This would be an immediate objective source of information . . . There are a number of electromagnetic effects known in the evidence—car-stopping cases, for instance."

As to pilot sightings, Dr. McDonald asserted, ". . . Once the Air Force began to discredit—and they have, in some cases unmercifully discredited them—that source of information pretty much dried up."[29]

At the same conference, astronomer and astrophysicist Donald Menzel outlined many IFO sources, from physical to optical to hallucinatory.

> I think it is time for the Air Force to wrap up Project Blue Book. It has produced little of scientific value. Keeping it going only fosters the belief of persons that the Air Force must have found something to substantiate belief in the UFO's. . . . [I]t's time that we put an end to chasing ghosts, hobgoblins, visions, and hallucinations.[30]

Further considerations pro and con: UFO accounts had no credence because they violated principles of science. Reported UFOs could not be under extraterrestrial control if the laws of physics were valid. Presumably, intelligent life forms existed elsewhere, some of them perhaps more advanced technically than humans. Hynek had asserted that some of the most coherent UFO reports arose increasingly from scientifically trained witnesses, many of whom were at close range, within roughly 500 feet, of the unconventional vehicle or aerial display. Newton explained the effects of gravitation, while Einstein developed equations for relativity at high speeds. A vehicle moved only if its thrust exceeded its mass. Acceleration increased as fuel/propellant was expelled and the mass reduced. Manned exploration of the planets would be difficult indeed with chemical rockets alone. Ion propulsion and nuclear engines were better suited. But to land and lift off again using, say, nuclear power, would produce substantial, detectable nuclear decay.

The October 1967 issue of *Flying Saucers, UFO Reports*, comprising a dozen articles and 68 pages, was submitted. The articles are briefly summarized:

> "If Anyone Asks." The author outlined landings at Cherry Creek, New York (8/19/65); Erie, Pennsylvania (8/1/66); and Pretoria, South Africa (9/65). Radar cases included Goose AFB, Newfoundland (6/19/52); Oneida AFB, Japan (8/5/52); Wichita, Kansas (8/1/65); Gulf of Mexico (12/6/52); and Custer, Washington (1/12/65).
>
> Astronomers with personal sightings included Frank Halstead, Walter Webb, and Clyde Tombaugh. Among pilot sightings, the Kenneth Arnold event, Mount Rainier, Washington, (6/24/47) was detailed. The author added, "Airline pilots have been the source of some of the most informative reports that are on record with the Air Force . . ." The July 1952 radar, pilot, and ground sightings around Washington, D.C., were also reviewed.
>
> "5 That Will Curl Your Hair." A series of controversial/dubious accounts of Close Encounters of the Third Kind (entity sightings) was outlined.
>
> "Like the Flight of a Bat." The alleged January 16, 1958, Trindade Island encounter by the crew of the Brazilian Navy ship Almirante Saldanha was portrayed.
>
> "I'm Still Climbing." This account concerned the January 7, 1948, aerial pursuit and death of F-51 pilot Thomas Mantell. His plane exploded in mid-air, but the cause of the crash was listed as oxygen debt. The Air Force initially called his alleged target Venus then changed that to a Skyhook balloon. Note: Whether Mantell had an oxygen supply onboard has been long debated.
>
> "Maybe I've Seen the Devil." Socorro, New Mexico, police officer Lonnie Zamora's CE-3 (entity encounter), April 24, 1964, was reviewed. Project Blue Book left his account unchallenged.

"The Missing Hours between Indian Head and Ashland." The account of a CE-4 (abduction) of Betty and Barney Hill on September 19-20, 1961, was outlined.

"Flap in Michigan." The Michigan events of March 20 and 21-22, 1966, on a Dexter farm and near a Hillsdale College dormitory, respectively, were detailed. Dispatched by the USAF's Project Blue Book hurriedly to the scenes, astronomer J. Allen Hynek's "swamp gas" conclusion was mocked by the 100+ witnesses including the Hillsdale coeds, police, and local government officials. Note: Seven years later, Hynek founded the Center for UFO Studies, which now bears his name.

"Hello, Out There." Speculations were offered on the prospect of intelligent life elsewhere and the chance of humankind making contact.

"If You Can't Sight 'em—Coin 'em." The article outlined hoax scenarios, using dinner plates and a garbage can lid.

"Coming In for a Charge." Electrical outages connected to UFO incidents were discussed. The Exeter, New Hampshire, incident of an object physically touching a power line was featured. In a November 1957 flap, NICAP recorded electrical outages at Levelland, Texas; Ararangua, Brazil; Kodiak, Alaska; Fort Olgethorpe, Georgia; Santa Fe, New Mexico; Hammond, Indiana; and Lemmon, South Dakota.

"Anatomy of a What'Zit." Notable 1960s cases from Project Blue Book were highlighted. Among them: February 23, 1965, Williamsburg, Virginia, mushroom/lightbulb shape where two observers' vehicles stalled; and September 3, 1965, Damon, Texas, triangular shape with two witnesses (both sheriff deputies). Courtesy of NICAP, ten vehicle shapes were drawn—all showing the bottom view, bottom angled, and side view—plus prominent historical dates for each: flat disc, domed disc, Saturn disc, hemispherical disc, sphere, flattened sphere, ellipse/football, triangle, and cylinder/cigar.

"Worth 1,000 Words." Intriguing photos over the years were featured, including the August 1951 "Lubbock Lights"; June 1950 McMinnville disc; October 1957 cigar shape near the White Sands Proving Grounds, New Mexico; and a 1951 domed disc near Riverside, California.[31]

Near Pueblo, Colorado, sometime in mid-October 1967, two 19-year-olds reportedly drove to the King Ranch to photograph a rumored UFO. At 1:20 a.m. they took two photos of a brilliant white light—apparent size of a penny. The light moved about the area, changing color and intensity until 3:04 a.m. when it winked out. No mention was made of whether the photos would be examined.[32]

From a personal journal, on the 28th of November a request had been received from a congressman's assistant who, on behalf of a constituent, asked for a copy of the 1953 Robertson Report. The writer had referred the staffer to the Air Force.[33]

By late 1967 *Playboy* was emerging as a serious, avante-garde literary magazine. Its December issue featured an essay by astronomer Dr. J. Allen Hynek, observatory director and astronomy department chairman at Northwestern University. In his provocative piece titled "The UFO Gap," Hynek noted that earlier Russian dismissals of the possibility of interstellar life were softening. A Russian magazine article posed questions (referencing the *Cmena* article described on page 195) and called for "a many-sided, careful scientific investigation." But because the US establishment was not taking the subject seriously enough, Hynek feared the Soviets would beat the West in making first contact with an ET. "From my own official involvement, I know that the United States is only now beginning to *consider* treating the problem seriously."[34]

"I had scarcely heard of UFOs in 1948 and, like every other scientist I knew, assumed that they were nonsense," Hynek began. "For the first few months of my association with what is now Project Blue Book . . . I had

no reason to change this opinion." Sighting reports were uniformly identifiable or the witness was unreliable. "But over the years cases began to
accumulate for which I could find no satisfactory physical explanation."
Blue Book did not debunk many cases outright, but its annual reports
leaned toward IFO conclusions. Its miniscule staff led by one or two
low-ranked officers echoed a skeptical Air Force officialdom, he asserted.

Needless to say, with this article Hynek left no doubt he had phil-
osophical differences with the Air Force and was completely out of the
UFO closet.

An official at the Moscow Aviation Institute declared that intelligent
life probably resided on other planets in our solar system. Over the previous two years, UFOs were sighted in "ever-increasing numbers" and in
ten countries. "It is becoming apparent that this is not an optical illusion."
The USSR instituted an observation service to assess UFO speeds and
acceleration beyond that of modern aircraft.[35]

On December 7, 1967, a form letter to an Auburn, Washington, resident acknowledged receipt of his inquiry and suggested he contact the
Air Force.[36]

Dr. Robert Low of the Condon Committee wrote to Dr. J. Thomas
Ratchford of the USAF Office of Scientific Research on December 8, 1967,
to ask that he convey a message. Low wanted Arthur Lundahl, Director of
the National Photographic Interpretation Center (NIPC) to know that Low
had spoken with Carl Sagan regarding the Soviet military's establishment
of a UFO commission. ". . . Sagan is very interested in the UFO problem
and in what we're doing and also in the recent developments in Russia . . ."[37]

Two days hence on the 10th, a Mr. Vitolniyek, Director of the (Soviet)
Station for the Radio Observation of the Ionosphere and Artificial Earth
Satellites, related that the Soviet press that night reported "luminescent
objects in the form of balloons and convex disks" in the sky. Further,
radar detected circular objects tens of kilometers high. Astrophysicists
postulated plasma phenomena.[38]

While you were away from your desk . . .

January 6, 1967

Dr. J. Allen Hynek spoke to an overflow crowd at the Goddard Space Flight Center, Maryland, telling the audience he had revised his thinking on aerial phenomena. He urged scientists to take an active role in UFO investigations. He confirmed reports that NORAD and SAC radars had tracked unknowns and cited one incident in which SAC radar followed an object at 4,000 mph on an erratic path.[39]

January 25, 1967

Colorado UFO Project director Condon spoke to the American Chemical Society in Corning, New York. Though his assembled scientists were not scheduled to complete their work for another year, he declared that the government should get out of the UFO business, since there was apparently nothing to it.[40]

Unspecified Date, January 1967

At the Algerian Hammaguir military base, a group of scientists and engineers was driving in two sedans one night toward a launch tower in preparation for a morning desert missile launch. The first car reached a row of buildings and the driver stopped, leaving the engine running. Momentarily he and his three passengers saw an approaching light in the sky. "And then something happened to my engine—it started running 'rough' and stopped by itself," the driver said later. They all exited. "We watched as the light slowly came closer, without making any sound. . . . It seemed to come within about 500 meters from us, and remained stationary at an elevation of 45 degrees."[41]

Cylindrical and dark, the men estimated it to be gigantic, 300–400 meters in length. Along its fuselage were "flames" of multiple colors. A later testifying witness said that was from ionization of the air. At a point they felt a "tinkling" deafness and paralysis for minutes. The second vehicle arrived, carrying the astrophysicists. Astonished, they watched the object for 20–30 minutes as it continued slowly on the same trajectory. Eventually it angled upward and out of sight.

March 5, 1967

North American Air Defense Command (NORAD) radar tracked an uncorrelated target descending over a Minuteman missile site at Minot AFB, North Dakota. Strike teams sighted a metallic disc with bright flashing lights slowly circling over the launch control facility. They chased the intruder in armed trucks until it stopped and hovered at 500 feet. Before F-106 Delta Dart jets could be scrambled, the ship climbed vertically and flew out of sight.[42]

Hours later, from 12:01 to 12:40 a.m. in Benton Harbor, Michigan, a radio station newsman and his wife watched a hissing oval or saucer shape, airborne and motionless. Red, green, and yellow lights around the bottom rim pulsated. A second object approached and halted above the first for 30 seconds then seemed to vanish. At 4:25 a.m. in Galesburg-Moline, Illinois, a deputy sheriff came upon a domed disc. Its bottom portion spun rapidly and the rim pulsated red. The saucer passed close overhead with a hissing sound. Both accounts were listed as unexplainable in the USAF Project Blue Book files.[43]

March 8, 1967

At 1:05 a.m., a couple was nearing their home in Leominster, Massachusetts when they entered an unexpected and dense fog. The husband noticed a bright light 400–500 aloft; he stopped the car and stepped out. As he pointed toward it, his engine and headlights failed and a force pulled his arm backward onto the roof. He was frozen in place by what he later said "felt like shock or numbness." His panicked wife was unable to pull him back inside. Half a minute passed before the object rocked back and forth and ascended with a humming sound. The engine easily restarted, but the man remained sluggish afterward.[44]

April 4, 1967

The Federal Aviation Agency published Notice N7230.29 that established procedures for reporting UFOs to the Colorado UFO Project.[45]

May 17, 1967

A group of Russian scientists convened in Moscow to form an unofficial scientific UFO investigating team. Several months later, on November 11, the establishment of the Russian UFO Commission was announced. It consisted of a network of observatories with 200 personnel, including eighteen scientists and military officers, led by a major general.[46]

June 7, 1967

Atmospheric physicist Dr. James McDonald spoke to the United Nations Outer Space Affairs Group. Concurrently, UN Secretary General U Thant expressed deep concern over the UFO situation.[47]

July 30, 1967

An Argentine steamer was 120 miles off the Brazilian coast in the evening, when the captain was called to the deck. Below the water's surface was a cylindrical object over 100 feet long but with no sign of a periscope, railing, conning tower, or other superstructure indicative of a submarine. The anomaly emitted a powerful blue and white glow while pacing the ship for 15 minutes before diving under it, not to be seen again. Argentine maritime authorities classed it an "Unidentified Submarine Object."[48]

October 4, 1967

At Shag Harbour, Nova Scotia, following reports earlier in the evening of odd lights at or near the water, at 11:20 p.m. something plunged into the sound. Mounted police were among the witnesses. Believing an airplane had crashed, they and other locals alerted authorities, including the RCAF, and gathered at the shore. Some type of dark object, about 60 feet across with a pale yellow light, floated on or hovered very near the water some 800–900 feet away. As they watched, it submerged out of sight. A boat sent out to investigate encountered thick bubbly foam, yellow in color and greasy, stretching for half a mile. The smell of sulfur was pervasive. A Coastguard cutter joined the search but nothing was found. Two days later, four divers from the Royal Canadian Navy's Fleet Diving Unit scoured the seabed and at one point brought something up to the surface, as seen by a number of area fishermen. It was rumored to have been sent to the Naval Armament Depot.[49]

Decades later a priority message was discovered, originating from the Rescue Coordination Centre in Halifax and sent to the Canadian Forces Headquarters. The message advised that a UFO had impacted the waters of Shag Harbour. Other official documents about the 1967 incident were retrieved as well.[50]

October 17, 1967

Congressman Louis Wyman of New Hampshire introduced House Resolution 946 calling for the Committee on Science and Astronautics to "conduct a full and complete investigation and study of unidentified flying objects."[51]

November 1, 1967

The US Weather Bureau issued Letter 67-16, amending its Operating Manual to encourage personnel to report UFO sightings to the Colorado UFO Project. Later that month, on the 24th, a Memorandum to Forest Service supervisors from the US Department of Agriculture followed suit.[52]

Chapter 21

1968:

Return to Relative Calm

Bruce Cathie, a New Zealand commercial airline pilot, had written several books theorizing a planet-wide grid (electrodynamic field) powering UFOs. Cathie stated many New Zealand sightings went unreported. He told an American military attaché that, on January 14, 1968, four UFOs were detected at high speed and great altitude by Auckland Air Traffic Control radar. Having been advised to submit verifying materials, he did so on January 18 (additional commentary illegible).[1]

Robert Low of the Colorado UFO Project (a.k.a. Condon Committee) wrote to J. Thomas Ratchford at the Air Force Office of Scientific Research on January 17, 1968. He attached a letter exchange with Commander Alvin Moore regarding Moore's 1952 UFO encounter and the disposition of materials related thereto. Low said Moore claimed he sent a report— plus many "stones" he had collected that were somehow tied to the UFO subject—to Wright-Patterson AFB (Project Blue Book). Low speculated that the original Project Blue Book chief, Captain Edward Ruppelt, might possibly have confiscated them, but Ruppelt's widow denied that. Low suggested that Ratchford discuss the matter with his superiors.[2]

A non-sourced report concerned a January 20, 1968, news article in *Komsomolskaya Pravda* entitled "Fantasy or Reality (Unidentified flying objects)." Various Soviet scientists had been interviewed on the UFO subject. "Although opinions varied, eyewitness accounts were cited and the necessity of studying the UFO phenomenon stressed."[3] Originally in a Hungarian newspaper, a January 31 news abstract in *Leninskaya (illegible)* reviewed British, Russian, Yugoslav, and US eyewitness accounts. A worldwide conference would be held in August 1968. Soviet astronomer Felix Ziegel said UFOs may have been optical illusions, earthly flying objects, natural phenomena, or objects from other planets. The ET hypothesis was "supported by the fact that UFO's exhibit a tremendous speed, which presupposes highly developed remote control." But few physical traces or photos existed.[4]

The Astronomic Council of the Soviet Academy of Sciences, on March 6, 1968, issued a report in *USSR Scientific Affairs*, "Scientists Refute Claims of 'UFO' Sightings." The authors lauded Donald Menzel's "painstaking analysis of phenomena." Claimed irrefutable facts by "scandalmongers," when examined, were of three basic types: deliberate misinformation, anecdotal accounts of no scientific value, and misidentifications of known objects or phenomena. Neither Soviet nor US scientists concluded any claims were credible. All the Soviet sightings, the academy concluded, evolved from "unscientific sensationalism." (The remainder of the file was redacted or unrelated.)[5]

From various eyewitness accounts, the author or authors of an article in *Pravda Ukrainy* determined that UFOs were a myth. Stereoscopic photography was not reliable. Pictures that did not initially raise doubts were usually ball lightning, the nature of which was unknown. The November 1957 "saucer" over Sofia, Romania, was actually a NATO scouting balloon. When the Western public was distracted from politics or economics, "there appear flying saucers, Loch Ness monsters, or Snowmen."[6]

Novosti (a.k.a. APN) was a Soviet unofficial news agency with close ties to the periodical *Soviet Life*. On April 9, 1968, it offered ten pages of material presenting opposing views on the UFO subject, including:[7]

- "'Flying Saucers'? They're a Myth!" (unknown date), by an APN science commentator. The United States publicized UFO events to divert attention from its failures and aggressions, it was argued.

- "Unidentified Flying Object." Dr. Felix Ziegel of the Moscow Aviation Institute offered a serious perspective that the subject deserved continuing attention.

In *Lyustiberg Moskovsky*, February 16, 1968, the 1948 crash of Captain Thomas Mantell while pursuing an unknown was argued as "undoubted proof of the existence of mighty forces still unknown to us." But the saucer was only a Skyhook balloon, and Mantell died of careless asphyxiation. Other UFO stories over the years bore the hallmarks of hoaxes. Flying saucers were like the Virgin Mary, appearing only to believers. Experiments were not repeated or the chance appearance of a phenomenon excluded the possibility of investigation.

No stereoscopic photos of an anomalous flying object were ever taken. "Modern photographic techniques allow photographs to be produced which no expert will ever prove to be counterfeit." Ball lightning accounted for some unretouched photos. Others were reflections of electric welding, airplane warning lights, high-altitude balloons, or solar plasmas. The anonymous eyewitness accounts were unconvincing. UFO lecturers were either frauds (for example, Adamski) or sincere but deluded.

Numbers of sightings always rose on the eve of US presidential elections or to divert attention from ruthless warfare—Korea and Vietnam. When US newspaper circulation dropped, American businessmen resorted to stories of UFOs, sea monsters, and the Yeti, drawing attention away from a wage freeze, rising prices, or unemployment. For statesmen in imperialistic countries, "the flying saucers are not a myth, but a well-camouflaged means for misinforming the people."

In this posting by an Agency operative, the *Novosti*/APN articles continued. On July 26, 1967, three Latvian astronomers observed a bright disc with a raised center, surrounded by three spheres rotating around it, as seen through a telescope and binoculars. After 15–20 minutes the spheres moved away in different directions.

On August 2, 1967, at 11:30 p.m. Moscow time in the Norwegian Sea, three sailors saw a very bright white light moving rapidly southward. A few minutes later a light high in the sky rushed angularly westward, stopped abruptly, displayed rainbow colors, threw off sparks, then was enveloped in a white shroud and moved south. This procedure was repeated four times over an hour. On the final time the unknown stopped and showed an egg shape. A white jet of liquid squirted downward, then the object grew pale and moved away.

Two weeks earlier, on the night of July 17–18, 1967, several Russian astronomers viewed a reddish unknown enveloped in a milky white cloud, reported by the area newspapers. The cloud dispersed, leaving a red nucleus. It remained until dawn. Photos were taken at various points. At 3:40 p.m., August 8, ten scientists at the same observatory witnessed a bright, moving white light in front of a red disc. Both disappeared.

Many thousands of such reports were recorded in many nations over 20 years, too many to be lightly dismissed. Publicity seekers would always surround the subject. "But we do not stop using money because there are counterfeiters. The task of science is, precisely, to distinguish between the false and the true." [Most of the remainder is illegible.]

An April 11 Information Report noted various sightings in Asia. On March 4, 1968, at 1:00 p.m. a bright white light flew over south Ladakh (a region of northern India) accompanied by two "blasting" sounds. Also, one reddish light was observed trailing white smoke. Two weeks earlier on February 19 at 11:00 p.m. over northeast Nepal and north Sikkim, a fast-moving, long, thin object emitted red and green light bright enough to rival daylight over a wide area. Two nights later on the 21st in western Bhutan, at 9:30 p.m. a bluish light brightened the terrain as it passed overhead at high speed without a sound. On March 4 back in south Ladakh, an unknown traveled a circular path, trailing smoke. Three weeks later on March 25 at 9:50 p.m., also in Ladakh, a rocket-like object passed overhead, leaving a prominent yellowish-white trail.[8]

A May 8, 1968, airgram from the American Embassy in Paris to the State Department clarified the official French response to the UFO problem. Though France had many interested amateur investigators, a foreign affairs official in France's aeronautics research group, ONERA, plus a general engaged in military research agreed that no government-sponsored program existed to formally study the subject.[9]

The University of Colorado UFO Project, on February 9, 1968, experienced "a near-mutiny by several staff scientists, the dismissal of two PhDs on the staff" (Dr. David Saunders and Dr. Norman Levine) for alleged incompetence "and the resignation of the project's administrative assistant." The tumult was recounted by John G. Fuller in an article titled "The Flying Saucer Fiasco" in the May 14, 1968, issue of *Look* magazine.[10] Apart from the Condon charge of incompetence, it might have been more than coincidence that Saunders and Levine intended to make public Robert Low's earlier comments to university officials that the UFO study would be a "trick" on the public regarding the committee's objectivity.

Dr. Edward Condon's record of leadership had seemed to promise scientific integrity. However, chief assistant Dr. Robert Low, outlining the upcoming project, told university principals:

> Our study would be conducted almost exclusively by non-believers who . . . would add an impressive body of evidence that there is no reality to the observations. The trick would be, I think, to describe it so that, to the public, it would appear a totally objective study but, to the scientific community, would present the image of a group of nonbelievers trying their best to be objective, but having an almost zero expectation of finding a saucer.

Soon after the committee was underway, Condon had told the press: "It is my inclination right now to recommend that the Government get out of this business. My attitude right now (1967) is that there is nothing to it, but I'm not supposed to reach a conclusion for another year."[11]

On August 1, 1968, Air Force Major A.P. Heard, an assistant air attaché stationed in Argentina, sent along a Defense Department Information Report, attaching a news article from the Buenos Aires newspaper *La Razon* with the provocative headline, "Alleged Activities of USAF and CIA Regarding UFOs." The article was in Spanish and not translated.[12]

As of August 9, 1968, the Taiwan Ministry of National Defense (MND) planned to dispatch a team of electronics experts to the islands of Kinmen and Matsu to investigate recent daily high-altitude appearances of UFOs over those offshore islands. The unknowns appeared in pairs or threes at the same approximate hour each afternoon, remaining in sight for about two minutes. ". . . MND suspects the UFOs may be some form of electronic spying device used by the Chinese Communists."[13]

A Chinese Nationalist team of technical officers concluded on October 14, 1968, that unknowns observed since July 17 were "man-made satellites, 'flying saucers,' electronic jamming devices, or psychological warfare balloons."[14]

Felix Ziegel was the cosmology expert at the Moscow Aviation Institute. He authored dozens of popular books on astronomy and space exploration and was generally regarded as a founder of Russian ufology. In an article for the November 2, 1968, issue of *Soviet Life*, he contended that the prevailing Soviet view of UFOs as fantasies and misidentified optics was wrong, due to a dearth of observational data collected. In October 1967 scientists, writers, public figures, and the military had begun a preliminary investigation. Named the UFO Section of the All-Union Cosmonautics Committee, it was headed by an Air Force major general. Ziegel said, "The hypothesis that UFOs originate in other worlds, that they are flying craft from planets other than earth, merits the most serious examination," said Ziegel.[15]

UFOs acted "sensibly," flying in formations and maneuvering to avoid contact with earthly aircraft, Ziegel noted. They were most often seen over airfields, atomic stations, and newly engineered installations. Strikingly similar sightings had occurred throughout human history. Well-documented cases included a large saucer seen widely in 1882 and a "procession of bolides" in 1913. Soviet scientists concluded that the 1908 Tunguska event met the criteria of an atmospheric nuclear blast, supported by a study published in 1967 declaring that it "left considerable residual radioactivity."[16]

"If we are indeed being studied by creatures from other planets, what is their purpose?" Ziegel pondered. "Why are they so studiously avoiding direct contact? . . . The important thing now is for us to discard any preconceived notions about UFOs and to organize on a global scale a calm, sensation-free, and strictly scientific study of this strange phenomenon."[17]

While you were away from your desk . . .

February 9, 1968

At 3:20 a.m. near Groveton, Missouri, a farmer checked on his bawling cattle. From 300 feet away, he saw a 100-foot disc hovering near the animals. Yellow-green light from portholes along its edge lit up the entire area. He heard a rhythmic sound like a whirling wire. Soon one cow bolted for the barn and the remainder followed. The whirling sound grew louder and the disc left rapidly at a 45-degree angle into the night. The farmer connected the UFO with cows earlier missing from his herd. USAF Project Blue Book left the case unidentified.[18]

Sometime in early 1968

At the Chinese Navy garrison at Luda, in the northern province of Liaoning, four artillerymen observed a luminous gold, oval-shaped object flying at a low altitude and leaving a thin trail. Soon it proceeded to climb steeply, but before it was out of sight, all of the fleet's radar systems and communications failed. The fleet commander put every ship on high alert and ordered the sailors to prepare for combat. Half an hour went by before everything returned to normal. Later it was learned that a two-man coastguard patrol saw the UFO land along the south coast. They fired on it with an automatic rifle and a machine gun but to no avail.[19]

Mid-April 1968

At a Gobi Desert construction site, a battalion of Chinese soldiers witnessed the landing of a luminous red-orange disc, just 10 feet in diameter. The commander dispatched a team of motorcycle soldiers from headquarters to investigate the vehicle. Upon the team's approach, the disc rose vertically out of sight. Most of those present wrote the incident off as a Soviet reconnaissance device, since the USSR's northern frontier passed through that region.[20]

May 13, 1968

The new issue of the journal *Scientific Research* contained an article titled, "Libel Suit May Develop from UFO Hassle," a report on the aftermath of Dr. Condon's February 9 firings of Drs. Saunders and Levine. The same theme carried over to a July 26 release of *Science*, which included an article titled, "UFO Project: Trouble on the Ground."[21]

July 29, 1968

The House Committee on Science and Astronautics held a hearing in symposium form. Presentations were made by Carl Sagan, James McDonald, J. Allen Hynek, James Harder, Robert Hall, and Robert Baker. This was the first congressional hearing that included testimony by scientists favoring UFO investigation.[22]

October 31, 1968

The Colorado UFO Project released its final report (a.k.a. the Condon Report) to the Secretary of the Air Force for review by the National Academy of Sciences.[23]

Note: In 1969 a frustrated Dr. James McDonald offered a controversial lecture he called "Science in Default" to the American Association for the Advancement of Science (AAAS). It was a summary of the then-current UFO evidence and a critique of the infamous, UFO-debunking Condon Report. Thereafter, McDonald was hounded by critics, in particular the author of the study, Edward Condon, and aviation journalist Philip Klass, who had declared that nearly all UFO sightings were really ball lightning. Professionally isolated, McDonald gradually slipped into a deep depression and finally took his own life in June 1971.[24] Rest in peace, Dr. McDonald; you did some good.

Chapter 22

1969:

Where'd All the UFOs Go?

No news accounts, information reports, or correspondence to, from, or within the Agency were filed in 1969. Not surprisingly, the wrap-up of the Colorado UFO Project in 1968 coincided with a renewed disengagement from the UFO subject by the CIA. In that 2017 release of files to the CIA website, not a single entry was dated 1969. The Company had really never embraced the pursuit, insisted on strict anonymity over the two decades of involvement, and wiped its hands of the whole affair when the Condon Report offered the opportunity. Going forward, written correspondence on UFO-related matters would be kept to a minimum to avoid any embarrassment later.

The journal *Science* decried the untenable position faced by physical scientists in "Beings from Outer Space—Corporeal and Spiritual," by Hudson Hoagland. The author compared UFO research to the practice of psychic research in the 1920s and beyond. The problem for scientists was the impossibility of proving a negative. "The Condon report rightly points out that further investigations of UFO's will be wasteful. In time we may expect that UFO visitors from outer space will be forgotten, just as ectoplasm as evidence for communication with the dead is now forgotten."[1]

The journal *Bulletin of the Atomic Scientists* piled on with "UFOs I Have Loved and Lost," by the controversial Edward Condon, in its December 1969 issue. The Air Force had long before concluded UFOs were not a defense problem, he wrote. After the first 4–5 years, Air Force attention to them was minimal. Concerning the University of Colorado study group, "All that can be said is that, of the cases we looked into carefully, we found no evidence in support of the hypothesis of their extraterrestrial origin." Objective investigative approaches did not work. Even when the source was incontrovertible (for example, the March 3, 1968, reentry of rocket debris), witness testimony differed markedly. "[N]o great certainty attaches to the specific details of any of the reports."[2]

"I continue to be astonished at the fervor with which many people hold views that are totally unsupported by objective evidence of any kind," Condon continued. Charlatans preyed on gullible people for book sales and speaking fees. Most people accepted even solid scientific ideas completely on faith. Astrology, to many, was just as credible as the hard science they accepted without any understanding. America had 10,000 astrologers but only 2,000 professional astronomers. Other pseudosciences included spiritualism, ESP, psychokinesis, and dowsing. "Perhaps we need a National Magic Agency to make a large and expensive study of all these matters, including the future scientific study of UFOs, if any," he added sarcastically. Publishers and teachers who promoted pseudoscience should have been "publicly horsewhipped" then banned from their professions.[3]

While you were away from your desk . . .

January 6, 1969

Around 7:15 to 7:30 p.m., waiting outside a church where he would make a campaign speech in Leary, Georgia, Governor Jimmy Carter and numerous others there observed what he concluded was a UFO. He told reporters soon thereafter, "It was big, it was very bright, it changed colors and was about the size of the moon. . . . One thing's for sure; I'll never make fun of people who say they've seen unidentified objects in the sky."[4]

Seven years later, during his 1976 presidential campaign, Carter vowed, "If I become President, I'll make every piece of information this country has about UFO sightings available to the public and the scientists."[5] Note: After assuming office, Carter did approach NASA about assuming a role like Project Blue Book, but he was rebuffed.

January 25, 1969

At Platteville, Illinois, a couple was driving past a farm when it was approached by a machine shaped like an ice cream cone, two or three stories tall with a "lattice" across the bottom which "shone like diamonds." It halted a quarter-mile from them as the car's engine stalled and headlights went out. A yard light at the farm was also extinguished. After remaining motionless for a moment, the anomaly suddenly spun around and halted, repeated that sequence twice then emitted a light beam. As it was executing those actions, the front end of their car lifted three feet off the ground. The anomaly finally tilted up and glided away.[6]

March 19, 1969

That night near Gladstone, Queensland, Australia, a disc-shaped aerial vehicle swooped down over a pair of cars as the drivers pulled to a stop. The object hovered over one and emitted pulsating light. As it brightened, the field of light cast by both autos' headlights broadened. When the disc dimmed, the headlights returned to normal. The cars' engines operated normally and the drivers pulled away, but the saucer remained nearby, pacing them. The drivers stopped a second time and watched as the anomaly remained in place, rocking gently. A moment passed before it finally flew off.[7]

June 17, 1969

At a Turkish air base on the night of the 17th, an alert went out regarding a UFO in the area. A pilot was ordered to scramble in his F-5A Freedom Fighter jet and intercept the intruder.

> It was gray, and like an upside-down lightbulb. I flew
> above it and reported that it was probably a meteorological

balloon. As I continued describing it, it moved to my left and moved off at a fantastic speed. Obviously it wasn't a balloon! . . . I also proposed firing at the object—but they forbade that. Eventually it disappeared.[8]

October 20, 1969

In a memorandum recommending that USAF Project Blue Book be closed, Brigadier General Carroll H. Bolender clarified that reports of UFOs that could affect national security were to be made in accordance with Joint Army/Navy/Air Force Publication (JANAP) 146 or Air Force Manual 55-11, not as part of the Project Blue Book system.[9]

October 24–27, 1969

For four days, Turkey's capital Ankara was inundated with sightings. The Turkish Air Force repeatedly scrambled interceptors from Murtad Air Base. The jets would close to within several miles, but the unknowns always climbed higher to escape. After days of cat-and-mouse, the base commander himself flew along. His report afterward noted that an object at 50,000 feet was oval and silvery, with three round portholes on the facing side. He added that no other country's traffic was in the area at the time and no prototype was under test. The interceptors took gun-camera film, which was never released.[10]

November 14, 1969

The Apollo 12 moon mission apparently had company. Telescopes at multiple European observatories spotted two flashing unknowns, one leading the space capsule, the second trailing. NASA announced that nothing they experienced was abnormal in a space environment.[11]

November 30, 1969

On State Highway 96, 13 miles southeast of Quincy, Illinois, at 7:30 p.m., three people in a car spotted an object shaped like a rounded triangle. It proceeded to swoop over the auto, raising it 10 feet off the roadway momentarily. Its engine and headlights continued functioning, but the steering was inoperable until the intruder left.[12]

Chapter 23

1970:

AIAA Weighs In

Throughout January and February 1970, South Korean (ROK) radar stations tracked numerous large balloon/dirigible-shaped unknowns at high altitudes over the Korean demilitarized zone (DMZ), on occasion penetrating ROK airspace. They invariably exploded. ROK military was concerned that the unknowns might possibly drop propaganda or even a chemical or germ agent.[1]

In November 1970, the journal *Astronautics and Aeronautics* published a piece titled "UFO: An Appraisal of the Problem"—a statement of the UFO Subcommittee of the AIAA (American Institute of Aeronautics and Astronautics). The subcommittee concluded there was no scientific basis to study the probability of an extraterrestrial hypothesis. The Condon Report was "the most scientifically oriented investigation published on the UFO problem." Condon's summary of the study also portrayed his personal conclusions. "Making value judgments was no doubt one reason why Condon was asked to handle the project," the writer stated. ". . . The UFO Subcommittee did not find a basis in the report for his prediction that nothing of scientific value will come of further studies."[2] Instead, the authors of the articles held out for continued investigation of UFO sightings.[3]

While you were away from your desk . . .

August 13, 1970

At 10:50 p.m. in Kastrup, Denmark, a policeman in his cruiser confronted a metallic disc, 30 feet in diameter, that stopped and hovered 60 feet overhead. When it cast a blue-white beam on the vehicle, the engine and lights failed and the body's metal heated. Momentarily the beam retracted—slowly, as if it were a solid. As the disc departed, the cruiser's lights came back on and the engine easily restarted.[4]

A security guard at a hydroelectric plant in Itatiaia, Brazil, noticed a row of lights over the dam and walked over to investigate. He stopped 15 meters short of the (undescribed) UFO, whereupon the noise it generated was deafening. He pulled out his revolver and began firing at it. Between the second and third shots he was hit by a flash of light and blinded, also experiencing intense heat and paralysis. He was hospitalized overnight and did not regain his sight for two weeks.[5]

October 29, 1970

At 4:40 p.m., a motorist outside Jæren, Norway, spotted a bright light approaching and pulled off the road for a better look. As it neared, the light was revealed as disc-shaped, 10 meters in diameter, with a steely blue body and dome above. When it stopped overhead, the car's engine quit. The driver exited and stood next to the vehicle, looking up at the intruder. After a few minutes, the disc left swiftly, somehow knocking the witness to the ground and breaking the auto's windshield.[6]

November 17–20, 1970

At a radar meteorology conference in Tucson, Arizona, atmospheric physicist James McDonald presented "Meteorological Factors in Unidentified Radar Returns," advancing the understanding of radar-visual UFO cases.[7]

Chapter 24

1971:

Science Journals— More to Say

Since 1968, UFO reports and general public interest had declined. The *Wall Street Journal* opined this was caused by publication of the Condon Report in 1968, which concluded that "nothing has come from the study of UFO's in the last 21 years that has added to scientific knowledge." A Stanford University academic, meanwhile, concluded that people simply lost interest. They turned to drugs, astrology, Oriental religions, and other philosophic subjects. National and international events drove people inward for answers to universal questions, he added, but as a recurring fad, interest in UFOs would inevitably return. A University of Michigan social work professor viewed UFOs as a form of escape. "One expression of this escape is the possibility of other lives, other planets, other beings like or unlike oneself."[1]

Curiously, the Condon study, having preselected specific cases, found 35 out of 117 unexplainable. Among the entire population, unexplained sightings would be a small but not negligible number. *Science News* reporters concluded, ". . . [W]e find it difficult to ignore the small residue of well-documented but unexplainable cases which form the hard core of the UFO controversy . . . characterized by both a high degree of credibility and a high abnormality ('strangeness' in Hynek's terminology)." The Colorado group made no serious attempt to find commonalities among the 35 unexplained cases; hence, any conclusions it reached were not necessarily the final word on the subject: "... [I]t is unacceptable to simply ignore substantial numbers of unexplained observations and to close the book about them on the basis of premature conclusions." Given the Air Force decision to divorce itself from the UFO subject, its files should be archived by a civilian agency, the author reported.[2]

The journal *Astronautics and Aeronautics* in September 1971 outlined the events on the night of August 13–14, 1956, at two air bases in England's interior—RAF Lakenheath and the US Air Force's Bentwaters AFB—as supported by radars at both.

> At 9:30 p.m., an unidentified radar echo (URE) was picked up east-southeast of Bentwaters, moving at least 4,000 mph. Contact was lost west-northwest of the base.
>
> At roughly 9:35, 12–15 UREs appeared southwest of Bentwaters. A check of the radar found no technical problem. Individual targets moved 80–125 mph. In 10–15 minutes, when 40 miles northeast of the base, the targets merged into one that was first stationary, traveled 5–6 miles, stopped again, then moved beyond the 50-mile radar range.
>
> At 10 p.m., Bentwaters plotted an unknown for 16 seconds, moving over 4,000 mph, perhaps up to 12,000 mph.
>
> At 10:55 p.m., Lakenheath targeted an unknown moving 2,000–4,000 mph that "disappeared" in the few seconds of one radar sweep. Bentwaters personnel saw a bright light move overhead at "terrific speed."
>
> At 12:10 a.m., Lakenheath radar again targeted unknowns. Visual sightings by base personnel were inconclusive. Before midnight, Waterbeach RAF station had scrambled a fighter jet to investigate. The plane's onboard radar locked onto a target for several seconds, so "there was something there that was solid." The pilot was vectored to one of the unknowns and made visual

contact coincidental with radar detection, calling it a "bright white light." He locked weapons on the target then lost sight of it; seemingly in an instant the unknown had circled around behind the plane and was following it.

The pilot returned to the base and a second fighter was vectored to the area, where the unknown was shown as a stationary object on both bases' radars. It then moved away at 400–600 mph. Radar operators reported no apparent acceleration/deceleration of any target. "[T]here was no build-up to this speed—it was constant from the second it started to move . . ."[3]

J. Allen Hynek ruled out a meteor hypothesis as UFO identifiers, despite the ongoing Perseids meteor shower: "The Condon Report in its analysis of this incident had stated: 'In conclusion, although conventional or natural explanations certainly cannot be ruled out, the probability of such seems low in this case and *the probability that at least one genuine UFO was involved appears to be fairly high*' (emphasis added)." Condon's conclusion: "In summary, this is the most puzzling and unusual case in the radar-visual files. The rational, intelligent behavior of the UFO suggests a mechanical device of unknown origin as the most probable explanation of the sighting."[4]

The article's author was quick to declare that Condon's probable-UFO assessment did not imply an extraterrestrial origin. Soon Philip Klass of *Aviation Week* suggested the Lakenheath radar was malfunctioning, but the author remarked, "[T]he coincident observation of the URE by the Lakenheath GCI radar, a different type (than Bentwaters' RATCC radar), and later by the Venom's (i.e., fighter jet's) airborne radar seems to rule out this hypothesis."[5]

Conclusions reached by the article's author:

- Meteors could be ruled out.

- A visual mirage was not possible.

- Anomalous radar propagation could not explain most of the instances.

"Taking into consideration the high credibility of information and the cohesiveness and continuity of accounts, combined with a high degree of 'strangeness,' it is also certainly one of the most disturbing UFO incidents known today."[6]

Note: Readers might think, "Let me get this straight . . ." Of the Condon Committee's 117 *preselected* UFO cases to study, 35 (*30 percent*) were left unresolved. Condon's group threw up its hands on the 1956 Bentwaters-Lakenheath airbases case, suggesting the objects in question were technologically advanced. "Puzzling," they wrote. Still, they had the *cojones* to call for an end to the government's UFO involvement: "Move along, nothing to *see* here," as it were. Once again, it would seem the fix was in. (Emphasis added.)

While you were away from your desk . . .

January 3, 1971

That night, at Aberdeen, Washington, three fuzzy round objects, two feet in diameter, moved over a bridge and hovered as an auto approached. The vehicle's engine quit and the radio had heavy interference, but the headlights remained on. The three objects then rose somewhat and drifted slowly down the river. The car could then be restarted.[7]

September 19, 1971

A young man at Bahia Blanca, Argentina, witnessed an anomalous object moving over pasture fields, unable to move as he watched. The object stirred up whirlwinds of dust, while cows appeared to change color in its presence. Afterward, his face was severely burned and he suffered from a persistent migraine headache.[8]

September 30, 1971

Secretary of State William Rogers and Soviet Foreign Minister Andrei Gromyko signed a bilateral agreement, to reduce the risks of nuclear war. Article 3 read: "The Parties undertake to notify each other immediately in the event of detection by missile warning systems of unidentified objects, or in the event of signs of interference with these systems or with related communications facilities, if such occurrences could create a risk of outbreak of nuclear war between the two countries."[9]

Chapter 25

1972:

The Government Remains Quiet

In an Information Report of April 10 from somewhere behind the Iron Curtain, five of the six topical discussions were redacted. As to the one shown, a member of a Soviet committee to study unusual phenomena gave a talk that was received with much humor. This "flying saucer committee" consisted of politicians, theorists, historians, and others with little scientific background.[1]

While you were away from your desk . . .

June 26, 1972

On a farm outside Fort Beaufort, South Africa, the owner was called out by a laborer who pointed to a fiery red sphere a short distance away. It moved into the open a second time, now fiery green, about 2½ feet in diameter. Then it turned to a yellowish white. The farmer raced into the house, alerted authorities, and returned with a rifle. He fired several rounds, believing at least one struck the intruder with a thud. It moved up and down then behind some trees. In time a warrant officer and a sergeant from the local fort arrived. After several more shots were fired, the ball emerged, shiny black. It maneuvered away and back again, apparently unfazed by the gunfire. One of the men snuck up from behind and fired once more, whereupon it turned gray-white and issued a whirring sound. Finally, it darted over treetops, parting the foliage with an unseen force as it went, and moved out of sight.[2]

August 21, 1972

At 2:30 a.m. a man was driving in Waukesha County, Wisconsin, when he spotted an object hovering over trees near the road. Its shape was undefined in the darkness, but it appeared to be 20–30 feet in diameter. Just then his engine and headlights failed and the radiator boiled over as he felt a buildup of heat. Before the anomalous vehicle departed he heard beeping sounds. In the aftermath, the car's lights, radio, and horn were inoperable.[3]

Chapter 26

1973:

MUFON's Year of the Humanoid

Dr. Jacques Vallee, a French mathematician and UFO researcher, said in conversation that as people experience increasingly strange phenomena, such as in UFO encounters, they tell fewer people. The mind is shocked by high strangeness and subconsciously adds to the incoming data, resulting in a mix of reliable information and conjecture. If the experience is severely stressful, one's mental state might not return to normal. Thus, in such a circumstance, "the mind should be centered on a reality so substantial and yet so far beyond form that no particular form will disturb its equilibrium." Many cultures across the ages had suggested centering the mind on this depth of reality. The report writer suggested balancing the person's mind first; otherwise the information brought forth thereafter would be useless.[1]

The Agency had intentionally shifted its focus away from UFOs toward other aspects of, broadly speaking, paranormal activity—extrasensory perception (ESP), remote viewing—amid rumors that the Soviets had a head start in those areas.

NICAP's Donald Keyhoe spoke to *The Oregonian* on the 1st of December, 1973, remarking to Portland readers that the only unanswered questions regarding UFOs were: (a) whether the crews resemble humans physically or mentally, (b) where in space they come from, and (c) their motive in surveilling Earth.

The continued government cover-up, Keyhoe emphasized, was prompted by a fear of public panic and chaos if the truth about alien visitors were admitted. A secrecy directive by the Joint Chiefs of Staff, JANAP-146, kept thousands of military and commercial pilots "strictly muzzled" by threat of fine and jail. Keyhoe's book, *Aliens from Space*, presented "Operation Lure" to coax UFOs to land for long enough to allow TV crews and linguists to intervene.[2]

Note: Joint Army-Navy-Air Force Publication (JANAP) 146(E), first issued on March 31, 1966, by the Joint Chiefs of Staff, required pilots and related personnel to immediately report sightings of, or encounters with, unidentified flying objects through established formal channels. Concurrently, it forbade personnel from communicating with anyone in the media or other member of the public about such incidents. A substantial fine, imprisonment, or both would result from any violation of the regulation. The rules were extended to commercial pilots informally by pressuring their airlines, stipulating that UFO reports were an intelligence matter, protected from disclosure by the Espionage Act.[3]

In an article in the journal *Science*, "Beings from Outer Space—Corporeal and Spiritual," the author, Hudson Hoagland, compared UFO research to the practice of psychic research in the 1920s and beyond. The problem for scientists was the impossibility of proving a negative. "The Condon report rightly points out that further investigations of UFO's will be wasteful. In time we may expect that UFO visitors from outer space will be forgotten, just as ectoplasm as evidence for communication with the dead is now forgotten."[4]

While you were away from your desk . . .

February 14, 1973

At 2:30 a.m., east of McAlester, Oklahoma, the pilots of a DC-8 cargo jet spotted a light a mile away, below them on the same path, confirmed by onboard radar. It suddenly rose up, rushed the plane, then resumed pacing from 300 yards. An oval shape was now evident, 75 feet by 40 feet, with small fins, a transparent dome, and three figures inside. The captain vainly radioed to keep a safe distance. The craft slid in front of the jet, arcing gracefully up and down before flying away. Air Force officers twice interviewed the pilots, first cordially, then later arguing that they had been mistaken.[5]

October 3, 1973

In the predawn light at 6:30 a.m., a husband and wife driving team in a trailer-tractor rig was south of Cape Girardeau, Missouri, on Interstate 55, nearing their terminal. The man saw something in his rearview mirror approaching rapidly without headlights. Then it slowed and began pacing right behind them. The overall shape was "like a turnip or top," its mass covering both lanes of the interstate. The upper and lower sections looked silvery and seemed to be spinning. A band of glittering "rainbow lights" shone in the middle. When the ship cast a beam of light onto the rear wheels of the trailer, the man leaned his head out for a better look, but "something like a red flash of fire hit me across the face and forehead."

He managed to bring the truck to a panic stop but was totally blind for the next 2½ hours. His wife drove them to the terminal, where they called an ambulance. A week of hospitalization and months of rest restored most of his sight. His glasses, blistered and warped, were tested by a prominent physicist who concluded that high heat was the cause.[6]

October 17, 1973

The Falkville, Alabama, police chief took a call about an unknown with flashing lights that had landed in a farm field that evening. When he arrived, he saw a figure, human-size, dressed in what appeared to be aluminum foil, with an antenna on its head. He snapped four Polaroid pictures. When he turned on the cruiser's overhead lights, the creature ran down the dirt road nearby. The chief gave chase on the primitive road but was unable to keep up, saying later, "He was running faster than any human I ever saw." Several residents in the area phoned the next day with their own UFO sightings of that night. However, the event soon turned sour for the chief. In short order his wife divorced him and the mayor asked for his resignation.[7]

October 18, 1973

The next night, an Army Reserve UH-1 (a.k.a. Huey) helicopter with a four-man crew was headed back to Cleveland, Ohio, from a day trip to Columbus. Captain Lawrence J. Coyne commanded the team. The sky was clear, starry, and moonless. The chopper was cruising at 90 knots and 2,500 feet. Both men in the rear seats noticed a single red light unlike an aircraft running light, apparently pacing them; one of them brought it to Captain Coyne's attention. Then the light closed on the Huey, seemingly on a collision path. Coyne took the controls and began a steep descent—2,000 feet per minute. The light slowed but continued to pace them, now above and in front of the Huey. It was discernible as cigar-shaped and gray metallic; it filled their windshield. A red light was at the nose, a white light was at the rear, and a green beam emanated from the bottom. The beam swung around and bathed the cockpit and men in green light. All sounds ceased for the crew; they felt no turbulence. After a few more seconds the anomaly accelerated, turned sharply 45 degrees, and sped away.

The crewmen now checked the altimeter and were astonished to find they were at 3,500 feet and climbing. The collective was still in the full *down* position. The magnetic compass was also malfunctioning. They were able to level off and continued their journey with no further incident. Afterward, seven other witnesses on the ground, from two families, were located. They had watched the Huey and the unknown in close proximity and had seen them separate.[8]

October 20, 1973

At an undisclosed location a woman was abducted from her car and taken aboard a UFO. Nonhuman beings conducted medical tests including taking blood samples and skin scrapings, and performing a rectal exam. Needles were inserted in her arms and abdomen. During the extended event she was given food and water. Afterward she experienced weight loss, depression, and sleep disturbances.[9]

November 6, 1973

At 9:45 p.m., air police at Kirtland AFB East were alerted to a breach of security in the Manzano Laboratory area. (Manzano carried on America's atomic weapons research, development, design, testing, and storage following the Manhattan Project.) The intruder was later described by an APRO investigator as "oblate spherical in shape, 150 feet in diameter, golden in color, and absolutely silent." The object hovered 100 feet over Plant No. 3, which stored atomic weapons. In moments, four F-101 Voodoo interceptors of the New Mexico Air National Guard were scrambled at the far end of the base. As those were assembling in the sky, the UFO began moving away at treetop level (under the radar floor). It quickly crossed over the Manzano Mountains east of the base. By the time the Voodoos arrived, there was nothing to intercept. Per one of the MPs in a later interview, officials at the base were greatly upset at coming up empty and chose to treat the incident as if it never happened. Intelligence briefs thereafter made no mention of it.[10]

Chapter 27

1974:

Gemini 4 Photos

Bruce Lowe, Executive Secretary of the National Security Council, sent a November 5, 1974, letter to researcher Brad Sparks—who in 1977 would cofound Citizens Against UFO Secrecy (CAUS). Lowe enclosed: (a) the minutes of a December 4, 1952, meeting of the Intelligence Advisory Committee, and (b) the declassified January 1953 Robertson Panel Report. The panel had concluded, Lowe stipulated, that UFOs offered no direct threat to national security. As a consequence, a National Security Council Intelligence Directive was not drafted.[1]

While you were away from your desk . . .

April 12, 1974

NBC network's episode of the *Today* show featured a UFO discussion including former astronaut James McDivitt, Congressman Edward Roush, and two civilian UFO researchers. McDivitt reported that, while aboard the Gemini 4 on June 4, 1965, he had seen a "cylindrical object with a long pole sticking out" that did not fit the position of any US or USSR space vehicle. In 1972 McDivitt had remarked that he twice photographed the object that day; the photo released by NASA showing the sun's reflection on the Gemini window, he asserted, had nothing whatsoever in common with what he had seen.[2]

May 17, 1974

Now surely, the Agency would have been curious about an alleged UFO crash on American soil. But judging by the official records released to its website in 2017, no, it was apparently not interested.

An apparent UFO crash occurred at 10:10 p.m., approximately 30 miles southwest of Albuquerque, New Mexico. At Kirtland AFB, technicians at the Manzano Laboratory on the base suddenly lost total control of their equipment coincident with a burst of energy never before experienced. Every instrument throughout the facility malfunctioned in seemingly dissimilar ways. Before the energy dissipated, a trajectory was plotted, and a recovery team was dispatched to the presumed impact site. An area surrounding the small mountain village of Chilili, New Mexico, was cordoned off from the public. Within a few hours an object described as metallic, circular, and about 60 feet in diameter (when reassembled) was transferred into a hangar at Kirtland.[3] Nothing further was ever openly mentioned concerning the incident.

May 31, 1974

Outside Umvuma, Zimbabwe, at 2:30 a.m., soon after a couple set out on a 179-mile journey, the car's headlights suddenly failed as a blue beam from above took control of their vehicle. The interior became extremely cold. They realized they were traveling at very high speed without lights. When they arrived at their destination the UFO was gone. They soon noticed that the auto's odometer had advanced only 11 miles; the gas tank remained nearly full.[4]

September 16, 1974

Near St. Helens, Tasmania, at 9:00 p.m., a woman and her two small children were driving home through a drizzle when static filled the car radio. A bright light appeared before them in the sky as the engine, headlights, radio, and heater all quit. Seconds later a "vibrating" noise surrounded the auto. All three felt painful electric shocks. Then the interior filled with a choking smell. The three abandoned the car and fled to the nearest home. An hour later when they returned to their vehicle, nothing was amiss. The mother, however, now had swollen arms and fingers, and the right side of her face was numb. Those symptoms gradually cleared.[5]

October 27, 1974

A British family of five was returning from an outing. At 9:50 p.m. as they neared Aveley, Essex, a bright light swooped down from the sky before them. The radio sparked as the engine quit and the headlights went out. They rolled into a thick green mist, whereupon they experienced several hours of missing time. Following the incident, the husband had a nervous breakdown. The wife and children thereafter could no longer tolerate meat. The husband and wife both gave up alcohol. The husband also quit smoking.[6]

Chapter 28

1975:

Ignoring Base Intrusions

Had the US Forecast Center, a division of the National Weather Service within the National Oceanic and Atmospheric Administration (NOAA), ever bothered with UFO sightings? (Redacted) said at one time many calls and questions were received. Scientific balloon flights had prompted some of those.[1]

"NMCC (National Military Command Center) notified the Operations Center that DDO (CIA Deputy Director of Operations) talking points contained an update concerning penetration of Loring AFB, Maine, by unidentified helicopter(s) flying out of Canada. Received copy via LDX and disseminated" October 28, 1975.[2]

While you were away from your desk . . .

May 3, 1975

A young Mexican pilot in a Piper PA-24 Comanche was harassed by three diminutive discs, each only 10–12 feet in diameter. Two positioned themselves at the wingtips, the third underneath where it struck and damaged the hull. His controls froze and he was unable to lower the landing gear.

He then radioed a Mayday. When the saucers finally left, he fixed the control lever with a screwdriver, was thereby able to lower the landing gear, and made an emergency landing at Mexico City International.[3]

May 5, 1975

At 9:15 p.m., a man was driving to his Pleasanton, Texas, home when an amber luminescent disc rose from the ground and approached with a whirring sound. He detected two figures inside the craft as it moved over his truck. A beam of light enveloped his vehicle and turned cherry red, heating the interior. When the intruder flew away, the driver's eyes were smarting and his hands and feet were numb.[4]

August 13, 1975

Air Force Sergeant Charles Moody was in the New Mexico desert outside Alamogordo, taking in the Perseids meteor shower at 1:15 a.m. He noticed a luminescent metallic object seemingly falling from the sky a football field's distance away. He adjudged it to be about 50 feet long and 18 or 20 feet wide. Wobbling, it stopped short of the desert floor and moved laterally toward him. He was now frightened and jumped into his car, but it wouldn't start. The intruder stopped about 70 feet away with a high-pitched hum. Through a rectangular window shadowy figures were evident inside. The humming stopped and he felt a pervasive numbness. The next thing he remembered was seeing the vehicle rising into the air. His car started without trouble. Arriving home, he realized he could not account for 1½ hours. The next day he experienced back pain; a few days hence, a rash broke out over much of his body. On the advice of a physician, he practiced self-hypnosis for his back discomfort and, to his satisfaction, recalled the particulars of an abduction experience aboard the craft.[5]

October 27, 1975

About 8:00 p.m., at Loring AFB, Maine, the white strobe and red-orange lights of an unknown accompanied by a whirring sound hovered 300 yards over stored nuclear weapons. It departed 90 minutes later after maneuvering over and around the base, tracked on radar. Two nights later, radar controllers detected an unknown intruder over the weapons storage area again. A helicopter was directed to within 1,000 yards of the unknown, but the pilot failed to detect it visually. On October 31 it was back once more, again interested in the weapons storage. This time it was detected three times by a pursuing helicopter that carried members of the USAF Office of Special Investigations. Despite having it in sight, the chopper crew was not able to intercept it.[6]

October 30, 1975

Wurtsmith AFB, Michigan, was intruded. As with Loring, its nuclear weapons underground were the apparent target. At 10:10 p.m., families in the base housing section noticed what they supposed was a low-flying helicopter with no running lights. By 10:25 p.m., security police at the base's back gate reported the same. Guards inside the Weapons Storage Area reported seeing an airborne vehicle low in the sky above. They were unable to identify it but heard a sound similar to a helicopter. Radar Approach Control tracked the object both over the base and up to 35 miles away over Saginaw Bay (Lake Huron). Staff in the tower did not *see* it—and never attempted to contact it.

In due course, a KC-135 tanker aircraft returning from a refueling run was vectored toward the intruder. Cat-and-mouse ensued as the tanker, flying at 2,700 feet and 200 knots, was unable to overtake it. A captain onboard who was a flight instructor recounted the final minutes of the encounter:

> I remember seeing lights similar to strobe lights which were flashing irregularly. . . . [A]fter observing the lights we determined that there were in fact two objects and the irregular flashing appeared to be some sort of signal being passed from one to the other . . .

Low on fuel and losing sight of the lights amid all the fishing boat lights on the lake, the crew turned back toward the base.

> On the way back we picked up the UFO again . . . [W]e turned back in the direction of the UFO and it really took off in the direction of the Bay area. I know this might sound crazy, but I would estimate that the UFO sped away from us doing approximately 1,000 knots. . . . On final approach we saw the lights again near the Weapons Storage Area.

The captain was questioned by the USAF Office of Special Investigations and cautioned not to discuss the incident.[7]

The next day, October 31, a note for the record was generated at the Alert Center Branch, USAF Aerospace Intelligence Division: "Contacted CIA OPS (Operations) center and informed them of U/I (unidentified) flight activity over two SAC bases near Canadian border. CIA . . . requested they be informed of any follow up activity."[8]

Chapter 29

1976:

An Uptick in Agency Interest

In an April 14, 1976, teletyped message, a source (name/place redacted) requested his report be classified confidential. "Source seeks guidance from CIA UFO experts as to material in his report that should remain classified."[1]

Also in teletyped form the next day, April 15, came a message (to/from redacted); the recipient, undoubtedly a superior, marked up the teletyped text to "waffle" on certain statements and redact identifiers. The message referred to the UFO (redacted—apparently a named study), which was given to (redacted), the Assistant Deputy Director for Science and Technology (A/DDS&T), "who was also briefed on the developments to date. Dr. (redacted) said he would show the study to a few people to determine possible implications of the information and would be back to us soon on this matter."[2]

Then, on page 2, came something of a blockbuster admission: "At the present time there are offices and personnel within the Agency who are monitoring the UFO phenomena, but again, this is not currently on an official basis." The particular phrasings leading up to this acknowledgment lent credence to the notion that some units within the Agency maintained an interest in aerial phenomena and that the CIA was involved with some manner of research already conducted—presumably in the recent past or perhaps ongoing. Seven years and change after its release, the Condon

Report was shopworn. This read like something newer. Then came that stark utterance, ". . . offices and personnel within the Agency who are monitoring the UFO phenomena . . ." A more obvious admission would never be made. The message ended, "In view of Dr. (redacted's) willingness to review additional information received on the UFO phenomena we will keep subject case open to your office for the present." Hence, the A/DDS&T, that is the CIA's Office of Science and Technology, would remain open for business—UFO business.[3]

On April 22, 1976, within an internal Domestic Communications Division memo, the writer said he "attempted to obtain analytical guidance on the UFO (redacted) subject." The A/DDS&T was asked if he knew of any official UFO program to answer questions posed by (redacted). After examining the materials, (redacted) said he would personally look into it. In a follow-up contact he said it did not appear the Government had any formal program to identify or solve the problem.

He continued, "Independent researchers (redacted) are vital for further progress in this area. At the present time there are offices and personnel within the Agency who are monitoring the UFO phenomena" unofficially. Open channels with outside sources were advised to keep the CIA apprised of any security threat or foreign applications. The writer offered to disseminate any further developments.[4]

On June 25, 1976, (redacted) met with (redacted) of the Agency's Office of Resource Development regarding ORD's possible interest in a UFO case. Copies of (redacted) materials were provided. ORD's potential interest depended on its evaluation of the materials. Additional information on the (redacted) system was requested. (Redacted) asked that ORD interest be kept quiet until analysis was complete but indicated he would stay in contact.[5]

On July 14, a redacted party sent a revealing note to the deputy chief of the Office of Development and Engineering (OD&E), who had expressed interest in the UFO subject:

> As you may recall, I mentioned my own interest in the
> subject as well as the fact that DCD (Domestic Collection

Division) had been receiving UFO related material from many of our S&T (science and technology) sources who are presently conducting related research. These scientists include some who have been associated with the Agency for years and whose credentials remove them from the "nut" variety.

The writer included attachments (not shown) from S&T sources and would provide additional material if the recipient were interested.[6]

September 10, 1976, sometime after 6:00 p.m., a London-bound British European Airways (BEA) airliner at 33,000 feet encountered an anomaly over Lithuania. A brilliant, stationary, yellowish light was 10–15 miles away and 5,000 feet or so below the plane. Difficult to look at, it illuminated a cloud below. The pilot alerted the passengers to his concern via intercom, saying he had asked Soviet authorities for an explanation. The light was in view for 10-plus minutes until the aircraft had flown past and left the light source behind. The Soviet respondent told the pilot he "should not ask questions."[7]

In a September 24 document, almost entirely redacted, is one visible and pertinent line: "23 September (redacted) with personal request to investigate UFO sighted Morocco."[8]

A November 18, 1976, information report, almost entirely redacted, had a revealing comment in paragraph 6:

> (Redacted) asked for (redacted's) personal opinion of the UFO phenomenon. He was told that 99 percent of these occurrences were traceable to either natural or man-made phenomena such as celestial movement, aircraft, or artificial satellites and that the other one percent cannot be explained—possibly hallucinations. (Redacted) then asked, "Do you think it is possible . . . could there be something coming from outer space?[9]

While you were away from your desk . . .

January 21, 1976

A Memorandum for the Record was filed at the National Military Command Center in Washington, D.C., concerning an incident at 5:55 a.m.: "Two UFOs are reported near the flight line at Cannon AFB, New Mexico. Security Police observing them reported the UFOs to be 25 yards in diameter, gold or silver in color with blue light on top, hole in the middle, and red light on bottom."[10]

April 22, 1976

At 11:10 p.m., an Elmwood, Wisconsin, patrolman drove over a hill to check out an orange glow and confronted an object some 500 feet away that he figured to be 250 feet in diameter. Hovering 100 feet over the ground, the ship had fin-like projections, landing legs, and six blue windows revealing figures moving inside. When it gave off a blue flash, the cruiser's engine, headlights, and two-way radio failed. The object departed quickly with a loud sound. Area residents reported that their TV sets malfunctioned in that time frame. The stunned policeman was hospitalized for several days. His cruiser needed a new condenser and spark plugs.[11]

July 11, 1976

Two Indian Air Force MiG-21 jets were sent to the Pakistani border, presumably to handle a border violation. Instead they came upon something crossing the sky at an estimated 2,600 mph. They described it as amber in color and saucer-shaped. It easily outdistanced them as they tried in vain to catch up.[12]

August 6, 1976

Near Gaspesie, Quebec, on a foggy day, a family was driving when a red "spotlight" descended over their car. Immediately the engine and headlights failed and the interior became uncomfortably hot. They pulled to a stop and climbed out, confronting a huge oval object with windows facing them. Strange-looking entities with huge eyes were inside. Momentarily the object flew away without further incident.[13]

August 13, 1976

About 5:00 p.m., a private pilot was flying a Piper Arrow between Diepholz and Petershagen, Germany, when he noticed a strange light on his left. Over the next 3–5 minutes it inched continually closer and assumed a position a short way off his left wingtip. It appeared oval-shaped with a yellowish center and a flame-orange perimeter. After several more minutes of pacing, the Piper suddenly went into two 360-degree barrel rolls. The pilot was able to manually recover a level attitude but not until the plane had dropped 500 feet. His magnetic compass was spinning wildly. He contacted Hannover Airport and was told that his plane and another object were being tracked and that help had been dispatched. In minutes two F-4 Phantom jets streaked by as the intruder accelerated forward then up, out of sight in seconds.

The pilot was told to land at Hannover and taxi to a special area. He was taken to an underground office and questioned for three hours. The interrogators would not identify whom they represented. Ultimately, he refused to sign a non-disclosure form, though threatened with the loss of his pilot's license for failing to cooperate.[14]

September 19, 1976

The Iranian Air Force case outlined below was reported by major media outlets at the time and has been a topic of multiple UFO documentary films. One day after the incident, an urgent meeting of US and Iranian generals was held. Later a Department of Defense document about the incident was released to FOIA petitioners. Yet the CIA made no mention of the matter in its 2017 files dump. This only substantiates a contention that cases with national security implications, even those half a century old, were withheld.

In the predawn hours, an Iranian Air Force F-4 Phantom was sent aloft from its Mehrabad Air Base outside Teheran to intercept an unknown over the city. Momentarily, while in pursuit the pilot lost both instrumentation and communications and so returned to base. A second F-4 was scrambled, piloted by an Iranian top gun, who proceeded to arm his AIM-9 Sidewinder guided missile. Immediately the plane lost power to the weapons control system. The pilot and copilot attempted to eject but that circuit malfunctioned as well. They were nonetheless able to land—followed overhead by the UFO.[14] It was spotted 25 minutes later by an Egyptian Air Force jet over the Mediterranean Sea, then later by a KLM crew and its passengers in the Lisbon area. It was ultimately revealed that a Defense Support System satellite had picked up signals of an "unidentifiable technology" over Iran that night.[15]

After the incident, a top-secret meeting was attended by the air base vice commander and a USAF major general, chief of the US contingent in Iran. The air-traffic supervisor at Mehrabad remarked afterward, "When they heard our report and the report of the pilots, they concluded that no country is able to have such a technology, and all of them believed it [must] be [an] object from outer space."[16]

Obtained under the Freedom of Information and Privacy Act, an August 31, 1977, DoD release recounted the events surrounding the Iranian jet chase incident. It added little to what was already reported but did reiterate the puzzling nature of the event. Given the multiple witnesses, the final report conceded, the circumstances had yet to be satisfactorily explained.[17]

Chapter 30

1977:

Start Spreading
the News

A non-sourced report from the Soviet Union on March 21, 1977, declared that, in 1976, Dr. Inal Akcyev was studying cosmic ray particles called phosphenes that caused Aeroflot pilots to *see* flashes of light while in flight, a possible cause of UFO claims.[1]

The opening statement of an untitled April 18, 1977, article in *US News & World Report* read:

> Before the year is out, the Government—perhaps the President—is expected to make what are described as "unsettling disclosures" about UFO's—unidentified flying objects. Such revelations, based on information from the CIA, would be a reversal of official policy that in the past has downgraded UFO incidents.

(The remainder of the article was deleted.)[2]

An April 27 article in *The Washington Post* related that, for scientists with a UFO interest, there was some "increasing hard evidence of recurrent, worldwide events that cannot be explained conventionally. The question, they say, is not 'is it real,' but how, through which discipline—astronomy, psychology, physics or social science—the phenomenon must be examined." At Northwestern University, astronomer J. Allen Hynek, a noted UFO authority, said more scientists and engineers were seeking to be involved—but anonymously. Despite a 1973 poll showing 51 percent of adults affirmed a UFO reality, researchers complained that the government remained "decidedly uncooperative." In earlier years as a USAF Project Blue Book consultant, Hynek said "military pilots told me they had their (cockpit camera) film confiscated, were debriefed, and told not to take it seriously or discuss it further."[3]

The *Houston Chronicle* on May 18 quoted CIA Director George H.W. Bush as complaining that the Agency "has been attacked for everything from 'hiding relics of Noah's Ark to capturing two humanoids and then letting them die.'"[4]

On June 3 the Agency's general counsel for the Deputy Director of Science and Technology (DDS&T) remarked that an acquaintance proposed a UFO research program as outlined in the attached letter (not shown):

- Analysis of existing policy

- Analysis of selected data and research

- Alternative policy strategies

- National research plan[5]

The secretary for a (redacted) Agency official sent a note to a White House liaison, attaching a letter (not shown). The correspondence was being forwarded since the letter writer sought to chair a new Presidential commission for UFO research.[6]

According to a September 22, 1977, report by TASS, in the regional capital of Petrozavodsk at 4:00 a.m., September 20, a huge flaring star appeared. "This star moved slowly toward Petrozavodsk and, spreading out over it in the form of a medusa, hung there, showering the city with a multitude of very fine rays which created an image of pouring rain." Minutes later all ceased and it formed into a semicircle of bright light, "red in the middle and white at the sides, then formed in this shroud." Witnesses said the incident lasted 10–12 minutes.[7]

An October 12 journal entry in the Office of Legislative Counsel indicated that Senator Daniel Patrick Moynihan's office telephoned on behalf of a constituent who requested all unclassified information on (a) Soviet gold production and sales, and (b) UFOs. The staffer said OLC had nothing to offer. (Twelve other topics were redacted.)[8]

As part of a heavily redacted December 22, 1977, Foreign Intelligence Information Report, paragraph 14 stated that, in late summer 1973, a Soviet man stepped outside one evening and spotted a bright green circular light high above. Over 10–15 seconds the circle expanded then displayed several concentric green circles. Minutes later it disappeared. No sound was heard.[9]

According to a December 20 report in the *Chicago Tribune*, the White House, State Department, and CIA all requested a private screening of the Columbia Pictures film, *Close Encounters of the Third Kind*.[10]

While you were away from your desk . . .

January 11, 1977

Forty-two miles west of Varanasi (a.k.a. Benares), India, the crew of an Indian Air Force jet transport encountered three luminous discs. The trio "flew past, circled once as if inspecting my airplane, then continued eastward toward Varanasi," according to the pilot. Shortly, thousands in the town saw the anomalous objects overhead.[11]

March 7, 1977

A French Mirage IV-A supersonic bomber capable of hauling a small nuclear weapon to its target was on a routine nighttime bombing exercise, headed toward the city of Bordeaux, when it encountered unknown traffic. At 8:34 p.m., the crew was surprised by a bright light ahead in the vicinity. The pilot, a colonel, said afterward, "I thought it was the landing light of a Mirage III interceptor jet. But we had not been warned about any other traffic." The Mirage bomber was clipping along at .95 of Mach 1 (approximately 700 mph). The pilot made a hard turn starboard but the light remained nearby, about a kilometer away, moving faster. "We had the feeling that there was a heavy mass behind the light—something at least as big as a Boeing 747." After they executed another sharp right turn, then a reversal, the unknown left at "I think at least 6,000 to 7,000 km/h—which is not possible for a plane. And there was no supersonic bang and no shock." The radar staff afterward prompted the crewmen to share their account.[12]

May 21, 1977

At 10:20 p.m., three British airmen at RAF Waddington, Lincolnshire, England, home to a Vulcan B.2 bomber squadron, saw a triangle of light moving erratically in the sky. In minutes it was on radar scopes at RAF Patrington, 50 miles northeast, moving in a zigzag pattern. It registered for four minutes, then suddenly the screens were "partially obliterated by high-powered interference." These returned to normal once the anomaly left.[13]

June 17, 1977

At a recreation camp on Cotile Lake, Louisiana, a father and two daughters heard and felt a sound characterized by the man as "ultra-low frequency." He later remarked, "I heard it and felt it vibrate my sternum." Nearby hovered a disc, 75 feet in diameter with a bubble top and blinking lights, suspended 50 feet in the air. The ship directed onto each of them a thin silver-blue beam that crackled the air. Their entire bodies glowed in an "eerie blue aura." Their movements were sluggish "as in a dream— slow, heavy." After 10 seconds the beams and auras vanished, and the craft glided away.[14]

Also on June 17, a young pilot in the Portuguese Air Force was flying a Dornier light aircraft in poor weather. Suddenly a dark object loomed out of the clouds nearby. The pilot veered left, radioed to ask about other traffic in the area, and was told there was none. Suddenly the object was right in front of him, pacing the plane from no more than six meters away. He estimated it to be 13–15 meters in diameter. On its lower section, he noticed, were four or five "panels." His directional gyroscope was now rotating wildly. The plane vibrated violently and went into an uncontrolled dive. He regained control at nearly treetop level and was able to land safely.[15]

June 18, 1977

The next day, two South African Air Force Mirage F1-CZ jets were airborne off the coast of Namibia. The weather was good. Both pilots had 15 years of flying experience. Following a routine 10:48 a.m. radio contact, at 11:15 both planes vanished from radar screens. Evidently, the pilots were pressing their radio call buttons in the final moments but nothing was transmitted. A Navy ship arrived at the last known location within an hour and a helicopter in two hours, but neither the pilots nor any traces of the planes were ever found.[16]

June 23, 1977

At 5:15 a.m. a newspaper delivery van was traveling between Noupoort and Middelburg, South Africa, when the driver noticed a dull glow emanating from a stone quarry he was passing. Immediately a phosphorescent object of indeterminate shape rose from the quarry and moved in front of the truck as its engine died and lights went out. Without further incident, in a moment the UFO left the scene with a buzzing sound. The van's engine restarted itself, quit, then started again when the accelerator was pressed.[17]

July 16, 1977

An Air India Boeing 747 was on final approach to Calcutta's Dum Dum Airport at 11:15 p.m., when the tower's air traffic control staff noticed a second object closing on the jet's position. No other aircraft had requested clearance for an approach. Witnesses on the ground described a saucer shape with a breadth equal to the 747's wingspan, rushing toward the airliner. Now dangerously close, the passengers and crew became aware of it. When the plane was two miles from touchdown, the intruder departed. Afterward the captain said it was a "strange-looking apparition . . . but a thing of real substance."[18]

Chapter 31

1978:

The New Zealand Film

The chief of the Agency's Minneapolis office contacted the Domestic Collection Division to relate the account of a man, somewhere in Canada, who claimed that as he was headed to work on January 27, he observed an "odd object coming down in the sky." No further description was given. Note: A Soviet satellite crashed in Canada on January 24.[1]

According to a non-sourced report from South America, the Argentine government announced that an object seen falling from the sky on May 14, 1978, was a satellite (no indication of origin). The crash site was located in Bolivia; the surrounding area was cordoned off.[2]

An anonymous person sometime in June 1978 sent a note titled "Parapsychology" to a major at the Office of the Assistant Chief of Staff for Intelligence (OACSI), Department of the Army. The state of "investigation of unconventional discrimination techniques" was outlined, in reference to the Stanford Research Institute (SRI) and parapsychologists Harold Puthoff and Russell Targ on remote viewing. A parapsychology course was offered at the University of Alabama, Huntsville, which included the UFO subject. Athens State University, Athens, Alabama, also offered a parapsychology course in its psychology department.[3]

Sociologist Marcello Truzzi of Eastern Michigan University resigned as editor of a magazine on paranormal events. That periodical was reorganized as *The Skeptical Inquirer*, with the Committee for the Scientific Investigation of Claims of the Paranormal (CSICP) skeptics at its core.

Truzzi in turn founded the *Zetetic Scholar*. He said interest in the paranormal meant abandoning the supernatural, seeking answers via science. Astronomer J. Allen Hynek's UFO research was an example, he offered. Instead of condemning UFOs, Truzzi called for serious examination by qualified persons. Paul Kurtz and CSICP, by contrast, were "tarring everybody with the same brush," Truzzi accused. "When you do that, you're cutting yourself off . . . from what I would call a protoscience."[4]

Bill Spaulding of Ground Saucer Watch decried official secrecy on UFOs. His group sued the CIA under the Freedom of Information Act (FOIA) provisions to reveal all its files. "It appears now that all intelligence agencies had something to do with this. We consider the Air Force to be merely the data collecting house. It appears when one goes through Project Blue Book, some of the better military cases are missing."[5]

Ground Saucer Watch had issued a FOIA request for all CIA materials on UFOs. A House committee did not object to their release.[6]

An investigative journalist for *The Washington Post* requested a copy of the approximate 900 pages of government UFO-related material released to Ground Saucer Watch in the previous week.[7]

While you were away from your desk . . .

January 15, 1978

On a flight from Evansville, Indiana, to Cincinnati, Ohio, the pilot of a cargo aircraft encountered two bright lights while at 5,500 feet, 20 miles north of Louisville, Kentucky. One of the lights was stationary ahead, the other circling nearby. Suddenly the latter shot toward the plane on a collision course. The pilot dove 1,000 feet as the anomaly passed overhead and out of sight. He then radioed the control tower at Louisville's Standiford Field Airport and was told that area residents had been reporting a UFO.[8]

January 18, 1978

At Fort Dix, New Jersey, three nights later, a bluish-green oval object approached and hovered over an MP's patrol car. The MP confronted a short being and fired five rounds. The being ran to the adjacent McGuire AFB fence line as the UFO ascended to join eleven more intruders overhead. A sergeant and others found the entity's body on an old runway and stood guard nearby. The sergeant described it as four feet long, unclad, and hairless. The being had a large head, slender torso, gray-brown scaly skin, and an ammonia smell. Blue Berets prepared it for removal to a C-141 aircraft dispatched from Wright-Patterson Air Force Base, Dayton, Ohio.[9]

April 23, 1978

At 7:30 p.m. near Goleta, California, a woman saw a bright airborne light nearby and heard a "zinging" sound while driving. Instantly her radio went silent and the engine lost RPMs, dropping the car's speed from 55 to 35 mph. The light's intensity decreased somewhat, revealing two green and two blue lights revolving around some sort of structured object. After a few minutes she had driven beyond sight of the craft, at which point the car's engine and radio worked normally.[10]

May 14, 1978

Just past 10:00 p.m., a man called the Navy's Pinecastle Electronic Warfare Range in the Ocala Forest of Florida to report a close encounter with a 50–60-foot, oblong UFO. Jacksonville air traffic control told the duty officer no conventional aircraft was in the area. While radar equipment warmed up, personnel observed a cluster of lights a few miles away. At 11:20 p.m. the radar detected a jetliner-sized object, 50–100 feet off the ground, which abruptly vanished. The same or a similar object was briefly detected at 11:40. About midnight, a target decelerated from 500 to 2 knots in one second, reversed direction, and disappeared.[11]

November 19, 1978

Around 3:30 a.m. at an undisclosed location in Italy, three individuals in a parked car were trying out a CB radio when they heard a sound like a harvester. The CB quit working as their vehicle was enveloped in red glaring light. They quickly decided to pull away then realized the car was 20 meters from where it had been and facing the opposite direction. With the red light fading, they drove off, catching sight of a sphere flying into the night.[12]

December 22, 1978

Over New Zealand's Canterbury Coast, on December 22 and again on the 30th and 31st, extraordinary aerial events captured the attention of the public as well as the Royal New Zealand Air Force, which placed fighter interceptors on standby. Never before had there been simultaneous radar, visual, and photographic connections in a UFO incident. At 12:30 a.m., December 22, an Argosy cargo airplane was heading up the eastern coast of the South Island toward Christchurch when the captain reported "a number of white lights similar to landing lights" in the distant sky. In due course, Wellington Air Traffic Control radar confirmed five objects for which it had no explanation.[13]

About three hours later, a second Argosy cargo plane following the same route also encountered five unknowns in the distance. Wellington requested the pilots to help identify them. The radar station located one particularly strong return in the vicinity of the plane. Shortly, the pilot shouted into his mike, "Something is coming toward us at a tremendous speed on our radar. It has traveled some twenty-four kilometers in five seconds" (equivalent to 10,800 mph). "Now it has abruptly veered off. It was moving so fast it was leaving a tail behind it on the radar screen." A Wellington controller reported that an unknown paced the freighter for 12 miles along the coast before leaving the radar screens.[14]

Whether announced or leaked, the dual encounters along the same route were an instant press sensation. Channel 0 in Melbourne spearheaded an experiment with the objective of a feature story. On the night of December 30, a recruited reporter and camera crew boarded another Argosy four-engine turbo-prop—leaving a side door open—for the same trip to Christchurch. The three-person media crew in the cargo bay was filming its lead-up commentary when the pilot sighted unfamiliar lights and shouted, "Get up here quick!" [15]

The reporter said later, "There were bright globules of light pulsating and expanding, lighting up the foreshore and town of Kaikoura." Wellington also saw the radar targets, about 13 miles from the plane. A spectacular light display ensued over the next 50 minutes, some of it captured on film. Individual objects' repeated disappearance and reappearance rendered filming difficult, though. [16]

The next night, December 31, 2:15 a.m., the special-cargo Argosy left Christchurch for the return to Blenheim. Almost immediately a bright object out of place was observed, confirmed by onboard radar. Over time its distance ranged from 20 miles initially to 10 miles away. The filming went better this time as the object neither faded nor seemed to disappear. Through the lens it had a brightly lit base and perhaps a transparent dome. Soon the pilot decided to turn toward it, but the anomaly kept its relative distance. When he turned to get back on course, it approached and passed beneath the plane. From that point until their landing, the pilots and media crew saw occasional bright pulsating lights in their vicinity. Some of these were picked up on radar. Channel 0 chose NICAP to analyze the film. It was thereafter shown to multiple scientific gatherings. No scientist came forward to explain these radar/visual/photographic sightings as prosaic. [17]

Chapter 32

1979:

Three Decades of Lies

CIA documents acquired by Ground Saucer Watch showed continuous CIA involvement since 1949, despite its repeated claim that it ceased interest in UFOs in 1952. An August 1, 1952, memo to the field called for continued surveillance while ordering that "no indication of C.I.A. interest or concern reach the press or public, in view of their probably alarmist tendencies . . ." An October 2, 1952, report had revealed the Agency's concern that UFO sightings could mask Russian air attacks or possibly "psychological warfare." Several documents detailed Air Force attempts to intercept or destroy UFOs, for example the 1976 incident over Iran. Spaulding of GSW pointed to patterns of sightings around military and research installations. He claimed that two retired Air Force colonels admitted on record the recoveries of crashed UFOs in Mexico (1948) as well as near Kingman, Arizona (1953). A thousand files verified that "the government has been lying to us all these years," Spaulding added.[1]

A January 18, 1979, article in the *St. Paul Pioneer Press* quoted William Spaulding, who declared the Air Force and CIA conspired to cover up UFO surveillance of military bases. He said he could back the charge with 1,000 pages of documents released under the FOIA. Further documents, film, and landing site residue were pending release. "We have information to categorically prove the government is lying and that significant findings have been suppressed." He added, "We have five ex-intelligence officers who will testify to this cover-up." Spaulding asserted US embassies were used to gather UFO data and send it to the CIA, NSA, and the White House.[2]

Likewise, on January 18, the British Parliament's House of Lords debated whether to establish an official government study of UFOs. Lord Davies of Leek was among those who supported the motion to advance a proposal to examine the subject: "If one human being out of the tens of thousands who allege to have seen these phenomena is telling the truth, then there is a dire need for us to look into the matter." In the end, the House of Lords voted not to pursue the subject.[3]

The next day, January 19, the *Philadelphia Inquirer* reported that GSW's Spaulding accused the Air Force and CIA of hiding UFO surveillance of military bases. He said documents obtained via FOIA supported his allegation.[4]

On NBC, host Jane Pauley of the *Today Show* on January 24 discussed the UFO subject with Spaulding. Pauley said the Defense Department had confirmed that unidentified objects visited nuclear missile and weapons sites in 1975. But *unidentified* did not necessarily mean saucers. Who was it? The intrusions were kept secret until Ground Saucer Watch used the FOIA. Who saw these UFOs in 1975? Spaulding's reply: The intruders were observed mostly by military security, on radar tracks at the bases, and by NORAD. They were also seen by sabotage alert teams and missile site personnel; people and equipment confirmed the reality of it. The remainder of the transcript was deleted.[5]

In a March 15, 1979, letter to ABKCO Films, Charles Wilson, Chief of the Agency's Plans and Policy Branch, emphatically asserted, "There is no organized effort to do research in connection with the UFO phenomena, nor has there been an organized effort since the 1950's."[6]

In the August 1979 issue of *Second Look* magazine, two letter writers discussed disparate personalities George Adamski, John Keel, and Jacques Vallee plus the December 31, 1978, New Zealand aerial sighting.[7]

The New York Times Magazine, in its October 14, 1979, issue, retold the account of October–November 1975 Air Force base intrusions in "U.F.O.

Files: The Untold Story." The author outlined the incidents at Loring, Wurtsmith, Minot, and Malmstrom USAF bases across the northern tier of the United States plus the Falconbridge, Ontario, RCAF base. The unknowns were verified visually and on radar from 200 to 15,000+ feet, sometimes as slow as 7 mph. Officials referred to the Loring and Wurtsmith incidents as helicopters but offered no firm identification. One report said the unknown "demonstrated a clear intent in the weapons storage area."[8]

The Joint Chiefs, NSA, CIA, and DIA were informed daily by the Air Force. FOIA-released papers showed that government agencies "remained perplexed about the nagging residue of unexplained U.F.O. sightings"— about 10 percent of all reports. Over three decades, UFOs had concerned the entire military, intelligence, and State officialdom. "But it is the CIA that appears to have played the key role in the controversy, and may even be responsible for the Government's conduct in U.F.O. investigations throughout the years."[9]

While you were away from your desk . . .

January 3, 1979

At approximately 7:00 p.m., three adults and a teen were driving near Hialeah, Florida, when the engine died. The driver got out and immediately saw a fast-approaching bright object emitting a buzzing sound. He found himself surrounded by blinding light. Two hours later police found him ten miles away. The others in the car verified the buzzing noise, the bright light, and the driver's disappearance.[10]

April 11, 1979

At Gormanston Saddle, Tasmania, a taxi driver was on his way to a passenger pickup when he came upon an oddity hovering over gravel by the road. The greenish light, about 30 inches in diameter, was tinged in purple. The light proceeded directly over his vehicle, illuminating the interior. His engine died and the two-way radio was inoperable for one minute until the light slid in front of the taxi and abruptly vanished. The driver was able to continue without further incident.[11]

July 10, 1979

Near Pinheiro, Brazil, at 1:00 a.m., a wealthy farmer was walking close to home when he was chased by a bright bluish light. He shone his flashlight on it and in turn was struck by a powerful beam that knocked him to the ground. When he regained consciousness in the morning, one arm was completely numb; his spine, kidneys, and right side were painful; his right leg would not support him without a cane. He had no appetite for the next eight days.[12]

August 27, 1979

At 1:40 a.m., in Marshall County, Minnesota, a deputy sheriff was driving toward a brilliant light near a stand of trees. Still a mile away, the light suddenly rushed and hit the cruiser in an instant. The deputy awoke across the road, his head on the steering wheel and skid marks on the pavement. He radioed in at 2:19 a.m. His windshield, hood, left headlight, overhead light, and two antennas were damaged. Both the dashboard clock and his wristwatch were 14 minutes slow. He was treated for flash burns to his eyes. Extensive investigation could not account for the effects.[13]

Chapter 33

1980-81:

Disclosure at Home and Away

In October 1980 came a translation of "Flying Saucers in China," a compilation of detailed letters by eyewitnesses of distant encounters years before.[1]

Translated from Russian, a 1980 edition (no calendar date given) of the voluminous journal *Bibliography of Parapsychology* included two articles of interest: "Methodology of Search for the Manifestation of the Activity of Space Civilizations on Earth," by V. I. Avinskiy, 1974; and *Sovetskaya Etnograftiya* No. 2, "UFO and UFO-nauts in the Light of Folklore," by Sanarov, March-April 1979.[2]

On January 26, 1981, a Foreign Broadcast Information Service report included a translation of an article in *Nature Journal* titled "Preliminary Survey of Unidentified Aerial Phenomena in China." In the previous half-year, nearly 100 eyewitness accounts were collected. The objects could be divided into three shapes:

1. Disc or globe, including ovular and egg-shaped. In daylight they appeared silvery; at night they emitted a red-orange brilliance. These appeared in about 80 percent of all reports. They were frequently accompanied by a white cloud or vapor mass.

2. Huge, long objects, even exceeding 1,000 meters. These rarely made an appearance.

3. Spiral nebula, consisting of a brightly lit central core and revolving arms composed of small points of light radiating from the core. Their volume was sometimes enormous.

Summaries of incidents from the late 1970s involving each type were offered.[3]

"Prior to 1978, 'flying saucer' incidents were virtually unheard of in China," though numerous reports from earlier time periods were recorded. Eyewitnesses included scientists, technicians, pilots, teachers, and other reliable observers. Frequently tens, hundreds, or even thousands of witnesses were present. "Possibilities that they were fabricated, imagined, or were rare psychological phenomena are not great." Recognizing all the known objects and phenomena that could be mistaken, applying such resolutions to some cases was "extremely farfetched." China's UFO reports were "pedestrian" in terms of strangeness: no power outages or interrupted communications, no photos or movies taken, no trace material, no peril to individuals or to social order, and no entity sightings.[4]

The assistant director of OSI, Herbert Scoville, drafted a reply to Congressman Joseph Karth for approval by the legislative counsel. OSI had received numerous letters from Leon Davidson in recent years and referred all of them to the Air Force, the executive agent on such matters. In the attached letter, Scoville stated further, "In summary, Mr. Davidson's belief that this Agency is involved in the 'flying saucer furor' and is using this as a tool in psychological warfare is entirely unfounded."[5]

As reported by *The Washington Post* on November 3, 1981, the National Security Agency squared off again with a citizen group demanding that its files on the UFO subject be opened to the public. This time the setting was the federal appeals court for Washington, D.C. An NSA spokesperson denied having any related documents: "The US government says it keeps no records on unidentified flying objects, because they don't exist." Yet, over 10 million Americans claimed to have seen a UFO. The court battle contested 131 specific NSA files claimed to be UFO-related.[6]

Would disclosure hurt NSA eavesdropping? District Judge Gerhard Gesell, upon privately reading a 21-page NSA summary of the contested files, ruled they were too sensitive to release. In federal appeals court, Citizens Against UFO Secrecy (CAUS) argued that the Agency, having for years argued UFOs posed no security risk, "cannot have it both ways." The FOIA suit challenged NSA, CIA, and DIA (Defense Intelligence Agency) policy "to withhold virtually anything they want under the guise of national security." The 1978 FOIA release of USAF and CIA documents revealed 1975 intrusions of missile sites and nuclear storage sites by unconventional objects unsuccessfully pursued by Air Force fighters.[7]

In a November 3 CBS Radio Network report, Peter Gersten of CAUS said UFOs pose "a real military threat." In 1977 he had argued in federal court that intelligence agencies must open their UFO files to the public. In 1979, the CIA released 900 UFO-related documents. In its file search the Agency found 131 documents originating in the NSA and thereafter returned them. The newest CAUS lawsuit was seeking those.[8]

In a "Viewpoint" opinion in the *Fairfax Journal*, November 30, 1981, Larry W. Bryant of CAUS followed up Peter Gersten's earlier remarks. Critics simplistically demanded infallible proof of UFOs, he said, but private investigative groups had no resources to provide it. Accepted legal proof was a valid substitute. Gersten, at the 12th annual MUFON International Symposium, detailed FOIA court actions to counter "a systematic effort by the federal government to suppress its hard-core evidence of UFO reality." The CIA might have been excused from FOIA rules. The National Security Agency declined in court to release 131 documents via FOIA "on the grounds that to do so would jeopardize national security." Earlier, government agencies had said UFOs posed no security threat. Bryant thus invited principals in the cover-up to please come forward.[9]

While you were away from your desk . . .

US District Judge Gerhard Gesell signed a court decision supporting the refusal by the National Security Agency to declassify and release

131 UFO-related documents that had been requested under the Freedom of Information Act. Judge Gesell remarked that such a release "could seriously jeopardize the work of the agency and the security of the United States." The judge himself had seen only a 21-page summary of the documents, prepared by the NSA for his review. In response to a later FOIA request for a copy of that summary, the NSA blacked out the great majority of the verbiage then allowed its release.[10]

Chapter 34

1982-85:

Habeas Corpus and Hudson Valley

On June 24, 1947, the modern UFO era began. In the same week 35 years later, Fred Whiting of the Fund for UFO Research (FUFOR) said, "There is considerable evidence to support the theory that some of these unidentified flying objects are extraterrestrial spacecraft, but there isn't any proof of it." FUFOR had sued both the CIA and NSA and obtained 3,000 pages of government documents.[1]

In a September 30, 1982, letter to CIA Deputy Director John McMahon, Sid Zins of MGM/UA Entertainment invited McMahon to a showing of the film "Endangered Species," which addressed the topic of ongoing cattle mutilations. Some ascribed responsibility to UFO involvement.[2]

In July 1983 Larry Bryant, for Citizens Against UFO Secrecy (CAUS), filed an application for a writ of habeas corpus in Washington, D.C., federal district court, demanding that the Air Force release "the remains of the extraterrestrial being or beings" allegedly held in secret custody. Said captives, if they were still alive, were allegedly subjected to "unwarranted deprivation of their right to travel." Bryant named the Pentagon, Air Force, Army, attorney general, CIA, and other national security agencies in the action.[3]

The year 1984 was devoid of any official CIA involvement in the UFO controversy.

Calendar year 1985 began quietly in terms of the frequency of UFO events reported. One incident in January raised eyebrows, however. At 4:10 a.m. on an undetermined date sometime before January 30, an Estonian airliner 120 km from Minsk, Belarus, encountered a bright light in the distance which, momentarily, shone a cone of light toward the ground, then a second and third. Then it appeared to become a green cloud. After first hesitating, the flight engineer contacted ground control. Immediately the unknown approached the plane, shining a blinding beam onto it. The controller on the ground said he found nothing on radar.

The unknown suddenly stopped in the air, dropped below the plane, then rose vertically, darted about, and finally paced the airliner at 10,000 meters and 800 km/hr. Lights within the cloud now twinkled. A tornado-like tail came out of it before it changed from elliptical to quadrangular in shape, then to a sharp-nosed "cloud airplane." The crew discussed what to tell the passengers—surface lights, the aurora, or something else normal? There were simply no easy explanations.[4]

An airline crew approaching from the opposite direction first saw nothing then described the cloud precisely. As the targeted plane passed over Riga and Vilnius, ground controllers detected the tandem of plane and cloud. They passed by two lakes and the nucleus within the cloud shone a beam toward the ground, allowing the crew to determine its size as equal to one of the lakes.

After the plane's safe landing came a statement by the deputy chairman of the Commission on Aerodynamic Phenomena of the [Soviet] All-Union Council of Scientific and Technical Societies:

> The fact that the object instantly changed its movement to the opposite direction and reached the ground with a beam of light from a very high altitude is unquestionably atypical. It was really very huge. It was natural to assume that somewhere distant, *many thousands of kilometers away, a global atmospheric or geophysical process of a type still unknown to science is taking place* (emphasis added). But it seemed to the aviators only that it was somewhere close by—a typical optical illusion, so to speak.[5]

What can one say? Wow.

In March of 1985, Ernest Volkman wrote an article for *Penthouse* magazine about the United States and high-tech espionage. He began the article with a recap of the June 24, 1947, Kenneth Arnold sighting. Volkman drew his own conclusions, asserting: "[O]nly a handful of people knew exactly what Arnold had seen. They knew that he had inadvertently spotted America's most secret intelligence operation." As part of an intercontinental aerial spying program called Moby Dick, Skyhook balloons had been outfitted with cameras. Arnold witnessed a Skyhook test flight, the author claimed. The remainder of the article covered advancements in spy planes and satellites. Note: Arnold recalled counting nine objects in a line. Nine stories-tall balloons in such close proximity—indeed formation—is highly improbable.[6]

While you were away from your desk . . .

February 26, 1983

About 8:00 p.m., three women and four men converged at White Pond, near Kent, New York, where a boomerang-shaped object was hovering silently. The black surface had red, blue, and amber lights. One woman noted crisscrossed tubing on the bottom. The airship soon moved away and minutes later stopped 1,000 feet above an I-84 exit. A teacher and two air traffic controllers present agreed that no known aircraft was this large.[7]

March 17, 1983

From 8:40 to 8:55 p.m., a huge, dark structure, generally described as either triangular or boomerang-shaped, hovered and moved slowly over a 10-mile area including Brewster and Carmel, New York, as well as Danbury and New Fairfield, Connecticut. The vehicle glided just over Brewster rooftops at jogging speed, then stopped above nearby I-84 as drivers gawked. All noted rows of multicolored lights and a centered strong amber light. Some detected a faint hum. One man, a private pilot, noticed a complex of piping on the underside. When another wished mentally for a better look at it, the ship pivoted and came directly to him. Police were flooded with calls all night.[8]

March 24, 1983

A week later, from 7:30 p.m. until 10:00 p.m. across New York's Westchester and Putnam counties, a huge dark boomerang or triangle was seen by thousands—300 phoning a local UFO hotline. Most said the ship was quiet and noted multiple light configurations and colors. A family in Carmel reported that a small reddish object shot out of its brilliant white beam. Near Millwood it paced an auto and hovered over a stoplight. Taconic Parkway traffic snarled as the anomaly zigzagged, made tight circles, hovered, and illuminated cars. Witnesses included several policemen, a meteorologist, and an aircraft designer.[9]

September 1, 1983

Outside the village of Weaverham in Cheshire, England, a man was riding his motorcycle at 11:45 p.m., when he noticed some kind of aerial light approaching. Cautious, he stopped on the road and turned out his headlamp. A dark wedge-shaped object loomed overhead. At his next realization, the lights of a car were coming down the road toward him. But it was a different road, and his watch indicated two hours had passed.[10]

February 3, 1984

Near Tingsryd, Sweden, at 1:00 a.m., a driver was beset by a huge object hovering low over the road just ahead. He slid on the icy road surface and nearly collided with it. His engine died in the process and would not restart. Eight small beings came out of the machine and took him from his car. The abduction was foiled and the man escaped when a lumber truck approached. When police arrived, they found him collapsed and in a state of shock.[11]

March 25, 1984

One year and a day after the flood of Hudson Valley sightings, once again a huge, dark, delta-shaped vehicle with multicolored lights was seen by hundreds of onlookers. From 8:20 p.m. on, police in Peekskill, Bedford, Carmel, and Kent, New York, plus Danbury, Connecticut, took continuous calls about a quiet structure moving parallel to the Taconic Parkway, gliding low and slowly. Attempts to reassure callers with the FAA's explanation that stunt pilots were responsible only angered many. A Carmel PD patrolman chased the UFO several miles to the Connecticut border.[12]

July 14, 1984

At 10:15 p.m., three security guards at New York's Indian Point nuclear power plant watched a massive dark boomerang shape approach. With an array of ten brilliant lights, it moved slowly over the facility. After hovering in gusty wind for 15 minutes, the structure pivoted 90 degrees and left. Ten nights later the same or identical intruder made another appearance. This time the guards, their supervisors, other personnel, and a security camera followed its path at walking speed directly over one of the reactors. When the facility's alarm system failed, a call was placed to Camp Smith, a New York National Guard base, to send a helicopter gunship. Moments later the intruder slowly moved away.[13]

The CIA did not record any UFO-related activity for 1985.

1986-88:

Claims and Counterclaims

No internal or external UFO-related communications were recorded for 1986 by the Central Intelligence Agency.

At the outset of 1987, three reputable publishing firms were poised to release nonfiction works of alleged human interaction with presumed extraterrestrials. Following the Japan Airlines 747 encounter with a UFO in November 1986 (see pages 277–78), the FAA was selling a package of the crew's audiotapes, air controller statements, pilot drawings, and radar images. MUFON membership was up 10 percent in two months. Author Budd Hopkins remarked: "I can understand the rationale of a cover-up. The whole economy—stocks, bonds, mortgages, capital investment—is based on the idea that 20 years from now, things are gonna be pretty much the same."[1]

Contemporaneously, an entrenched debunking organization, CSICOP (Committee for the Scientific Investigation of Claims of the Paranormal), declared that the alleged Truman-era documents concerning the 1947 UFO crash and recovery of four alien bodies were "clumsy counterfeits." The report was released by Phillip J. Klass, an editor for *Aviation Week & Space Technology* magazine. The committee's chairman Paul Kurtz, a University of Buffalo philosopher, called the UFO claims "one of the most deliberate acts of deception ever perpetrated against the news media and the public." Those efforts countered documents released by William L. Moore, which implied that Truman created a secret group, Majestic 12 (a.k.a. MJ-12) to study the downed saucer and its contents. A National Archives spokesman said the documents had an improper designation. Another alleging Truman ordered the MJ-12 creation was a fraud, Klass insisted.[2]

Apart from those wranglings, on the island of Barbados, on September 2, 1987, scores of residents observed several glowing spheres moving north to south in a moonlit sky for over ten minutes. They were also reportedly seen elsewhere in the eastern Caribbean—up to eighteen balls of light, each with a long, illuminated tail. Weather officials had no explanation.[3]

While you were away from your desk . . .

May 15, 1986

An elderly farmworker in Belo Horizonte, Brazil, watched as an unconventional vehicle hovered near his house for 30 minutes. A brilliant beam of light flashed across surrounding hills. More than once it swept over him. He tried to shield his eyes but one remained exposed. After the anomaly left the area, the man was diagnosed with 80-percent loss of sight in that eye. The arm shielding his gaze had a sunburn effect.[4]

August 1, 1986

Two men were fishing on Banksons Lake in southwestern Michigan at 10:30 p.m., when a gigantic anomalous airborne machine arrived and moved slowly over the lake. The air behind it had a wavy appearance. Abruptly there was a great flash and the intruder was gone. Though not seriously harmed, both men's eyes watered for several days thereafter.[5]

November 17, 1986

At 5:10 p.m., a Japan Airlines 747 cargo jet was crossing Alaska en route to Tokyo. The captain noticed lights pacing the plane from 2,000 feet below. He banked away, but the intruder—a rectangle of amber and whitish lights, with pulsating jets of fire and a dark vertical center—rose and positioned itself directly before the plane. He radioed the Anchorage tower, but the transmission was garbled. A huge object dwarfing the jumbo jet now appeared in the distance. The Anchorage controller notified Elmendorf Air Force Base, and both radars detected the unknowns. Rather than continue the intrigue, the captain decided to land at Anchorage and did so uneventfully.[6] Note: This incident has been the focus of numerous televised UFO documentaries.

August 6, 1987

At 11:00 p.m., between Barcis and Cimolaid, Italy, an auto and its three occupants were suddenly enveloped in a beam of red light from above. The car lost power and came to a stop. Within the beam it was as bright as day. When the light was extinguished, the car operated fine, but now they were at San Daniele, 40 km from the location they were last aware of. Ten minutes had passed. They drove to a hospital, all suffering from conjunctivitis (pink eye) and nausea.[7]

September 22, 1988

At 7:30 p.m., three people in an auto near Walcha, New South Wales, Australia, noticed a red undefined object in the sky. Suddenly the auto lost power while the interior's temperature *dropped* significantly. Though nothing specific was recalled as happening next, afterward all three related that they were fatigued for a week.[8]

October 24, 1988

Likewise in Australia, late at night, an Adelaide resident awoke, aware that someone was in his bedroom. Suddenly he felt an overwhelming fatigue and fell back asleep. At his next awareness he was undergoing a medical examination in what seemed to be a sterile environment, but the lighting was so brilliant that he could not *see* his surroundings. After another skip in consciousness, he woke up back in his bed two hours later. In the morning one of his arms was fundamentally though temporarily paralyzed.[9]

Chapter 36

1989

Lots of Activity . . . Elsewhere

An April 1989 Joint Publications Research Service (JPRS) Report emanating from Estonia related a national survey of its youth concerning their views on religion and other esoteric subjects. One comment related to the UFO subject: "While traditional, canonical religious culture attracts the attention of about half of the respondents, a majority (80 percent) are interested in questions linked to mysterious phenomena of nature and the human mind (UFOs, telepathy, telekinesis, the biofield, and the like)."[1]

An April 25 article in *Pravda* centered on an interview with Valentinas Artsishauskas, a noted parapsychologist at a laboratory in Vilnius, Lithuania. He defined "psychocerebronics" as the art of knowing the psyche. As a separate study, a device had allegedly been developed there to communicate with UFOs.[2]

A May 1 JPRS Report (no source shown) covered the activities and perspectives of a Soviet scientist, a winner of the prestigious Lenin Prize. He offered that persons with a religious aspiration may also gravitate to topics such as mysticism and "flying saucers."[3]

The June 1989 edition of the Journal of Scientific Exploration offered two articles by MUFON principals. In "Analysis of a UFO photograph," Dr. Richard F. Haines reviewed the investigation of a 35 mm photo taken on Vancouver Island, British Columbia, at 11:00 a.m., October 8, 1981. When shooting, the photographer was not aware of a disc-like object in the frame. Later microdensitometry, computer enhancement, and other techniques failed to reveal a hoax or a misidentified known object. The photo remained unexplained.

Dr. Bruce Maccabee authored "Analysis and discussion of the images of a cluster of periodically flashing lights filmed off the coast of New Zealand." The strengths of the December 31, 1978, event were the presence of seven witnesses, a radar track, two tape recordings, and 16 mm film shot with a professional camera. No known phenomenon could adequately explain the lights.[4]

The August 11, 1989, issue of a Bulgarian journal carried an article titled "Farmers Burning Straw to Make Up for Delays." One topic concerned a recent reported UFO landing near Moscow. "Unprejudiced investigations produced a perfectly prosaic explanation, namely the combustion of a large amount of dry grass."[5]

Another JPRS Report was devoted to "English Summaries of Major Articles" in China over July and August 1989. Paragraph 39 was titled "Unidentified Flying Objects (UFO) in Ancient China." In the 1980s Chinese culture developed "societies of UFO fanciers." Scientists were making efforts to find evidence of a UFO presence in ancient China.[6]

As reported on September 13, 1989, by Beijing Xinhua, at 11:13 p.m., September 6, an unknown was witnessed over the capital of Xinjiang Uygur. A dark cloud suddenly lit up. Then, after a golden flash, a saucer "with a black gap on its edge" appeared with a sound louder than an auto's engine. Bathed in red and yellow light, it hovered and rotated quickly before moving swiftly beyond the horizon.[7]

An unclassified Argentina Notice in late September 1989 was titled "Rocket Found in Desolate Area." In response to a crashed rocket found in a salt pan of Cordoba Province, Argentina, residents remarked that several unusual events had occurred of late, including UFO sightings.[8]

Moscow's TASS carried forward a brief note initiated by *Komsomolskaya Pravda*. On September 27, 1989, in Voronezh, some local residents were eyewitnesses to a nondescript UFO. TASS added, "The newspaper prints a feature on its back page on UFO riddles and enthusiasts studying the problem."[9]

The Foreign Broadcast Information Service (FBIS, successor to JPRS), in its Foreign Press Note for November 22, 1989, announced, "USSR: Media Report Multitude of UFO Sightings." Leading Soviet news sources and journals were publishing numerous reports of UFOs sighted throughout the Soviet Union. Moscow, meanwhile, was establishing a "permanent center" for UFO studies.[10]

FBIS went on to recount that, in July 1989, the Russian newspaper *Sotsialisticheskaya Industriya* reported on several astounding cases:

An anomalous sphere had recently crashed on "Hill 611" near Dalnegorsk in the Primorskiy Kray (Maritime Province) of eastern Russia. Numerous scientists studied the remnants: "a fine mesh," "small spherical objects," and "pieces of glass." The case remained open. One scientist reported finding gold, silver, nickel, alpha-titanium, molybdenum, and compounds of beryllium at the site. Some of the scientists concluded the sphere was extraterrestrial. A chemist claimed the mesh had threads measuring 17 microns, in turn made of braided threads still thinner. "Extremely thin gold wires were discovered intertwined in the finest threads, evidence of an intricate technology beyond the present capabilities of terrestrial science . . ."

On July 25, 1989, an engineer and workers at a collective farm witnessed the landing of a disc with two beams of light. After 20 minutes it flew away silently. An astronomical society spokesman said that, at that and other landing sites, an oscillator and electronic watches were affected.

On September 30, media all over the Soviet Union were receiving reports of UFO sightings on the ground and in the air. Editors were reviewing hundreds of reports related to UFO incidents. A member of the All Union Astronomical and Geodesic Society, then responsible for investigating anomalous phenomena, said that at locations of claimed UFO landings "electronic timepieces run at rates that are either too fast or too slow."[11]

Sometime in 1988, over the city of Borisov, the crews of two Soviet aircraft spotted a disc with five light beams. One pilot was instructed to approach it. As he did, a beam was directed at the cockpit; the crew called it an unbearably bright 20-cm light and felt heat from it. Afterward the pilot and copilot were overcome and rendered "invalids." Deteriorating health forced the copilot to quit his job after episodes of prolonged loss of consciousness. The pilot contracted cancer and died a few months later. Radiation affecting internal organs was listed as a contributing factor.[12]

Another newspaper, *Stroitelnaya Gazeta*, reported on September 16, 1989, that in August a group including one physical scientist began investigating a circular depression in a forest near Surgut where a worker reported a UFO had visited.[13]

On October 9, 1989, TASS reported that a UFO had landed in a park in the city of Voronezh, and was observed by many people before it left. *Komsomolskaya Pravda* reported on October 12 that a group of scientists had visited a field in Perm Oblast where locals said an object landed and left behind a circular depression 62 meters in diameter.[14]

Sotsialisticheskaya Industriya weighed in again on October 21, carrying forward the observations of hundreds in Omsk, eyewitnesses to the aerial maneuvers of a metallic sphere above the city for over five minutes. Pilots reported seeing it as well but said that, as with the airport control tower radar, their onboard radars did not detect it. When it left, a nearby military post alerted another post 600 km away, which reported sighting it five minutes later.[15]

The October 19–25 issue of *Poisk* included the observations of a physicist at the Terrestrial Magnetism Institute. He said he doubted scientists' claims of finding remnants from a UFO crash at Dalnegorsk, that the materials found were instead from an unsuccessful rocket launch in that region. He added that many other reports were actually misidentified ball lightning. As for the Roswell, New Mexico, incident of 1947, the same physicist said the crash was of a USAF rocket with four rhesus monkeys aboard.[16]

In the wake of that flurry, SRI International announced in December 1989 that it had screened 256 persons for remote-viewing ability. Among those, just eight were chosen for second-stage screening.[17]

While you were away from your desk . . .

At 3:30 p.m., December 24, 1989, the pilot of a Czechoslovakian L-29 jet trainer was near Chelyabinsk, Siberia, when he encountered a dark-gray, cigar-shaped, airborne object some 500 meters below him. He decided to maneuver his L-29 to *see* it better through his transparent canopy. He stared at it for four minutes, realizing his face felt hot to the touch. After landing, he discovered a red coating of soft skin on the exposed (non-helmeted) parts of his face; they were sensitive when pressed. Within a day the affected skin was thicker and crust-like.[18]

Chapter 37

1990:

Back in the USSR

One brief entry in a JPRS Report from January 18, 1990: Chinese scientists were making efforts to find "historical evidences" of UFOs, which were of particular interest to Sinologists.[1]

In a February 21 program summary for the Moscow International Service, item 15 of 20 stated that "policy holders of insurance company in China can file claims if attacked by ufo."[2]

Moscow's TASS reported on April 15 that, since March 12, as per the *Rabochaya Tribuna*, several hundred people had seen distinct types of objects along the Yarovslavl Highway:

- Large shining spheres and discs
- Six-meter-long pineapple shapes with "characteristic pineapple platelets covering the hull"
- Huge triangular "milk cartons"
- Inverted basin shapes 12–15 meters across

The hulls of various objects would flare up then "shimmer and flicker with iridescent flames." The anomalies moved quickly, stopped suddenly, and darted sideways. No sound was ever heard. Sometimes a shining cloud emerged from a nearby forest. Many were spending their evenings on rooftops to watch the displays.[3]

TASS further reported on April 17 that the All-Union Inter-Industrial Ufological Scientific Coordination Center, the first of its kind, was established within the Soviet Academy of Sciences. A ufological commission in the previous year had received 10–15 reports per day from all over the world.[4]

An information specialist for the Soviet Council of Ministers decried the earlier removal of economics matters from the headlines. "The press, for example, enthusiastically discussed the escapades of a UFO, which obstinately appeared in full view but impudently ignored the radars."[5]

As conveyed by the Moscow Domestic Service in May, scientists of the USSR and the People's Republic of China had begun a joint study of UFOs. They mapped out a program to investigate known cases and exchanged video and photo materials on new incidents.[6]

The editor of a new Soviet periodical on aviation and cosmonautics alerted readers: "This magazine will be a one-of-a-kind source of information on the space program, on unidentified flying objects, and on puzzling phenomena."[7]

Johannesburg (South Africa) Television Service, in its program summary for July 20, 1990, alerted its viewers: "Report on strange land imprints found in the south of England and believed to have been caused by UFO's."[8]

A JPRS Report on August 1 included a Soviet astronomer's essay entitled "Boundaries of Cosmology." Included were the remarks: "[E]ven in an environment of people with higher educations, questions about 'flying saucers,' 'space aliens,' etc. are most widespread. A segment of the audience believes science studies these things."[9]

Also on August 1, a JPRS Report quoted an exchange related to the Soviet lunar program. A major asked a major general: "Did you *see* extraterrestrials on your films? UFO specialists assert that the first people on the Moon saw them and that extraterrestrials allegedly observed the astronauts. Is this true?" The general replied: "People fond of any sensations wrested a phrase from the astronauts' conversation and are building their fantasies on this." The general remarked, when Aldrin said to

Armstrong, "Look out, they're watching us," he meant Houston watching Armstrong take skipping steps, not observation by ETs.[10]

A September 1, 1990, JPRS Report included among a list of "Articles Not Translated" from a Russian journal, *Ekonomika, Politika, Ideologiya,* one titled "Official American Science and UFO's."[11]

At Murmansk, Russia, on September 2, as residents looked on, a "large illuminated ball suddenly appeared above the city, slowly moving . . ." The "airship" was at an estimated 25 km altitude. Air Defense soldiers were among the observers.[12]

A JPRS Report on October 1 concerned a survey of Moscow residents. Among various findings:

> One other trend in the mass conscience [*sic*] at present
> is its growing mysticalness [*sic*] and the appearance of
> this we are encountering everywhere. This involves both
> a belief in miracles, flying saucers, the growing influence
> of various prophets, including psychotherapists, and
> much else.[13]

On the 4th of October came word of a new Soviet news bulletin, *UFO and Anomalous Phenomena,* which was awaiting government permission to publish. The first edition would recount the sighting by two cosmonauts on separate space stations, including their transcribed conversation. All information in the bulletin was to be verified. The ten-person editorial staff would visit UFO-related sites and gather eyewitness accounts. But it was feared the military would use the accounts to gain new insights and ban open publication. The bulletin was intended to be printed in several languages but had not yet been approved by the state newspaper agency.[14]

A new Russian television program, *VID,* premiered on October 5, and was reported on a week later. As one segment, "El Dorado" detailed reports of a 1989 sighting in the Georgia republic, including an interviewee claiming he was controlled by aliens. The reporter announced, "Although aliens think people on earth are more attractive than themselves, the aliens find people on earth to be spiritually ugly."[15]

A series of brief mentions were made on the UFO subject in the Soviet society:

- Soviet Commentary List for November 5, 1990, included an anonymous source who discussed the Soviet magazine, *UFO and Us.*[16]

- The Television Program Summary for November 9, 1990, on Paris Antenna 2 stated: "UFO sightings reported over weekend turn out to have been of section of Soviet rocket."[17]

- Soviet Commentary List for November 13, 1990, announced the first issue of a new Soviet magazine, *We and the UFOs.*[18]

- Comlist: Moscow Consolidated (radio) for November 16, 1990. Scheduled during the "hour for youth" would be a 5-minute rundown of new publications in the USSR on UFOs.[19]

- Moscow *Krasnaya Zvezda*, press selection list, November 22, 1990. A military officer disclosed radar tracks of UFOs around the time of a November 15, 1990, "rogue launch" of multiple surface-to-air missiles.[20]

- Commentary List for December 5, 1990. Among the nine topics, "more UFO sightings by some Soviet citizens . . ."[21]

- Radio Peace and Progress program schedule for December 9, 1990. One of 19 subjects: "The Soviet Union through the eyes of an Arab." Journalist Ahmad Abu Rashad discussed the economic crisis in USSR in addition to the phenomenon of UFOs.[22]

- Hanoi Domestic Service, Program Summary (radio) for December 10, 1990. A report on America's intentions in UFO research.[23]

- Moscow Television Service, Video Selection List for December 12, 1990. A video report on paintings depicting the artist's encounters with UFOs and his extrasensory powers.[24]

- TASS on December 6, 1990, reported on a peculiarity seen by cosmonauts in space. "Asked about UFO sightings, Gennadiy

Strekalov said that the crew saw a huge ball of light for seven minutes on September 26. 'This is probably an unknown natural phenomenon,' he said."[25]

- Comlink, Moscow Consolidated, for December 21, 1990. In the "science & engineering" segment, Boris Belitskiy answered listeners' questions about circles in English fields, "noting U.S. speculation that they could be caused by winds, pranksters, or even UFO's, also commenting on changing Soviet attitudes toward UFO's with increasing interest on scientific basis."[26]

While you were away from your desk . . .

April 6, 1990

In rural southern Iowa, a couple was driving home when they noticed a single red light moving laterally in the distance. Curious, they decided to follow. The light soon halted above a stand of trees, so they tried to get closer, but it abruptly disappeared before their eyes. Repeatedly the light came on when they retreated, only to wink out upon their approach. They finally gave up and drove away. The next morning the farmer who owned that field found a tight grouping of three deep oval depressions, each 14 inches by 36 inches, evidently formed by something of great weight.[27]

April 6, 1990

Driving from Gulf Breeze, Florida, to Pensacola across the Escambia Bay Bridge, around 10:50 p.m., a couple's attention was drawn to an aerial object shaped like a long isosceles triangle. The structure was motionless or moving slowly above the Pensacola shore. It displayed a centered red light on the bottom and pairs of white lights at the points. Suddenly, they could neither *see* nor hear the bridge traffic around them. The triangle moved out over the bay as the couple drove cautiously forward, fearing a collision. They pulled into a parking lot at the bridge's end and climbed out to *see* the structure above the water. When it receded into the night, they became aware of normal traffic again.[28]

September 1, 1990

At Williams Lake, British Columbia, a couple rose from their bed at 4:10 a.m. Over the roof of their son's home next door was a red glow. Through a light fog they discerned a cone of red light overhead, some 75 feet across at the top. It remained over the yard for 20 minutes before leaving. Upon awakening later in the morning, the wife had a nosebleed that persisted for three weeks. Her doctor could only say it was a severe nasal irritation without offering a cause.[29]

Chapter 38

1991:

USSR—Nay, Russia

Among various Soviet-based TV and radio programming schedules, commentary lists, and the like for January 1991 were three of particular note:

- Moscow International Korean (radio schedule), January 19, 1991. "... on interest of world media in unidentified flying objects."[1]

- BBC Hungary Television Program Summary, January 21, 1991. Video report on unidentified flying object spotted in Kecskemet.[2]

- Comlist: Moscow Consolidated, January 21, 1991. Video discussed a local man's claims of repeated contacts with an alien life form, plus other paranormal topics.[3]

The January 22 edition of *Pravda* addressed a January 18 "report on observation of unidentified flying object in south Moravia, possibly a destroyed satellite."[4]

Also appearing on January 22, Moscow's *Rabochaya Tribuna* commented on the prospect of repurposing an obsolete radar station. Rather than demolishing it, the writer suggested retrofitting it as a center for UFO research. "Then, perhaps, we will figure out jointly who these 'strange guests' are and what they want."[5]

On the night of January 19, in south Moravia at 11:17 p.m., for three minutes, area residents saw a light like a comet's tail, debris occasionally falling from it.[6]

In the Moscow Consolidated Comlist's "Science & Engineering" segment on January 25, Boris Belitskiy answered a Kenyan listener's inquiry, "mentioning in USSR possibility of extraterrestrial research, confirmation that there has never been an official statement on capture of a UFO."[7]

On January 30, 1991, a new Cypriot Greek-language magazine, "Cruising—Greek-Language Magazine," included an article on Soviet UFO witnesses.[8]

A JPRS Report of March 11, 1991, implied a correlation between a Chinese government crackdown on pornographic magazines and the ascension of other periodicals that offered "healthy, forward-looking, colorful, and realistic content." Among those magazines that were gaining new readers was *Feidie Tansuo* (*Probing the Secrets of Flying Saucers*), which was printing 300,000 copies, a 25-percent increase (time period unstated).[9]

From Moscow's TASS on April 12, 1991, "A shattering explosion shook this small town in the heart of Russia." Occurring at 1:30 a.m. in Sasovo, it knocked out most windows in the town, injuring some residents. High rises rocked heavily, but earth tremors were ruled out. In a field 1.5 km outside the town, a crater 28 meters in diameter and 3.5 meters deep was discovered. Emergency crewmen on the scene detected no changes to radiation levels or airborne chemical composition. The unusual form of the crater dismissed notions of a bomb or artillery shell. The mayor suggested that stored saltpeter might have spontaneously exploded. An emergency task force was investigating the matter.[10]

On the 14th of April, Soviet Army General Ivan Tretyak, Deputy Minister of Defense, was interviewed on Moscow's main TV channel, CTV1, discussing a range of issues and viewpoints. On the matter of reported aerial phenomena, he said no UFOs had been recorded by air defense forces. Asked whether he personally accepted a UFO reality, Tretyak replied, "As yet I do not. I believe something else, that modern science and technology are capable of creating such spacecraft that could appear above us."[11]

Following up on the Sasavo tragedy, *Pravda* clarified that at midnight, April 12, a huge explosion ripped off roofs and blew in windows in the Ryazan area town. As yet unresolved, disparate public speculation included:

munitions left from war, an air bomb, a meteorite, and UFOs. A crater 28 meters in diameter and 4 meters deep was found one kilometer away.[12]

As reported by TASS on April 19, in Kazakhstan two militia patrols spotted "a kind of fire" near a mountain peak in a recreation area. An array of reds burst from its center. One of the vehicles was within 200 meters when "a few rays swept across the car and it stopped dead." The UFO dimmed its "searchlights" and flew away.[13]

Tretyak and Those Denials

On April 20, 1991—a week after being interviewed on Moscow's CTV1—Army General Ivan Tretyak spoke on television again on the UFO topic, expanding on his earlier remarks: "I have recently had a large article in *Literaturnaya Gazeta*. I would like to tell you that UFO questions involve a great number of myths. A great number of tall stories. In practice, in saying that they were here and [we] saw them and registered them, I couldn't say that at all.[14]

On May 21, Moscow Consolidated news service and Moscow International Service, both Russian news giants, reported on something that had happened on May 11 at the Mir space station. Summarizing the public's reaction, Consolidated announced, ". . . some (callers) want to know about unidentified flying objects . . ."[15]

On Moscow's CTV1, during a filming of the Mir from the Soyuz cargo craft before docking on May 11, 1991, a "phosphorescent" object had been seen on screen hovering near the space station. The Soyuz pilot speculated it might have been a piece from that craft. The commentator on the ground said ominously, "[T]here is nothing cheerful about the fact that an object of quite a considerable size is flying around the station, even if it is not a part of the Soyuz transport craft." He followed up, "The fact is quite interesting indeed and, perhaps, fairly alarming."[16]

The Moscow Russian Television Network (Vesti) TV Program Summary for June 2, 1991 announced: "Humorous video report from Astrakhan which is allegedly visited frequently by flying saucers."[17]

Johannesburg's SABC TV, in its program summary for July 9, included a video report on a UFO sighting locally (no details).[18]

Then on July 15 came an entry to the Soviet Commentary List: From *USSR Today*, "Report of sighting of UFO in Krasnoyarsk."[19]

At the village of Atsavan, Armenia, on August 4, an unknown object landed about 9:30 p.m. and remained, lights twinkling and changing shape, until 3:00 a.m.[20]

Contained in the August 31, 1991, JPRS Report was the headline "*Pravda* Urges Readers to Contribute News, Ideas." Given all newspapers' new status following the Soviet dissolution, *Pravda* urged readers to submit news stories: from encounters with "flying saucers" to interviews with politicians. "We will buy news."[21]

The Hanoi Television Program Summary for September 10, 1991, included "UFO's continue to be a myth for scientists."[22]

A commentary in the September 27, 1991, periodical *Sovetskaya Rossiya* by a Mr. Abalkin regarding the remaking of the USSR, expressed the writer's distress over the nation's institutions. "[I]n such crisis situations there begins a mass belief in aliens, UFOs, extrasensory perception, and much else."[23]

As the months of 1991 progressed, Russian newspapers increased their reporting of UFO incidents. The still-evolving Russian government, without the wider and burdensome Soviet Union to administer, encouraged all media to speak out on a great variety of topics and issues, not the least of which was the persistence of unidentified flying object reports. Meanwhile, Army General Tretyak showed the basic and necessary political skills of backtracking and playing both sides of the street.

Now Deputy Minister of Defense, General Tretyak gave a lengthy interview in the November 9, 1991, issue of the weekly newspaper *Literaturnaya Gazeta*. He confirmed that jet fighters had in recent years encountered UFOs in Soviet airspace. On March 2, 1991, a Russian interceptor obtained photographs plus both optical and thermal signals from an unknown. "[S]ome 'stealth-like' capacity prevented the recording of radar signals." Tretyak believed the narrow frequency band of the air defense forces radars prevented radar returns. Asked why he had not ordered the intruder shot down, he replied wryly, "It would be foolhardy to launch an unprovoked attack against an object that may possess formidable capacities for retaliation."[24]

General Tretyak related an event from an unspecified evening north-east of Moscow. For over three hours, two pulsating lights roamed the area in tandem, "moving as if they were fixed in position in relation to each other." He said it was premature to consider the unknowns visiting Earth a threat to security or sovereignty. He advised that the public adopt a critical, cautious attitude. "He emphasized, however, that some of the UFOs, as demonstrated by evidence obtained by his interceptor pilots, are real."[25]

In the town of Corrientes, Argentina, a 15 kg metal object fell through the roof of a home, landing on the couple's bed. (Presumably they were away.) The 35 cm object was green; no other details given. "It may be a cast iron piece that came loose from a satellite or a flying object," the writer said.[26]

The Russian television program summary for October 20, 1991, included a mention that the UFO Congress opened in Moscow that day.[27]

The JPRS Report for October 26, 1991, cited an article in *Izvestiya*, "'Sverdlovsk Syndrome' Studied." Among many potential causes of a mysterious illness overtaking the agricultural region were the "intrigues of UFO's."[28]

Moscow Central Television aired an October 28, 1991, segment on pollution in a Maritime Kray. Several years before, a UFO had allegedly crashed on a particular hill outside Dalnegorsk. As witnesses climbed toward it, the unknown vanished. Residents said UFOs were a common occurrence. What attracted the visitors? The moonscape of strip mined rubble must have been suitable for only a UFO landing, the voiceover said.[29]

In a non-sourced report by (redacted), the director of the Soviet Institute of Economics reflected on the USSR's breakup. He opined, UFO reports circulate during difficult times.[30]

While you were away from your desk . . .

At 8:30 p.m., April 23, 1991, in Plaistow, New Hampshire, a couple driving home saw a glowing disc with a hazy ring around the mid-section. The craft hovered, ascended and descended, turned abruptly, fluttered, and wobbled. Over the next four hours policemen in Plaistow and Atkinson tracked its movements. Once it appeared to land but quickly rose up and away when officers approached.[31]

Chapter 39

1992-94:

Spy Planes and Homemade Saucers

High-altitude testing of the U-2 in the mid-1950s led to a "tremendous increase" in UFO reports, according to Agency sources. A major CIA publication in 1992 recounted the period. Many airline pilots flying in early evening were fooled by the anomaly high above, its wings glinting in the sun's rays. The article's author declared (dubiously), "U-2 and later OXCART flights accounted for more than one-half of all UFO reports during the late 1950s and most of the 1960s."[1]

In a formal January 1992 visit to Ulyanovsk, Russian President Boris Yeltsin was shown a "thermoplane," a saucer-shaped vehicle with the promise of multiple uses.[2]

To quell a rumor that a Soviet submarine—temporarily grounded in a Swedish fjord a decade earlier—carried nuclear torpedoes, a Swedish Coast Guard commander said later, ". . . the racket raised over the last 10 years about invasions of Swedish skerries by foreign submarines was simply fantasy, like with flying saucers."[3]

On February 11, 1992, the South Korean Air Force scrambled 18 interceptors, a helicopter, and a cargo plane in response to an unknown intruder on radar tracked at nearly Mach 1. At a point, the unknown disappeared from radar. A search of the area found nothing. A spokesperson speculated that overlapping radars might have produced a phantom signal.[4]

Robert Durant on February 20, 1992, detailed the interests of former Naval Intelligence Commander Cecil B. "Scott" Jones in parapsychology and ufology. Jones was also a MUFON consultant.[5]

Moscow Radio's schedule for April 2, 1992, included a "Report on *Economic Weekly* Article on UFO's," April 2, 1992.[6]

The China UFO Research Organization (CURO) held a conference in Beijing in May. CURO, organized in 1978, was included in the China Association for Science and Technology.[7]

In other UFO-related material mentioned on the radio program:

- The Fourth National Congress of the China UFO Society reaffirmed it would always follow the dialectical materialist guiding principle and a practical, scientific attitude.

- A 1978 UN resolution had asked all nations to pay close attention to the UFO problem.

- Some 400,000 people worldwide claimed to have witnessed a UFO. In the previous decade plus, 5,000 reports were registered on the China mainland.

- Chinese scientists studied ball lightning, superconductivity, and other physical phenomena.

The UFO Society's president said "studying UFOs with a serious scientific attitude will contribute to the development of science and civilization as well as to maintaining social stability." China would seek more cooperation and exchanges with other countries.[8]

A June 16, 1992, JPRS Report featured an article in Moscow's *Rabochaya Tribuna,* "On 'Flying Saucer'" that stated: "The rumors that the military industrial complex . . . is rather seriously interested in 'flying saucers' are justified." The essay referred to "Mohammed's Tomb," a Russian-built saucer-shaped object from a cooled superconductor freely levitating in a magnetic field. Technical problems were resolved using a "fast electron flux," which allowed speeds faster than the eye could follow. Aboard a space vehicle, a superconductor surrounded by such fluxes could create both a current and an electromagnetic field. "The vehicle will soar, as if floating in the electron medium which is itself created around itself." . . . "The sphere is the perfect shape for interstellar travel. Yet for moving in an atmosphere, it is difficult to find anything better than the 'saucer.'"[9]

Moscow's *Krasnaya Zvezda* newspaper, in its August 6, 1992, edition, reported that aircraft and ground crews had searched for a missing SU-27 jet interceptor that disappeared July 25. The aircraft was at 7,500 meters altitude when it was lost from radar. No trace of a crash or even a radio beacon distress signal had been found. Air Defense Headquarters noted that "a UFO had been sited [*sic*] in the crash area during the SU-27's flight."[10]

An August 26, 1992, JPRS Report described a weeklong air show near Zhukovskiy, Russia. "Some of the aircraft had radical new designs suggestive of flying saucers."[11]

Moscow's Central Television First aired an interview with an official of the Ministry of Defense Space Units that included this intriguing quote:

> I personally do not believe in the existence of UFO's in the form described as some kind of mysterious apparatus from which humanoids appear. However, I can confirm that there are real, to date incomprehensible and unidentifiable phenomena, inasmuch as I have seen such phenomena during a flight in an aircraft . . . in the form of a ray of light which performed definite movements in the air . . .[12]

As reported on October 23, 1992, by the Khabarovsk Radio Network, on July 24, a Russian SU-27 pilot returning from antiaircraft and missile training went missing near the Okhotsk Sea coast when contact was suddenly lost. The plane had experienced an engine malfunction during the flight but was deemed flyable. Possible explanations put forward included an accident, loss of consciousness, escape to another country, or abduction by a UFO. Investigation revealed no trace of the interceptor in Japan, South Korea, or the United States.[13]

An unknown aerial object near the Shetland Islands was observed at high speed and drew speculation about a top-secret American spy plane (SR-71 Blackbird successor), rumored to reach 5,500 mph. The local police, coast guard, and observatory recorded sightings of a large white, low-flying object at 9:00 p.m., December 12, 1992.[14] Note: Somewhere in rumor or myth was the Aurora, with a triangular outline, the supposed next in line. Whether the Aurora was actually built or flown was never confirmed.

Reported by *Krasnaya Zvezda* on January 14, 1993, the circulation of Russian military newspapers had declined in recent years. To restore readership to prominence, their editors had broadened the subjects covered. "It is true that some military publications, in trying to attract readers, are filling their pages with light fiction, detective stories, and yarns about UFO's."[15]

Moscow Central Television First furthered speculation on human-created discs. A "large" saucer-shaped structure was filmed—exterior only—at the Saratov aviation factory. The developer claimed that it could lift half its weight and, with its air cushion, land on snow or water. No mention was made of the propulsion system or any performance data.[16]

From a non-sourced report, the Japanese Ministry of International Trade and Industry (MITI) planned to form a research institute to study parapsychology, including telepathy and clairvoyance, plus UFOs, for application to next-generation industry. The goal was an industry more sensitive to human needs for art, inner peace, and other intangibles. Brain wave checks of claimed telepaths, enhanced plant growth via music, and other correlative scientific examinations would be applied. Virtual reality applications for audio-visual equipment would logically be a target.[17]

The first test models of a high-velocity, economically efficient "flying saucer" aircraft were being developed at the Saratov Aviation Plant, as reported by Radio Moscow World Service on March 9, 1993. With its air cushion, the aircraft could land anywhere. Passenger models would carry from 20 to, eventually, 2,000 people.[18]

The *Canadian Weekly World News* reported on March 27, 1993, that US intelligence had obtained a 250-page report of a UFO attack on a Russian military unit in Siberia. Per the KGB, the unit was conducting routine training when a saucer arrived overhead. Someone fired a surface-to-air missile, which struck the disc, causing it to crash. Five short beings with oversized heads and eyes emerged from the wreckage, joined together and transformed into a brilliantly lit sphere. It issued buzzing and hissing sounds then grew much larger and "exploded," turning 23 soldiers into sandstone. Two men a distance away survived. The debris and "petrified" men were taken to a secret facility near Moscow.[19] Note: As has often been said, consider the source.

An April 1, 1993, JPRS Report quoted the chief of the Russian Ministry of Defense Space Units, who said some UFO sightings were Soviet space launches. However, about five years before, an incident wherein three unknowns passed over the Baykonur facility (Russia's Cape Canaveral) was not resolved. As expressed by the head of Russia's space personnel, ". . . I cannot deny the possibility of the existence of UFO's as many people do."[20]

The Moscow periodical *Argumenty I Fakty* for April 1, 1993, included discussions of certain facilities, for example, Baykonur, plus the budget and UFOs.[21]

Per ITAR-TASS World Service, a prominent Russian economics minister predicted that "'flying saucers' could become a normal form of air transport in Russia."[22]

The Moscow Russian Television Network addressed the Saratov Aviation Plant's most unusual project, the "flying saucer," on July 8, 1993. It would, in theory, be able to land anywhere without a runway, carry passengers and cargo, help fight fires, prospect for minerals, and provide a normal living environment in extreme weather conditions.[23]

Izvestiya reported on July 14, 1993, that the Ekip firm had built an economical, saucer-shaped prototype aerial vehicle. The 2.5-meter drone flew over the plant's airfield at Saratov in 1992. A full-scale model would be 25 meters in diameter and weigh 120 tons, capable of carrying half that weight in cargo. It would fly at 8–10 km altitude over 8,500 km at 650–700 km/hr. The production model would cost $70 million per copy. Several countries had expressed interest, but Russian authorities had not offered funding for its assembly.[24]

Izvestiya again addressed the prospect of human-created flying discs:

> Yermishin's office contained . . . a machine of an intrinsi-
> cally new design that is reminiscent of a fantastic 'flying
> saucer.' The series-produced machine would soon receive
> its international certificate and join 'Boeing'; it cost $21
> million. The saucer had already been made up in metal,
> and preparation for series production was supposedly
> underway.[25]

As reported by *Pressfax* on the final day of August 1993, a renewed
Pravda intended to cover, among many topics, "encounters with 'flying
saucers' . . ."[26]

Radio Moscow World Service announced on September 3, 1993,
"Russian scientist from Khabarovsk claims in local press article that aliens
cause explosions on earth to use the energy for boosting the operation of
their UFOs."[27]

A non-sourced December 7, 1993, document reported that a jointly
produced Taiwan-Mainland UFO symposium in Beijing had concluded.
In their tallies of sightings over the years, nearly 6,000 UFOs had been
reported across the Taiwan Straits. Over 5,000 sightings had occurred
on the Chinese mainland. Some "defied rational explanation." Witnesses
included observatory staff plus civilian and military pilots. Four months
earlier on August 7, "two rim-linked, hat-like objects" soared over Taipei
International Airport for 15 minutes, media reported. The world over, an
estimated 400,000 reports had been made since World War II. In 1978
the UN had called on all nations to be alert and to form UFO investigative bodies. China's group was part of the government-supported China
Association for Science and Technology.[28]

On Moscow Ostankino Television came some criticism aimed at
Russia's investor class, decrying the absence of investors in the Saratov
factory's saucer-shaped aerial vehicle.[29]

On December 19, 1993, the Moscow Russian Television Network
aired film of a Russian-made flying disc. The voiceover intoned: "This
is secret footage of a laboratory for the production of UFO's. . . . It is a

modern Russian airship, our 'thermoplane.' . . . It is designed for installation work in Siberia." The vehicle was saucer shaped.[30]

As reported in a non-sourced message two days later, December 21, just before 7:00 p.m. a group of Matanzas City, Cuba, residents, including the writer, observed a bright white light with a tail, likened to a comet, on a trajectory from north to south. It then divided into several such lights. The sighting lasted 30 seconds.[31]

From January 7, 1994, a non-sourced message announced that the town of Hakui, in Ishikawa Prefecture, Japan, sought to build a center for the study of UFOs and other space phenomena. It would feature a library with 10,000 plus documents. A city employee with thousands of files led the effort.[32]

The Moscow Ostankino Television First Channel Network on January 24, 1994, reported on a trip to England by Saratov Aircraft officials to find financing for their prototype flying disc. On a visit to Birmingham to interest potential investors, Saratov principals showed video and stills of a "flying saucer" from various angles in a hangar. The prospective 120-passenger craft, supported by an air cushion, would need no airstrip and could land on either the ground or water.[33]

The March 23, 1994, edition of the Moscow *Robochaya Tribuna* newspaper took its place in the press selection list with an "Article on flying saucers containing information 'from our secret archives.'"[34]

On May 28, 1994, *Pravda* speculated on the cause of two unexplained craters discovered near Kursk. Specialists initially concluded only a 500 kg bomb could have caused the craters, 7–8 meters across, in a ravine near the Kursk nuclear power station. But no related sound was heard and no damage reported. However, locals had observed a fiery body in the sky. Civil defense and emergencies staff considered two possibilities: a large meteor or a UFO.[35]

While you were away from your desk . . .

January 10, 1992

From a classified Department of Defense letter, at an unnamed US Army base in Germany, a disc-shaped object hovered near three adults and two infants. Following the encounter, they received ten days of medical care for severe headaches, burns on their hands, faces, and genital areas, and loss of hair. Radiation from the intruder was noted as the cause of their conditions.[36]

February 24, 1993

A Sylvania, Alabama, farm wife awoke around 2:00 a.m. to *see* a red-orange light the size of a full moon pulsing over the pasture. Later that day her husband discovered a dead cow, its udder excised. Microscopic cellular analysis of the wound indicated the cuts were "consistent with sharp dissection" rather than "tearing or chewing as would be seen by predator attack."[37]

Chapter 40

1995-1998:

Psychic Woo Woo

No UFO-related CIA documents were filed and subsequently released to the Agency's website for 1995, 1996, or 1997.

In a journal prepared at California State College, Sonoma, a psychic fair was attended by 1,200 on November 5, 1998. Included were lectures and workshops on Kirlian photography, biofeedback, psychic development, UFOs, dream theory, palmistry, astrology, and humanistic parapsychology.[1]

In a lengthy essay published on December 7, 1998, the Guangdong, China, Somatic Sciences Research Committee addressed what to some would be an exotic topic: "Some Brief Notes on the Development of Research into Human Paranormal Capabilities in Guangdong." "In 'hyper time and space flight,' real flight time has no meaning. . . . [O]bjects effectively 'break through the time barrier.'" Separately "Research into 'unidentified flying objects' (UFOs) has provided a type of indirect data. . . . [W]e can *see* a number of reports of abnormal circumstances surrounding UFO flights. . . . [T]he almost simultaneous occurrences of UFOs over China's Xizang and California . . . remind us of the 'hyper time and space flight' . . ." The brain emits a "thought field" which breaks through spatial barriers, disassembling and reassembling matter, the writer then asserted.[2]

While you were away from your desk . . .

May 25, 1995

During a night flight aboard an America West Boeing 757 over Texas, the captain, his first officer, and lead flight attendant noticed a line of brilliant lights somewhat below their 39,000-foot altitude. The lights strobed continuously in sequence from left to right. Momentarily, silhouetted by lightning flashes from a thunderhead, the structure was revealed as wingless and cylindrical. They kept the object in view for five minutes while contacting the Albuquerque Air Route Traffic Control Center and NORAD. Neither facility was able to identify the intruder as a conventional aircraft.[3]

July 31, 1995

At 8:10 p.m., an Aerolineas Argentinas Boeing 727 was on approach to the San Carlos de Bariloche airport, when a blinding white light rushed the airliner head on. It halted in the air 100 meters away, turned, and flew parallel to the aircraft, revealing itself as an inverted saucer shape, with a pair of green lights on either side and an orange light at the center. Its diameter equaled the expanse of the 727. The pilot climbed back to 3,000 feet with the intruder still nearby. When once more on approach, suddenly the runway lights went out, as did those in the control tower. The entire city, in fact, experienced the blackout. Then the saucer flashed away and out of sight, all the lights came back on, and the pilot was able to land safely.[4]

January 20, 1996

In the predawn hours, two persons near Varginha, Brazil, reported sighting a submarine-shaped object apparently experiencing difficulty—flying slowly and close to the ground with smoke or vapor pouring out. At daylight, a number of nonhuman entities were observed by multiple witnesses as they wandered within the town. Military police were called out, capturing two without resistance and shooting a third to death.[5]

March 15, 1997

At 5:00 a.m. an object that was not described was seen exploding in the sky over Wegorzewo, Poland. Soldiers immediately removed the remains of the structure.[6]

October 19, 1998

In China's Hebei province, radars at four locations tracked an unknown moving target approaching. At least 140 people on the ground served as eyewitnesses, describing the object as having a flat bottom covered in bright rotating lights and an overlying dome in the shape of a mushroom. A base commander ordered a Shenyang JJ-6 interceptor trainer into the air. When it was still a few miles away, the object abruptly shot upward, only to descend again and pace the aircraft from above. This maneuver was repeated multiple times, outdistancing the plane then returning. At a point, the pilots requested permission to fire their cannon at the saucer, but that was denied. Low on fuel, the JJ-6 was forced to land. The intruder left the area before two more modern interceptors were airborne.[7]

Chapter 41

1999:

A Fitting Climax

On July 1, 1999, historian Gerald Haines of the National Reconnaissance Office in the Defense Department published a paper on the Central Intelligence Agency's continuous, covert involvement in the UFO subject.[1] Dr. Haines' account, broadly paraphrased, with direct quotes where appropriate, follows.

The June 1947 pilot sighting near Mount Rainier, Washington, was followed only a week later by the alleged Roswell, New Mexico, saucer crash. Soon came a rash of sighting reports across the country. In January 1948 Air Force General Nathan Twining established Project Sign. It would collect, evaluate, and distribute all flying saucer data—on the premise of a national security concern. The Technical Intelligence Division of the Air Material Command at Wright Field (soon thereafter Wright-Patterson AFB), Dayton, Ohio, assumed control of the project.

The Air Force soon concluded that almost all UFO reports were easily explained and not extraordinary. Most stemmed from mass hysteria or hallucination, hoaxed accounts, or misinterpretation of known objects or atmospheric effects. Still, the ten percent left unexplained included "a number of incredible reports from credible observers." Project Sign called for continued military intelligence involvement and "did not rule out the possibility of extraterrestrial phenomena."

For reasons not well explained since, attitudes changed within Air Force officialdom. In just a year Project Sign was disbanded. "Under new management"—menacingly renamed Project Grudge—the Air Force would seek to allay public anxiety via education, that UFOs were actually IFOs. Grudge officers reported no evidence of any foreign weapons design or a national security threat and suggested reducing the project's scope. Continued official interest, the Grudge officers contended, would only encourage hysterical belief by the American populace in a UFO reality. On December 27, 1949, that project was terminated as well.

Then in early 1952, perplexed by an unexpected increase in UFO reports by the general public, the USAF director of intelligence ordered a new effort, Project Blue Book. Never intended to include a considerable staff, the office would consist of one or two low-ranking officers or one officer and a noncom, plus a secretary. It would be housed in the Air Technical Intelligence Center (ATIC) at Wright-Patterson, Dayton, Ohio. Its mission did not specifically include persuading the public that all UFO reports had prosaic origins, not of any unusual nature or design. Still, "only a voice or two at ATIC believed there was even a remote possibility of interplanetary aircraft."

The CIA quietly monitored Air Force efforts for security reasons. The 1952 spate of sighting reports, culminating in radar tracks on July 19, 20, and 27 in and around Washington, D.C., was not immediately identifiable, and a clearly bungled military response failed to allay the public's concerns. After repeated hours-long logistical delays, jet interceptors proceeding from Delaware had found nothing amiss—friendly or otherwise.

In the absence of anything substantive to account for all the D.C. radar returns, all were eventually reasoned to be the products of temperature inversions. But that weak attempt to explain all the occurrences across three nights as meteorological was lost amid headlines of unidentified intruders in the skies over our very capital.

As a consequence of those and other flying saucer sightings across a wide expanse throughout 1952, principals in the CIA came to realize that only a scientific study would satisfy the public. Reaching into universities, especially, a small cadre was formed in December 1952 with input from the Office of Scientific Intelligence (OSI). In doing so, the Agency acknowledged the public's probable alarmist tendencies if that were known. It thereby concealed its involvement. This decision was later interpreted as an interagency conspiracy and cover-up.

The study group, headed by physicist Howard P. Robertson, feared the Soviets might use UFO reports to panic the American public or overload warning systems as a nuclear attack ensued. The OSI assistant director believed those concerns should be taken to the National Security Council. Ultimately, no such document for NSC consideration was prepared.

OSI had regularly studied the Soviet press for UFO accounts but found none; it concluded that must be due to official government policy. Great Britain, meanwhile, had its own wave underway. The British press and public were convinced of a UFO reality. Whether these phenomena originated here on the planet or untold light years away was the question.

The Agency's hand-picked physical scientists met for 12 hours over four days in January 1953, reviewing two controversial amateur films and a dozen or so written anomalous accounts in some detail. They concluded that all of those and most, if not all, UFO reports arising elsewhere were explainable.

The so-named Robertson Panel declared that such cases were neither extraterrestrial in origin nor a national security threat. It was concerned that the government's "orderly functioning" could be threatened by clogged communications channels, inducing "hysterical mass behavior" harmful to constituted authority. The Robertson Panel called on the National Security Council to debunk UFO reports and educate the public on the lack of related evidence. It suggested using mass media, advertising, business clubs, schools, even Walt Disney to get the message across. The panel further recommended monitoring APRO and other civilian UFO research groups for possible subversive activities.

Mounting reports in Europe prompted Agency concern that the Soviets were operating saucer-type vehicles, built by captured German scientists and engineers. A British-Canadian saucer construction project was also underway.

The advent in 1955 of secretive U-2 flights at 60,000 feet prompted UFO reports by airline pilots and ground controllers. CIA officials who worked on the U-2—or subsequent SR-71 Blackbird—project later claimed (dubiously) that those accounted for half of all UFO reports through the late 1960s.

In 1956 USAF Captain Edward Ruppelt, the original Blue Book chief, called for release of the 1953 Robertson Panel Report. Both NICAP and APRO followed suit, but the Agency's OSI refused. Instead, a very brief sanitized version was released which made no mention of the CIA or any psychological warfare component.

A flap involving a code recorded from a radio broadcast drew in civilian groups and individuals over an extended period. The CIA called it simple Morse code, but the incident deepened public distrust.

Another situation the Agency handled poorly involved five photos of an unknown taken by an employee of a TV station. CIA staff acquired the photos then ignored requests for their return. This aggravated suspicions that they were hiding the truth. Although the Agency had a lessened interest in the subject, it continued to monitor UFO sightings. Agency officials felt the need to keep informed on such incidents if only to alert the CIA Director (DCI) to the more sensational UFO reports and flaps.

In 1964, at the DCI's request, OSI obtained a sampling of NICAP's recent compelling cases but found nothing new. That year, the USAF Scientific Advisory Board, with help from astronomer Carl Sagan, reached the same conclusions: no security threat and nothing obviously beyond terrestrial origin. Again in 1966 the Air Force requested the CIA to release the entire Robertson Panel Report, but the Agency refused.

University of Arizona atmospheric physicist James E. McDonald by chance read the original Robertson Report at Wright-Patterson AFB in June 1966—including an instruction to the Air Force to debunk future reports arising from the public. On returning to the base three weeks later for a printed copy, he was denied access. Over the next few years McDonald spoke out against CIA secrecy and its dictating of Air Force policy.

In August 1966, the Air Force announced its intent to contract with a university for an intensive scientific review of its UFO files, "to blunt continuing charges that the US Government had concealed what it knew about UFOs." Two months later, on October 7, an 18-month, $325,000 agreement with the University of Colorado was signed. Physicist Edward

U. Condon would head the effort. Calling himself "agnostic" and open-minded, he stated extraterrestrial origins were "improbable but not impossible." USAF coordinators were Brigadier General Edward Giller and J. Thomas Ratchford from the Office of Research and Development (ORD).

General Giller enrolled the CIA's National Photographic Interpretation Center (NPIC) for photographic analysis, without public mention of the arrangement. Dr. Condon and four committee members visited the Center on February 20, 1967. NPIC Director Arthur Lundahl emphasized that its help would be strictly technical—no report writing—and that the CIA would remain anonymous. Impressed by NPIC briefings, they met again in May 1967 to hear the Zanesville, Ohio, photos debunked. Condon intended to ask citizens for more UFO photos and to provide guidelines to taking useful shots. Whatever his real intentions, those initiatives were not acted upon.

In April 1969 the Condon committee released its findings. "The report concluded that little, if anything, had come from the study of UFOs in the past 21 years and that further extensive study of UFO sightings was unwarranted." It called for Project Blue Book to end. A National Academy of Sciences panel concurred with the report. On December 17, 1969, Air Force Secretary Robert Seamans dissolved Blue Book.

Continued UFO reports by the public elicited more cover-up claims. In 1975, an Agency spokesman wrote brusquely that the Robertson Report was "the summation of Agency interest and involvement in UFOs." A September 1977 Freedom of Information Act (FOIA) request tested that statement, seeking all CIA UFO-related files. Fourteen months later in November 1978 came the release of 355 documents, while 57 others were withheld "on national security grounds and to protect sources and methods." Though the release showed only low-level CIA interest, the press treated it sensationally. An FOIA request for the 57 retained files and any others followed. "No matter how much material the Agency released and no matter how dull and prosaic the information, people continued to believe in a [sic] Agency coverup and conspiracy," one principal wrote. The CIA soon requested a federal district court to intervene. In May 1980 that court dismissed the FOIA lawsuit.

In the 1980s Agency analysts in OSI's Life Science Division were concerned with: (a) the KGB using UFO groups to get information on sensitive US weapons programs (for example, stealth aircraft), (b) American air defense network's vulnerability to missiles mimicking UFOs, and (c) evidence of advanced Soviet technology related to UFOs. ". . . Agency officials purposely kept files on UFOs to a minimum to avoid creating records that might mislead the public if released."

The 1980s also brought renewed assertions of secret documents on the alleged 1947 crash at Roswell, New Mexico—that the government had recovered debris and alien bodies there, and that it refused to divulge its investigation results and research.

Such was the case for secrecy made by the DoD historian Haines. Nothing nefarious was at work, he argued. Instead, the Agency's reasoning for its anonymity was borne of a distrust within the general public. Permitting the CIA's tempered interest in the subject to become widely known would tend to add false credence to further UFO matters in the press. Hence, Haines argued, discretion was indeed the better part of valor.

Chapter 42

2000 and Beyond

A German parapsychology journal carried an entry titled "The Spectrum of UFO Sightings" on May 17, 2000. It argued that scientists' collective prejudice against UFO phenomena was socio-psychological. Most reports were by laypersons, were anecdotal, lacked physical evidence, and did not appear in science journals. Scientists eschewed UFO claims due to unreliable data, the premature public opinion that UFOs were ET spaceships, and their overall disrespect for obscure events involving untrained observers. Condon and others in the late 1960s traced all UFO reports to natural phenomena, conventional aircraft, hallucinations, illusions, and frauds. But only when 50,000 computerized cases were tested could one say UFO phenomena were primarily physical or "parapsychical."[1]

To fulfill requirements for a master's degree, one individual developed a survey on various topics within parapsychology. "The purpose of this study (was) to ascertain the subjects, frequency, and degree of information exchanged between US and Warsaw Pact scientists concerning the field of parapsychology . . ." The UFO subject was among dozens of paranormal topics.[2]

At the University of Edinburgh, in August 2000 an experiment was conducted on belief in parapsychology (psi). Subjects were asked to rate a list of psi and anomalous phenomena, including UFOs.[3]

While you were away from your desk . . .

January 5, 2000

About 4:00 a.m., police officers in Lebanon, Millstadt, Shiloh, and Dupo, Illinois, observed a UFO 2–3 stories in height and of football field proportions. One officer within 1,000 feet described it as a silent, "massive elongated triangle" emitting intense white light. Another called it a fat arrowhead, 500–1,000 feet aloft. The object's speed was generally slow, punctuated by pivots and extreme acceleration. After traveling generally southeast, it turned northwest toward Scott AFB, Illinois. Air Force and Boeing Corporation spokespersons subsequently denied responsibility.[4]

May 3, 2000

A "Fact Sheet" released by NASA explained why it had turned down President Jimmy Carter's 1977 overture to that agency to assume a role in UFO investigations similar to Project Blue Book's. In response came some NASA plain talk:

> From 1947 to 1969, the Air Force investigated UFOs; then in 1977, NASA was asked to examine the possibility of resuming UFO investigations. After studying all of the facts available, it was determined that nothing would be gained by further investigation, since there was an absence of tangible evidence.[5]

In effect, NASA had proclaimed to President Carter, "No, we won't, and you can't make us."

Postscript

The New York Times published a front-page article on December 16, 2017, curiously titled "Glowing Auras and 'Black Money': The Pentagon's Mysterious U.F.O. Program." The *Times'* authors outlined the functioning of an obscure research office originating in DoD's Defense Intelligence Agency (DIA). Its benefactors were former Senate majority leader Harry Reid and Robert Bigelow, founder and CEO of Bigelow Aerospace.

As revealed by personnel records therein, once again, a post-century UFO investigative team effort was contemplated. The futurist Robert Bigelow and his staff were agreeable initially to a contractor role, prepared to analyze an array of any undefined materials acquired from civilian-reported UFO sites. Even after federal funding ended and its head was reassigned, that individual—likely Luis Elizondo—reportedly continued a part-time effort around his unrelated official duties. In recent years he left federal civil service to continue his research into this peculiar subject, now under the aerospace umbrella.

Sixty years after the Central Intelligence Agency endeavored to discover whether claims of uninvited otherworldly visitors were real or not, the effort briefly shifted next door, to the DIA, before moving into the quasi-private sector implicitly in cooperation with volunteer investigative organizations such as MUFON. Dedicated to the best energies of APRO and NICAP before us, MUFON contends we're not all wrong! Above the highest scientific principles and phrasings is this ever-common assertion: "I know what I saw."

Endnotes

Chapter 1 **The 1940s: War and Beyond**

1. Arlington National Cemetery website, last updated June 11, 2015, *www.arlingtoncemetery.com*.

2. Central Intelligence Agency, CIA Library, "The Office of Strategic Services: America's First Intelligence Agency," last updated September 6, 2017, *www.cia.gov*.

3. Ibid.

4. Ibid.

5. Ibid.

6. Ibid.

7. Central Intelligence Agency, Library, Center for the Study of Intelligence, last updated January 11, 2008, *www.cia.gov*.

8. "Glorious Amateurs: The Spies of World War II's OSS Celebrate a Birthday," *NBC News*, aired July 1, 2017.

9. Jerome Clark, *The UFO Book* (Detroit, MI, Visible Ink Press, 1998).

10. Central Intelligence Agency, *About CIA*, "History of the CIA," last updated September 18, 2017, *www.cia.gov*.

11. Ibid.

12. C. Thomas Thorne Jr. and David S. Patterson, eds., "Foreign Relations of the United States, 1945–1950, Emergence of the Intelligence Establishment." Office of the Historian, 1996, *https://www.state.gov*.

13. "History of the CIA," *https://www.cia.gov*.

14. Doc # 0000015471, IFDRB, March–May 1953, "Engineer Claims Saucer Plans Are in Soviet Hands; Sightings in Africa, Iran, Syria," distributed August 18, 1953.

15. Allen Hall, "Roswell was not aliens, it was the Nazis, according to a German documentary," *Sunday Express* (London), October 4, 2014, *www.express.co.uk.*

16. Ibid.

17. Wikipedia, "Operation Paperclip," last updated December 15, 2017, *https://en.wikipedia.org.*

18. Ibid.

19. Clark, *The UFO Book.*

20. Bruce Maccabee, "How It All Began: The Story of the Arnold Sighting," *MUFON 1997 International UFO Symposium Proceedings,* pp.99–120.

21. Lawrence Fawcett and Barry J. Greenwood, *Clear Intent: The Government Coverup of the UFO Experience* (Englewood Cliffs, NJ: Prentice-Hall, 1984).

22. Timothy Good, *Need to Know: UFOs, the Military and Intelligence* (New York: Pegasus Books, 2007), p. 45.

23. Ibid., p. 62.

24. Ibid., p. 103.

25. Fawcett and Greenwood, *Clear Intent*, pp. 156–59.

26. Clark, *The UFO Book,* "Mantell Incident," pp. 351–353.

27. Ibid.

28. Good, *Need to Know.*

29. Margaret Sachs, *The UFO Encyclopedia* (New York: Perigee Books/G. P. Putnam's Sons, 1980).

30. Don Berliner, Fund for UFO Research, *The Blue Book Unknowns* (1995), available at *www.nicap.org.*

31. Sachs, *The UFO Encyclopedia.*

32. Ronald D. Story, *The Encyclopedia of UFOs* (Garden City, NY: Dolphin Books/ Doubleday & Co., 1980).

Chapter 2 **1949: Curiouser and Curiouser**

1. Sachs, *The UFO Encyclopedia.*

2. Don Berliner, Unidentified Flying Objects Briefing Document (The UFO Research Coalition, 1995), *www.openminds.tv.*

3. Berliner, *The Blue Book Unknowns.*

4. Fawcett and Greenwood, *Clear Intent*, pp. 151–61.

5. Story, *The Encyclopedia of UFOs.*

6. Bob Gribble, "Looking Back," *MUFON UFO Journal,* September 1989.

7. Wikipedia, "Green Fireballs," last edited November 30, 2017, *https://en.wikipedia.org/wiki/Green_fireballs.*

8. Ibid.

9. Ibid.

10. Gregory W. Pedlow and Donald E. Welzenbach, *(1992), The Central Intelligence Agency and Overhead Reconnaissance: The U-2 and OXCART Programs, 1954–1974, www.gwu.edu.*

11. Thorne and Patterson, "Foreign Relations of the United States, 1945–1950."

12. "History of the CIA," *www.cia.gov.*

13. Doc # 0000015337, "Flying Saucers," internal OSI memo from Dr. Stone to Dr. Machle, March 15, 1949.

14. Berliner, *The Blue Book Unknowns.*

Chapter 3 **1950: Escalation**

1. Berliner, Unidentified Flying Objects Briefing Document.

2. Berliner, *The Blue Book Unknowns.*

3. Wikipedia, "Gordon Cooper," updated December 13, 2017, *https://en.wikipedia.org/wiki/Gordon_Cooper.*

4. Fawcett and Greenwood, *Clear Intent,* page 69.

5. Bob Gribble, "Looking Back," *MUFON UFO Journal,* May 1990.

6. Doc # 0000015283, Information Report (heavily redacted), "German Scientist's Article on 'Flying Discs,'" July 31, 1950.

7. Doc # 0005516578, Information Report from (redacted), "Unidentified Airborne Object," August 18, 1950.

8. Doc # CIA-RDP80R01731R003500010009-8, Office Memorandum from Assistant Director, OCD(?), to (various), "Unconventional Aircraft," September 26, 1950.

9. Central Intelligence Agency, "Taking Stock: 15 DCI's First 100 Days," *www.cia.gov.*

10. Good, *Need to Know.*

11. Sachs, *The UFO Encyclopedia.*

12. Bob Gribble, "Looking Back," *MUFON UFO Journal,* April 1990.

13. Ronald D. Story, *The Encyclopedia of Extraterrestrial Encounters* (New York: New American Library, 2001), pp. 644-645. *See* also Wikipedia; "McMinnville UFO Photographs," last updated December 6, 2017, *https://en.wikipedia.org.*

14. Bob Gribble, "Looking Back," *MUFON UFO Journal,* August, 1990.

15. Good, *Need to Know.*

16. Berliner, *The Blue Book Unknowns.*

17. Berliner, Unidentified Flying Objects Briefing Document.

Chapter 4 **1951: Calm Before . . .**

1. Good, *Need to Know.*

2. Berliner, *The Blue Book Unknowns.*

3. Sachs, *The UFO Encyclopedia.*

4. Good, *Need to Know,* pp. 162–163.

Chapter 5 **1952: A Genuine Wave**

1. Doc # 0000015282, Information Report, "Light Phenomena East of Tashkent" (Uzbekistan), February 11, 1952.

2. Doc # 0000015467, IFDRB, "'Saucers' Sighted Over Spain and French Africa," April–August 1952," distributed September 27, 1952.

3. Doc # 0000015464, IFDRB, "'Flying Saucers' in East Germany," July 9, 1952.

4. Doc # 0000015467, IFDRB, "'Saucers' Sighted Over Spain and French Africa," April–August 1952," distributed September 27 1952.

5. Doc # 0005515704, Information Report, "Flying Saucers," heavily redacted, September 2, 1952.

6. Doc # 0000015276, Information Report, heavily redacted, "Flying Saucers," undated, distributed September 2, 1952.

7. Berliner, *The Blue Book Unknowns.*

8. J. Allen Hynek, *The Hynek UFO Report* (New York: Dell Publishing, 1977).

9. Berliner, *The Blue Book Unknowns.*

10. Ibid.

11. Ibid.

12. Sachs, *The UFO Encyclopedia;* Story, *The Encyclopedia of Extraterrestrial Encounters.*

13. Story, *The Encyclopedia of Extraterrestrial Encounters.*

14. Doc # 0005515934, memorandum for Deputy Director, Intelligence, "Recent Sightings of Unexplained Objects," July 29, 1952.

15. Doc # 0000015341, memorandum for Deputy Assistant Director/SI from Acting Chief, Weapons & Equipment Division, "Flying Saucers," August 1, 1952.

16. Ibid.

17. Doc # 0000015443, untitled note regarding phone call from the FBI, August 8, 1952.

18. Doc # 0000015441, draft "Minutes of Branch Chief's Meeting of 11 August 1952."

19. Doc # 0000015340, interagency transmittal, "Recent Sightings of Unexplained Objects," 20 August 1952.

20. Ibid.

21. Ibid.

22. Doc # 0000015342, memorandum from the Assistant Director of Operations to the Deputy Director (Intelligence), "USSR and Satellite Mention of Flying Saucers," August 22, 1952.

23. Doc # 0005516118, non-sourced, "The Air Force Stand on Flying Saucers—As Stated by CIA, in a Briefing on 22 August 1952."

24. Ibid.

25. Ibid.

26. Ibid.

27. Ibid.

28. Ibid., emphasis added.

29. Ibid.

30. Doc # 0000015465, Information from Foreign Documents or Radio Broadcasts, "Flying Saucers in Spain and North Africa," May–June 1952, distributed August 27, 1952.

31. Ibid.

32. Ibid.

33. Doc # 0000015276, Information Report, "Flying Saucers," undated, distributed September 2, 1952.

34. Doc # 0000015466, IFDRB, "Unidentified Flying Objects over Morocco and French West Africa," July 1952, distributed September 2, 1952.

35. Doc # 0000015467, IFDRB, "'Saucers' Sighted Over Spain and French Africa," April–August 1952," distributed September 27, 1952.

36. Doc # CIA-RDP81R00560R000100020011-8, draft memorandum from James Q. Reber, Assistant Director, Intelligence Coordination, for the DD/I, "Flying Saucers," October 13, 1952.

37. Ibid.

38. Doc # 0005515935, memorandum from H. Marshall Chadwell, OSI Director, to Director of Intelligence, "Unidentified Flying Objects," December 2, 1952.

39. Doc # 0000015345, memorandum for Record, by P. G. Strong, OSI Acting Deputy Assistant Director, December 3, 1952.

40. Doc # 0005516074, Intelligence Advisory Committee Minutes of Meeting Held in Director's Conference Room, Administration Building, Central Intelligence Agency, on 4 December 1952.

41. Doc # 0005516214, memorandum from V. P. Keay to A. H. Belmont (titles not shown), December 5, 1952.

42. Doc # 0000015346, Office Memorandum from H. U. Graham to OSI Deputy Assistant Director, "FCC Monitoring and Flying Saucers," December 9, 1952.

43. Doc # 0000015347, memorandum from H. Marshall Chadwell, OSI Director, for the Director of Central Intelligence, "Unidentified Flying Objects," December 10, 1952.

44. Doc # 0005515943, memorandum from H. Marshall Chadwell, OSI Director—signed by H. L. Clark—to Director of Central Intelligence, "Unidentified Flying Objects," with enclosures, December 13, 1952.

45. Doc # 0005515711, letter from H. Marshall Chadwell, OSI Director, to J. Allen Hynek, Ohio State University, December 29, 1952.

46. Doc # 0000015470, IFDRB, July–November 1952, distributed February 9, 1953, "Reports of Unconventional Aircraft in French Africa, Corsica, and Western Europe."

47. J. Allen Hynek, *The Hynek UFO Report*.

48. Good, *Need to Know*.

49. Ibid.

50. Ibid.

51. Berliner, *The Blue Book Unknowns*.

52. Story, *The Encyclopedia of Extraterrestrial Encounters*.

53. Good, *Need to Know;* Sachs, *The UFO Encyclopedia*.

54. Good, *Need to Know*, p. 152.

55. Story, *The Encyclopedia of Extraterrestrial Encounters*, p. 397.

56. Ibid.

57. Ibid.

58. Sachs, *The UFO Encyclopedia*. *See* also Doc # 0000015470.

59. Good, *Need to Know*.

Chapter 6 **1953: Cold Water from Robertson and Others**

1. Doc # 0000015351, memorandum from H. Marshall Chadwell, OSI Director, to the Director of Central Intelligence, "Consultants for Advisory Panel on Unidentified Flying Objects," January 9, 1953.

2. Wikipedia, "Robertson Panel," last edited December 16, 2017, *https://en.wikipedia.org*.

3. Ibid.

4. Ibid.

5. Ibid.

6. Doc # 0000015458, non-sourced, "Comments and Suggestions of UFO Panel" (Robertson Report), January 21, 1953.

7. Ibid.

8. The Computer UFO Network, "Seven Status Reports for Project STORK" (n.d.), *www.cufon.org*.

9. Ibid.

10. Ibid.

11. Ibid.

12. The Computer UFO Network, "Seven Status Reports for Project STORK"; see also Above Top Secret, "The 1952 Tremonton, Utah UFO Fleet," 2017, *www.abovetopsecret.com*.

13. Sachs, *The UFO Encyclopedia*.

14. Ibid.

15. Ibid.

16. Doc # 0005515715, letter from H. Marshall Chadwell to Dr. H. P. Robertson, California Institute of Technology, January 28, 1953.

17. Doc # 0005515715, letter from H. P. "Bob" Robertson, California Institute of Technology, to H. Marshall "Chad" Chadwell, January 20, 1953.

18. Doc # 0000015470, IFDRB, July–November 1952, distributed February 9, 1953, "Reports of Unconventional Aircraft in French Africa, Corsica, and Western Europe."

19. Ibid.

20. Ibid.

21. Doc # 0000015287, letter from H. Marshall Chadwell, OSI Director, to Julius Stratton, Provost, Massachusetts Institute of Technology, January 27, 1953.

22. Doc # RDP79B00752A000300100010-4, "Report of Meetings of Scientific Advisory Panel on Unidentified Flying Objects Convened by the Office of Scientific Intelligence, CIA," February 16, 1953.

23. Ibid.

24. Doc # RDP79B00752A000300100010-4, "Report of Meetings of Scientific Advisory Panel on Unidentified Flying Objects Convened by the Office of Scientific Intelligence, CIA," February 16, 1953. Note: This file is also shown as Doc # 0005516128 and 0000015459, both largely illegible.

25. Ibid.

26. Doc # 0000015353, Memorandum for Record, by Philip G. Strong, OSI Acting Deputy Assistant Director, "Briefing of ONE Board on Unidentified Flying Objects," January 30, 1953.

27. Doc # 0000015355, Office Memorandum from (redacted) to the OSI assistant for operations, Contact Division, "California Committee for Saucer Investigation," February 9, 1953.

28. Doc # 0000015455, non-sourced report, "National Investigations Committee on Aerial Phenomena," January 4, 1953.

29. Ibid.

30. Doc # 0000015354, memorandum from Alan M. Warfield, Chief, FEIS (?) to bureau chiefs, "Unidentified Flying Objects," February 6, 1953; see also Doc # 0000015352.

31. Doc # 0005516124, letter from (redacted), Secretary, Intelligence Advisory Committee (IAC), to (redacted), March 12, 1953.

32. Doc # 0005517565, letter from Richard Drain, IAC Secretary, to the Secretary of Defense, March 13, 1953.

33. Doc # 0000015357, Office Memorandum from F. C. Durant to P. G. Strong, "Unidentified Flying Objects," March 31, 1953.

34. Doc # 0005515716, untitled letter from OSI Director H. Marshall Chadwell to Samuel A. Goudsmit, Brookhaven National Laboratory, April 7, 1953.

35. Doc # 0000015358, draft by Richard D. Drain, IAC Secretary, "Item for Director's Log," April 21, 1953.

36. Doc # 0000015359, Memorandum for Record, by Philip G. Strong, OSI Acting Deputy Assistant Director, "FCDA Meeting," April 23, 1953.

37. Doc # 0000015360, Memorandum for Record, by Philip G. Strong, "Further to FCDA Meeting," April 24, 1953.

38. Doc # 0000015361, Office Memorandum from H. Marshall Chadwell, OSI Assistant Director, to the chief of the Physics and Electronics (P&E) Division, "Unidentified Flying Objects," May 27, 1953.

39. Doc # 0000015362, Office Memorandum, from Todos M. Odarenko, Chief, OSI Physics and Electronics Division, to the OSI Assistant Director, "Unidentified Flying Objects," July 3, 1953.

40. Doc # 0005516159, IFDRB, *Morgon Tidningen*, "Danish Defense Leaders Take Serious View of Flying Saucers," July 13, 1953.

41. Wikipedia, "Air Base Karup," updated October 13, 2016, *https://en.wikipedia.org*.

42. Doc # 0000015472, IFDRB, October 1952–July 1953; distributed July 13, 1953.

43. Doc # 0000015471, IFDRB, March–May 1953, "Engineer Claims Saucer Plans Are in Soviet Hands; Sightings in Africa, Iran, Syria," distributed August 18, 1953.

44. Ibid.

45. Ibid.

46. Doc # 0000015290, letter from John S. Warner, Legislative Counsel, to Congressman Gordon H. Scherer, undated.

47. Doc # 0005515713, undated (post-8/24/53) letter from Philip G. Strong, OSI Deputy Assistant Director, to Thornton Page, Johns Hopkins University.

48. Wikipedia, "Donald Keyhoe," updated September 12, 2017, *https://en.wikipedia.org*.

49. Ibid.

50. Ibid.

51. Ibid.

52. Doc # 0000015363, Office Memorandum from P. G. Strong, OSI Deputy Assistant Director, to the OSI Assistant Director, "Report on Book Entitled 'Flying Saucers from Outer Space'," December 8, 1953.

53. Doc # 0000015364, memorandum from the Chief, OSI Operations Staff, to staff, "Flying Saucers," December 16, 1953.

54. Doc # 0000015365, memorandum from Chief of OSI's P&E Division to the OSI Assistant Director, "Current Status of Unidentified Flying Objects (UFOB) Project," December 17, 1953.

55. Ibid.

56. Ibid.

57. Ibid.

58. Ibid.

59. Ibid.

60. Doc # 0000015473, IFDRB, "Unidentified Aircraft Reported over Spain, Greece, North Africa," July–November 1953, distributed January 11, 1954.

61. Doc # 0000015475, IFDRB, "Sightings of Unidentified Flying Objects," May 1953–January 1954, distributed April 20, 1954.

62. Clark, *The UFO Book*.

63. Wikipedia, "Douglas C-47 Skytrain," updated November 8, 2017, *https://en.wikipedia.org*.

64. Doc # 0000015476, IFDRB, "Non-orbit Sightings of Unidentified Flying Objects, December 1953–March 1954," distributed May 26, 1954.

65. Ibid.

66. Ibid.

67. Doc # 0005516171 (identical to Doc # 0000015476), distributed May 26, 1954.

68. Doc # 0000015474, IFDRB, December 1953, "Veteran Swedish Airmen Observe, Describe Disk-Shaped Aircraft Over Skanne," distributed April 1, 1954.

69. Ibid.

70. Berliner, *The Blue Book Unknowns*.

71. Ibid.

72. Good, *Need to Know,* pp. 183–184.

73. Berliner, *The Blue Book Unknowns*.

74. Good, *Need to Know,* p. 199.

75. Ibid.

76. Ibid.

77. Wikipedia, "List of reported UFO sightings," updated December 11, 2017, *https://en.wikipedia.org*.

Chapter 7 **1954: Through a Long Winter's Night**

1. Doc # 0000015475, IFDRB, "Sightings of Unidentified Flying Objects," May 1953–January 1954, distributed April 20, 1954.

2. Doc # 0005516171, IFDRB, December 10, 1953–March 2, 1954, "Non-Orbit Sightings of Unidentified Flying Objects," distributed May 26, 1954.

3. Doc # 0005515720, untitled letter from H. Marshall Chadwell, OSI Director, to Walter Pforzheimer, OSI Assistant Director and General Counsel, May 4, 1954.

4. Doc # 0000015477, IFDRB, "'Flying Saucer' Theories and Experiments," December 1953–January 1954, distributed May 27, 1954; also shown as Doc # 0005516188.

5. Doc # 0000015477; *see* also Doc # 0000015471.

6. Ibid.

7. Doc # 0000015367, Memorandum for the Record, by Sidney H. Graybeal, T. M. Nordbeck and T. M. Odarenko, "Intelligence Responsibilities for Non-Conventional Types of Air Vehicles," June 14, 1954.

8. Doc # 0000015366, Memorandum for the Record, by Herbert Scoville Jr., AD/SI, "Office Responsibilities for Non-Conventional Types of Air Vehicles," June 14, 1954.

9. Doc # 0000015478, IFDRB, "Sightings of Unidentified Flying Objects, 19 January–15 May, 1954," distributed July 30, 1954.

10. Ibid.

11. Ibid.

12. Ibid.

13. Doc # 0005516189, IFDRB, "Sightings of Unidentified Flying Objects, 19 January–15 May, 1954," distributed July 30, 1954.

14. Ibid.

15. Ibid.

16. Doc # 0005516190, IFDRB, "Military—Unidentified flying objects," May–June 1954, distributed August 25, 1954.

17. Doc # 0000015481, IFDRB, "Sightings of Unidentified Flying Objects," distributed October 25, 1954.

18. Doc # 0000015478, IFDRB, "Sightings of Unidentified Flying Objects, 19 January-15 May, 1954," distributed July 30, 1954.

19. Doc # 0000015479, IFDRB, "Military—Unidentified Flying Objects," May 7–June 20, 1954, distributed August 25, 1954.

20. Ibid.

21. Doc # 0000015479. *See* also Doc # 0005516190 above.

22. Wikipedia, "Solar eclipse of June 30, 1954," updated September 23, 2017, *https://en.wikipedia.org*.

23. Doc # 0000015480, IFDRB, "Sightings of Unidentified Flying Objects," June–July 1954, distributed September 22, 1954.

24. Ibid.

25. Ibid.

26. Doc # 0000015481, IFDRB, "Sightings of Unidentified Flying Objects," distributed October 25, 1954.

27. Ibid.

28. Ibid.

29. Ibid.

30. Doc # 0000015482, IFDRB, "Sightings of Unidentified Flying Objects," July–September 1954, distributed October 29, 1954.

31. Doc # 0000015481, IFDRB, "Sightings of Unidentified Flying Objects," distributed October 25, 1954.

32. Ibid.

33. Ibid.

34. Doc # 0000015482, IFDRB, "Sightings of Unidentified Flying Objects," July–September 1954, distributed October 29, 1954.

35. Ibid.

36. Ibid.

37. Ibid.

38. Ibid.

39. Ibid.

40. Ibid.

41. Computer UFO Network, "JANAP 146(C) Communication Instructions for Reporting Vital Intelligence Sightings from Airborne and Waterborne Sources—10 March 1954," available at *www.cufon.org*.

42. UFO Research Network, *http://uforesearchnetwork.proboards.com*.

43. Bob Gribble, "Looking Back," *MUFON UFO Journal,* May 1989.

44. Sachs, *The UFO Encyclopedia.*

45. Wikipedia, "List of reported UFO sightings," updated December 11, 2017, *https://en.wikipedia.org.*

46. Ibid.

47. Ibid.

48. Ibid.

49. Good, *Need to Know*, pp. 154–155.

50. Ibid., p. 207.

Chapter 8 **1955: The Ham Radio Flap**

1. Doc # 0005515984, memorandum from (illegible), Deputy Chief, OSI Support Staff, to Chief, Contact Division, Office of Operations (OO), "Unusual Wire Recording," February 25, 1955.

2. Doc # 0000015371, untitled memo from the Chief, Contact Division, to the Chief, Chicago Office, "New Case (redacted)—Radio Code Recording," March 4, 1955.

3. Doc # 0000015372, untitled memo from the Chief, Contact Division, to (illegible), OSI, "Radio Code Recording—Case (redacted)," March 17, 1955.

4. Doc # 0005515987, memorandum from the Chief, P&E Division, to the Chief, OO Contact Division, "Radio Recording," April 6, 1955.

5. The Project Blue Book Archive, "Special Report 14," available at *www.ufocasebook.com.*

6. Battelle website, 2017, *www.battelle.org.*

7. Project Blue Book archive, "Special Report 14."

8. Ibid.

9. Ibid.

10. Ibid.

11. Ibid.

12. Clark, *The UFO Book*, pp. 482-486.

13. Doc # 0000015374, memorandum from Todos Odarenko, Chief, P&E Division, to the Acting Assistant Director for Scientific Intelligence, "Unusual UFOB Report," July 12, 1955.

14. Doc # 0000015375, Office Memorandum from the Chief, P&E Division, to the OSI Acting Assistant Director, "Responsibility for 'Unidentified Flying Objects' (UFOBs)," August 8, 1955.

15. Doc # 0000015264, Information Report by (redacted), "Flying Objects Seen in Shakhty Area," August 9, 1955.

16. Doc # 0000015377, memorandum from Herbert Scoville Jr., AD/SI, to the CIA Director, "Flying Saucers or Unconventional Aircraft," September 4, 1955.

17. Doc # 0000015277, Information Report, "Sighting of Unconventional Aircraft," October 2, 1955.

18. Doc # 0000015293, letter from Allen Dulles, CIA Director, to Congressman Gordon Scherer, October 4, 1955.

19. Wikipedia, "John Carver Meadows Frost," updated August 28, 2017, *https://en.wikipedia.org.*

20. Doc # 0000015378, memorandum for Information, by W. E. Lexow, Chief, OSI Applied Science Division, "Reported Sighting of Unconventional Aircraft," October 19, 1955.

21. Doc # 0000015381, memorandum from Herbert Scoville Jr., AD/SI, for the Director of Central Intelligence, "Interview with (redacted)," October 20, 1955.

22. Doc # 0000015382, memorandum from Herbert Scoville, AD/SI, for the OSI Director, "Sightings of Flying Saucers or Unconventional Aircraft," October 31, 1955. *See* also Doc # 0000015277.

23. Doc # 0005515997, Memorandum from Herbert Scoville Jr., AD/SI to (redacted), "Guided Missiles in Afghanistan," November 10, 1955.

24. National Investigations Committee on Aerial Phenomena, *www.nicap.org.*

25. Berliner, Unidentified Flying Objects Briefing Document.

26. Bob Gribble, "Looking Back," *MUFON UFO Journal,* April 1990.

27. Bob Gribble, "Looking Back," *MUFON UFO Journal,* June 1990.

28. Ibid.

29. Wikipedia, "List of reported UFO sightings."

Chapter 9 **1956: Transitive**

1. Doc # CIA-RDP79B00752A000300120001-2, non-sourced, photographs, "UFO Photos," undated, 1956.

2. Doc # 0000015444, untitled, non-sourced handwritten note, undated, 1956.

3. Doc # 0000015266, Information Report by (redacted), "Report of Unidentified Flying Objects," January 6, 1956.

4. Doc # 0005515999, Memorandum for the Record, by Herbert Scoville Jr., AD/SI, "Office Responsibilities for Non-Conventional Types of Air Vehicles," January 9, 1956.

5. Doc # 0000015387, Memorandum for the Record, by W. E. Lexow, Chief, OSI Applied Science Division (ASD), "Responsibility for 'Unidentified Flying Objects,'" February 9, 1956.

6. Ibid.

7. Doc # 0000015387; *see* also Doc # 0000015366.

8. Doc # 0000015384, memorandum from Robert Amory Jr., DD/I for the AD/SI, "Flying Saucers," March 26, 1956.

9. Doc # 0000015390, memorandum from Herbert Scoville Jr., AD/SI, to the CIA DD/I, "Flying Saucers," April 13, 1956.

10. Doc # 0005515706, Information Report, by (redacted), "Report of Unusual Flying Object Sightings and Attendant Scientific Activity," April 17, 1956.

11. Doc # 0000015280, Information Report by (redacted), "Fast-moving Flying Objects Over Stalingrad in Spring 1954," August 2, 1956.

12. Doc # 0000015491, draft memorandum from J. P. Anderson for OSI executives, "Report of Unidentified Flying Object," December 10, 1956.

13. Coral and Jim Lorenzen, *UFOs: The Whole Story* (New York: Signet Books/ New American Library, 1969).

14. Good, *Need to Know.*

15. Clark, *The UFO Book*; Story, *The Encyclopedia of Extraterrestrial Encounters.*

16. Ibid.

Chapter 10 **1957: Ham Sandwich**

1. Doc # CIA-RDP81R00560R000100080013-0, letter from (redacted), OSI Deputy Assistant Director, to Thornton Page, Johns Hopkins University, January 1, 1957.

2. Doc # 0000015247, teletyped message (to/from redacted) March 4, 1957.

3. Doc # 0000015241, heavily redacted informal note (to/from redacted), March 5, 1957; *see* also Doc # 0000015295.

4. Doc # 0005515707, Information Report by (redacted), "Objects Observed Over Budapest," April 1, 1957.

5. Doc # 0000015392, memorandum from (redacted), Deputy Assistant Director for Operations, to Assistant to the Director, "Leon Davidson Letter to the DCI," May 8, 1957; *see* also Doc # 0000015241.

6. Phillip Coppens, "A lone chemist's quest to expose the UFO cover-up," accessed December 19, 2017, *www.eyeofthepsychic.com*

7. Doc # 0000015295, letter from J. Arnold Shaw, Assistant to the Director, to Leon Davison [*sic*], May 10, 1957; *see* also Doc # 0000015241.

8. Doc # 0000015393, memorandum from (redacted), Chief, Contact Division, to the Chief, Chicago Office, May 10, 1957.

9. Doc # 0000015248, note (to/from redacted), July 2, 1957; *see* also Doc # 0000015241.

10. Doc # 0000015391, memorandum from (redacted), Director, Planning and Coordination, for (redacted), "Unidentified Flying Saucers (UFO)," June 11, 1957.

11. Ibid.

12. Ibid.

13. Ibid.

14. Doc # 0000015251, Information Report by (redacted), "Unidentified Flying Object Observed on Iran/USSR Border," July 2, 1957.

15. Doc # 0000015395, memorandum from Philip G. Strong, OSI Deputy Assistant Director, to Deputy Director for Coordination, "Flying Saucers," (date illegible, post-7/8/57).

16. Wikipedia, "Wayne Sulo Aho," updated August 31, 2017, *https://en.wikipedia.org*.

17. Doc # CIA-RDP68-00046R000200090042-3, news article, Charleston, West Virginia, newspaper (not identified), "Group Says Radar Traced Saucers at 3,600 MPH," July 12, 1957.

18. Ibid.

19. Doc # CIA-RDP68-00046R000200090041-4, news article, Harlan, Kentucky, newspaper, July 20, 1957.

20. Doc # CIA-RDP68-00046R000200090041-4; *see* also Doc # 0000015455

21. Doc # 0000015394, memorandum from (redacted) to the OSI Deputy Assistant Director, Collection, "Interview with (redacted) on the subject of Unidentified Flying Objects," July 26, 1957.

22. Ibid.

23. Doc # 0005515655, note from Support (to/from redacted), August 20, 1957.

24. Wikipedia, Flight airspeed record, updated December 16, 2017, *https://en.wikipedia.org*.

25. Doc # 0000015396, memorandum from Herbert Scoville Jr., AD/SI, to the Acting Director, Central Intelligence, "Unidentified Flying Object Reported on 20 September 1957," September 21, 1957.

26. Doc # CIA-RDP81R00560R000100080016-7, letter (to/from redacted), October 1, 1957.

27. Doc # 0000015297, letter from Philip G. Strong, OSI Deputy Assistant Director, to Lloyd V. Berkner, President, Associated Universities, October 2, 1957.

28. Doc # CIA-RDP81R00560R000100080015-8, letter (to/from redacted), October 5, 1957.

29. Doc # 0000015397, Office Memorandum from P. G. Strong, OSI Deputy Assistant Director, to the OSI Assistant Director, October 26, 1957.

30. Doc # 0000015243, message (to/from redacted), November 3, 1957; *see* also Doc # 0000015241.

31. Doc # 0000015249, note from (redacted) to (unknown), November 4, 1957; *see* also Doc # 0000015241.

32. Doc # 0000015244, teletyped message from (redacted) to (unknown), November 5, 1957; *see* also Doc # 0000015241 and related files.

33. Doc # 0000015302, Letter from Philip G. Strong, OSI Deputy Assistant Director, to Luis Alvarez, University of California at Berkeley, November 5, 1957.

34. Doc # 0000015300, untitled letter from Philip G. Strong to Lloyd Berkner, Associated Universities Inc., published November 5, 1957.

35. Doc # 0000015301, untitled letter from Philip G. Strong to Thornton Page, Johns Hopkins University, Operations Research Office, published November 5, 1957.

36. Doc # 0000015398, memorandum from (redacted) to (illegible), "Case (redacted)—Photographs and Background of Unidentified Flying Object Seen by Ralph L. Mayher," November 7, 1957.

37. Doc # CIA-RPD68-00046R000200090038-8, news article (publisher not shown), "Will Sputniks Solve Flying Saucer Puzzle?" by Douglas Larsen, November 18, 1957.

38. Doc # CIA-RDP81R00560R000100080009-5, letter from Thornton Page, The Johns Hopkins University, to Philip Strong, OSI Deputy Assistant Director, December 4, 1957.

39. Doc # 0000015399, memo from (redacted) to Chief, (illegible), December 12, 1957.

40. Doc # 0005515656, teletyped message, (to/from redacted), December 19, 1957.

41. Doc # 0000015298, letter from Philip G. Strong, OSI Deputy Assistant Director, to Howard P. Robertson, Chairman, Defense Science Advisory Board, Department of Defense, December 20, 1957.

42. Doc # 0000015299, 0005515771, 0005515772, 0005515773.

43. Doc # 0005516035, letter from Philip G. Strong, OSI Deputy Assistant Director, to USAF Assistant Chief of Staff, Intelligence, "Declassification of the 'Report of the Scientific Panel on Unidentified Flying Objects," December 20, 1957.

44. Doc # 0005515651, teletyped message, (to/from redacted), December 20, 1957.

45. See *www.cia.gov.*

46. Ibid.

47. Timothy Good, *Above Top Secret* (Kent, England: Quill Books, 1988).

48. Wikipedia, "List of reported UFO sightings."

49. NICAP, "UFO Updates," (n.d.), *www.nicap.org.*

50. Ibid.

51. Ibid.

52. Clark, *The UFO Book.*

53. Good, *Need to Know.*

54. Story, *The Encyclopedia of Extraterrestrial Encounters.*

55. Infogalactic, "UFO sightings in Portugal," updated January 14, 2015, *https://infogalactic.com.*

56. Story, *The Encyclopedia of Extraterrestrial Encounters,* pp. 306-308.

57. Sachs, *The UFO Encyclopedia.*

58. Story, *The Encyclopedia of UFOs;* Lorenzen and Lorenzen, *UFOs: The Whole Story.*

Chapter 11 **1958: Insurgencies Peak**

1. Doc # 0000015304, letter from Philip G. Strong, OSI Deputy Assistant Director, to Samuel Goudsmit, Brookhaven National Laboratory, January 3, 1958.

2. Doc # 0000015402, one-page memorandum from (redacted) to Support Branch Chief, Chicago Office, "Case (redacted) closed and Dr. Leon Davidson," January 9, 1958.

3. Doc # 0000015245, teletyped message (to/from redacted), January 31, 1958.

4. Doc # CIA-RDP81R00560R000100040072-9, Air Force Regulation 200-2, "Unidentified Flying Objects (UFO)," Department of the Air Force, February 5, 1958.

5. Doc # CIA-RDP81R00560R000100040072-9, Air Force Regulation 200-2, "Unidentified Flying Objects (UFO)," Department of the Air Force, February 5, 1958.

6. Ibid.

7. Ibid.

8. Ibid.

9. Ibid.

10. Doc # 0005515657, note (to/from redacted), February 5, 1958.

11. Doc # 0000015403, memorandum from Herbert Scoville Jr., AD/SI, to the Assistant Director, Office of Operations, "Unidentified Flying Objects," March 21, 1958.

12. Doc # 0000015305, letter from C. P. Cabell, CIA Deputy Director, to Major Donald Keyhoe (Retired), March 21, 1958.

13. Doc # CIA-RDP80B01676R0004000110007-1, memorandum from (redacted), Acting Assistant Director for Operations, for the AD/SI, "Unidentified Flying Objects," (date illegible, post-3/21/58).

14. Doc #0005516038, memorandum from Herbert Scoville Jr., AD/SI, for the Assistant Director, Office of Operations, "Unidentified Flying Objects," March 23, 1958.

15. Doc # 0005516039, memorandum from (redacted), Acting Assistant Director for Operations, to the Office of Scientific Intelligence (recipient name/title illegible), "Unidentified Flying Objects," April 1, 1958.

16. Doc # 0000015306, letter from J. S. Earman, Executive Officer, CIA Director's office, to Major Donald Keyhoe (Retired), April 4, 1958.

17. Doc # 0000015408, Office Memorandum from the Chief, OSI Applied Science Division, to the OSI Assistant Director, "Comments on Letters Dealing with Unidentified Flying Objects," April 4, 1958.

18. Ibid.

19. Ibid.

20. Doc # 0000015409, Memorandum for Record, by W. E. Lexow, Chief, OSI Applied Science Division, April 4, 1958.

21. Doc # 0000015308, letter from J. S. Earman, CIA Executive Officer, to USAF Major Lawrence J. Tacker, Information Service, Office of the Air Force Secretary, April 4, 1958.

22. Doc # 0000015303, letter from J. S. Earman, Executive Officer, to Donald Keyhoe, April 17, 1958.

23. Doc # 0000015410, Memorandum for Record, by W. E. Lexow, Chief, OSI Applied Science Division, "Meeting with Air Force Personnel Concerning

Scientific Advisory Panel Report on Unidentified Flying Objects, dated 17 January 1953 (Secret)," May 16, 1958.

24. Ibid.

25. Ibid.

26. Doc # CIA-RDP91-00965R000400050068-8, Memorandum for the Record, by (redacted), Assistant to the Legislative Counsel, "Meeting with Air Force Representatives concerning Unidentified Flying Objects," May 16, 1958, pp. 1–4.

27. Ibid.

28. Ibid.

29. Doc # 0000015411, Memorandum for Record, by LaRae L. Teel, Deputy Division Chief, OSI Applied Science Division, "Meeting with Mr. Chapin on Replying to Leon Davidson's UFO Letter, and June Subsequent Telephone Conversation with Major Tacker," May 22, 1958; *see* also Docs # 0000015295 and 0000015241.

30. Doc # 0000015311, letter from J. S. Earman, Executive Officer, to Leon Davidson, May 26, 1958.

31. Doc # 0000015312, letter from Philip G. Strong, Deputy Assistant Director, to Samuel Goudsmit, Brookhaven National Laboratory, May 29, 1958; *see* also Doc # 0000015313 and 0000015314.

32. Doc # 0000015310, letter from Philip G. Strong to Lloyd Berkner, discussing Berkner's letter of April 21, 1958.

33. Doc # 0000015315, letter from Philip G. Strong, OSI Deputy Assistant Director, to Lloyd V. Berkner, President, Associated Universities, May 29, 1958.

34. Doc # 0000015316, letter from Philip G. Strong, OSI Deputy Assistant Director, to USAF Major Lawrence J. Tacker, USAF Office of Information, June 4, 1958.

35. Doc # 0000015295, letter from Arnold Shaw to Leon Davidson, dated May 10, 1958; Doc # 0000015241, untitled report (two letters received from Davidson asking information on UFOs), date stamp April 26.

36. Doc # 0000015317, letter from Philip G. Strong, OSI Deputy Assistant Director, to Thornton Page, July 30, 1958.

37. Doc # CIA-RDP68-00046R000200090036-0, news article, *Pittsburgh* (PA) *Press,* "Saucer Data Suppressed, Admiral Says," August 2, 1958.

38. Doc # CIA-RDP68-00046R000200090032-4, Fred A. Kirsch, reply to letter to the editor, *Akron Beacon Journal,* "Seeks More Data on UFOs," August 11, 1958.

39. Doc # 0000015318, letter from Philip G. Strong, OSI Deputy Assistant Director, to Samuel Goudsmit, Brookhaven National Laboratory, August 19, 1958.

40. Doc # 0000015412, Office Memorandum from W. E. Lexow, Chief, OSI Applied Science Division, to USAF Major Tacker, August 22, 1958; *see* also Doc # 0000015318.

41. Doc # 0000015413, Memorandum for Record, by W. E. Lexow, Chief, Applied Science Division, "Reply to Leon Davidson's Letter of 3 July 1958," August 22, 1958.

42. Doc # 0005516198, Official Routing Slip from (illegible) to F. M. Chapin, assistant to the CIA Director, (post-8/22/58—log date incorrect).

43. Ibid.

44. Doc # 0000015319, letter from J. S. Earman, Executive Officer, to Donald Keyhoe, NICAP, October 10, 1958.

45. Doc # 0000015414, memorandum (to/from redacted), "Reported Photography of Unidentified Flying Objects," October 1, 1958 (names redacted throughout; part of one paragraph deleted).

46. Ibid.

47. Doc # 0000015267, Information Report by (redacted), "Sighting of Unidentified Airborne Objects Near Leningrad," October 10, 1958 (five of seven numbered paragraphs redacted); *see* also Doc # 0000015268, below.

48. Doc # 0000015268, Information Report by (redacted), "Unexplained Traveling Bright Light Seen in the Sky," October 27, 1958; *see* also Doc # 0000015267, above.

49. Doc # 0000015415, memorandum from Philip G. Strong, OSI Deputy Assistant Director, for the Director, National Photographic Interpretation Center, "Reported Photography of Unidentified Flying Objects," October 29, 1958.

50. Doc # 0000015320, unsigned letter from F. M. Chapin, CIA director's office, to George Popowitch, UFO Research Committee, December 2, 1958.

51. Doc # 0000015495, Teletyped Information Report (to/from redacted), "Unidentified Flying Object Observed in the Sky," December 11, 1958.

52. Doc # 0000015321, letter from Philip G. Strong, OSI Deputy Assistant Director, to Larry W. Bryant, Citizens Against UFO Secrecy, December 17, 1958.

53. David M. Jacobs, *The UFO Controversy in America* (New York: New American Library, 1975), p. 119.

54. NICAP, "UFO Casebook: 1958," (n.d.): *www.nicap.org*.

55. NICAP, "UFO Casebook: 1958"; *see* also Think About It, "1958: May alien UFO sightings," 2017, *www.thinkaboutitdocs.com*.

56. NICAP, "UFO Casebook: 1958."

57. Project 1947 (n.d.), *www.project1947.com.*

58. Jan Aldrich, *www.nicap.org.*

59. NICAP, "UFO Casebook: 1958."

60. NICAP, "UFO Casebook: 1958"; Patrick Gross, "Project Blue Book unexplained cases summaries with witness names: Year 1958": *www.ufologie.patrickgross.org.*

61. NICAP, "The Monon RR UFO Incident" (n.d.): *www.nicap.org.*

62. Ibid.

63. Ibid.

Chapter 12 **1959: Same Cast of Characters**

1. Doc # 0000015416, memorandum from (redacted) to Assistant to the Director, "Inquiry by Major Donald E. Keyhoe," January 22, 1959.

2. Doc # 0000015322, letter from J. S. Earman, Executive Officer, to Donald Keyhoe, USMC (Retired), January 27, 1959.

3. Doc # 0000015323, letter from John S. Earman, Executive Officer, to George Popowitch, The Unidentified Flying Objects Research Committee, February 6, 1959.

4. Doc # 0000015486, Official Routing Slip from (redacted) to Frank Chapin, February 6, 1959.

5. Doc # CIA-RDP80B01676R004000110015-2, letter from Frank Chapin, Assistant to the Director, to Fred A. Kirsch, UFO Research Committee, February 18, 1959.

6. Doc # CIA-RDP80R01731R000300040016-2, letter from Richard Ogden to Allen Dulles, CIA Director, February 22, 1959.

7. Doc # 0000015324, letter from J. S. Earman, Executive Officer, to Major Donald E. Keyhoe, USMC (Retired), March 5, 1959. *See* also Doc # 0000015306.

8. Doc # 0000015446, FDD (Foundation for Defense of Democracies) note by (redacted), "Flying Saucers Seen Over Sweden," citing a news article from the January 20, 1959, *Stockholms-Tidningen*, "Eight Persons Saw Flying Saucer," ("March '59" handwritten).

9. Doc # 0005516086, FDD Note, "Unusual UFOB Report," March 1959.

10. Doc # CIA-RDP9100965R000400050014-7, Journal, Office of Legislative Counsel, May 28, 1959.

11. Doc # 0000015326, letter from Herbert Scoville Jr., AD/SI to George Wyllie, June 30, 1959.

12. Doc # CIA-RDP80R01731R000300010089-5, letter from (redacted—Frank Chapin), Assistant to the Director, to Major L. J. Tacker, Secretary of the Air Force, Information Service, July 30, 1959, with buckslip to (redacted).

13. Doc # 0000015487, Official Routing Slip, from (redacted), Chief (illegible), to Assistant to the Director, October 2, 1959.

14. Doc # 0000015252, Information Report, by (redacted), "Possible Unidentified Flying Object," October 22, 1959.

15. Doc # CIA-RDP80R01731R000300010057-0, letter from Assistant to the Director to C. H. Marek Jr., November 10, 1959.

16. Doc # 0000015327, letter from Philip G. Strong, OSI Deputy Assistant Director, to Dr. Thornton Page, Wesleyan University, November 25, 1959.

17. Doc # 0000015328, letter from Alnora Belt, secretary to Philip Strong, December 10, 1959.

18. Above Top Secret, "A quote from Werner von Braun" (posted October 25, 2005): *www.abovetopsecret.com.*

19. Lorenzen and Lorenzen, *UFOs: The Whole Story.*

20. Jacques Vallee, "Vallee classification system" (2011), *www.ufoevidence.org.*

21. See "UFO Evidence," *www.ufoevidence.org;* Clark, *The UFO Book.*

22. NICAP, "UFO Casebook: 1959" (n.d.), *www.nicap.org.*

23. Ibid.

24. Sightings Archive, "Huge UFO Sighted—1959, USAF SAC Base, Goose Bay, Labrador, *www.sightings.com.*

25. NICAP, "UFO Casebook: 1959."

26. John E. Bortle, "The Bright-Comet Chronicles," 1998, available at *www.icq.eps.harvard.edu.*

27. NICAP, "UFO Casebook: 1959."

28. Ibid.

29. Ibid.

30. Good, *Need to Know.*

Chapter 13 **1960: What's This All About?**

1. Doc # 0000015417, non-sourced instruction sheet, anonymous, "Guidance to UFO Photographers," January 1, 1960 (approximate).

2. Wikipedia, "Film speed," updated November 8, 2017, *https://en.wikipedia.org.*

3. Doc # 0000015418, instructions, anonymous, "UFO Photographic Information Sheet," January 5, 1960.

4. Doc # 0000015419, Office Memorandum, from W. E. Lexow, Chief, OSI Applied Science Division, to Deputy Assistant Director, OSI Collection, "Flying Saucers—Student Papers Thereon Received from Dr. Thornton Page," January 26, 1960.

5. Doc # CIA-RDP6800046R000200090030-6, news article, Fairmont (WV) *Times-West Virginian* (UPI), "Air Force Says Unidentified Flying Objects Are 'Serious,'" February 28, 1960.

6. Ibid.

7. Ibid.

8. Doc # CIA-RDP6800046R000200090029-8, editorial, (source stated only as *Telegram*), "Another Jab at the Air Force," February 29, 1960.

9. Doc # CIA-RDP6800046R000200090027-0, news article, *Journal* (city not shown), "Flying Saucer Alert," March 4, 1960.

10. Doc # 0000015253, Information Report, (to/from redacted), "Rumored Unidentified Flying Objects in the Sary Ozek Region," March 9, 1960 (handwritten).

11. Doc # 0000015447, FDD Note, anonymous, "UFO's Sighted, Photographed in Sweden; Unidentified Satellite Seen," March 17, 1960.

12. Doc # CIA-RDP68-00046R000200090024-3, news article, *Hartford Times*, "UFO's—Visitors from Space? Food for Future Thought," June 9, 1960.

13. Ibid.

14. Doc # CIA-RDP68-00046R000200090025-2, news article, *Worcester* (MA) *Evening Gazette*, "Ex-C.I.A. Chief Wants UFO Probe," June 12, 1960.

15. Ibid.

16. Doc # CIA-RDP81R00560R000100040013-4, News Release, Department of Defense, Office of Public Affairs, "Fact Sheet Air Force UFO Report," July 21, 1960.

17. Ibid.

18. Ibid.

19. Ibid.

20. Doc # CIA-RDP68-00046R000200090023-4, news article, *Chicago Daily News*, "Hill Group Eyes 'Flying Saucers,'" August 5, 1960.

21. Doc # 0005516055, memorandum from Philip G. Strong, OSI Deputy Assistant Director, to G. L. Cary, Deputy Assistant Director for Collection, "Reply to Your Note Regarding Gordon H. Scherer," August 31, 1960.

22. Doc # CIA-RDP81R00560R000100040011-6, "Reply to Your Note Regarding Gordon H. Scherer," August 31, 1960.

23. Ibid.

24. Ibid.

25. Doc # 0000015330, letter from John S. Warner, Legislative Counsel, to Coral Lorenzen, International Director, Aerial Phenomena Research Organization, December 13, 1960.

26. Doc # CIA-RDP68-00046R000200090022-5, news article, *Worcester* (MA) *Evening Gazette*, "Inquiry into UFOs Still Held Needed," December 15, 1960.

27. Ibid.

28. Doc # 0005516056, memorandum from the Chief, Detroit Office, to (illegible), "Sighting of Unusual Object," December 16, 1960.

29. Clark, *The UFO Book*, pp. 508–509.

Chapter 14 **1961: Old News**

1. Doc # 0000015331, letter from Brig. Gen. Philip G. Strong (Retired) to Lt. Colonel Lawrence J. Tacker, USAF Office of Information, January 10, 1961.

2. Doc # CIA-RDP68-00046R000200090019-9, news article, Worcester (MA) *Evening Gazette*, "McCormack Asks Hearing on UFOs," February 16, 1961.

3. UFO Evidence, "Congressional Hearings on UFOs," 2011, available at *www.ufoevidence.org*.

4. Doc # 0000015332, letter from Philip G. Strong, OSI Deputy Assistant Director, to Robert J. Palmer, The Americana Institute, April 5, 1961.

5. Doc # 0000015492, Congressional Correspondence (routing slip), from Legislative Counsel Lawrence Houston to (unnamed) "Exec" and (illegible), June 4, 1961; *see* also Doc # 0000015333 and related files.

6. Doc # 0005515877, letter from Lawrence E. Houston, CIA General Counsel, to Congressman Joseph Karth, post-June 30, 1961.

7. Ibid.

8. Doc # 0000015488, Official Routing Slip, from (illegible) to the Legislative Counsel, July 5, 1961; *see* also Doc # 0000015492.

9. Doc # 0000015423, letter from Herbert Scoville Jr., AD/SI to the Legislative Counsel, "Reply to the Honorable Joseph E. Karth," July 12, 1961.

10. Doc # 0000015333, letter from Lawrence R. Houston, General Counsel, to Congressman Joseph E. Karth, (post-7/12/61—log date incorrect).

11. Doc # CIA-RDP79T00936A000200260001-6, The White House, Outgoing Message, September 11, 1961.

12. Doc # CIA-RDP68-00046R000200090014-4, news article, *Roanoke* (VA) *World-News*, "Congress Is Being Pressed for Flying Saucer Probe," October 23, 1961.

13. Doc # CIA-RDP68-00046R000200090017-1, editorial, *Bangor* (ME) *News*, "Mystery Makes Life More Interesting," November 17, 1961.

14. Sachs, *The UFO Encyclopedia*.

15. Clark, *The UFO Book*.

Chapter 15 **1962: Blinders**

1. Doc # 0005516059, memorandum from Philip Strong, Deputy Assistant Director, to USAF Hq, "Transmittal of Letter from Thomas B. Scott," April 23, 1962.

2. Doc # 0000015254, anonymous, non-sourced multi-topic report from Argentina, May 25, 1962.

3. Ibid.

4. Good, *Need to Know*; Clark, *The UFO Book*.

5. Good, *Need to Know*, p. 247.

6. Ibid.

7. Lorenzen and Lorenzen, *UFOs: The Whole Story*.

Chapter 16 **1963: Cooper Spills the Beans**

1. Doc # CIA-RDP6800046R000200090008-1, letter to editor, *Hartford* (CT) *Courant*, "Aerial Phenomena," May 2, 1963.

2. Sachs, *The UFO Encyclopedia*, pp. 72–73.

Chapter 17 **1964: From a Lull to a Quickening**

1. Doc # CIA-RDP81R00560R000100010001-0, 195 pages, publication, National Investigations Committee on Aerial Phenomena (NICAP), "The UFO Evidence," January 1, 1964.

2. Doc # CIA-RDP75-00149R000400460035-3, news article, Passaic (NJ) *Herald-News*, "Unidentified Flying Objects," January 22, 1964.

3. Doc # CIA-RDP75-00149R000400460034-4, letter to editor, *Atlanta Constitution*, "An Earthly Explanation? CIA Must Have Brainwashed You," March 3, 1964.

4. Doc # CIA-RDP75-00149R000400460033-5, letter to editor, *Cleveland Plain Dealer*, "If You *See* an Unidentified Flying Object (UFO) Land Here—Dial CD" (presumably Civil Defense), March 16, 1964.

5. Doc # CIA-RDP75-00149R000400460032-6, letter to editor, *Amarillo Globe-Times*, "People Are Talking about . . . Little Green Men," April 27, 1964; *see also* Doc # CIA-RDP75-00149R00400460033-5.

6. Doc # CIA-RDP75-00149R000400460031-7, letter to editor, *Dayton* (OH) *News*, "Unidentified Flying Objects Kept under Cover Officially," April 30, 1964; *see also* Doc # CIA-RDP75-00149R00400460033-5.

7. Doc # CIA-RDP75-00149R0004000460030-8, letter to editor, Binghamton (NY) *Sun-Bulletin*, "Space tests branded as propaganda," May 13, 1964; *see also* Doc # CIA-RDP75-00149R00400460033-5.

8. Doc # 0005516023, non-sourced handwritten notes by (redacted), January 19, 1965; *see also* Doc # 0005516109.

9. Good, *Need to Know*.

10. Sachs, *The UFO Encyclopedia*.

11. John Schuessler, *UFO-Related Human Physiological Effects*, published by GEO Graphics, La Porte, TX, 1996.

Chapter 18 **1965: A Gathering Storm**

1. Doc # CIA-RDP80B01676R001500060109-2, Memorandum for the Record by (redacted), January 18, 1965.

2. Doc # 0000015426, memorandum from (redacted), Chief, (redacted), to the Chief, Contact Division, "National Investigations Committee on Aerial Phenomena (NICAP)," January 25, 1965.

3. Doc # 0000015425, memorandum from Donald F. Chamberlain, OSI Deputy Director, for the CIA Director, "Evaluation of UFO's," January 26, 1965.

4. Doc # 0000015427, memorandum from Donald F. Chamberlain, OSI Deputy Director, for the Assistant Director for Special Activities, February 11, 1965.

5. Doc # CIA-RDP69B00596R000100190086-2, letter from (redacted), NICAP, to CIA Director John McCone, February 26, 1965.

6. Doc # 0000015255, non-sourced report from Argentina, post-July 6, 1965.

7. Doc # CIA-RDP68-00046R000200090003-6, letter to editor, *Hartford Courant*, "Let's Get the Facts about the UFOs," July 26, 1965.

8. Sachs, *The UFO Encyclopedia.*

9. Good, *Need to Know.*

10. Story, *The Encyclopedia of UFOs.*

11. Good, *Need to Know*, p. 253.

12. Sachs, *The UFO Encyclopedia.*

13. Story, *The Encyclopedia of UFOs.*

14. John G. Fuller, "Incident at Exeter" (New York: Berkley Books, 1978); Story, *The Encyclopedia of Extraterrestrial Encounters.*

15. Story, *The Encyclopedia of Extraterrestrial Encounters*, pp. 568–570.

16. Lorenzen and Lorenzen, *UFOs: The Whole Story;* George Fawcett, "What We Have Learned from UFO Repetitions," *MUFON 1985 UFO Symposium Proceedings.*

17. Story, *The Encyclopedia of Extraterrestrial Encounters.*

Chapter 19 **1966: All Hell Breaks Loose**

1. Berliner, *The Blue Book Unknowns.*

2. Doc # CIA-RDP73-00475R000100150001-0, news article, *New York Journal-American*, "Boomerang Feared in 'Saucer' Probe," March 30, 1966.

3. Doc # CIA-RDP88-01365R000300080004-5, letter from (redacted), to Jerry Fairbanks Productions, Hollywood, CA, April 12, 1966.

4. Doc # 0005517743, CIA report (heavily redacted), "Exploitation of Metallic Fragment from Unidentified Flying Object," May 4, 1966.

5. Doc # 0005515698, Information Report by (redacted), "Sighting of Unusual Phenomenon on Horizon Near Iranian/USSR Border," September 18, 1966.

6. Doc # 0000098713, teletyped message, Moscow ITAR-TASS World Service, "Lithuania—Police Officers Spot UFO; Rapid Reaction Force Alerted," June 26, 1966 (log date incorrect).

7. Doc # 0000015428, memorandum from David B. Stevenson, OSI, for Chief, OSI Defensive Systems Division, "Air Force Request to Declassify an OSI Paper on UFO's," July 20, 1966.

8. Doc # CIA-RDP81-R00560R000100010009-2, news article, Hammond (LA) *Sunday Star*, "Flying Saucers Again: Do You Believe in Them?" August 7, 1966.

9. Doc # 0000015334, letter from Karl Weber, OSI Deputy Director, to USAF Col. Gerald Jorgensen, Chief, Community Relations Division, Office of Information, August 16, 1966.

10. Doc # 0000015431, draft memo from Walter L. Mackey, Executive Officer, for the CIA Director, "Air Force Request to Declassify CIA Material on Unidentified Flying Objects (UFO)," September 1, 1966.

11. Doc # 0000015430, Memorandum for Record, by David B. Stevenson, "Air Force Request to Declassify CIA UFO Report," August 23, 1966.

12. Doc # CIA-RDP81R00560R000100040001-7 (identical to Doc # 0000015431), memorandum from the Executive Officer, for the Director of Central Intelligence, "Air Force Request to Declassify CIA Material on Unidentified Flying Objects (UFO)," September 1, 1966.

13. Identical to Doc # 0000015429, "Air Force Request to Declassify CIA UFO report," from D. B. Stevenson, August 11, 1966.

14. Doc # CIA-RDP81-R00560R000100010003-8, magazine article, *Look*, "Aboard a Flying Saucer," by John G. Fuller, October 4, 1966.

15. Doc # CIA-RDP71B00364R000500220018-0, Journal, Office of Legislative Counsel, by (redacted), October 7, 1966.

16. Doc # CIA-RDP75-00149R000100910003-1, (publisher unknown) news article, "National U.F.O. Probe Slated," October 7, 1966.

17. Doc # CIA-RDP75-00001R000200450001-6, news article, *Arizona Republic*, "UFO Hush Blamed on CIA Men," October 7, 1966.

18. Doc # CIA-RDP75-00149R000100910004-0, news article, *The New York Times*, "Campus Engaged for Saucer Study," October 7, 1966. *See* also page 189.

19. Doc # CIA-RDP75-00149R000500070006-7, news article, *Baltimore Sun*, "'Debunking' Charged on UFO Stories," October 8, 1966.

20. Doc # CIA-RDP75-00149R000500070008-5, news article, *Chicago Daily News*, "Air Force Probe of UFOs Called 'Scientific Scandal,'" October 8, 1966.

21. Doc # CIA-RDP75-00149R000100910001-3, news article, *Washington Star*, "Fearless Physicist Tackles Mystery of UFOs," October 9, 1966.

22. Doc # CIA-RDP75-00149R000500070005-8, news article, *Los Angeles Times*, "UFO Reports Throttled by CIA, Physicist Says," October 9, 1966.

23. Story, *The Encyclopedia of Extraterrestrial Encounters*, pp. 435–437.

24. Doc # CIA-RDP75-00149R000500070005-8, news article, *Los Angeles Times*, "UFO Reports Throttled by CIA, Physicist Says," October 9, 1966.

25. Doc # CIA-RDP80B01675R001800080054-7, Memorandum for the Record, by L. K. White, (title redacted), "Morning Meeting of 12 October 1966," (principals redacted).

26. Doc # CIA-RDP79B00314A000300010030-5, Memorandum for the Record, by (redacted), Deputy Director of Research and Development, "Meeting with Drs.

Price, Sander, Savely, and Finch of the Air Force Office of Scientific Research (AFOSR) on 28 October 1966," October 29, 1966.

27. Doc # CIA-RDP78T05929A002200090006-2, news article, *Chicago Daily News*, "UFO Spaceman 'Conversed' without Words," November 4, 1966.

28. Doc # 0000015335, letter from (redacted) to an Auburn, WA, resident, December 7, 1966.

29. Doc # CIA-RDP75-00149R000700390033-0, Radio TV Reports, memorandum from (not shown) for Public Affairs Staff, "Joe Pyne Show"—WAVA Radio, Washington, D.C., December 23, 1966, 10:00 a.m.

30. Story, *The Encyclopedia of UFOs*.

31. Ibid.

32. Ibid.

33. Clark, *The UFO Book*, pp. 476–477

34. Story, *The Encyclopedia of Extraterrestrial Encounters*, pp. 435–437.

35. Ibid.

36. Ibid.

37. Distant Suns 5.0, *http://distantsuns.com*.

38. Raymond E. Fowler, *Casebook of a UFO Investigator* (Englewood Cliffs, NJ: Prentice-Hall, 1981).

39. Good, *Need to Know*, pp. 265–266.

Chapter 20 **1967: The Tempest Rages**

1. Doc # CIA-RDP7500149R000100270013-1, letter to editor, *Syracuse Post-Standard*, "1966 Good Year for UFO Reports," January 7, 1967.

2. Doc # CIA-RDP79B00752A000300090001-6, translated article from Russian magazine *Cmena* (*Change*), No. 7: "UFOs—What Are They," by Felix Ziegel, February 1967.

3. Ibid.

4. Ibid.

5. Doc # 0000015432, Memorandum from Arthur C. Lundahl, Director, National Photographic Interpretation Center, for the Deputy Director for Intelligence, "U.S. Air Force Contract with the University of Colorado to Report on the UFO Situation," February 7, 1967.

6. Ibid.

7. Doc # CIA-RDP80R01284A001800010034-0, Memorandum for the Record, by L. K. White, February 10, 1967.

8. Doc # 0000015433, memorandum from (redacted) for Director, NPIC, "Photo Analysis of UFO Photography," February 17, 1967.

9. Ibid.

10. Doc # 0000015434, memorandum (to/from redacted), "Answer to Request of Speed Letter (redacted) dated 30 January 1967," February 21, 1967.

11. Doc # 0000015435, Memorandum for the Record, by (redacted), "Visit of Dr. Condon to NPIC, 20 February 1967," February 23, 1967.

12. Doc # CIA-RDP81S00991R000300150001-4, Intelligence Subject Code and Area Classification Code, March 1, 1967.

13. Doc # 0000015442, non-sourced (heavily redacted) "Monthly Report for February 1967," March 13, 1967. *See* also Doc # 0000015436.

14. Doc # CIA-RDP81R00560R000100010005-6, magazine article, *Look*, "Flying Saucers," by Warren Rogers, March 21, 1967 (attachment).

15. Ibid.

16. Ibid.

17. Doc # CIA-RDP75-00149R000500070003-0, news article, *Washington Star*, "Secret of 14 Years UFO Debunking Laid to CIA by Scientist," April 23, 1967.

18. Ibid.

19. Ibid. *see* also Doc # CIA-RDP69B00369R0002000240055-8.

20. Doc # CIA-RDP75-00149R000500070002-1, editorial, *Boston Herald*, "UFO's and the CIA," April 24, 1967.

21. Doc # 0000015436, Memorandum for the Record, "UFO Briefing for Dr. Edward Condon, 5 May 1967," by (redacted), Chief, Technical Intelligence Division, NPIC, May 8, 1967.

22. Ibid.

23. Doc # CIA-RDP75-00149R000500070001-2, news article, *Philadelphia Inquirer*, "Scientist Accuses CIA of World Plot to 'Debunk' UFOs," July 9, 1967.

24. Doc # CIA-RDP71R00140A000100100220-1, non-sourced note from (redacted) to "Walt" at OSI, July 17, 1967.

25. Doc # CIA-RDP71R00140A000100100216-6, memorandum from (redacted) to "Mr. Duckett," "1000 Meeting on UFO—19 July," July 18, 1967.

26. Doc # CIA-RDP80B01676R001600010004-2, letter from John A. Larson, The Brookings Institution, to Vice Admiral Rufus L. Taylor, CIA Deputy Director, July 18, 1967.

27. Doc # CIA-RDP71R00140A000100100215-7, memorandum from (redacted) for Mr. Duckett, July 19, 1967; *see* also Doc # CIA-RDP71R00140A000100100216-6.

28. Doc # 0000015273, Information Report, "Report on Conversations with Soviet Scientists on Subject of Unidentified Flying Objects in the USSR," August 18, 1967.

29. Doc # CIA-RDP69B00369R0002000240055-8, news article, *The Arizona Daily Star*, "Scientists Debate the Question of UFO's," September 6, 1967; *see* also Doc # CIA-RDP75-00149R000500070003-0.

30. Ibid.

31. Doc # CIA-RDP81R00560R000100010002-9, 68 pages, magazine, *Flying Saucers, UFO Reports*, (12 articles), October 1967.

32. Doc # CIA-RDP81R00560R000100010005-6, news article, *The Pueblo* (CO) *Chieftain*, "Pair of Pueblo Youths Photograph Strange Light in San Luis Valley," October 17, 1967.

33. Doc # CIA-RDP69B00369000200180005-0, journal, by (redacted), Office of Legislative Counsel, November 28, 1967.

34. Doc # CIA-RDP81R00560R000100010006-5, magazine article, *Playboy*, vol. 14, no. 12, "The UFO Gap," December 1967, by J. Allen Hynek.

35. Doc # 0005517744, *Leninskaya* (illegible), "Study of UFO's," December 2, 1967.

36. Doc # 0000015335, letter from (redacted) to Auburn, WA, resident, December 7, 1967.

37. Doc # CIA-RDP79B00752A000300100002-3, letter from Robert J. Low, U of Colorado, to J. Thomas Ratchford, Headquarters, Air Force Office of Scientific Research, December 8, 1967.

38. Doc # 0005517736, *Sovetskaya Latviya*, "Flying Phenomena (UFO's)," by R. Vitolniyek, Director of the Station for the Radio Observation of the Ionosphere and Artificial Earth Satellites, December 10, 1967.

39. Story, *The Encyclopedia of UFOs*.

40. Good, *Need to Know*, pp. 296–297.

41. Ibid.

42. Good, *Above Top Secret*.

43. Berliner, *The Blue Book Unknowns*.

44. Clark, *The UFO Book*.

45. Story, *The Encyclopedia of UFOs.*

46. Ibid.

47. Ibid.

48. Good, *Need to Know.*

49. Ibid.

50. Ibid.

51. Story, *The Encyclopedia of UFOs.*

52. Ibid.

Chapter 21 **1968: Return to Relative Calm**

1. Doc # CIA-RDP81R00560R000100070025-8, source illegible, by US Defense Attaché, "UFO Global Grid Theory," Wellington, NZ, February 1, 1968.

2. Doc # CIA-RDP79B00752A000300100001-4, letter from Robert J. Low, University of Colorado, to J. Thomas Ratchford, Air Force Office of Scientific Research, January 17, 1968.

3. Doc # 0005517735, news article, *Komsomolskaya Pravda*, "Fantasy or Reality (Unidentified flying objects)," January 20, 1968.

4. Doc # 0005517747, news abstract, *Leninskaya (illegible)*, "Hypothesis about Flying Plates," January 31, 1968.

5. Doc # CIA-RDP81R00560R000100010014-6, non-sourced retyped report, USSR Scientific Affairs, "Scientists Refute Claims of 'UFO' Sightings," by Ye. Mustel et al, USSR Academy of Sciences Astronomic Council, March 6, 1968.

6. Doc # 0005517734, abstract, *Pravda Ukrainy*, "Are flying saucers a myth?" (date uncertain, post-3/25/68).

7. Doc # 0000015452, non-sourced report with attachments (author not shown), "Nothing But the Facts on UFOs, or Which Novosti Writer Do You Read?" April 9, 1968.

8. Doc # CIA-RDP81R00560R000100070007-8, Information Report, "(redacted) Sightings of Unidentified Flying Objects in Ladakh, Nepal, Sikkim, and Bhutan," April 11, 1968.

9. Doc # CIA-RDP81R00560R000100070024-9, Airgram from American Embassy Paris to Department of State, "No Serious Studies of Unidentified Flying Objects (UFO's) in France," May 8, 1968.

10. Doc # CIA-RDP81R00560R000100010008-3, magazine article, *Look*, "The Flying Saucer Fiasco," by John G. Fuller, May 14, 1968.

11. Ibid.

12. Doc # CIA-RDP81R00560R000100070019-5, Defense Department Information Report, "Alleged Activities of USAF and CIA regarding UFOs," by USAF Major A. P. Heard, Assistant Air Attaché, August 1, 1968.

13. Doc # CIA-RDP81R00560R000100070020-3, Taiwan Department of Defense Intelligence, Information Report, "Sighting of UFO's Over Off-Shore Islands," August 15, 1968.

14. Doc # CIA-RDP81-R00560R000100070028-5, Taiwan Department of Defense Intelligence Information Report, "Investigation of UFO Sightings Over Off-Shore Islands and Taiwan Strait," October 14, 1968.

15. Doc # 0000044116, *Soviet Life*, "Unidentified flying object," by Felix Ziegel, November 2, 1968.

16. Ibid.

17. Ibid.

18. J. Allen Hynek, *The Hynek UFO Report*.

19. Good, *Need to Know*.

20. Ibid.

21. Story, *The Encyclopedia of UFOs*.

22. Ibid.

23. Ibid.

24. Wikipedia, "James E. McDonald," updated November 20, 2017, *https://en.wikipedia.org*.

Chapter 22 **1969: Where'd All the UFOs Go?**

1. Doc # CIA-RDP81ROO560R000100010011-9, journal article, *Science*, "Beings from Outer Space—Corporeal and Spiritual," by Hudson Hoagland, February 14, 1969.

2. Doc # CIA-RDP81ROO560R000100010011-9, journal article, *Bulletin of the Atomic Scientists*, "UFOs I Have Loved and Lost," by Edward U. Condon, December 1969.

3. Ibid.

4. Story, *The Encyclopedia of UFOs*, pp. 63–65.

5. Ibid.

6. Mark Rodeghier, *UFO Reports Involving Vehicle Interference* (Evanston, IL: Center for UFO Studies, 1981).

7. Ibid.

8. Good, *Need to Know*, p. 299.

9. Good, *Above Top Secret*, 1988.

10. Ibid.

11. Sachs, *The UFO Encyclopedia*.

12. Rodeghier, *UFO Reports Involving Vehicle Interference*.

Chapter 23 **1970: AIAA Weighs In**

1. Doc # CIA-RDP81R00560R000100070026-7, Defense Intelligence Information Report, "Sighting of Unidentified Flying Objects (UFO)," March 7, 1970.

2. Doc # CIA-RDP81ROO560R000100010011-9, journal article, *Astronautics and Aeronautics*, "UFO: An Appraisal of the Problem," November 1970.

3. Story, *The Encyclopedia of UFOs*.

4. Rodeghier, *UFO Reports Involving Vehicle Interference*.

5. Schuessler, *UFO-Related Human Physiological Effects*.

6. Rodeghier, *UFO Reports Involving Vehicle Interference*.

7. Story, *The Encyclopedia of UFOs*.

Chapter 24 **1971: Science Journals—More to Say**

1. Doc # CIA-RDP81ROO560R000100010011-9, journal article, *Science News*, "Whatever Happened to UFO's?" June 26, 1971.

2. Ibid.

3. Doc # CIA-RDP81R00560R000100010010-0, journal article, *Astronautics and Aeronautics*, "UFO Encounter II, Sample Case Selected by the UFO Subcommittee of the AIAA," September 1, 1971.

4. Ibid.

5. Ibid.

6. Ibid.

7. Rodeghier, *UFO Reports Involving Vehicle Interference*.

8. Schuessler, *UFO-Related Human Physiological Effects*.

9. Berliner, Unidentified Flying Objects Briefing Document; *see* also Antonio Huneeus, "The famous Rockefeller Briefing Document," September 3, 2010, available at *www.issuu.com*

Chapter 25 **1972: The Government Remains Quiet**

1. Doc # 0000015270, Intelligence Information Report, (subject redacted—USSR), April 10, 1972.

2. Sachs, *The UFO Encyclopedia.*

3. Schuessler, *UFO-Related Human Physiological Effects.*

Chapter 26 **1973: MUFON's Year of the Humanoid**

1. Doc # NSA-RDP96X00790R000100040013-0, non-sourced, anonymous report, "The Importance of Substance in ESP Research," October 20, 1973.

2. Doc # CIA-RDP90-00552R000303250002-8, news article, Portland, *The Oregonian*, "U.S. officials persist in secrecy, but UFOs real, claims authority," December 1, 1973.

3. UFO Research Network, "JANAP 146," 2011, www.*uforesearchnetwork. proboards.com.*

4. Doc # CIA-RDP81ROO560R000100010011-9, journal article, *Science*, "Beings from Outer Space—Corporeal and Spiritual," by Hudson Hoagland, February 14, 1969.

5. Raymond E. Fowler, *Casebook of a UFO Investigator.*

6. John Schuessler and Edward F. O'Herin, "Truck Driver Injured by UFO: The Eddie Doyle Webb Case," *MUFON 1993 International UFO Symposium Proceedings.*

7. Sachs, *The UFO Encyclopedia.*

8. Story, *The Encyclopedia of Extraterrestrial Encounters.*

9. Schuessler, *UFO-Related Human Physiological Effects.*

10. Good, *Need to Know*, p. 321.

Chapter 27 **1974: Gemini 4 Photos**

1. Doc # 0000015336, draft letter from Bruce A. Lowe, NSC Executive Secretary, to Brad C. Sparks, November 5, 1974.

2. Story, *The Encyclopedia of UFOs,* Appendix A.

3.Good, *Need to Know,* p. 321.

4. Schuessler, *UFO-Related Human Physiological Effects.*

5. Ibid.

6. Ibid.

Chapter 28 **1975: Ignoring Base Intrusions**

1. Doc # 0000028609, non-sourced memorandum (to/from redacted), content heavily redacted, May 8, 1975.

2. Doc # 0005516212, (mostly redacted), CIA, The Operations Center, "Event and Action" record, by (anonymous), Watch Officer, October 28, 1975, 6:10 a.m.

3. Good, *Need to Know,* p. 321

4. Schuessler, *UFO-Related Human Physiological Effects.*

5. Sachs, *The UFO Encyclopedia; see* also Doc # 0005516212, above.

6. Sachs, *The UFO Encyclopedia.*

7. NICAP, "UFO Chased by KC-135 Tanker," (n.d.), *www.nicap.org.*

8. Good, *Need to Know,* p. 325.

Chapter 29 **1976: An Uptick in Agency Interest**

1. Doc # 0000015237, note from (redacted), Defense Communications Division, to DCD Hq, April 14, 1976.

2. Doc # 0000015451, non-sourced note by (redacted), April 15, 1976.

3. Ibid.

4. Doc # 0000015235, teletyped message from DCD to (redacted), "DCD Case (redacted)—UFO Research," April 22, 1976.

5. Doc # 0000015437, Memo for the File, June 25, 1976.

6. Doc # 0000015490, note from (redacted) to Deputy Chief, OD&E, July 14, 1976.

7. Doc # 0000015275, Foreign Intelligence Information Report, Domestic Collection Division, Directorate of Operations, "Aerial Observation of Intense Source of Light," September 10, 1976.

8. Doc # 0000015238, teletyped message, from (redacted) to "Immediate Director," September 24, 1976.

9. Doc # 0000015274, Foreign Intelligence Information Report, Domestic Collection Division, Directorate of Operations, "(Redacted) UFO Phenomena," November 18, 1976.

10. Peter A. Gersten, JD, "What the Government Would Know about UFOs if They Read Their Own Documents," *MUFON 1981 UFO Symposium Proceedings.*

11. Schuessler, *UFO-Related Human Physiological Effects.*

12. Good, *Need to Know.*

13. Rodeghier, *UFO Reports Involving Vehicle Interference.*

14. Good, *Need to Know.*

15. Ibid.

16. Ibid., pp. 302–303.

17. Story, *The Encyclopedia of Extraterrestrial Encounters.*

Chapter 30 **1977: Start Spreading the News**

1. Doc # 0005517733, USSR, non-sourced report by (redacted), March 21, 1977.

2. Doc # CIA-RDP11M01338R000400480018-9, news article (untitled), *US News & World Report*, April 18, 1977.

3. Doc # CIA-RDP88-01315R000300070010-4, news article, *The Washington Post*, "UFO Buffs Say Respect Is Replacing Ridicule," April 27, 1977.

4. Doc # CIA-RDP99-00498R000100050092-8, news article, *The Houston Chronicle*, "Bush shunning Nixon Series of Interviews," May 18, 1977.

5. Doc # 0005516220, memorandum from Anthony A. Lapham, General Counsel, for Director of Research and Development, DDS&T, "Proposed Research Project," June 3, 1977.

6. Doc # CIA-RDP80M00165A002200090013-8, letter from the Executive Secretary for (redacted), Deputy (?), to the White House Agency Liaison Chief, August 12, 1977.

7. Doc # 0000015256, Moscow TASS International Service, "Unusual Natural Phenomenon Observed in Karelia," September 22, 1977.

8. Doc # CIA-RDP82M00345R000700040168-0, journal, Office of Legislative Counsel, by (anonymous), October 12, 1977.

9. Doc # 0000015262, Foreign Intelligence Information Report, Domestic Collection Division, Directorate of Operations, (to/from, subject, and nearly all text redacted), December 22, 1977.

10. Doc # CIA-RDP88-01365R000300040038-2, news article, *Chicago Tribune*, "Tempo People," December 20, 1977.

11. Good, *Need to Know*, p. 303.

12. Ibid., pp. 304–305.

13. Ibid.

14. Alan C. Holt, "UFO Light Beams: Space-Time Projections, *MUFON 1984 International UFO Symposium Proceedings.*

15. Good, *Need to Know.*

16. Ibid.

17. Rodeghier, *UFO Reports Involving Vehicle Interference.*

18. Good, *Need to Know*, p. 304.

Chapter 31 **1978: The New Zealand Film**

1. Doc # 0000015438, memorandum from the chief, Minneapolis office to the chief, Domestic Collection Division, "Report of UFO at Time of Soviet Satellite Failure," February 9, 1978.

2. Doc # 0000015257, non-sourced report, "Argentina Authorities Report Satellite Down in Bolivia," May 15, 1978.

3. Doc # CIA-RDP96-00788R02000010001-9, note from (anonymous) to Major Bill Stoner, Office of the Assistant Chief of Staff, Intelligence (OACSI), "Parapsychology," June 1978 (calendar date not shown).

4. Doc # CIA-RDP96-00787R000200080024-8, news article, *The New York Times,* "Skeptics Criticized on Paranormal Issue," June 25, 1978.

5. Doc # CIA-RDP88-01315R000300070009-6, news article, *Midnight Globe,* "Revealed: The CIA's Secret UFO File," November 7, 1978.

6. Doc # CIA-RDP81M00980R000300010021-5, letter from Office of Legislative Counsel to (redacted name and agency), December 13, 1978.

7. Doc # CIA-RDP88-01315R000300070008-7, letter from Art Harris, investigative journalist, *The Washington Post,* to George W. Owens, CIA Information Privacy Coordinator, December 20, 1978.

8. Leonard Stringfield, "The Fatal Encounter at Ft. Dix-McGuire: A Case Study," *MUFON 1985 UFO Symposium Proceedings.*

9. Ibid.

10. Rodeghier, *UFO Reports Involving Vehicle Interference.*

11. Clark, *The UFO Book.*

12. Rodeghier, *UFO Reports Involving Vehicle Interference.*

13. Story, *The Encyclopedia of Extraterrestrial Encounters,* p. 663–665.

14. Ibid.

15. Ibid.

16. Ibid.

17. Ibid.

Chapter 32 **1979: Three Decades of Lies**

1. Doc # CIA-RDP88-01315R000300070007-8, news article, *The New York Times*, "C.I.A. Papers Detail U.F.O. Surveillance," January 14, 1979.

2. Doc # CIA-RDP88-01315R000300070003-2, news article, *St. Paul Pioneer Press*, "CIA, Air Force cover-up of UFOs claimed," January 18, 1979.

3. Sachs, *The UFO Encyclopedia*, page 149.

4. Doc # CIA-RDP88-01315R000300070005-0, news article, *Philadelphia Inquirer*, "The Air Force and the CIA were accused of covering up UFO reports," January 19, 1979.

5. Doc # CIA-RDP88-01515R000300070002-3, Radio TV Reports Inc. NBC, *The Today Show*, "UFOs Discussed by Spaulding and Zackle of Ground Saucer Watch," January 24, 1979.

6. Doc # CIA-RDP88-01365R000300020001-4, letter from Charles E. Wilson, Chief, Plans and Policy Branch, to John Fielding, Producer, ABKCO Films, March 15, 1979.

7. Doc # CIA-RDP88-01314R000300010021-9, letters to editor, *Second Look*, August 1979.

8. Doc # CIA-RDP88-01315R000300070001-4, magazine article, *The New York Times Magazine*, "U.F.O. Files: The Untold Story," October 14, 1979.

9. Ibid.

10. Schuessler, *UFO-Related Human Physiological Effects*.

11. Rodeghier, *UFO Reports Involving Vehicle Interference*.

12. Schuessler, *UFO-Related Human Physiological Effects*.

13. Rodeghier, *UFO Reports Involving Vehicle Interference*; Clark, *The UFO Book*.

Chapter 33 **1980-81: Disclosure at Home and Away**

1. Doc # 0005516655, non-sourced report, "Eyewitness Accounts of UFO Sightings Published."

2. Doc # CIA-RDP96-00788R001300230001-3, *Bibliography of Parapsychology*, translation from Russian by the Parapsychological Association, 1980.

3. Doc # 0005516652, Foreign Broadcast Information Service, *China Report Science and Technology No.79*, "UFO Phenomenon in China Analyzed," January 26, 1981.

4. Ibid.

5. Doc # 0005516058, memo from Herbert Scoville Jr., AD/SI, to Lawrence R. Houston, Legislative Counsel, "Reply to Honorable Joseph E. Karth," July 12, 1981.

6. Doc # CIA-RDP90-00806R000100200075-6, news article, *The Washington Post*, "Suit Seeks to Lift Secrecy Veil from Agency's UFO Documents," November 3, 1981.

7. Ibid.

8. Doc # CIA-RDP90-00806R000100200029-7, Radio TV Reports, CBS Radio Network, Bob Schieffer, "UFOs, a Military Threat," November 3, 1981.

9. Doc # CIA-RDP92B00478R000800340008-9, opinion, *The Fairfax* (VA) *Journal*, "The federal government is suppressing UFO evidence," by Larry W. Bryant, CAUS, undated (11/30/81 handwritten).

10. Don Berliner, UFO Research Coalition, UFO Briefing Document, 1995, *www.anomalyarchives.org*.

Chapter 34 **1982-85: Habeas Corpus and Hudson Valley**

1. Doc # CIA-RDP90-00806R000100390037-8, news article, *The New York Times*, "35 Years of U.F.O.'s," June 23, 1982.

2. Doc # CIA-RDP83M00914R002700220076-0, letter from Sid Zins, MGM/UA Entertainment, to John M. McMahon, CIA Deputy Director, September 30, 1982.

3. Doc # CIA-RDP90-00806R000100200074-7, untitled news release, Reuters, July 14, 1983.

4. Doc # 0005516658, newspaper article, "Airliner crew reports UFO sighting," Moscow *Trud* (in Russian), January 30, 1985.

5. Ibid.

6. Doc # CIA-RDP90-00965R000707000002-9, magazine article, *Penthouse*, "High-Tech Espionage," by Ernest Volkman, March 1985.

7. Dr. J. Allen Hynek, Philip Imbrogno, and Bob Pratt, *Night Siege: The Hudson Valley UFO Sightings* (New York: Random House, 1987).

8. Ibid.

9. Ibid.

10. Schuessler, *UFO-Related Human Physiological Effects*.

11. Ibid.

12. Hynek, Imbrogno, and Pratt, *Night Siege*.

13. Ibid.

Chapter 35 **1986-88: Claims and Counterclaims**

1. Doc # CIA-RDP91-00901R0005000180001-6, news article, *The Washington Post*, "Take Me to Your Reader," March 9, 1987.

2. Doc # NSA-RDP96X00790R000100040025-7, news article, *The New York Times*, "Report of U.F.O. Crash in '47 Called False by Science Panel," August 26, 1987.

3. Doc # 0000112351, teletyped message, "Barbadians Report Several UFO Sightings," September 2, 1987.

4. Schuessler, *UFO-Related Human Physiological Effects.*

5. Ibid.

6. Story, *The Encyclopedia of Extraterrestrial Encounters.*

7. Ibid.

8. Schuessler, *UFO-Related Human Physiological Effects.*

9. Ibid.

Chapter 36 **1989: Lots of Activity . . . Elsewhere**

1. Doc # 0000042352, JPRS Report (Estonia), "Results of Youth Poll on Religious Issues Reported," April 4, 1989.

2. Doc # CIA-RDP96-00792R000500610012-3, news article, *Komsomolskaya Pravda*, "Laboratory of Psychocerebronics Contemplates Close Encounters of the Third Kind," April 25, 1989.

3. Doc # 0005517516, JPRS Report, "A Rational-Metaphorical Picture of the World," May 1, 1989.

4. Doc # CIA-RDP96-00792R000700990001-2, *Journal of Scientific Exploration*, June 1989.

5. Doc # 0000042347, journal article, *Sofia Rabotnichesko Delo*, "Farmers Burning Straw to Make Up for Delays," August 11, 1989.

6. Doc # 0005516674, JPRS Report, "English Summaries of Major Articles," July–August 1989.

7. Doc # 0000112355, teletyped message, Beijing Xinhua, "UFO Sighted over Urumqi Evening of 6 September," September 13, 1989.

8. Doc # 0005517525, notice, "Rocket Found in Desolate Area," September 28, 1989.

9. Doc # 0005516572, teletyped message, "TASS Reviews Soviet Central Press for 12 October," *Komsomolskaya Pravda*, "Voronezh eyewitnesses described a UFO on September 27."

10. Doc # 0000042346, news article, FBIS, Foreign Press Note, "USSR: Media Report Multitude of UFO Sightings," November 22, 1989.

11. Ibid.

12. Ibid.

13. Ibid.

14. Ibid.

15. Ibid.

16. Ibid.

17. Doc # CIA-RDP96-00789R002200590001-3, SRI International, "Screening for Remote Viewing Talent," December 1989. *See* also Doc # CIA-RDP96-00789R002200430001-0.

18. Schuessler, *UFO-Related Human Physiological Effects.*

Chapter 37 **1990: Back in the USSR**

1. Doc # 0000042351, JPRS Report, "Unidentified Flying Objects (UFO) in Ancient China," January 18, 1990.

2. Doc # 0005516579, program summary, Moscow International Service in Mandarin, February 21, 1990.

3. Doc # 0000112331, Moscow TASS International Service, "UFO's Reported near Moscow," April 15, 1990.

4. Doc # 0000112332, teletyped message, Moscow Television Service, "State Center for Study of UFO's Established," April 17, 1990.

5. Doc # 0005516675, JPRS Report [USSR], "Council of Ministers Official Urges Improved Economics Reporting," May 1, 1990, paragraph 34.

6. Doc # 0000043370, Moscow Domestic Service, "USSR, PRC Scientists in Joint Study of UFO's," May 21, 1990.

7. Doc # 0005517533, JPRS Report, editor's column, *Aviatsiya I Kosmonavtika*, June 1, 1990, paragraph 8.

8. Doc # 0005517460, Johannesburg Television Service, program summary, July 20, 1990, paragraph 20.

9. Doc # 0005517534, JPRS Report, essay, "Boundaries of Cosmology," August 1, 1990, paragraph 5.

10. Doc # 0005516669, JPRS Report, "Maj Gen Avn. Leonov on Soviet Lunar Program Details," August 1, 1990, paragraph 20.

11. Doc # 0005516668, JPRS Report, "Articles Not Translated" from Russian, Moscow SSHA, *Ekonomika, Politika, Ideologiya*, September 1, 1990.

12. Doc # 0005516711, non-sourced teletyped message, September 4, 1990.

13. Doc # 0005517538, JPRS Report, "Muscovites on Elections," October 1, 1990, paragraph 36.

14. Doc # 0005517798, teletyped message (to/from not shown), "UFO News Bulletin Publication Planned," October 4, 1990.

15. Doc # 0005517679, teletyped message [USSR], "'Vid' Program Premiers 5 October," October 13, 1990.

16. Doc # 0005516723, Soviet Commentary List for November 5, 1990, paragraph 15.

17. Doc # 0005517684, Television Program Summary 110990, paragraph 16.

18. Doc # 0005517496, Commentary List–Moscow Turkish 131400/1830, paragraph 5.

19. Doc # 0005516730, Moscow Consolidated, November 16, 1990.

20. Doc # 0005516731, Press Selection List: PAU Pressfax Three, paragraph 21.

21. Doc # 0005516732, Commentary List–Moscow Creek, December 5, 1990.

22. Doc # 0005516752, Comlist: Radio Peace and Progress, December 9, 1990.

23. Doc # 0005517497, Hanoi Domestic Program Summary, paragraph 7.

24. Doc # 0005517686, Video Selection List: Moscow Mos 90:1152.

25. Doc # 0005517789, TASS, "Japanese Cosmonaut's Observations from Space," December 6, 1990.

26. Doc # 0005516659, Comlist: Moscow Consolidated, December 21, 1990, paragraph 70.

27. Dr. Jack Kasher, "A Scientific Analysis of the Videotape Taken by Space Shuttle Discovery on Shuttle Flight STS-48," *MUFON 1994 International UFO Symposium Proceedings*.

28. Dan Wright, *MUFON UFO Journal*, August 1990.

29. Schuessler, *UFO-Related Human Physiological Effects*.

Chapter 38 **1991: USSR Nay Russia**

1. Doc # 0005516753, Commentary List—Moscow International Korean.

2. Doc # 0005527991, Television Program Summary 191830 Bud 91-01801211991, paragraph 16.

3. Doc # 0005516693, Comlist Moscow Consolidated, January 21, 1991, paragraph 75.

4. Doc # 00055167754, Press Selection List—East Europe, *Pravda*, January 22, 1991, paragraph 25.

5. Doc # 0005517689, commentary, *Moscow Rabochaya Tribuna*, "Alternative Uses for Krasnoyarsk Site," January 22, 1991; *see* also Doc # 0005517701.

6. Doc # 0000112350, teletyped message, "Moravian UFO Thought to Be Satellite," January 24, 1991.

7. Doc # 0005516663, Comlist: Moscow Consolidated, January 25, 1991, paragraph 102.

8. Doc # 0005517691, non-sourced teletyped message, January 30, 1991.

9. Doc # 0005517535, JPRS Report, "Magazines Increasing after Anti-Pornography Purge," March 11, 1991.

10. Doc # 0005516243, Moscow TASS, "'Strange Roar' Precedes 'Mysterious Blast' in Sasovo," April 12, 1991.

11. Doc # 0005517695, Moscow CTV1, "Air Defense Forces Chief Interviewed," April 14, 1991.

12. Doc # 0005517791, *Pravda*, "Diverging Opinions on Cause of Sasovo Explosion," April 15, 1991.

13. Doc # 0005517792, teletyped message, TASS, "ALMA-ATA Patrolmen Report UFO Sighting," April 19, 1991.

14. Doc # 0005517719, Moscow, BBC feed, "Air Defense Forces Chief Interviewed," April 20, 1991.

15. Docs # 0005517509 and 0005517520, Moscow Consolidated, May 11, 1991; Commentary List—Moscow International Korean.

16. Doc # 0005517793, Moscow Central Television First Program Network, "Object Discovered Floating around Mir Station," May 21, 1991; Doc # 0005517697, Moscow Central Television First Program Network, "'Strange Object' Filmed Floating around Mir Station," May 21, 1991.

17. Doc # 0005517521, FYI–Vesti Television Program Summary, 2000 GMT June 2, 1991, paragraph 13.

18. Doc # 0005517698, Johannesburg SABC TV, Television Program Summary, July 9, 1991, paragraph 10: Video report on a UFO sighting in Johannesburg.

19. Doc # 0005517701, Soviet Commentary List for July 15, 1991. *See* also Doc. # 0005517689.

20. Doc # 0005517731, non-sourced teletyped message, "UFO Reportedly Lands in Mountain Pass Near Yerevan," August 5, 1991.

21. Doc # 0005517540, JPRS Report, "*Pravda* Urges Readers to Contribute News, Ideas," August 31, 1991.

22. Doc # 0005516722, Hanoi Television Program Summary, September 10, 1991, paragraph 21.

23. Doc # 0005517797, commentary, *Sovetskaya Rossiya*, "Abalkin Condemns '500 Days' Recovery Program," September 27, 1991.

24. Doc # 0005517677, teletyped message, FBIS, "UFO Sightings No. 3—Deputy Minister of Defense Interview," May 1, 1991.

25. Ibid.

26. Doc # 0005516593, Buenos Aires, TELAM, "Metal Object Falls on Private House," pre-10/10/91.

27. Doc # 0005517708, Television Program Summary 192100: MRT91-163 created June 24, 2015.

28. Doc # 0005517548, JPRS Report, "'Sverdlovsk Syndrome' Studied," October 26, 1991.

29. Doc # 0005517795, Moscow Central Television, "Strip Mining Pollutes Dalnegorsk, Maritime Kray," October 28, 1991.

30. Doc # 0005516710, non-sourced report by (redacted), "Abakin 15 Nov News Conference," November 18, 1991.

31. Bob Gribble, "Looking Back," *MUFON UFO Journal*, July 1993.

Chapter 39 **1992-94: Spy Planes and Homemade Saucers**

1. Doc # 0000190094, CIA publication, "The Central Intelligence Agency and Overhead Reconnaissance: The U-2 and OXCART Programs, 1954-1974," Chapter 2, Developing the U-2, "U-2s, UFOs and Operation Blue Book," 1992.

2. Doc # 0005517495, Moscow TASS, "Yeltsin Begins Visit to Ulyanovsk," January 1992.

3. Doc # 0005517547, JPRS Report, "On Claims of Commander of Submarine Grounded off Sweden in 1981," January 29, 1992.

4. Doc # 0005527992, teletyped message, Yonhap News Agency, "Unidentified Plane 'Might Have Been a Phantom.'" February 11, 1992.

5. Doc # CIA-RDP96-00792R000400300004-7, monograph by Robert J. Durant, "Will the Real Scott Jones Please Stand Up?" February 20, 1992.

6. Doc # 0005517120, Program Summary—Moscow Manderin 021200.

7. Doc # 0005517741, non-sourced teletyped message, April 16, 1992.

8. Doc # 0000112346, report, Beijing Xinhua Domestic Service, "China UFO Society Meets to Continue Scientific Study," May 13, 1992.

9. Doc # 0005516643, JPRS Report, *Moscow Rabochaya Tribuna*, "On 'Flying Saucer'," June 16, 1992.

10. Doc # 0005517758, teletyped message, *Moscow Krasnaya Zvezda*, "Search for Missing SU-27 Continues," August 6, 1992.

11. Doc # 0005517546, JPRS Report, "Russian Arms, Aircraft Displayed at Air Show," August 26, 1992.

12. Doc # 0005516726, Moscow Central Television First Program Network, "Studio Interview with Major General Yuriy Grigoriyevich Gusev, deputy commander of the Russian Ministry of Defense Space Units," October 1, 1992.

13. Doc # 0005516728, Khabarovsk Radio Network, "Search Continues for Downed Su-27 Pilot," October 23, 1992.

14. Doc # 0005517757, teletyped message, "Shetland UFO Sighting Prompts Spy Plane Speculation," December 14, 1992.

15. Doc # 0005516712, report, *Krasnaya Zvezda*, "Military Papers' Circulation Declines," January 14, 1993.

16. Doc # 0005516713, Moscow Central Television First Program Network, "New 'Saucer-Like' Aircraft Developed in Saratov," January 26, 1993. *See* also Doc #s 0005516714, 0005516715, 00055716, 0005516717, 0005516720, 0005517786, and related files.

17. Doc # 0000112348, non-sourced teletyped message, "Ministry to Study Psychic Powers, UFO's for Future Industry," February 19, 1993.

18. Doc #0005516714, Radio Moscow World Service, "Government to Patent New 'Flying Saucer' Airliner," March 9, 1993. *See* also Doc #s 0005516713, 00055715, 0005516716, 0005516717, 0005516720, 0005517786, and related files.

19. Doc # 0005517761, anonymous teletyped message, "Paper Reports Alleged Evidence on Mishap Involving UFO," March 27, 1993.

20. Doc # 0005516639, JPRS, "Space Forces Chief on Funding, Baykonur," April 1, 1993.

21. Doc # 0005517464, Moscow *Argumenty I Fakty*, April 1, 1993.

22. Doc # 0005517523, ITAR-TASS World Service, "Minister's Predictions on Satellites, 'Flying Saucers'," April 27, 1993.

23. Doc # 0005516716, Moscow Russian Television Network, "Saratov Plant's Successes, Future Plans Reported," July 8, 1993. *See* also Docs #s 0005516713, 0005516714, 0005516715, 005516717, 0005516720, 0005517786, and related files.

24. Doc # 0005516715, *Izvestiya*, "'Flying Saucer' Financial Problems Viewed," July 14, 1993. *See* also Doc #s 0005516713, 0005516714, 0005516716, 005516717, 0005516720, 0005517786, and related files.

25. Doc # 0005516717, Moscow *Izvestiya*, "Saratov Oblast's Reform Plans Explained," August 13, 1993. *See* also Doc #s 0005516713, 0005516714, 0005516715, 000556716, 0005516720, 0005517786, and related files.

26. Doc # 0005516796, *Pressfax*, "Pressfax carries 31 August *Pravda*," August 31, 1993.

27. Doc # 0005517466, Radio Moscow World Service, September 3, 1993.

28. Doc # 0005517760, non-sourced report, "Taiwan, Mainland UFO Symposium Closes in Beijing," December 7, 1993.

29. Doc # 0005516720, Moscow Ostankino Television First Channel Network, "Saratov Committee to Prioritize Industrial Investment," December 8, 1993. *See* also Doc #s 0005516713, 0005516714, 000551615, 0005516716, 0005517786, and related files.

30. Doc # 0005516721, Moscow Russian Television Network, "Report Details Planned Use of Aerostats in Mars Exploration," December 19, 1993. *See* also Doc #s 0005516713, 0005516714, 000551615, 0005516716, 0005516717, 0005517786, and related files.

31. Doc # 0005517759, teletyped message, "Unidentified Flying Objects Sighted in Matanzas (Cuba) Skies," December 23, 1993.

32. Doc # 00055517787, non-sourced teletyped message (Japan), "Seaside Town to Build Center for UFO Study," January 7, 1994.

33. Doc # 0005517786, Moscow Ostankino Television First Channel Network, "Plane Makers in England to Advertise Their Wares," January 24, 1994. *See* also Doc #s 0005516713, 0005516714, 0005516715, 0005516716, 0005516717, 0005516720, and related files.

34. Doc # 0005517504, press selection list, *Moscow Robochaya Tribuna*, March 23, 1994.

35. Doc # 0005517765, teletyped message, *Pravda*, "Meteorites May Have Caused Mysterious Craters Near Kursk," May 28, 1994.

36. Schuessler, *UFO-Related Human Physiological Effects*.

37. Linda Moulton Howe, "Moving Lights, Disks, and Animal Mutilations in Alabama," *MUFON 1993 International UFO Symposium Proceedings*.

Chapter 40 **1995-98: Psychic Woo Woo**

1. Doc # CIA-RDP96-00787R000500230001-3, journal, California State College, Sonoma, *Ubiquity Interchange*, Vol. 1, No. 8, November 5, 1998

2. Doc # CIA-RDP96-00792R000200440002-6, 71 pages, essay, The Guangdong Somatic Sciences Research Committee [China], "Some Brief Notes on the Development of Research into Human Paranormal Capabilities in Guangdong," December 7, 1998, 13.

3. Story, *The Encyclopedia of Extraterrestrial Encounters.*

4. Good, *Need to Know.*

5. Ibid.

6. Ibid.

7. Ibid.

Chapter 41 **1999: A Fitting Climax**

1. Doc # 0005517742, Department of Defense, National Reconnaissance Office, by Gerald K. Haines, Historian, "CIA's Role in the Study of UFOs, 1947–90," July 1, 1999.

Chapter 42 **2000 and Beyond**

1. Doc # CIA-RDP96-00792R000700680001-6, German journal entry, *Parapsychology Abstracts International*, "The Spectrum of UFO Sightings," May 17, 2000.

2. Doc # CIA-RDP96-00787R000500250002-0, questionnaire, Naval Postgraduate School, August 7, 2000.

3. Doc # CIA-RDP96-00792R000701020004-4, abstract, "An Experimental Evaluation of a Belief in Psi," by Kenneth Reed, University of Edinburgh, August 15, 2000.

4. Colm Kelleher, "Research at the National Institute for Discovery Science," *MUFON 2000 International UFO Symposium Proceedings.*

5. Story, *The Encyclopedia of Extraterrestrial Encounters*, 385–386.

Index

Canterbury Coast, aerial events over, 261
Cape Girardeau, Missouri, encounter in, 237
Carroll, General Joseph, 15–16
Carter, Jimmy,
    UFO investigations and, 313
    UFO sighting of, 222–223
Casablanca, sightings over, 38
Cascade Mountains, sighting in the, 26
Cathie, Bruce, 213
Central Intelligence Agency Act of 1949, 14
Central Intelligence Group, 4
Chadwell, H. Marshall, 40, 41, 48, 55, 56, 61, 62, 75, 93
    communications with, 48
Chapin, Frank, 129
    letter to Fred Kirsch, 140
    response to Donald Keyhoe, 132
Cherlbourg, France, unknown in, 183
Cheshire, England, aerial lights over, 274
China,
    aerial phenomena in, 267–268
    UFOs witnessed in, 296
Chop, Albert, 65–66
Christchurch, lights over, 262
Ciampino air base, mysterious object spotted over, 82
cigar-shaped
    mass sighting in Tiaret, Algeria, 28
    object over Oloron, France, 46
circular object spotted over Helsinki, Finland, 82
Citizens Against UFO Secrecy, 134, 240, 269, 271
clairvoyance, MITI study of, 298
Clark, H. L., 41–42
Clark, Ralph, 31
    memo from Todos Odarenko from, 66
close encounter
    in French Equatorial Africa, 63
    on the Monon Railroad, 136
clothing, sightings of men dressed in shiny metallic, 27–28
Coast Guard, 18, 171, 295, 298
Cochise, New Mexico, disc-shaped object over, 93
Cold War, sightings during the, 114–115
Colorado UFO Project,
    final report from the, 220
    Operating Manual amendment for the, 212
    problems within the, 216–217
    procedures for reporting to the, 211
    wrap-up of the, 221
comet-like light seen over Matanzas, Cuba, 301
Commission for the Scientific Investigation of Claims of the Paranormal, see CSICOP
Commission on Aerodynamic Phenomena (Soviet), 272
Condon, Edward U., 185, 199, 220, 221
    record of leadership for, 217
    NPIC and, 197
    public security risk of, 188
    sightings theories of, 200
    visit to NPIC, 198

Condon Committee, 189, 208, 213, 231
    formation of the, 192
    released findings of the, 310
Condon group, Project Blue Book and the, 187
Condon Report, 116, 220, 221, 226, 230, 236
    effect on public interest of UFOs and the, 228
confidentially offered by NICAP, 107
congressional hearings on UFOs, secret, 130
contactees, 108, 140, 190
    and extraterrestrial beings, 107
conventional aircraft mistaken for UFOs, 114
Cooper, Gordon L., 114
    object spotted by, 168
    sighting by, 24
Coordinator of Information, evolution of the, 3
Corning, California, encounter near, 157–158
cosmic ray particles, UFO explanations and, 253
Cotile Lake, Louisiana, sound heard near, 256–257
Coyne, Lawrence J., 238
CSICOP, 276
cylindrical object sighting at Eglin Air Force Base, 12

D

Dakar, Senegal, gray object over, 81
Dalnegorsk, Russia, UFO crash in, 294
Danish Defense Command, 63
Darmstadt, West Germany, flying saucers over, 80
Davidson, Leon, 160
    ATIC and, 105
    correspondence with Allen Dulles, 103
    cover-up allegation of, 112
    ham radio transmission and, 104
    letters to OSI from, 268
    recording sent to, 103–104
    tape recording translation and, 120
Davis-Monthan Air Force Base,
discs over, 44
    incident at, 30
daytime sightings, shapes of, 13
DCI, 33, 40, 91, 112, 128, 129, 132, 141, 197, 309
DDI, message from W&E to the, 31
DDS&T, 173, 247, 248
    UFO research program and the, 254
debunking efforts
    by the Robertson Panel, 49–50
    for the public, 56
declassified statement of the Robertson Panel, 113
Defense Department
    activities regarding UFOs, 66
    response to UFOs, 131
    warning to airline pilots, 83
Defense Intelligence Agency, 269
Defense Science Advisory Board, 113
Defense Support System satellite, 252
Denmark, sightings over, 62–63
Department of Defense, see DoD
depression after abduction, 239

Federal Communications Commission and unexplained radio signals, 41

fiery
  discs over the mines in Elisabethville District, 27
  object seen over Arras, France, 70
  red sphere over Fort Beaufort, South Africa, 233–234

fireball
  phenomena, Project Sign and, 13
  spotted by Sabena Airlines pilot, 70

fireball-observation installations, Project Twinkle and, 13

flame-colored discs over Yuma, Arizona, 29

flat disc sighting at Farnborough, England, 21

flat-bottomed saucer, sightings of a, 20

flying disc patent, 76

"Flying Discs" memorandum, 6–7

flying formations of UFOs, 217

flying saucer
  plans of Nazi engineers, 63
  reports to J. Edgar Hoover, 13

flying saucer, origin of the term, 6

flying wing over Santa Barbara Channel, 74

Ford, Gerald, 180, 189
  UFO-related hearings and, 191

foreign attack, USAF's concern regarding a, 150

foreign CIA reports about UFOs, 16

Foreign Documents or Radio Broadcasts, 4

Foreign Technology Division, 184, 197

formation of discs over Gaillac, France, 47

Fort, Charles, 50

Fort Beaufort, South Africa, fiery red sphere over, 233–234

Fort Bliss, Texas, sighting, 15

Fort Bragg, North Carolina, circular object above, 136

Fort Dix, New Jersey, oval object hovering over, 260

Fort Itaipu, Brazil, unknown over, 118–119

Fortean Society, 55

fourth dimension, Wayne Sulo Aho and travel to the, 108

Freedom of Information Act, 259, 270, 310

French Air Force, admittance of flying saucers and the, 76

French Equatorial Africa close encounter, 63

French response to the UFO problem, 216

Frost, John, 92

Fuller, John, G., 178, 182, 185, 217

Fund for UFO Research, 271

G

Gaillac, France, formation of discs over, 47

Galesburg-Moline, Illinois, domed disc seen over, 210

Gaspesie, Quebec, entity encounter in, 251

Gemini 4 photos, 240

geographic locations of unexplained sightings, 53

geophysics, study of UFOs and, 121

George Air Force Base,
  discs in a V formation over, 43–44
  matte-white discs spotted over, 30

German flying saucer plans, Soviet theft of, 63

Germany, glowing discs over, 79

Gersten, Peter, 269

Gesell, Gerhard, UFO-related documents and, 269–270

ghost rocket anomaly, sightings of a, 6

Giller, Edward, 196–197

Glen Burnie, Maryland, silver disc over, 43

glowing discs over Germany, 79

glowing saucer over Redondo Beach, California, 100

Goldwater, Barry, 162

Goleta, California, airborne light near, 260

Goodman Air Force Base, 9

Gormanston Saddle, Tasmania, incident in, 265–266

Goudsmit, Dr. Samuel A., 61, 102, 105, 113
  correspondence with Philip Strong, 120, 129–131

Graham, H. U., 41

gray metallic object sighting near Ladd Air Force Base, 23

gray object over Dakar, Senegal, 81–82

gray-white saucers in Beverly, Massachusetts, 193

Great Falls, Montana, footage from, 52–53

green
  ball over Tananarive, Madagascar, 84–85
  fireballs, sightings of, 12
  object over Larson Air Force Base, 72

Griffin, Bulkley, appeal of, 156–157

Griffiss Air Force Base, tragedy at, 84

Grogan, Colonel Stanley, 123

Gromyko, Andrei, nuclear war agreement and, 232

Ground Saucer Watch, 259

Groveton, Missouri, yellow-green light over, 219

H

Haines,
  Dr. Richard F., photograph review by, 279–280
  Gerald, paper written by, 306

Hall, Richard, 151–152, 169, 173, 174, 185, 220

Hallein, Austria, unknown over, 79

hallucinations,
  sightings resulting from, 35
  UFO reports and, 306, 312
  UFOs and, 186
  UFO sightings, 56

Halstead, Frank, 205

ham radio flap, the 87–95

ham radio transmission and Leon Davidson, 104

Hamilton Air Force Base, flying disc at, 20

Hammaguir military base, 209

Hardin, Charles A., 66–67

hardware aspects of flying craft and ASD, 106

Hartman, William K., 20, 201

Hassleholm, Sweden, saucer seen over, 71

Mehrabad Air Base, 252
Melsbroek, Belgium, fireball spotted over, 70
Memorandum for Record, 58
Menzel, Donald, IFO sources and, 204
Mersin, Turkey, unknown object over, 78–79
metallic disc
    encounter in Kastrup, Denmark, 227
    over Karup Field, Denmark, 46
metallic silver object seen by L. Gordon Cooper, 24
metallic sphere, aerial maneuvers of a, 282
meteor hypothesis, J. Allen Hynek and the, 230
meteors mistaken as UFOs, 33
Michigan, sightings in southeast, 195
military bases, Air Force conspiracy to cover up
    UFO surveillance of, 263–264
military threat, UFOs as a, 269
Millikan, Max, 40
Minot Air Force Base, aerial intruders at, 193–194
Minuteman missile site, 210
Miramar Naval Station, sphere seen over, 93
misidentification of conventional aircraft, 56
misidentifications, UFO-related, 161–162
misidentified natural phenomena, 42
misinterpretations of known objects, sightings
    resulting from, 35
missile silo, 166
missile site,
    aerial intruders at a, 193
    intrusions of, 269
    Minuteman missile site, 210
    Titan, 165
missing time, Charles Moody and, 244
MITI, 298
Moby Dick spying program, 273
Moncla, Lieutenant Felix, 69
Monon Railroad, close encounter on the, 136–138
Montluçon, France, luminous white disc over, 71
Moody, Charles, missing time of, 244
Moore, Alvin, disposition of materials by, 213
Moore, William, 276–277
Morocco, sightings over, 29
Morse code, 103, 110, 112, 120, 309
Moscow Aviation Institute, 195
Moscow, Russia, pulsating lights over, 294
Moscow radio show transcript, FBI interception
    of a, 34
Mount Rainier, Washington,
    event, 205
    incident in, 182–183
Mount Taylor, New Mexico, orange circle near, 73
MUFON membership, increases in, 276
MUFON Photographic Cases, 148
Murmansk, Russia, illuminated ball over, 286
Muroc Army Air Field, sighting at, 8
mutual interference, 54

N

National Academy of Sciences, 186, 200, 220, 310
National Aeronautical Association, 58

National Bureau of Standards, 188
National Investigations Committee on Aerial
    Phenomena, see NICAP
National Military Command Center, see NMCC
National Oceanic and Atmospheric
    Administration, see NOAA
National Photographic Interpretation Center, see
    NPIC
national security,
    Scientific Review Board review of, 62
    sightings and, 53
    UFOs and, 49, 192
national security agencies, Robertson Panel and,
    49–50
National Security Agency, see NSA
National Security Council, 4, 33, 57, 170, 240, 308
NATO scouting balloon over Sofia, Romania, 214
natural phenomena, 56–57
    misidentified, 42
    UFOs and, 186
Navy, 18, 22, 32, 45, 51, 52, 56, 68, 83, 105, 107,
    155, 162, 224, 236
Navy Hill, Washington, D.C., 4
Nazi engineers, flying saucer plans of, 63
Nazi-founded saucer-building program, 91–92
Nazis, American victories over the, 25
Nazis and UFOs, 4–6
Nederland, Texas, encounter in, 180–181
Nellis Air Force Base, object spotted at, 165
Netherlands, sightings in the, 29
Newhouse, Delbert, footage taken by, 52
NICAP, 59–60, 130–131
    Air Force allegations from, 150–151
    confidentiality offered by, 107
    US Air Force and pressure from, 102
NICAP, 59–60, 65, 102, 111, 124, 125, 128, 130,
    131, 139, 141, 150, 151, 153, 154, 167, 173, 174,
    180, 185, 188, 191, 202, 206, 235, 262, 309
    article outlining the UFO problem, 170
    claim of supersonic airborne jets, 107
    letter-writing campaign, 170
    published document, 169–171
nighttime sightings, features of, 13–14
NMCC, 243, 250
NOAA, UFO sightings and, 243
nonhuman entities observed in Varginha, Brazil,
    303–304
NORAD, 57
    cylindrical object tracked by, 304
    intruders tracked by, 264
    renaming of, 57
    J. Allen Hynek and confirmed reports from,
        209
    tracking of a missile by, 210
NORAD radars, tracking unknowns with, 209
North Africa, anomalies in, 37
North American Air Defense Command, see
    NORAD
Norway, V formation spotted over, 77
Nova Scotia, sighting near, 16–17

pillow balloon, 51
pilots, requirements for sighting reports by, 236
Plaistow, New Hampshire, glowing disc over, 294
planet-wide grid, UFOs powered by a, 213
plasma phenomena as a reason for UFO sightings, 208
plate-shaped object sighting in Boukanefis, Algeria, 28
Platteville, Illinois, encounter in, 223
polygraph exams, CIA employees and, 7
Popowitch, George, 139
Port Gentil, Gabon, orange luminous object over, 27, 39
Port Huron, Michigan, 48
Portage County, Ohio, incident in, 192
Portalegre, Portugal, anomalous light over, 117
Practica di Mare military air base, 82
Presque Isle weather station, 42
Prince Christian Sound, Greenland, lens-shaped object over, 85
procedures for identifying unknown aerial objects, 33
Project Blue Book, 11, 307
    dissolving of, 310
    sighting at Holloman Air Force Base and, 10
    transfer of, 57
Project Blue Book
    accumulated date on UFO reports, 113–114
    and Captain Edward Ruppelt, 19
    and new reports, 67
    and radar-visual sightings, 144
    and the Condon group, 187
    and the Davis-Monthan Air Force Base incident, 30
    and the Fort Bliss sighting, 15
    and the George Air Force Base incident, 30
    and the Ladd Air Force Base sighting, 23
    and the San Antonio, Texas, sighting, 30
    investigations, fallacies of, 187
    quarterly statistical reports by the ATIC, 68
    review, 42
    staff, 106
    transfer to the ADC, 67
Project Blue Book's ruling of the incident at Glen Burnie, Maryland, 43
Project Grudge, 11, 50, 199, 307
    sighting reports to, 16
Project Grudge and Oak Ridge, Tennessee, sighting, 21
Project Lothar, 5
Project Magnet, 21
Project Pounce, 51
Project Saucer, 35
Project Sign, 13
    declaration of, 11
    disbanding of, 306–307
Project STORK, 68
Project Twinkle, establishment of, 13
Project "Y," 91, 92

psychiatric evaluations of UFO witnesses, 187
psychic research and UFO research comparisons, 236
psychological
    explanations for UFO sightings, 56
    factors contributing to sightings, 36
psychological warfare, 35
    UFOs and accusations of, 160–161
psychological warfare
    accusations and Lawrence Tacker, 161
    and Soviet government policy, 36
public interest in UFOs, the Condon Report and, 228
published saucer reports, validity of, 83
Pueblo, Colorado, white light sighting in, 207
pulsating lights over Moscow, Russia, 294
Pyne, Joe, interview with Frank Stranges, 189–190

Q
Queensland, Australia, disc-shaped aerial vehicle seen in, 223
Quincy, Illinois, object spotted in, 225
Quintanilla, Hector, 187

R
radar
    jamming, explanations for, 108
    problems, 54
    stations used for UFO research, 290
radar-visual sightings, Project Blue Book and, 144
radio recording, ham, 87–88
radio signals, unexplained, 41
radio teletype of the UFO crash in Spitsbergen, Norway, 32
RAF
    Lakenheath, 101, 229, 230–231
    Little Rissington, 47
    Manston, 115
    Patrington, 256
    Topcliffe, 45
    Waddington, 256
Randolph Air Force Base, 44
rapid identification by OSI, 42
Ratchford, Dr. J. Thomas, 196–197
    correspondence with Dr. Robert Low, 208
Reber, James, 39
recording sent to Leon Davidson, 103–104
rectangular
    flight path, flat disc sighting in a, 21
    object over Lynchburg, Virginia, 135
red light over Williams Lake, British Colombia, 289
red object, sightings of a, 20
red object over Andujar, Spain, 39
red undefined object over Walcha, New South Wales, 278
red-orange
    light over Sylvania, Alabama, 302

W

W&E message to DDI, 31
Walcha, New South Wales, red undefined object over, 278
Walesville, New York, tragedy at, 84
Warfield, Alan, 59–60
Warner, John S., 64
    letter from Coral Lorenzen to, 155
Washington, D.C.,
    anomalous objects over, 175
    sightings in, 29
Washington National Airport, objects flying over, 30
Waukesha County, Wisconsin, hovering object in, 234
Weapons and Equipment Division, see W&E
weather balloons, 52, 55, 94, 117, 183
    misidentification of, 34, 153
weather balloons mistaken as UFOs, 33, 114
Webb, Walter, 205
Weber, Karl, 183
Wheelus Air Force Base, round object at, 136
White, L. K., 188
white mass sighting at the Algiers factory, 28
white object spotted over Tuscany, Italy, 82
White Pond, New York, boomerang-shaped object in, 273
White Sands incident, 14
White Sands Proving Grounds, New Mexico, series of encounters at, 118
Whiting, Fred, 271
Wilcox Field, oncoming unknown over, 114
Williams Lake, British Colombia, red light over, 289
Williamsburg, Virginia, incident in, 206–207
Wilmington, Delaware, sightings over, 31
Wilson, Lieutenant Robert, 69
windblown objects mistaken for UFOs, 36
Witkowski, Igor, 5
witness, aerial anomalies and the earnestness of a, 36
witness
    accounts, evaluating, 122
    interviews conducted by James E. McDonald, 202
    reliability, the ATIC and, 34
witnesses,
    scientifically trained, 204
    silencing of UFO, 124
Worcester, South Africa, 77
World War II and the OSS, 3
Wright-Patterson Air Force Base, 18, 58, 184, 186, 187, 213, 260, 306, 309
    ATIC and, 42, 103, 104, 123, 307
    investigations by, 19
    OSI meeting at, 43
    Skyhook balloon at the, 36
written correspondence on UFO-related matters, 221

Wurtsmith Air Force Base, low-flying helicopter at, 245
Wyllie, George, letter from Herbert Scoville to, 141–142
Wyman, Louis, House Resolution 946 by, 212

Y

Yaak, Montana, 48
Yarovslavl Highway, objects along the, 284–285
yellow object sighting in Lodi, Algeria, 28
Yeltsin, Boris, 295
Yuma, Arizona, flame-colored discs over, 29

Z

Zamora, Lonnie, 172, 205
Zanesville, Ohio, testing of photographs taken at, 201
Zeider Zee, sightings at, 2
Zhukovskiy, Russia, airshow display in, 297
Ziegel, Dr. Felix,
    and UFOs as optical illusions, 214
    theories of, 195–196, 218

About the Author

Dan Wright is retired from Michigan civil service where he was a senior analyst and technical writer in the state department of social services.

In 1978 he joined the Mutual UFO Network (MUFON), a multinational organization comprising thousands of volunteer field investigators and researchers to address cases of aerial phenomena reported by the public. Following his ascension to the Michigan state directorship, he was further elevated to the international board of directors in 1986. He subsequently served two terms as MUFON's deputy director in charge of all North American investigations. He authored multiple chapters for its manual of investigative procedures, he was instrumental in devising computerized case reports, and he conducted a 5-year study involving 300+ cases of alleged alien abduction. In 1995, 1997, and 2003 he was selected to speak to members gathered at the MUFON International UFO Symposium.

In 2014 Dan published *Winter Solstice*, a novel shedding light on Islam and Christianity and corresponding Middle East and American politics, while introducing a superior nonhuman intelligence.

Dan Wright holds a Master of Arts degree in political science from the University of Illinois, Springfield.

TO OUR READERS

MUFON BOOKS

The mission of MUFON BOOKS, an imprint of Red Wheel Weiser, is to publish reasoned and credible thought by recognized authorities; authorities who specialize in exploring the outer limits of the universe and the possibilities of life beyond our planet.

ABOUT MUFON

The Mutual UFO Network *(www.MUFON.com)* was formed by concerned scientists and academic researchers in 1969 for the specific purpose of applying scientific methods to the serious study of UFO sightings and reported human/alien interactions. MUFON's mission is "The Scientific Study of UFOs for the Benefit of Humanity" with the intent to unveil and disclose credible information free of distortion, censorship, and lies, and prepare the public for possible implications.

ABOUT RED WHEEL/WEISER

Red Wheel/Weiser *(www.redwheelweiser.com)* specializes in "Books to Live By" for seekers, believers, and practitioners. We publish in the areas of lifestyle, body/mind/spirit, and alternative thought across our imprints, including Conari Press, Weiser Books, and Career Press.